Ideology and Politics in Contemporary China

Studies in
Chinese Government and Politics

1. CHINESE COMMUNIST POLITICS IN ACTION
Edited by A. Doak Barnett

2. CHINA: MANAGEMENT OF A REVOLUTIONARY SOCIETY
Edited by John M. H. Lindbeck

3. ELITES IN THE PEOPLE'S REPUBLIC OF CHINA
Edited by Robert A. Scalapino

4. IDEOLOGY AND POLITICS IN CONTEMPORARY CHINA
Edited by Chalmers Johnson

Sponsored by the Subcommittee on
Chinese Government and Politics
of the Joint Committee
on Contemporary China of the
American Council of Learned Societies
and the Social Science Research Council

MEMBERS OF THE SUBCOMMITTEE

Robert A. Scalapino, *Chairman*

A. Doak Barnett   John W. Lewis
Chalmers Johnson   George E. Taylor

MEMBERS OF THE JOINT COMMITTEE, 1970–71

Albert Feuerwerker, *Chairman*

Thomas P. Bernstein   James R. Townsend
Chalmers Johnson   Ezra F. Vogel
Dwight H. Perkins   Arthur P. Wolf
John Creighton Campbell, *staff*

Ideology and Politics
in
Contemporary China

EDITED BY CHALMERS JOHNSON

CONTRIBUTORS

JOHN ISRAEL

RICHARD H. SOLOMON

JEROME CH'EN

LAWRENCE SULLIVAN

SUZANNE PEPPER

MERLE GOLDMAN

BYUNG-JOON AHN

RENSSELAER W. LEE III

PHILIP L. BRIDGHAM

BENJAMIN I. SCHWARTZ

UNIVERSITY OF WASHINGTON PRESS

SEATTLE & LONDON

Library of Congress Cataloging in Publication Data
Main entry under title:

Ideology and politics in contemporary China.

(Studies in Chinese government and politics, 4)
Based on papers from the 5th conference sponsored by the Subcommittee on Chinese Government and Politics of the Joint Committee on Contemporary China of the American Council of Learned Societies and the Social Science Research Council, held at Santa Fe, N. M., Aug. 2–6, 1971.
Includes bibliographical references.
1. China (People's Republic of China, 1949–   )—Politics and government—Addresses, essays, lectures. 2. Communism—China (People's Republic of China, 1949–   )—Addresses, essays, lectures. I. Israel, John. II. Johnson, Chalmers A., ed. III. Joint Committee on Contemporary China. Subcommittee on Chinese Government and Politics. IV. Series.
DS777.55.I3   320.9'51'05   72-11514
ISBN 0-295-95247-4
ISBN 0-295-95255-5 (pbk)

CHALMERS JOHNSON

Introduction

One of the most persistent problems, even failings, in the scholarly study of Communist societies has been a simplistic treatment of the influence of ideology on those societies. Scholars regularly play a "zero-sum" game with ideology: it either dominates everything that happens in a Communist system, or else it is mere window dressing and an observer who calls attention to its presence is, in fact, offering evidence of his own "anti-Communist" bias. Thus, for example, in the analysis of the Chinese Communist movement during the 1940's, foreigners tended to dispute whether Chinese Communist behavior or Chinese Communist ideology offered the best evidence about the true nature of the Chinese Communist movement. The evidence from behavior indicated that the Communists were moderate reformers, addressing themselves to real social grievances; the evidence from ideology suggested that they were Leninists, carefully disguising their long-term goals in order to promote a "united front" through which they hoped to seize power. Both propositions were true, but only error resulted from advancing one to the exclusion of the other.

This problem is not just one of the need to synthesize the evidence of behavior and ideology, but rather of the need to conceptualize ideology properly. In its vulgarized version, ideology in a Communist system is thought to function analogously to a blueprint. In Michael Oakeshott's words: "A political ideology purports to be an abstract principle, or set of related abstract principles, which has been independently premeditated. It supplies in advance of the activity of attending to the arrangements of a society a formulated end to be pursued, and in so doing it provides a means of distinguishing between those desires which ought to be encouraged and those which ought to

v

be suppressed or redirected." [1] The issue here is the "premeditation" of ideology, not its capacity to prescribe or disallow various desires. Oakeshott believes that "instead of an independently premeditated scheme of ends to be pursued, [ideology] is a system of ideas abstracted from the manner in which a people have been accustomed to go about the business of attending to the arrangements of their societies. The pedigree of every political ideology shows it to be the creature, not of premeditation in advance of political activity, but of meditation upon a manner of politics. In short, political activity comes first and a political ideology follows after." [2]

Although Oakeshott was not thinking particularly about Communist movements or Communist societies, it seems to me that his understanding of the origins of ideology—as a "meditation upon a manner of politics"—finds greater support from the history of Chinese communism than does the theory of a premeditated blueprint. It is true that the early leaders of the Chinese Communist Party sought to apply in China a Russian "blueprint," but it was in fact a Leninist meditation on the Bolshevik revolution and its aftermath. Mao Tse-tung's early revolutionary strategy grew out of his reflection on the failure of the imported Leninist blueprint. His more fully developed "theory of people's war" was written during the Yenan period and was explicitly conceived in light of the defeat of the Kiangsi Soviet and of the Long March. The initial, postliberation conception of "socialist transformation and construction" in China was, again, a distillation from a Soviet "manner of politics." The ideology of the Great Leap Forward, as many observers have pointed out, made sense only in light of many earlier—particularly of the Yenan period—organizational precedents. And finally, the ideology of the Cultural Revolution was indubitably the product of Mao's meditations on the failure of the Great Leap, on the Sino-Soviet dispute, and possibly on much of the history of the Chinese manner of politics and the international Communist movement. Needless to add, ideology as the summing up of the heritage of the past plays a prescriptive role for the present. Equally true, meditations on past politics may lead to positive insights—or to illusions, to the mistaking of "fact" for "not-fact," or of "not-fact" for "fact." [3] That Chinese Communist ideological summations have been both pre-

[1] Michael Oakeshott, *Rationalism in Politics* (New York: Basic Books, 1962), p. 116.
[2] *Ibid.*, pp. 118–19.
[3] *Ibid.*, p. 207.

scriptive for the present and occasionally illusionary is made abundantly clear in the papers that follow in this volume.

The essays and reports of recent research collected here are not about either "ideology" or "politics" but about the interaction between the two. In the conference that preceded the writing of this book, the participants addressed themselves in general and in detail to the influence of Chinese Communist ideology on the Chinese revolution and to the influence of the Chinese revolution on Chinese Communist ideology. All of the papers are concerned more or less explicitly with this theme. In the initial paper, on continuities and discontinuities between pre-Communist Chinese ideologies and the latest outpourings of the current regime, John Israel "sinicizes" the problem of ideology for us, reminding the student of "Marxism-Leninism-Mao Tsetung Thought" of the manifold Chinese influences that he is likely to ignore if he abstracts current ideology from its true political setting. Israel's playful language and open questioning of how one discovers a "continuity" provide a welcome antidote to the customary portentousness that accompanies the study of any Communist ideology.

In the next two papers, Richard Solomon and Jerome Ch'en take up directly the relationship between political activity and ideological innovation. Solomon studies the various functions that ideology has performed for the Chinese Communists—legitimacy, identity, solidarity, agitation, communication, and goal-specification—and indicates when and why one function has been dominant over others during different periods of the Chinese Communist movement. Ch'en documents the development of Mao's Marxism and his "heresies," including his reliance on the masses, his commitment to protracted struggle, and his attack on ideological dogmatism, in terms of Mao's contests with other claimants to ideological leadership.

In Part II, "Ideology and the Intellectuals," our authors invite us to witness directly the most insightful of politicized Chinese actually meditating on the Chinese manner of politics, in each case on what was wrong with that manner rather than on its special genius. Sullivan and Solomon describe in detail how and why many Chinese came to the ideological conclusion that political change in China had to be accompanied by a "cultural revolution." Suzanne Pepper, in exploring the mordant meditations of Chinese intellectuals during the Civil War on the Kuomintang, traces the development of their rationale for supporting the Communists despite their own deep-seated doubts about the desirability of communism. Merle Goldman looks at Communist intellectuals in the period following the Great Leap Forward, when they were trying desperately to reintroduce certain ideological principles that had suffered during the Leap but whose continued validity seemed reinforced by the failure of the Leap.

The papers of Part III, "Maoism in Action," all deal with specific instances in which previous politics or changes in the political environment led to changes in ideology and to new ideological distillations of the past. Utilizing the valuable new materials made available by the Cultural Revolution, Byung-joon Ahn recreates the Great Leap Forward in startling detail. He documents the extent to which the Party "de-Maoized" itself in attempting to recover from the Leap, and he points to a major function of ideology in describing Mao's ability to stop the drift toward private farming and material incentives by defining these trends in terms of a renascent "class struggle." During the conference in which these papers were critically discussed, Mao's counterattack against the Party's "crisis managers" was likened to what it would have been like if Herbert Hoover had come back into politics in 1936 and had condemned the New Dealers for "revisionism" against the capitalist system—although perhaps a comparison with Napoleon's return from Elba would be more appropriate in light of the Chairman's place in history.

Rensselaer Lee leads us through Mao's meditations on the customary roles of scientists and technicians in modern China, and he outlines the ideology of technological innovation by the masses that resulted. Philip Bridgham describes a particularly apt instance of the interaction of ideology and politics: what the ideology of the Cultural Revolution did to China's foreign relations and how Mao's and Chou En-lai's meditations on that dangerous outcome led quickly to a change in ideology. Finally, Benjamin Schwartz brilliantly takes up the problem of the possibility of illusion emerging from an ideological summary. He discusses critically two of the latest ideological positions of the Chinese Communists, namely, their beliefs that they have discovered effective substitutes for both bureaucrats and scientists. His essay is particularly noteworthy for its exploration of Maoism as a contribution not just to Chinese ideology but to a universal ideology, a meditation on everyone's manner of politics.

To my mind each of these papers makes an important and original contribution to the continuing study of modern Chinese politics, but it goes without saying that this volume is neither a comprehensive analysis nor an encyclopedia of Chinese Communist ideology. It was not intended to be. This volume grew out of a scholarly "conference," one of those devices for promoting a new area of learning that have played such an important role in the study of modern China. As a first step in this procedure, a committee of scholars appoints an organizer, who in turn invites—within the limitations of his budget—all the promising participants he knows of to present papers. The group then gathers for a week of intensive debate and criticism of each other's work, and the organizer returns to his study to fabricate a book derived from the conference and addressed to a wider audience of readers than the conference itself.

This particular conference, the fifth sponsored by the Subcommittee on Chinese Government and Politics of the Joint Committee on Contemporary China of the American Council of Learned Societies and the Social Science Research Council, met in Santa Fe, New Mexico, between August 2 and 6, 1971. As organizer and editor for the conference, I made the selection of papers to be published here. I am painfully aware that not all of the major research presented at this conference is represented in this volume, but I believe that all the papers contained herein reflect the high level of research and inquiry that distinguished the conference.

The nineteen scholars who participated in the Santa Fe conference are: Byung-joon Ahn, Western Illinois University; A. Doak Barnett, Brookings Institution; Robert Bedeski, Ohio State University; Philip Bridgham, Central Intelligence Agency; Parris Chang, Pennsylvania State University; Jerome Ch'en, York University; Merle Goldman, Boston University; John Israel, University of Virginia; Chalmers Johnson, University of California, Berkeley; Rensselaer W. Lee III, City College of New York; Klaus Mehnert, Institut für Politische Wissenschaft, Aachen; Mineo Nakajima, Tokyo University of Foreign Studies; Suzanne Pepper, University of California, Berkeley; Robert Rinden, University of California, Berkeley; Robert Scalapino, University of California, Berkeley; Benjamin Schwartz, Harvard University; Richard Solomon, University of Michigan; George Taylor, University of Washington; and Noriyuki Tokuda, Institute of Developing Economies, Tokyo.[4]

[4] Parris Chang's paper on "The Role of Ch'en Po-ta in the Cultural Revolution" has been expanded and published as *Radicals and Radical Ideology in the Cultural Revolution* (New York: Research Institute on Communist Affairs, Columbia University, 1972).

Mr. Tokuda's valuable paper for the conference on the rise of Mao Tse-tung and on the emergence of his ideology to a place of dominance in the Party has been published

I should like to acknowledge the valuable assistance in the organization of this conference and in the editing of this volume that I have received from Josephine Pearson and Jane Kaneko of the Center for Chinese Studies, University of California, Berkeley; from John Campbell of the Social Science Research Council; and from Ivars and Judy Lauersons, who served as rapporteurs for the conference.

partly in English and completely in Japanese. See N. Tokuda, "Yenan Rectification Movement: Mao Tse-tung's Big Push toward Charismatic Leadership during 1941–1942," *The Developing Economics* (Tokyo), IX (March, 1971), 83–99; and *Mō Taku-tō-shugi no keisei, 1935–1945* (The Formation of Mao Tse-tungism, 1935–1945) (Tokyo: Keiō Tsūshin, 1971).

Contents

PART III. MAOISM IN ACTION

ABBREVIATIONS USED IN NOTES

CB	*Current Background*
CFJP	*Chieh-fang jih-pao* (Liberation Daily)
CQ	*The China Quarterly*
HCN	*Hsin ch'ing nien* (New Youth)
JMJP	*Jen-min jih-pao* (People's Daily)
JPRS	*Joint Publications Research Service*
KJJP	*Kung-jen jih-pao* (Workers' Daily)
KMJP	*Kuang-ming jih-pao* (Bright Daily)
KTTH	*Kung-tso t'ung-hsün* (Work Bulletin)
NCNA	New China News Agency
SCMM	*Selections from China Mainland Magazines*
SCMP	*Survey of the China Mainland Press*
TKP	*Ta kung pao* (Impartial Daily)
URI	Union Research Institute
URS	Union Research Service

PART I

Origins and Functions

JOHN ISRAEL

Continuities and Discontinuities in the Ideology of the Great Proletarian Cultural Revolution

"Continuities in Chinese history" is a shopworn subject. Historians have launched a devastating series of assaults on the cliché of "5,000 years of changeless Chinese civilization." In regard to modern China, on the other hand, it has become fashionable to emphasize the heavy weight of tradition that imposed itself upon even revolutionists who championed radical change. To seek time-honored patterns in nineteenth- and twentieth-century history has gained the status of a popular parlor game, if not an academic cult.

The quest for continuities in post-1949 China has become even more complicated. From the first, politics seized command. Scholars sympathetic to Chinese communism (or at least critical of anti-Chinese-Communist American foreign policy) ferreted out continuities. The simplest argument suggested that Chinese traditions were functional, hence good; Chinese communism was traditional, ergo, Chinese communism was good. More subtle minds reasoned that hierarchical, authoritarian traditions, though "evil" from an American perspective, were historically understandable when they appeared in Chinese communism. If Mao had borrowed a few points from Stalin, he had done so "naturally," in a manner consistent with his heritage. Because it was "bad" in an indigenous way, Chinese communism did not have to be attributed to machinations of the Kremlin.

The continuities argument, however, could be double-edged. Karl Wittfogel contended that a despotic Chinese tradition had been inter-

3

rupted by a pluralistic republican effort, only to be reimposed by the Communists. By reverting to tradition, Mao was not only bad but, still worse, historically retrogressive. Many who shared Wittfogel's assessment of the present parted company over the past and favored a discontinuities approach: Chinese tradition was good; Chinese communism destroyed tradition; therefore Chinese communism was bad. The roots of evil were to be found not in China's past but in an external source—international communism, emanating from America's Cold War enemy, the Soviet Union. Hence Chinese communism was as dangerous as it was immoral. The policy position that followed centered around the alternative of a Taiwan-based model of modernization-within-tradition. All these arguments had become tediously familiar. The continuities versus discontinuities issue was both a dead dog and a red herring. One might well think twice before reviving this genre of historical analysis.[1]

Recent developments have redefined the problem without altogether decontaminating it. The deepening Sino-Soviet rift has made the domestic-roots-versus-Soviet-transplant debate increasingly irrelevant, and the Great Proletarian Cultural Revolution (GPCR) has made it difficult for sympathetic analysts to argue that seemingly revolutionary phenomena were, in fact, highly traditional. To be sympathetic to the Cultural Revolution, one should take its expressed goals seriously, and these were explicitly revolutionary in the most extremely antitraditional way. The most striking thing about GPCR ideology was its militant presentism—its refusal to pay homage to the past except insofar as the past was encapsulated in the thought and writings of the Chairman. Discontinuity was the key idea of the Cultural Revolution.

To be sure, iconoclastic criticism of the "feudal" past antedated the Cultural Revolution, but with Chinese historians culling their traditions to create a selective ancestral lineage, it had behooved the sympathetic foreigner to join the search. Now the past was execrated, when it was mentioned at all. Only the targets of the GPCR, like Wu Han and Teng T'o, harped upon the lessons of history, and what they found was denounced as subversive. Red Guards were urged to "destroy the Four Olds." "To rebel is justified"—an idea diametrically opposed to traditional concepts of loyalty and harmony—became the battle cry. Pre-

---

[1] Benjamin Schwartz suggests the following categorization of schools of thought on continuities and discontinuities: (1) bad present continuous with a bad past (Wittfogel) ; (2) good present discontinuous with a bad past (New Left); (3) good present continuous with a good past (Needham); (4) bad present discontinuous with a good past (Taiwan).

viously, by delineating parallels with the past, one could lend an aura of familiarity to aspects of communism that would otherwise seem mysterious and diabolical. Now those seeking reassurance from history were reduced to comparing the extremism of the GPCR with transient elements—paranoid founding emperors of peasant origin, fanatical but short-lived rebellious sects—rather than with enduring traditions. One could derive a small measure of comfort from the thought that even collective madness was very Chinese but that it too would soon pass away. Given this unhappy situation, it is little wonder that friendly writers have sought similarities to foreign experiences (excluding, of course, such phenomena as Stalin's purges), pointing to supranational processes such as modernization, populism, and the "Protestant ethic" to demonstrate that the Chinese were simply doing, in their own way, what others had done.[2]

Still undeterred, the dogged continuities buff may counter with three arguments. (1) No matter what the possible abuses of history, one cannot cease to communicate for fear of being misunderstood. (2) The study of continuity and discontinuity is at the very core of the historian's calling. The special problems of the Chinese case complicate the problem, but also make it more alluring. (3) Once anticipated, pitfalls may be avoided. One may cut through the glitter of surface similarities to seek deeper patterns, abjuring unintended political implications. With these caveats in mind, we set forth.

EXPLORING A FEW TRAILWAYS

"We learn to swim by swimming," saith the Chairman. May we not, then, learn to find continuities by looking for continuities? In this exploratory spirit, let us examine a few of the more prominent features of GPCR ideology that seem to have past precedents. We should then be able to identify some of the problems and to continue on our quest in a more sure-footed fashion.

PHILOSOPHY OF MIND

In times of crisis, notes Wing-tsit Chan, the philosophy of mind comes to the fore. Writing of the early Ming, Chan observes:

---

[2] On modernization, see "Comments by Michael Oksenberg" in Ping-ti Ho and Tang Tsou (eds.), *China in Crisis*, Vol. I: *China's Heritage and the Communist Political System* (Chicago: University of Chicago Press, 1968), Bk. 2, pp. 487–500. Also, papers by Charles Hoffman and Harry Harding, presented to the University Seminar on Modern East Asia: China, at Columbia University, March 10 and May 12, 1971, respectively. On populism, see Maurice Meisner, "Leninism and Maoism: Some Populist Perspectives on

It was a time not for dry and disinterested intellectual speculation but for moral choice and personal decision. In a climate like this, the philosophy of mind was an irresistible development. That was the case in mid-nineteenth-century Japan when the Meiji Restoration demanded determination and dedication. This is the case in present-day China, when the national crisis forces the best scholars to search within themselves for an explanation and a solution.[3]

In the GPCR, the key term is not *hsin* (mind) but *ssu-hsiang* (thought). As James Chieh Hsiung notes in his incisive explication of *ssu-hsiang,* there are significant differences in etymology and usage between the two terms, and there may or may not be lineal continuity from one to the other. Nonetheless, since both refer to the same conceptual realm, and since they have been used synonymously by no less an authority than Mao Tse-tung, they provide a fruitful field for our search for continuities.[4] Since the term "mind" has many usages and "philosophy of mind" numerous ramifications, our problems may be better delineated if we confine ourselves to three general propositions: (1) Truth is innate within the mind. (2) The values of the mind are more important than the needs of the body. (3) Spirit can transform matter.

Truth is innate within the mind. True knowledge comes from within, from a proper state of mind in mastery of a fundamental principle, not from the arduous "study of things." This idea is basic to the philosophy of *hsin* as expounded by Wang Yang-ming. Its social implications are highly equalitarian. Egalitarian, universalistic potentialities, as well as hierarchical and particularistic ones, are present in Confucian thought. The civil-service examination system theoretically made possible social mobility based upon intellectual accomplishment, but in fact maintained a hierarchy based largely upon economic advantage and family background. By de-emphasizing the costly, time-consuming memorization of texts and commentaries, Wang Yang-ming accentuated the more egalitarian side of the tradition. By equating knowledge and action, he tended to make correct behavior the proof of correct thought.

Chinese communism, likewise, contains both potentialities. From

---

Marxism-Leninism in China," *CQ,* No. 45 (January–March, 1971), pp. 2–36. On the Protestant ethic, see Maurice Meisner, "Utopian Goals and Ascetic Values in Chinese Communist Ideology," *Journal of Asian Studies,* 28, No. 1 (November, 1968), 101–10.

[3] Wing-tsit Chan, "The Ch'eng-Chu School of Early Ming," in William Theodore de Bary (ed.), *Self and Society in Ming Thought* (New York: Columbia University Press, 1970), p. 46.

[4] See James Chieh Hsiung, *Ideology and Practice: The Evolution of Chinese Communism* (New York: Praeger, 1970), pp. 138–43.

Marx it inherits the view that a man's thought derives from his social class, which is based upon his relationship to the forces of production. Chinese tradition, on the other hand, emphasized the ultimate goodness and educability of all men. Drawing upon such indigenous ideas, the Chinese Communists have practiced thought reform, hoping to proletarianize the ideas and behavior of all but the most benighted social elements. In fact, however, this reform has allowed members of "reactionary" classes to compete on equal terms with those of "revolutionary" classes and—because the educational system rewarded family origin, wealth, and prior educational opportunities—"reactionary" children were able to get ahead.

Tension between the doctrine of predestination by social class and the belief in universal salvation has created a fundamental ambiguity in the ideology of the Cultural Revolution. Mao has generally assumed support from the overwhelming majority of Chinese. Though an elastic term, "the people" has tended to be inclusive rather than exclusive. However, in the early stages of the GPCR, clear lines were drawn. "Black elements," including landlords, rich peasants, capitalists, rightists, and "bad elements," were fair game for young vigilantes. Membership in the Red Guards was restricted to the "Five Kinds of Red"—children of workers, poor peasants, revolutionary martyrs, revolutionary cadres, and revolutionary soldiers. Later on, however, such notions were anathematized as the "bourgeois reactionary Theory of Family Lineage." [5] The direction of the movement was away from a priori classifications toward a new kind of achievement-orientation based upon mastery of the basic writings of Mao and willingness to participate in revolutionary struggle. Though this did not represent a total abandonment of the notion of enlightenment through study, it reduced the objects of study to a minuscule proportion of what they had been, made them available to the masses, and emphasized the inseparability of knowing and doing. Like Wang Yang-ming, the GPCR has maximized some of the egalitarian potentialities in its own tradition.

The values of the mind are more important than the needs of the body. This idea is prominent in Chinese thought both before and after Wang Yang-ming. According to Confucius, a wise ruler should enrich his people before attempting to educate them. This did not mean that food was more important than correct ideas, at least for the *chun-tzu*

5 Gordon A. Bennett and Ronald N. Montaperto, *Red Guard: The Political Biography of Dai Hsiao-ai* (Garden City, N.Y.: Doubleday, 1971), pp. 94–95, 4.

(man of true virtue), for Confucius also said that the *chun-tzu* would value goodness more than life itself.[6] Though Confucius was no extremist, some of his followers advocated mortification of the flesh on the altar of absolute moral standards. These ideas reached their zenith —or their nadir, if you will—after the advent of neo-Confucianism. Moralists asserted that it was better for a woman to die than to remarry, and they carried on a tradition of edifying tales about children who cut off their own flesh to nurture ailing parents.

Now that "the people" have become functional equivalents of parents, we read similar stories in a new context. Quite aside from the breed of super-heroes who give their lives for the people, there are homier tales about ordinary men like the People's Liberation Army (PLA) soldier Liu Tso-yeh. One morning, Liu marched off with his unit from a village, forgetting that he had borrowed a needle from a peasant woman to prick painful blisters. Suddenly realizing his oversight, he convened a seminar on Chairman Mao's injunction, "Do not take a single needle or piece of thread from the masses." His duty was clear: to return the needle. "As he hurried on," writes the hagiographer, "the pain from his blistered feet shot through his legs but he paid them no heed. His single thought was to return the needle." [7]

In overpopulated and underindustrialized twentieth-century China, it has been easier for leaders to preach moral virtues to the masses than to satisfy their material needs. In expounding the principles of the New Life Movement, Chiang Kai-shek declared:

When these virtues (*li, i, lien,* and *ch'ih*) prevail, even if food and clothing are insufficient, they can be produced by manpower; or, if the granary is empty, it can be filled through human effort. On the other hand, when these virtues are not observed, if food and clothing are insufficient, they will not be made sufficient by fighting and robbing; or, if the granary is empty, it will not be filled by stealing and begging. The four virtues, which rectify the misconduct of men, are the proper method of achieving abundance.[8]

In March, 1942, in the midst of the war against Japan, Chiang declared that "victory will be due ninety per cent to spiritual factors and only ten per cent to material factors." [9] The GPCR's emphasis upon

---

[6] Arthur Waley (trans.), *The Analects of Confucius* (London: Allen and Unwin, 1938), pp. 173, 195.

[7] "A Single Needle," *Peking Review,* X, No. 1 (January 6, 1967), 31.

[8] Chiang Kai-shek, "Essentials of the New Life Movement," in William Theodore de Bary, Wing-tsit Chan, and Chester Tan (eds.), *Sources of Chinese Tradition* (New York: Columbia University Press, 1964), II, 140–41.

[9] Quoted in Norman D. Palmer, "Makers of Modern China, VI, Chiang Kai-shek: Immovable Stone," *Current History,* XVI, No. 89 (January, 1949), 5.

proper attitudes and on ideological motivation over material concerns
obviously has ample precedents, modern as well as traditional.

Spirit can transform matter. This idea is clearly expounded in the
above quotation from Chiang to the effect that virtue produces
abundance. It is reassuring to believe that man, in placing spiritual
values over material ones, will ultimately achieve both. This thought
leads to an extreme emphasis on the force of human will over nature
and technology, which Robert Jay Lifton has termed "psychism." [10]
The notion that practical skills are extensions of moral virtues was
voiced by the eighteenth-century literatus Chang Hsueh-ch'eng, who
believed (in the words of David Nivison) that "learning to write is
actually a species of Neo-Confucian self-cultivation." [11] In the nineteenth and twentieth centuries, the belief that all reforms begin with
the right state of mind appears in the ideas of the T'ung-chih restora-
tionists and is prominent in Liang Ch'i-ch'ao's stress on the attitudinal
qualities of the "new citizen." "Whether we succeed or fail," stated
Sun Yat-sen, "depends largely upon whether we think we can succeed
or not. If we have faith in what we do, we can move mountains and
level seas. If we have no faith, we cannot even raise our hands and
break a twig." [12] From Sun's declaration that faith could move mountains to Mao's "Foolish Old Man" is but a short distance.

THE INVESTIGATION OF THINGS

How about the investigation of things? Revolutionary experiences
unquestionably are "things" in the broader sense of the word, and
going from place to place to expound one's own and examine those of
others certainly looks like "investigation." Since there were seventy-
two explanations of the term *ko-wu* [13] (commonly translated as "investigation of things" in line with Chu Hsi's commentaries), why not
add a seventy-third? One can almost see the small type of simplified
characters in the commentary of an updated edition of the *Great
Learning: "ko-wu, ch'uan-lien yeh."*

When the historian does things like this, he is no longer hunting for

[10] Robert Jay Lifton, *Revolutionary Immortality* (New York: Vintage, 1968), p. xv
and *passim.*
[11] David S. Nivison, "The Problem of 'Knowledge' and 'Action' in Chinese Thought
since Wang Yang-ming," in Arthur F. Wright (ed.), *Studies in Chinese Thought* (Chicago: University of Chicago Press, 1953), p. 129.
[12] Quoted in Hu Shih and Lin Yu-t'ang, *China's Own Critics* (Tientsin, 1931), p. 49,
which is cited by Nivison in "The Problem of 'Knowledge' and 'Action,' " p. 138.
[13] Wing-tsit Chan, *A Source Book in Chinese Philosophy* (Princeton, N.J.: Princeton
University Press, 1963), p. 561.

continuities; he is fishing for analogies. What *is* worth noting is that, no matter how Confucianists interpreted the two characters, *ko-wu*, they generally confined themselves to the investigation of things ethical.[14] By the seventeenth century, this led men like Ku Yen-wu and Yen Jo-ch'ü to carry out highly "scientific" textual studies of the classics without showing any interest in applying their methodology to the natural world.[15] The preoccupation with ethical goals continues to absorb the Chinese Communists even though they encourage "scientific experimentation." To this extent they share not only the concerns of Chu Hsi but those of an honorable, though neglected, tradition in Western thought that refuses to divorce the world of science from fundamental human values.

KNOWLEDGE AND ACTION

Another duality which the GPCR attempts to reconcile is "knowledge" and "action." The history of this problem since Wang Yangming has been skillfully discussed elsewhere.[16] Therefore we will confine ourselves to some supplementary observations specifically relating to the Cultural Revolution. The significance of these terms and of their relationship to one another changes with historical context. For example, in discussing T'an Ssu-t'ung's ideas, Nivison notes that "the reason for making Confucius the founder of a 'religion' was to guarantee the priority of 'knowledge' *over* 'action,' that is, of the man of vision, who constructs an ideal, a blueprint for the future, over the defenders of traditional experience and practices actually in use." [17] Like the "Reformers of '98," the "ideologues of '66" sought to mobilize a religified orthodoxy to change established institutions. However, unlike K'ang Yu-wei and T'an Ssu-t'ung, they were less concerned with designing blueprints for the future than with spurring men to action here and now. Might their needs not be met, then, by Sun Yat-sen's dictum, "Knowledge is difficult, action is easy," which serves to glorify the Supreme Knower while discouraging *immobilism* among his followers? No. The message that comes through in the GPCR is rather different: *knowledge* is easy (the simplified thought of Mao being universally available via the "little red book"), but *action*—applying these thoughts in practice—is difficult. However, in a revolutionary

14 *Ibid.*, p. 562.
15 *Ibid.*, p. 612.
16 See Nivison, "The Problem of 'Knowledge' and 'Action,'" pp. 112–45.
17 *Ibid.*, p. 135.

age, heroic deeds must become commonplace. Hence it is the very
difficulty of acting that is supposed to inspire men to act.

There is essential continuity, nonetheless, in the idea that knowledge
and action (now called "theory" and "practice") should be intimately
interrelated. In his introduction to Mao's *Quotations,* Lin Piao says,
"In studying the works of Chairman Mao, one should do so with
specific problems in mind." [18] The strong antischolastic emphasis of
this idea is confirmed by the avalanche of articles about individuals and
groups that used Mao's thought to solve particular problems. However,
Lin goes on to say that such topical applications of the Chairman's
thoughts may be necessary mainly "to get quick results." "In order
really to master Mao Tse-tung's thought, it is essential to study many
of Chairman Mao's basic concepts over and over again," writes Lin,
"and it is best to memorize important statements and study and apply
them repeatedly." This sounds like an echo from the standard Confucian education. Lin then concludes that "to study selected quotations
from Chairman Mao with specific problems in mind is a good method
for learning Mao Tse-tung's thought, a method conducive to quick results." [19] The process is circular. Theory is good for solving problems,
but the application of theory in particular situations is also instrumental to mastering the theory. In rejecting logical opposites in favor
of mutually fulfilling *completes,*[20] Lin is adhering to a deeply ingrained principle of Chinese thought.

THE ROLE OF STRUGGLE

Theory is translated into practice, however, via struggle—a principle
alien to the mainstream of traditional Chinese thought. Nineteenth-
century China's brutal experience in the international jungle forced
many of her most perceptive minds to the conclusion that human affairs were governed not by the ancient principles of harmony and reconciliation but by a relentless contest for supremacy. Yen Fu, Liang
Ch'i-ch'ao, and the young intellectuals who came of age after the turn
of the century were tremendously impressed by Social Darwinism,
which so vividly described the world in which they lived. From that

[18] Lin Piao, "Foreword to the Second Edition," in Mao Tse-tung, *Quotations from
Chairman Mao Tse-tung* (Peking: Foreign Languages Press, 1968), p. ii.
[19] *Ibid.*
[20] "Completes" is a term suggested to me by Roderick Scott and included in some
of his personal manuscripts. I do not know whether it has found its way into the
literature on Chinese philosophy.

point on, the leitmotiv of struggle was a persistent one in the thought of diverse groups. Though anarchists saw individuals and voluntary associations confronting the state, only a rare maverick like Hu Shih interpreted Social Darwinism primarily as a struggle of individuals against one another rather than of groups. Nearly all agreed that China and other nations were locked in a struggle in which only the fittest would survive.

Chinese Marxists shifted the arena from nature to history and proclaimed that struggle was conducted through social classes. Mao, like many contemporary leaders of his generation, absorbed more than a little Social Darwinism en route to Marxism.[21] Struggle plays a prominent role in his writings. His earliest work, "An Essay on Physical Education," urges individuals to toughen themselves for the struggle of life. As James Hsiung observes, the theme of struggle is prominent in his Hunan report, in which he "obliquely challenged the *Analects* of Confucius by stating flatly that no real revolution could be carried out 'gently, kindly, politely, plainly, and modestly.' " [22] The "Three Great Revolutionary Movements" of the Cultural Revolution are "class struggle, struggle for production, and scientific experiment," and the spirit of struggle permeates even the third of these.

Nor is the struggle a thing of the moment. Contradictions, hence struggle, are to continue even under communism. Enemies of the masses, foes of the revolution, will always exist. There is a feeling of danger, both imminent and permanent. Mao is in danger. The revolution is in danger. They must be defended. By struggling against present enemies, men toughen themselves to become still stauncher revolutionists in future battles. Wherever there are men in motion, from the swim in the Yangtze to the fire in the Tach'ing oil fields, there is struggle. Struggle has become one of the central concepts of Chinese Communist thought.

There is only partial continuity between *yin-yang* reasoning and the dialectic. The *yin* and the *yang* oppose one another, but in the process they complete one another. Both survive. They produce no higher synthesis. The process is not one of struggle between them but of interaction, alternation, reconciliation, balance, and order. *Yin-yang* thinking may, as James Hsiung claims, have "influenced Mao's theory of contradictions as much as Marx and Lenin have"; but it is also true,

[21] Marian Galik, "From Chuang-tzu to Lenin: Mao Tun's Intellectual Development," *African and Asian Studies*, No. 3 (1967), p. 109.
[22] Hsiung, *Ideology and Practice*, p. 238.

as he notes, that only Mao's *non*antagonistic contradictions truly resemble *yin-yang*.[23] Antagonistic contradictions and the dynamic historical process that arises from them is far removed from *yin-yang* reasoning.

If one starts with the *chung-yung* (central harmony) of the Confucianists, one finds *tou-cheng* (struggle) at the other extreme. The former emphasizes reconciliation, the latter irreconcilability; the one moderation, the other excess; the former uniting two into one, the latter dividing one into two. The difference in spirit is evident in a quotation attributed to the Chairman: "What Confucius said about 'the compassionate loving the compassionate' actually meant loving the exploiters." [24]

There were, of course, limits to Confucian tolerance. Mencius gave short shrift to the "dangerous" thoughts of Yang and Chu, and the upright T'ang official Han Yü viewed Buddhism and Taoism much as Mao views feudal and bourgeois thought. Han Yü believed there could be no peaceful coexistence between truth and falsehood. If Confucianism were to survive, its rivals must be liquidated. "Let us man their sectaries, let us burn their books, let us secularize their temples," he advised.[25] There were literary proscriptions during the Sung, Yüan, and Ming dynasties, capped by the famous "literary inquisition of Ch'ien Lung," an emperor who could not tolerate the writings of an allegedly disloyal official who had died more than a century earlier. "Now Ch'ien Ch'ien-i is already dead, and his bones have long since rotted away," wrote the emperor, "but his books remain, an insult to right doctrines and a violation of [the principles of] loyalty. How can we permit them to exist and be handed down any longer. They must be done away with." [26] Censorship of plays, novels, essays, newspapers, and periodicals on Taiwan suggests that those who claim to be faithful guardians of traditional values have not failed in their mission.

The new element in the Cultural Revolution is not its narrowed tolerance for heterodoxy so much as (1) its broadened definition of public domain, hence of the kinds of literary and artistic expression that would fall under control; (2) its narrowed definition of orthodoxy,

---

[23] *Ibid.*, p. 103.

[24] "Chairman Mao's Conversation with Comrades Ch'en Po-ta and K'ang Sheng" (1965), in "Selections from Chairman Mao," *Translations on Communist China*, No. 90 (February 12, 1970) (*JPRS*, No. 49826), p. 26.

[25] Quoted in Luther Carrington Goodrich, *The Literary Inquisition of Ch'ien-Lung* (Baltimore, Md.: Waverly, 1935), p. 3.

[26] *Ibid.*, pp. 26, 102–3.

hence the kind of expression that would be permitted; and (3) its move toward virtually total control of the media of verbal and nonverbal expression.

If the world is in a process of eternal conflict, there can be no utopia. Here the ideology of the GPCR contrasts sharply with classical Marxist thinking as well as with the utopian strain in Confucian thought. Confucianists tended to find their utopias in the past, in the Golden Age of Yao, Shun, Yü, and the Duke of Chou. Radical reformers often suggested that the "well field" system and other elements of the ideal society found in the *Chou Li* (Rites of Chou) could be reestablished in the present. K'ang Yu-wei, interpreting Chinese history in a linear, progressive manner, anticipated a utopian Age of Great Harmony. And, as recently as the Great Leap Forward, Chinese Communist thinkers justified herculean efforts of the present so that everyone could live "at ease" in the future. Now, however, the Cultural Revolution has attempted to mobilize a nation of revolutionists without offering hope of a future nirvana. There is no reconciliation of antagonisms in the future, no respite from conflict. Sacrifice, service, and struggle will continue indefinitely, for they are the very substance of the eternal revolutionary process.

It is the process itself that is valuable. Precedents for this idea may be sought in the workaday, nonutopian notion that although men can never recreate the Golden Age, they must always strive to approximate its ideals. Though seldom expressed so explicitly, this is the underlying assumption of "Chinese realism"—a way of thought much more pervasive than utopianism, and also less revolutionary. Here, in the emphasis upon process, Mao finds himself in the company of the execrated Hu Shih. His "Foolish Old Man" may never have heard of Hu's notion of "bit by bit, drop by drop" progress or of "social immortality," but he behaved as if he had. There are differences (Hu would have given the old man a steam shovel), but the emphasis on inexorable process is shared.

ANTIBUREAUCRATISM

Another time-honored tenet of GPCR ideology is antibureaucratism. According to James Hsiung, "the Maoists complained that the Liu group had perpetuated the ancient tradition of *tso-kuan tang-lao-yeh* ("find a career in the bureaucracy and be a revered lord"). . . . Mao's countermeasures, known as *ching-pin chien-cheng* ("good men and simple government"), stressed the need for fewer and better personnel." [27] The new constitution of 1969, especially in its draft stage, established procedures by which Party members could communicate directly with Mao, bypassing intervening levels. This was in the tradition of "directly memorializing the emperor." [28]

There are ample antecedents for these manifestations of antibureaucratic thought. Bureaucrats were traditionally objects of suspicion both to the court and to the people. Reformers such as Wang An-shih had to run new policies through the gauntlet of bureaucratic hostility.[29] Active emperors, convinced that they represented the public interest (*kung*) as contrasted to the selfish and narrow-minded officials (*ssu*), fostered institutions intended to overcome the dead weight of bureaucracy and occasionally tried to circumvent the bureaucracy altogether in efforts to reach out to their subjects. One of the main purposes of the censorial system, writes Charles Hucker, was "to discover all violations of public policy, administrative regulations, and operational orders; thereby to purge the government of incompetence and malfeasance; and consequently to help maintain a governmental tone that accords as closely as possible with the Chinese ideal." [30]

The idea of a built-in check against lax and corrupt officials appealed to Sun Yat-sen, and the Nationalists followed his blueprint by establishing a governmental control apparatus. However, this failed to stifle the tradition of antibureaucratism. During the Sino-Japanese War of 1937–45, Chiang Kai-shek created his own instrument, the *San-min chu-i ch'ing-nien t'uan* (Three People's Principles Youth Corps), as a counterweight to the Kuomintang (KMT) party organization.

The Communists held periodic "rectification movements" and "sent down" officials who allegedly had lost touch with the masses, but these measures proved inadequate in face of the historic problems of promoting the moral virtues through a far-flung and unresponsive bureaucracy. Hence, one of the main targets of the Cultural Revolution has been the elitist, lethargic, careerist bureaucrat, a figure personifying the baneful influence of China's "feudal" culture. A document of uncertain origin but altogether in keeping with this antibureaucratic spirit is "Chairman Mao Discusses Twenty Manifestations of Bureaucracy."

[27] Hsiung, *Ideology and Practice*, p. 251.

[28] *Ibid.*, p. 286.

[29] James T. C. Liu, *Reform in Sung China* (Cambridge, Mass.: Harvard University Press, 1959), p. 7.

[30] Charles O. Hucker, *The Censorial System of Ming China* (Stanford, Calif.: Stanford University Press, 1966), p. 2.

Because this may be the most complete catalogue of antibureaucratic rhetoric in the history of China, it is worth quoting at length.

1. At the highest level there is very little knowledge; they do not understand the opinion of the masses; they do not investigate and study; they do not grasp specific policies; they do not conduct political and ideological work; they are divorced from reality, from the masses, and from the leadership of the Party; they always issue orders, and the orders are usually wrong; they certainly mislead the country and the people. . . .

2. They are conceited, complacent, and they aimlessly discuss politics. They do not grasp their work; they are subjective and one-sided; they are careless; they do not listen to people; they are truculent and arbitrary; . . . they maintain blind control. This is authoritarian bureaucracy.

3. They do not examine people and they do not investigate matters; they do not study policies; they do not rely upon the masses; they do not prepare their statements; they do not plan their work. This is brainless misdirected bureaucracy. . . .

4. Their bureaucratic attitude is immense; they do not have any direction; they are egotistic; they beat their gongs to blaze the way; they cause people to be afraid just by looking at them; they repeatedly hurl all kinds of abuse at people; their work style is crude; they do not treat people equally. This is the bureaucracy of the overlords.

5. They are ignorant; they are ashamed to ask anything; they exaggerate and they lie. . . . This is dishonest bureaucracy.

6. They do not understand politics; . . . they haggle; they put things off; they are insensitive. . . . This is irresponsible bureaucracy.

7. They are negligent about things. . . .

8. They do not completely learn politics; . . . their manner of speech is tasteless. . . . This is the deceitful, talentless bureaucracy.

9. They are stupid; they are confused; they do not have a mind of their own; they are rotten sensualists; they glut themselves for days on end. . . . This is the stupid, useless bureaucracy.

10. They want others to read documents; the others read and they sleep. . . . This is the lazy bureaucracy.

11. Government offices grow bigger and bigger; things are more confused. . . . This is the bureaucracy of government offices.

12. Documents are numerous; there is red tape; instructions proliferate. . . . This is the bureaucracy of red tape and formalism.

13. They seek pleasure and fear hardships; they engage in back-door deals. . . .

14. The greater an official becomes, the worse his temperament gets. . . . This is the bureaucracy of putting on official airs.

15. They are egotistical. . . .

16. They fight among themselves for power and money. . . .

17. A plural leadership cannot be harmoniously united; . . . there is no centralization, nor is there any democracy. This is the disunited bureaucracy.

18. There is no organization; they employ personal friends; they engage in factionalism; they maintain feudal relations. . . . This is sectarian bureaucracy. . . .

19. Their revolutionary will is weak. . . . This is degenerate bureaucracy.

20. They promote erroneous tendencies and a spirit of reaction; they connive with bad persons and tolerate bad situations; they engage in villainy and transgress the law; they engage in speculation; they are a threat to the Party and the state; they suppress democracy; they fight and take revenge; they violate laws and regulations; they protect the bad; they do not differentiate between the enemy and ourselves. This is the bureaucracy of erroneous tendencies and reaction.[31]

This document seems to suggest that Chairman Mao does not consider the bureaucracy to be altogether free of faults.

Revitalization of the bureaucracy, as reformers have generally realized, is impossible without reform of the educational and examination systems. We find in Mao something like the Taoist cynicism about the value of education *per se*. He is quoted as saying that "one who goes to school for several years becomes more stupid as he reads more books." [32] Mao's animus is not against all education, only against the wrong kind of education. Here he follows a long tradition of reformers. The early Ch'ing scholar Li Kung exclaimed that "the mere reading of books is not learning. People who read books in these times merely value the elucidation of unreal 'principles' and the memorization of 'empty words.' " [33] This finds more recent echoes in the complaints of students during the 1930's that it was criminal to read "dead books" in times of national crisis.

Mao is saddled with a system that rewards intellectual ability as exhibited in academic accomplishment. In spite of efforts to make education a handmaiden of ideology, as was attempted in imperial China with mixed results, the system has, in fact, created a skilled elite removed by schooling from the masses they are to serve. The problem is old, but the consciousness of it is new. Traditionally, the complaint was not that the elite was separated from the masses (an inevitable development, *vide* Mencius), but rather that there were inadequate opportunities for entrance into the elite. Hence the founder of the Ming dynasty simplified the examination system so that ordinary men could aspire to officialdom. But all that this did was to promote careerism on a lower level of intellectual proficiency based upon memorization of texts.[34] Proposals for educational reform during the Cultural Revolution seem to have taken this danger into account.

[31] "Chairman Mao Discusses Twenty Manifestations of Bureaucracy," in "Selections from Chairman Mao," *JPRS*, No. 49826, pp. 40–43.
[32] "Talk at Hangchow Conference" (December 21, 1965), *ibid.*, p. 3.
[33] Nivison, "The Problem of 'Knowledge' and 'Action,' " p. 124.
[34] William Theodore de Bary, "Introduction," in de Bary (ed.), *Self and Society*, p. 7.

None has suggested that simple memorization of Mao's quotations and popular writings will suffice. Practice must accompany theory.

However, mere acceleration of social mobility is not the goal. The aim is to break with the traditional paternalistic doctrine (encapsulated in Sun Yat-sen's *min-sheng*) that emperor, officials, and scholars are guardians of the public's welfare. The Maoist phrase, "serve the people," turns the traditional relationship on its head. No longer does a superior but benevolent elite place itself *in loco parentis* for the dependent masses. Now the masses are to be masters, and those with knowledge and skills are to be servants. To serve the masses, the educated elite must share the life of the masses. Fusion of work and study into an integrated life style was not unknown in premodern thought. A Ming scholar, Ch'en Hsien-chang, wrote:

> On market days at Chiang-men
> I buy hoes and I buy books
> Ploughing the fields and reading the books
> I am half farmer and half scholar.[35]

If this is an early version of "half-work, half-study," there is no evidence that the idea caught on. Ploughing the fields, for Ch'en, scarcely meant identifying with the world view of the masses. It signified, rather, a withdrawal from public life, a tacit protest against the political order. Now work-study has precisely the opposite implication. It is the epitome of orthodoxy, the most positive kind of participation in the system, a strong reaffirmation of official norms.

Maurice Meisner suggests that the explanation for recent Chinese populism "is more likely to be found in factors present in the modern Chinese historical environment" than in premodern traditions. He stresses the desire of alienated members of the intelligentsia "to bridge the gulf that separates them from society by finding roots in the vast peasant masses and speaking on their behalf." [36] Of course, the GPCR brand of populism goes far beyond merely speaking for the masses. However, is it not reasonable to assume that populist impulses find reinforcement in Chinese traditions that place moral responsibility for the well-being of the people squarely on the shoulders of the intellectual elite?

[35] Jen Yu-wen, "Ch'en Hsien-chang's Philosophy of the Natural," *ibid.*, p. 55.
[36] Meisner, "Leninism and Maoism," p. 32.

BACK HOME ON THE CONTINUITIES RESERVATIONS

The excursions we have undertaken remind us of the old adage about Chinese food. You gobble up what seem enormous quantities of ideas, but within an hour (and probably much sooner), you feel ignorant again. Some of the reasons for this unsatisfying experience are clear. The path of continuities is strewn with hidden ambiguities. What constitutes a meaningful continuity? How does one distinguish "continuities" from "precedents," "antecedents," "prototypes," and "patterns"? To qualify as a continuity, must a phenomenon be traceable in an unbroken line from its source to its most recent occurrence, or may it run part of its course underground? What is the process through which continuities are transmitted, and through what mechanism?

When an authority on Chinese philosophy tells us that "promote general welfare and remove evil" became the motto of the whole Mohist movement, we immediately note an affinity to the ideas of the Cultural Revolution. So what? Finding evidence of tradition in a movement that denounces tradition is a neat trick—if it can be done. What is the relationship between continuity and consciousness?

Of all categories of continuities, the ideological realm is the least promising. It is possible to argue that there are patterns in the *function* of ideology.[37] But the content is something else. Those who have discovered traditional patterns in Chinese communism have, more often than not, found them in spite of Communist ideological pronouncements. They argue to this effect: "The Communists say they are revolutionary [ideology], but their behavior proves they are traditional [practice]." Hence the problems of seeking continuities in Chinese history are magnified in the case of the Cultural Revolution. If we can find them here, we can find them anywhere.

However, if finding continuities is easy, finding meaningful ones is difficult. The possibility that traditional antecedents will be found for a given contemporary phenomenon increases as our picture of Chinese tradition becomes more complex. No longer is it necessary to relate our present-day observations to a monolithic Confucianism, a dualistic Confucianism-Taoism, or a trinitarian Confucianism-Taoism-Buddhism or Confucianism-Taoism-Legalism. We are acutely aware that there is a "little tradition," albeit less studied, in addition to the "great tradition." We are aware of protests within tradition, including such

[37] Hsiung, *Ideology and Practice*, p. 110.

exotic phenomena as Confucian protests against the (Confucian) examination system, to say nothing of rebel ideologies.[38] Even if contemporary thought were absolutely monolithic and self-consistent, we should be able to find *something* in it that related to *some* Chinese tradition. From this perspective, we can reverse our observation: if we cannot find continuities here, we cannot find them anywhere.

Another stumbling block in the search for meaningful continuities is the principle, so intricately worked out by Joseph Levenson, that significance changes with historical context. Similarities in form may well belie an underlying difference in spirit. Take, for example, Levenson's "amateur ideal." Superficially, this would seem akin to the Maoists' hostility to specialization. However, there is a vast difference between the amateurism of the Ming literatus and the omnicompetence of the Maoist *to-mien-shou*. The amateur ideal developed gradually and "naturally." It functioned well enough in the context of traditional political and social institutions. Unchallenged by scientism, technologism, or the cult of expertise, it was a life style unto itself—self-contained, self-sufficient, but quite unself-conscious. Contrast this to the Maoist master of all trades, a paradigm of paragons militantly asserted in a revolutionary age, painfully developed through the dichotomy of "Red and expert," and inextricably related to adulation of the working masses and hostility toward bourgeois-trained intellectuals. If we seek continuities between the two "amateur ideals," we find only negatives (both traditional and Communist China rejected rule by "experts") and high-level generalizations of dubious significance (both traditional and Communist China share the paradigm of the whole man, functionally integrated with himself and with his society).

Even more dubious is the revelation of "antecedents" or "precedents" or "continuities" to which the modern spokesman is palpably oblivious. Hence, when we read that certain rotters are "waving the red flag to oppose the red flag," it avails us little to recall that the *Ta Hsueh* (Great Learning) warns against the man who tries "to disguise himself, concealing his evil, and displaying what is good." [39]

When is an idea borrowed (either from inside or from outside a culture) and when is it the result of independent invention? How much

[38] For example, see David S. Nivison, "Protest against Conventions and Conventions of Protest," and Yuji Muramatsu, "Some Themes in Chinese Rebel Ideologies," in Arthur F. Wright (ed.), *The Confucian Persuasion* (Stanford, Calif.: Stanford University Press, 1959), pp. 177–201 and 241–67.

[39] James Legge (trans.), *The Chinese Classics* (2nd ed., rev.; Oxford: Clarendon Press, 1893), I, 366–67; quoted in Nivison, "The Problem of 'Knowledge' and 'Action,'" p. 115.

of Mao's thought comes from his readings in traditional literature? Take the heaven-storming imperial style that he displayed even as a youth. What is one to make of this? It would be easy to say that this posture was peculiarly Chinese were it not for other youths in other lands—Napoleon, for example. Is China the only country where young men boast they can lick the world, and where a few of them grow up to try it?

To become overly involved in these problems of cause would be to miss the larger questions of significance. There may be meaningful similarities between phenomena unconnected by any evident line of continuity. Since patterns exist in the mind of the beholder, why limit one's quest to China? For example, Chinese experience in dealing with large, impersonal institutions may enhance our understanding of analogous, though causally distinct, problems in our own society. The value of a cross-cultural approach is borne out in recent writings on Maoist ideology. Benjamin Schwartz attacks the notion that Mao's views are "peculiarly Chinese." Ideas coined by Rousseau, he argues, having gained general currency, became part of the thought of Mao via the Marxist-Leninist tradition. Similar, but not identical, ideas in the Chinese tradition provided reinforcement and a mechanism for selectivity.[40] Schwartz is concerned, then, with transcending the problem of Chinese uniqueness and constructing a more sophisticated model of intellectual provenance. Maurice Meisner, on the other hand, relegates the issue of provenance to a low order of importance.[41] Though he takes the trouble to argue that Chinese populism was not influenced by Russian populism and to assert an agnostic position on the traditional Chinese origins of Maoist populism, his concerns go beyond these questions. In contrast to Schwartz, who emphasizes men's capacities for misinterpreting the ideas of other men, Meisner is more impressed with the tendency for similar ideas to arise from similar historical conditions, in this case for intellectuals in "modernizing societies" to seize upon populist notions to resolve the problem of alienation. Nonetheless, both men agree that we must study the "transcultural significance" [42] of what used to be considered problems of China or, at most, problems of communism.

One final precaution before we resume our explorations. If we compare Chinese communism as a whole and the Cultural Revolution,

[40] Benjamin I. Schwartz, "The Reign of Virtue: Some Broad Perspectives on Leader and Party in the Cultural Revolution," *CQ*, No. 35 (July–September, 1968), pp. 1–17.
[41] Meisner, "Leninism and Maoism," *passim*.
[42] Schwartz, "Reign of Virtue," p. 17.

which is a selective part of that tradition, we shall find such a super-abundance of continuities that the question will be reduced simply to one of selectivity: what aspects of the Chinese Communist heritage have been emphasized in the Cultural Revolution and why? Though it is impossible to discuss the Cultural Revolution without touching upon this question, we shall leave detailed examination to others and shall, with some exceptions, focus our attention on the more tenuous relationship to China's non-Communist past, both traditional and modern.

SOME DEFINITIONAL PROBLEMS

We have discussed the nature of continuity, but we have yet to explain what we mean by "the ideology of the Cultural Revolution." Our evasiveness is not accidental. Have you ever looked for a simple, usable definition of the word, "ideology"? In a comprehensive article in the *International Encyclopedia of the Social Sciences,* Edward Shils tells us how to distinguish ideology from "outlooks and creeds, systems and movements of thought, and programs," to say nothing of things that go bump in the night.[43] A close reading of Shils's erudite essay will convince most readers that the "ideology of the Cultural Revolution" is a misnomer, if not a phantasm. Arguments over such things could easily throw our discussion into a state of suspended animation (more suspended than animated).

Seeking simplicity, we consult *Webster's Third New International Dictionary* (unabridged), which gives, among others, the following definition: "the integrated assertions, theories, and aims that constitute a sociopolitical program." If we add "or movement," this will meet our needs nicely enough.

We will treat GPCR ideology in a narrow, official sense. A study should be undertaken of the ideology (if one can call it that) of the Red Guards, but we will leave that herculean effort to others. In any case, there is some question as to whether Red Guard materials should be considered sources for "the ideology of the Cultural Revolution." Despite high-level advocacy of populism, antibureaucratism, and rebellion, we should not assume that ideological authority was meant to be subject to challenges from the masses. The ideology of the Cultural Revolution emanated from the official writings of Mao and those

---

[43] Shils, "The Concept and Function of Ideology," in David L. Sills (ed.), *International Encyclopedia of the Social Sciences* (New York: Macmillan and The Free Press, 1968), VII, 66–76. See also Harry M. Johnson, "Ideology and the Social System," *ibid.,* pp. 76–85.

around him. In studying the ideological aspects of this movement, an elitist approach needs no excuse.

In its centrist features, GPCR ideology is structurally similar to that of tradition. In Communist China, notes Hsiung, "the ideology is always imparted from the 'center,' from above. . . . The Communist elite transmits a single, all-unifying prescriptive system downward to the nation at large, to be 'internalized' and translated into reality by social mobilization. Ideology in Maoist tradition represents the 'general will' to which all particular wills . . . must bend." [44] The same author notes that official ideology in China has been centrist in a logical as well as a political sense, operating deductively from general principles to specific problems. It has also been central in a systemic sense, in keeping with "a favorite Chinese approach to leadership, *i-ssu-hsiang ling-tao* (to lead by ideology)." [45]

Hsiung identifies three basic dimensions of the ideological structure of the Chinese Communist Party (CCP): "(1) *kuan-nien hsing-t'ai* or conceptual order, the epistemological part of ideology; (2) *li-lun*, the theoretical part of ideology . . . ; and (3) *ssu-hsiang*, or thought, the absolutely indispensable link between theory and practice." The distinguishing features of GPCR ideology have been in its *ssu-hsiang* or, in the words of Daniel Bell, in "the conversion of ideas into social levers, . . . the commitment to the consequences of ideas." [46]

In this sense, GPCR ideology seems nearly identical with GPCR policy. However, if we accept Webster's proviso that the "assertions, theories, and aims" of an ideology must be integrated into a program, then ideology must be carefully distinguished from policy, which changes in response to unanticipated challenges. Alas, this is virtually impossible. Seemingly ideological sources (Mao's *Quotations*) have policy implications, and statements of policy (the "Sixteen-Point Decision" of August 8, 1966) are major sources of ideology. Nonetheless, failure to make some distinction between the policy-oriented and the ideological aspects of GPCR documents will lead to the erroneous conclusion that changes in policy are *ipso facto* changes in ideology.

Some things, such as the laudatory references to the writings of Liu Shao-ch'i prior to late 1966, are obviously inconsistent with the basic themes of the GPCR, and one cannot consider them part of GPCR

[44] Hsiung, *Ideology and Practice*, p. 6.

[45] *Ibid.*, pp. 300, 156.

[46] *Ibid.*, pp. 131–32. Daniel Bell, *The End of Ideology: On the Exhaustion of Political Ideas in the Fifties* (New York: Free Press, 1960), pp. 370–71.

ideology simply because they occurred during the period after May, 1966. Conversely, attacks on the principle of "self-cultivation" must be understood in context of the assault against the author of *The Self-Cultivation of a Communist Party Member* and do not necessarily possess independent ideological significance.

There is, however, more ideological consistency in the GPCR than one might expect. Most of the major motifs appeared during the first year, from the spring of 1966 to the spring of 1967. Since practice continually outran theory, seemingly drastic shifts in policy often lacked equally dramatic ideological implications. For example, in early 1967 we find warnings against "anarchism" and in mid-1968 injunctions against a theory of "many centers." These clearly were responses to a situation that was reeling out of control. Yet it is arguable that Mao never intended the GPCR to be anarchic or for authority to derive from many centers. If we examine the "Sixteen-Point Decision," we find that injunctions against extremism were present from the beginning. The more explicit and persistent statement of the law-and-order theme in 1967 and 1968 simply directed attention to an element that had been present all along.

CONTINUITIES WITH THE "GREAT" AND "LITTLE" TRADITIONS

The GPCR develops in an atmosphere of uninterrupted crisis, from the beginning when Red Guards step forth to "defend Chairman Mao" to Mao's recent plea, four years later, for heightened "vigilance" against the danger of "a capitalist restoration."[47] There is a sense of destiny, that China is at a historic crossroads. Men's ideas and acts here and now will have irrevocable consequences. Hence there is a total demand on the minds and bodies of all men, every minute of the day—even at night, when one dreams of Chairman Mao. The feeling of crisis, of *the* historic moment, of the need for total involvement, is unprecedented.

Perhaps we should look to rebel thought rather than official ideology for forerunners of a movement that proclaims, "To rebel is justified." Certainly the mood of GPCR ideology as interpreted by the Red Guards is captured in the rebel theme of *ta-kuan* (down with the officials!). However this may be, GPCR ideology cannot appropriately be compared to rebel ideology. Its fountainhead is at the center of the existing order, and its message to the people in terms of life style is

---

[47] *Important Documents on the Great Proletarian Cultural Revolution in China* (Peking: Foreign Languages Press, 1970), unpaginated.

to work hard and loyally within a purified version of the existing social order. Utopian visions of a better life under a new authority are lacking, as are eschatological promises of rewards in the hereafter.

Since its purpose is not to replace existing authority but to purify it, GPCR ideology may have more in common with restoration or revitalization movements than with rebellion. Confucian ideology had this potential—to purify the system as well as to justify it. Confucianism coexisted uneasily with imperial and bureaucratic institutions. The high standards of virtue to which Confucius failed to convert even the petty princes of his day were still less reachable for the rulers of a vast empire. What made the ideology vital and the system viable was the ability of the former to hold a critical mirror to the latter. Periodically throughout Chinese history one discovers a kind of Protestant fundamentalism—the mobilization of the ideas of officialdom against established institutions and practices. One finds echoes of this in Maoist fundamentalism which, like its Confucian parallels, is based upon a highly selective version of the Sacred Canon.

Heretofore we have sought continuities primarily in China's "great tradition," the sophisticated, written heritage of her literate, cultured minority. But we must not ignore the "little tradition," the popular, unwritten, diffuse heritage of the illiterate majority. Bridging the two traditions were genres of popular fiction such as the stories of knights-errant. In written form, they were accessible to a much wider and less educated audience than those who could understand the classics. The main means of transmission to the masses, however, was oral, through storytellers and the theater. As a boy, Mao read the most famous of these works, the *Shui-hu chuan* (Water Margin). The heroes of this saga practice acknowledged virtues in opposition to official institutions that stifle their realization.[48] Certain values from the knight-errant genre are prominent in the GPCR: courage, daring, loyalty to one's comrades-in-arms, and identification with the common people. These are the attributes of modern heroes like Lei Feng, paragon of Maoist virtues. However, since current hero literature is disseminated from above to serve official purposes, its heroes work within, and not against, established institutions such as the PLA.

One of Mao's goals is to destroy the barriers between the great and little traditions. According to traditional norms, the values of the great tradition were supposed to seep down to the people of the little tradi-

[48] Robert Ruhlmann, "Traditional Heroes in Chinese Popular Fiction," in Wright (ed.), *Confucian Persuasion*, pp. 173–74.

tion. Now things are reversed. Virtues attributed to the masses are expected to seep "upward" to the privileged urbanized elite. It may be true, as Franz Schurmann and Orville Schell argue, that Lei Feng's values of nobility, poverty, and sacrifice are diametrically opposed to the traditional trinity, *fu, lu,* and *shou* (happiness, high salary, and long life).[49] But it is no less true that certain work-oriented, thrift-inducing habits of the Chinese peasant have always enjoyed at least verbal support in the great tradition. During his suppression of the Taipings, Tseng Kuo-fan seized free moments to exhort his family back home to practice industry, simplicity, and frugality. Of course, nobody suggested that Tseng should take time off to *hsia-fang,* but it is worth noting that this paragon of Confucian virtues championed the same "industrious and simple style of work" for which Chiang Ch'ing recently congratulated an audience of Red Guards.[50]

In a sense, the ideology of the Cultural Revolution may be said to contain its own "great" and "little" traditions. The early stages of the GPCR, developing out of a dispute in the literary world, were definitely "great tradition" in that the literary and historical issues at stake were of interest primarily to the intellectual elite. The first of Mao's writings to be reissued for a mass public, moreover, were full-length philosophical and political works dating from the 1938–42 period. These too were initially composed for audiences of Party cadres, students, and other members of the Yenan elite. Much of the content of these writings reflects the needs of the wartime united front and is quite contrary to the general tenor of the Cultural Revolution. For example, Mao's classic "On New Democracy," highly recommended in the last of the "Sixteen Points," contains references to "the fine old culture of the people, which had a more or less democratic and revolutionary character." [51] Even with the qualifying clause, such an idea is very much at odds with the call for destruction of the "Four Olds." Later in the year the cult of Mao blossomed. The principal literary works of this cult were the "three constantly read articles" and the "little red book." [52] These became the core of what we might call the

49 Schurmann and Schell, *The China Reader,* Vol. III: *Communist China* (New York: Vintage, 1967), p. 435.

50 "Young Revolutionary Fighters of Long March Detachments Gather to Exchange Experiences," *Peking Review,* January 1, 1967, p. 5.

51 Mao Tse-tung, *Selected Works of Mao Tse-tung* (Peking: Foreign Languages Press, 1967), II, 381.

52 Even among these highly selective quotations, one finds some that seem to contradict basic tenets of the GPCR. For example: "Different forms and styles in art should develop freely and different schools in science should contend freely. We think that it is

"little tradition" of the Cultural Revolution—a corpus of brief quotations, homilies, and edifying stories that required no sophistication in philosophy or history to be understood. Aimed at a mass audience, this tradition was dominant during the greater part of the Cultural Revolution.

The most famous of these works, *Quotations from Chairman Mao Tse-tung,* has been compared to the *Analects (lun-yü) of Confucius.* This is a bit far-fetched. Granted, both are anthologies of brief selections illustrative of the teachings of the Master, intended as guidelines for moral behavior. Both contain the character *yü* (sayings or discourses) in their titles. Both require interpretation and application since they are distillations of decades of life and thought. Neither is very specific about methods of extrapolation to meet requirements of novel situations. Both presume, as Confucius said, that a student given one corner of a problem should be able to "come back . . . with the other three." [53]

The differences, however, are more fundamental. The *Analects* were strictly great tradition, intended for the moral education of an aristocracy of learning and virtue. Compiled by disciples of the Master, they consisted of stories about his life and sayings attributed to him. There was no apparent organization to them. The only way of bringing an apposite teaching to bear was to memorize the entire work in advance. In any case, the principles that could be drawn from the *Analects* were very general and were limited to the public and personal behavior of the *chun-tzu.* It was scarcely conceivable that one could master the art of *ch'in* strumming or overfulfilling his quota of bricks on the Great Wall by applying an appropriate aphorism from the Thoughts of Chairman K'ung.

Mao's "little red book" is aimed at the masses to be applied in precisely such earthy situations. Though its sayings are wrenched out of historical and textual context, the present generation has some idea of the revolutionary history from which they emerged. Nonetheless, their historical and textual background is unimportant and will probably become less so as these events fade from memory. What is vital is their application to present problems. Thus the chapter headings predefine the nature of the most important issues facing contemporary

---

harmful to the growth of art and science if administrative measures are used to impose one particular style of art or school of thought and to ban another." Mao, *Quotations,* p. 303.

[53] Waley (trans.), *Analects of Confucius,* p. 124.

man. However, the following observation, drawn from the Ming period, applies equally well to contemporary ideological works: "The integrity of [orthodox] teaching [has] constantly to be defended against the danger of debasement through its use as an official ideology or as mere professional qualification." [54] One purpose of the Cultural Revolution is to save Chinese Communist ideology from such a fate. However, *Quotations from Chairman Mao,* no less than the Four Books and the Five Classics, may easily fall victim to routinization and institutionalization. To prevent such an outcome may take more than collective study sessions—themselves a kind of institutionalization.

One thing that the *Analects* share with the *Quotations* is the fact that they are written. In this respect, works in the "little tradition" of the Cultural Revolution fall into a different category from the little tradition of premodern China. In other respects, however, the GPCR's "little tradition" resembles its namesake:

1. *Religious qualities.* Certainly the emulation of Chairman Mao is as much a religion as it is an ideology. Indeed, it seems expressly designed, among other things, to serve some of the functions of popular religions. Man's confrontation with nature, even with life and death, now is to be mastered through the thoughts of the Chairman. In retrospect, the attack on the "Four Olds" (including superstitious beliefs and practices of the "feudal" era) prepared the way for the establishment of the new religion.

2. *Ecstatic qualities.* As Max Weber observed, Confucianism was a sober school of thought, lacking the Dionysian element. "Confucianism," he wrote, "strictly rejected the emotional ecstasy to be found only among the popular magicians, the apathetic ecstasy among the Taoists, and every form of monachal asceticism." [55] "Nonapathetic ecstasy" in Chinese religious experience was to be found only in the little tradition among religious cults. In political terms, such beliefs were considered appropriate only as rebel creeds, never as bureaucratic ideology. It is not surprising, then, that the GPCR, which attempts to mobilize the masses against a bureaucracy, has created an ecstatic religious creed.

3. *As a conduit for great tradition values.* The kinds of literature available for popular consumption in the GPCR are akin to the traditional kinds of literary and nonliterary devices used to convey the

[54] De Bary, "Introduction," p. 6.
[55] Max Weber, *The Religion of China* (New York: Macmillan, 1964), p. 206; also pp. 181, 233.

ideas of the great tradition, in simplified form, to the people. During the Ch'ing dynasty, attempts at ideological indoctrination were more superficial. Nonetheless, Confucian doctrine (as well as political expediency) dictated that attempts be made to convey at least the fundamental precepts of political orthodoxy to the people. Through the *hsiang-yüeh* system, the public was exposed to semimonthly speeches on the "Sacred Edicts." [56] This system was based upon the *Liu yu* (Six Maxims of a Hortatory Edict) of the Shun-chih emperor. Like the sayings of Chairman Mao, these were very general moral precepts that needed elucidation before they could be put into practice. The maxims, notes Kung-chuan Hsiao, "represent as a whole the substance of the Confucian ethic reduced to the barest essentials." [57] This is precisely what the popular writings of the Cultural Revolution are trying to accomplish in terms of the Maoist ethic.

Shun-chih's maxims were superseded by the *Shen-yü* (The Sacred Edict), issued by his successor, K'ang-hsi.[58] Like the doctrinal charter of the Cultural Revolution, this manifesto had sixteen points. The idea was to persuade the people to apply the maxims to their own lives. An edifying example is the story of Chung-yeh, son of a ne'er-do-well family, who attended a lecture in his native village:

The preacher told the story of the Ch'en clan of Chiang-chou, one of the illustrations used in the Amplified Instructions, according to which some members of this clan achieved wealth by honest work and made it possible for its seven hundred kinsfolk to live together. The young peasant was moved to the depths of his heart and said to himself, "Can I not also achieve what the Ch'ens accomplished?" From that day on he worked harder than ever and accumulated a moderate wealth to bring together and support all his kin.[59]

This is akin to stories of those whose lives have been remodeled through the inspiration and application of Mao's teachings. Success stories were, nonetheless, rare since the system was practiced sporadically and superficially. Hsiao conjectures that "the fundamental obstacle that stood in the way of successful ideological control" was the deplorable living conditions of the masses that rendered the lofty Confucian pronouncements irrelevant and made the people vulnerable to the lure of " 'false doctrines'—the White Lotus, the Nien, or the God-worship-

[56] T'ung-tsu Ch'ü, *Local Government in China under the Ch'ing* (Stanford, Calif.: Stanford University Press, 1969), p. 162.

[57] Kung-chuan Hsiao, *Rural China: Imperial Control in the Nineteenth Century* (Seattle: University of Washington Press, 1960), p. 186.

[58] *Ibid.*, p. 185.

[59] *Ibid.*, pp. 194–95.

pers." [60] The brutal material realities of Chinese life remain to plague the ideologues of latter-day orthodoxies.

It should be evident from this brief discussion that, in function as well as in content, massive discontinuities separate traditional ideologies from that of the Cultural Revolution. While the GPCR's popular qualities seek to provide it with a broader social base than that of Confucianism (an objective which remains far from realization), in its ecstatic, Dionysian qualities it is closer to a total religious experience than anything in traditional Chinese political thought. Hence, it scarcely is possible to compare the ideology of the GPCR as a total system with anything in premodern China. This means that our quest cannot be for total continuities between whole systems, but only between discrete aspects of ideologies, past and present. In this regard, we should take heed of the well-known adage that "he who would bite off piecemeal comparisons may end up straining at gnats and swallowing camels."

IN HOT PURSUIT OF THE ELUSIVE CONTINUITIES

If we are bold enough to suggest continuities with the remote past, we must not shrink back before the more palpable continuities of recent history. Even in modern China, we are unlikely to find anything comparable to the Cultural Revolution in scope or intensity, but we may expect to find at least some linear continuities. Examination of several configurations of ideas in modern Chinese thought may help elucidate the issue of continuity and change: (1) the individual's problem of maintaining his Chinese identity while adapting his mind to new ideas—what Levenson called the problem of "history" and "value"; (2) the resolution of the syndrome of ideological questions that came to a head during the New Culture Movement of 1915–23; and (3) the series of attempts to create a focal point of legitimacy through the creation of personal cults.

"HISTORY" AND "VALUE"

The problem of maintaining a Confucian identity while modernizing has been a favorite topic for Western historians. It will not be rehashed here. However, we will discuss some of the episodes in this series of attempts to reconcile "history" and "value" insofar as they bear upon our problem of continuities in the Cultural Revolution.

The leaders of the Self-Strengthening Movement, who insisted that

[60] *Ibid.,* p. 199.

it was possible to have a "rich country and a strong army" without surrendering fundamental Confucian values, clearly recognized the problem—even if their solutions embraced philosophical and practical contradictions. The viability of their simple solution is evidenced by the large numbers of Chinese who have continued to accept it in some form. Indeed, it may well be the least common denominator for the thinking of a vast array of intellectuals, officials, and military leaders. Conservatives such as Wo Jen, on the other hand, feared that preoccupation with Western technology would undermine China's unique and sacred civilization. They drew upon deeply entrenched traditions, in popular literature as in the classics. The *Romance of the Three Kingdoms* (a favorite of Chairman Mao) expounds the idea, to borrow the words of Robert Ruhlmann, that "moral superiority is more important and essential for success in war as well as in other endeavors, than technical skill." [61] During the 1870's and 1880's, the *Ch'ing-i* (pure) faction argued that the barbarian could be ousted by application of what Benjamin Schwartz has dubbed "muscular Confucianism," an attitude that he traces back at least as far as the Southern Sung. *Ch'ing-i* stalwarts argued that "the barbarian could be expelled not by the use of cunning Western gadgets but by the militant and aroused spirit of the Chinese people." [62]

Is Mao a lineal descendant of the *Ch'ing-i* purists or of the Self-Strengtheners? Without surrendering that high, safe, middle ground where one can defend the proposition that he shares something with both without being completely like either, I would stress his affinity with Tseng Kuo-fan, precisely because it is so easily overshadowed by his more evident (though perhaps misleading) similarities with Wo Jen.

"The atom bomb is a paper tiger." Certainly this sounds more like the crusty conservative Wo Jen's condescending views of technology than the thought of a man like Tseng who placed confidence in steamship and cannon. Yet the vital point is that Mao wants to have both the ideological purity (though not that of Confucianism) *and* the benefits of modern technology—and he believes he *can* have both. He is convinced, furthermore, that men and ideas will run the machines and not the other way around. Wo Jen would have considered this a dangerous Tseng-like fallacy.

---

[61] Ruhlmann, "Traditional Heroes," p. 165.

[62] Benjamin I. Schwartz, *In Search of Wealth and Power: Yen Fu and the West* (Cambridge, Mass.: Harvard University Press, 1964), pp. 15–16.

Mao's affinities for Tseng go still further. Both men, though supreme moralists, insist that knowledge be put to practical use. Both champion the Chinese "Protestant ethic." Tseng "exhorted aspiring officials to heroism," writes Father Brière, "charging them to prepare themselves for service to the State by self-abnegation, abstinence and sacrifice." [63] An excellent capsulization, one would think, of the "three constantly read articles" of Chairman Mao. It was another Self-Strengthener, Feng Kuei-fen, who wrote that "the way to avoid trouble is to manufacture, repair, and use weapons by ourselves." This would enable China to "become the leading power in the world." [64] *Tzu-li keng-sheng* (Operation Bootstrap) with a vengeance!

After the turn of the century, the insistence that China preserve her unique cultural identity even while adopting modern ways continued in a line of thinkers from K'ang Yu-wei through Chang Chih-mai, while the idea of self-sufficiency on the level of political and economic policy was voiced on a popular level through boycotts and movements to promote native goods. From 1911 through the mid-1920's, scientism enjoyed a vogue, but its content—when it was not used as a metaphysical absolute—became increasingly social. Even Ting Wen-chiang, one of the few high priests of scientism who was a practicing scientist, turned his science to social problems after 1919.[65] However, to Ting and his fellow *"endeavor* pragmatists," scientism meant accepting "certain Confucian political structures" as "among the given facts of any political situation," leaning toward "a Confucian notion of political relevance" which meant "carefully devised purely administrative solutions" without challenging the basic structure.[66] Ting and his colleagues were handicapped too by their emphasis on another traditional value, leadership by an educated elite. This tenet, which denied them an independent source of popular support,[67] may be one reason why more and more intellectuals came to reject their version of science as a total solution. Writing in 1949, Father Brière noted that, for the previous two decades, intellectuals had subordinated science to "social realities." [68]

[63] O. Brière, *Fifty Years of Chinese Philosophy, 1898–1948* (London: Allen and Unwin, 1956), p. 16.

[64] De Bary *et al.* (eds.), *Sources of Chinese Tradition*, II, 47.

[65] Charlotte Furth, *Ting Wen-chiang: Science and China's New Culture* (Cambridge, Mass.: Harvard University Press, 1970), p. 33.

[66] *Ibid.*, p. 156.

[67] *Ibid.*, p. 157.

[68] Brière, *Fifty Years of Chinese Philosophy,* p. 105.

Thus GPCR ideologues followed a century of efforts to adapt foreign values to Chinese needs and especially to subordinate science and technology to social values. So fundamental is this theme to China's intellectual trauma that one can readily appreciate the strength of Mao's position when he reiterates the primacy of man over machine, mind over matter, human will over nature, and indigenous effort over reliance upon foreign countries.

NEW CULTURE AND CULTURAL REVOLUTION

Forces that produced an intellectual crisis in mid-twentieth-century China converged during the New Culture Movement of 1915–23. Like the Cultural Revolution of 1966–69, this movement was posited on the notion that radical social change had to begin with new fundamental principles and a new kind of man.[69] For purposes of analysis, we may divide the movement into two periods: 1915–19 and 1919–23. The watershed is May 4, 1919, the date of the epochal Peking student demonstration. During the first period the dominant themes were the questioning of the old culture *in toto* and the adulation of everything new, modern, and foreign. The key words were "science" and "democracy," which were regarded by Ch'en Tu-hsiu and others as panaceas for China's problems. The spirit of this period was liberal, cosmopolitan, international, and relatively apolitical.

During the second half of this era, the pre-eminent ideas were nationalism, anti-imperialism, radicalism, and political *engagement*. Although science and democracy had lost none of their appeal, science was more and more directed to social problems, and democracy ceased to be identified with the "bourgeois liberal" principles of the West and began to take on Marxist connotations of social and economic justice. Religious iconoclasm remained a strong theme, but the principal target of the antireligious movement switched from native anti-Confucianism to foreign Christianity, in keeping with the anti-imperialistic trend.

The post-May 4 period saw politics take command. Those like Hu Shih who had vowed to eschew politics for twenty years either changed their minds or suffered eclipse. Ch'en Tu-hsiu and Li Ta-chao, whose principal contributions to the earlier period had been literary and cultural, now devoted their energies to political organization. Nor was politicization restricted to a political elite. After May 4 the concept of mass organization spread from students to workers, peasants, mer-

[69] Furth, *Ting Wen-chiang*, p. 4.

chants, women, and other groups. Men of the great tradition were making a determined effort to break through to those of the little tradition.

Two men whose careers and ideas have come to symbolize the radical turn of the post-May 4 New Culture Movement are the fathers of the Chinese Communist Party, Ch'en Tu-hsiu and Li Ta-chao. In the configurations of ideas represented by Ch'en and Li, we discover twisted strands of intellectual continuities that have emerged most recently in the Cultural Revolution.

Contradictions among the dominant values of the New Culture tradition—science, nationalism, populism, rationalism, and iconoclasm—have produced many of the critical ideological problems of the Cultural Revolution. During the exhilarating years of the New Culture period, a panoply of theories could be accepted and often reconciled with one another because they had yet to be tested in practice. Thus, for Ch'en Tu-hsiu, eighteenth-century rationalism and nineteenth-century science provided an eminently rational frame of reference for modern Chinese life. Ch'en attributed the survival of religions and other irrational traditions to blind superstition and the interests of an oppressive minority. Truth to him was a universal commodity, and one need not be ashamed to use rational ideas and institutions—whatever their origin—for the benefit of China. After his conversion to Marxism, Ch'en was able to retain many of his earlier beliefs. Science now applied to history as well as to the natural world. Blind and covetous forces (capitalism and imperialism) still could be repelled by men of reason. And, since truth remained universal, China's best interests were well served by cooperation with sympathetic foreigners. The breakdown in Ch'en's synthesis came under the pressure of events leading to his rupture with the Party in 1927, his subsequent imprisonment, and anguished self-examination in the last years of his life. However, the ideas he had championed lived on, sometimes in new forms, and had to be dealt with by new generations of political and intellectual leaders.

For Li Ta-chao, a rather different synthesis held together until his execution of 1926. Though willing to believe in laws of history and human behavior, Li insisted nonetheless that human volition was ultimately free and historically decisive. Li placed a high value on the independent role of ideas and was reluctant to attribute all thought to predetermined class structures and relations of production. Nor was Li prepared to ascribe ultimate virtue to a single social class, much less to an elite party representing that class. Virtue, he contended, was to be found among the masses, and upon them would depend the success of China's revolution. Li's voluntarism, nationalism, and populism proved as serviceable during his Marxist period as they had been earlier. As Meisner has demonstrated, this ideological cluster survives today in the thought of Mao.[70]

For radicals like Ch'en and Li, faith in science could be expressed in revolutionary Marxist terms through the laws of history. On the other hand, for moderates like Hu Shih, science was a methodology suitable for gradual change. This interpretation of science was easily reconciled in Hu's mind with the Chinese tradition of painstaking scholarship. The national priorities that emerged from such a combination were quite clear: a modern, highly sophisticated educational system was in order. Elite education would have to receive precedence over mass education. Social rewards would fall disproportionately to people and places that were advanced, urbanized, and Westernized. Eventually the entire country would benefit, but the process would perforce be measured, systematic, and experimental. Though Hu's literary theories and political views were excoriated in the mid-fifties, his view of science and society was tacitly accepted by many in the Communist order. In the hands of a ruling party guided by its own "scientific" view of history, scientific methods could be used to promote rational planning, industrialization, and "modernization." The planning owed more to Lenin and Stalin, but the homage to science, functional rationality, and modernity was much in keeping with the heritage of Hu.

During its years in power, the CCP has borrowed quite broadly from the heritage of the New Culture. It has accepted elements of Ch'en's cosmopolitanism, Ch'en's and Hu's versions of scientism, and Li's amalgam of voluntarism, populism, and nationalism. Li's ideas, now championed by Mao, underly the revolutionary orthodoxy of the Cultural Revolution. However, even the proclamations of the GPCR testify to the fact that other elements of the New Culture heritage are deeply ingrained. Hence the trinity of "class struggle, struggle for production, and scientific experiment," all placed in an interpretive context that emphasizes ideology, will, and the masses. Class struggle continues indefinitely even under socialism. In discarding the Marxist view of a placid utopia for the doctrine of *pu-tuan ko-ming* (uninter-

[70] Maurice Meisner, *Li Ta-chao and the Origins of Chinese Marxism* (Cambridge, Mass.: Harvard University Press, 1967), pp. 261–66.

rupted revolution), Mao ironically seems to accept Hu's criticism that Marxism is untenable precisely because it demanded a halt in the historical process.[71] The struggle for production is spurred onward by nonmaterial incentives, and scientific experiment is carried out for ends determined by men loyal to the thought of Mao. It is the will and determination of these men, not the natural limitations of scientific laws, which will decree success or failure. This is an echo of Li. But in the distrust of institutionalized power, one senses the ghost of the much-reviled "Trotskyite," Ch'en Tu-hsiu.[72]

What is most striking about the transmutation of the New Culture heritage is the 180-degree turn from secular iconoclasm to theocratic absolutism. During the New Culture era men tried to desacralize the world. What was sacred was traditional. This they rejected. What they accepted was a rational, nonsacred modern world, as conveyed to them in varying strands of Western thought. Science frequently was treated as an absolute, but it never became sacred in a religious sense. That would have been too great a leap of faith for the men of reason.

The Cult of Mao re-establishes a sacred focal point within China. The first imperative is to believe. This is a jarring note in contrast to a New Culture that stressed doubt and iconoclasm. In the Manichaean world, all things contrary to the True Faith are bad. Hence the campaign against the "Four Olds." This slogan would have been recognizable in the May Fourth period when the key word was "new." But now the word is not "new" but "revolutionary," a far more explosive concept with a higher religious content. To the leaders of the New Culture Movement there could be no religion of Science and Democracy, much as these ideals may have seemed moral absolutes. Men of the great tradition to the core, Ch'en and his cohorts could scarcely have been so undignified as to worship anything. But the populist tradition demands the involvement of the masses, and mass movements are things of passion—even when they include members of a student lumpen-elite. Hence the Dionysian Cult of Mao, a substitute not just for a discarded *weltanschauung* of the great tradition but of the cultist ecstasy of the little tradition. From roots in a militant secularism, China has rediscovered the sacred. No longer is it possible to say, "I give my heart to the Party," because my heart now belongs to Daddy.

[71] Jerome B. Grieder, *Hu Shih and the Chinese Renaissance: Liberalism in the Chinese Revolution, 1917–1937* (Cambridge, Mass.: Harvard University Press, 1970), p. 211.
[72] See Richard Clark Kagan, "The Chinese Trotskyist Movement and Ch'en Tu-hsiu: Culture, Revolution, and Polity" (Ph.D. dissertation, University of Pennsylvania, 1969).

CULT-MAKING

"The year 1960," wrote Franz Schurmann, "marked the beginning of a period when China was without an ideology." [73] He might have said 1935 or 1916 or 1905, for the problem has been a persistent one. In a sense, nationalism has served as China's ideology throughout this turbulent half-century. However, simple nationalism has not been enough. Nationalism needs positive content, which is no easy thing for a country that is militarily, politically, economically, and culturally at the mercy of foreigners. China required a sense of identity that would tell her where she was and where she was going. Nationalism alone could not provide this. Most of all China needed a source of legitimacy—a symbol at the center to fill the void left by the Son of Heaven.

These needs of identity and legitimacy have led Chinese intellectual and political leaders into a series of attempts at cult-making. They hoped to lay a secure foundation for power and authority that would encapsulate both the uniqueness of China and her universality in the world order. The most notable effort at cult-making in premodern China was the creation, during the Former Han dynasty, of the State Cult of Confucius. Like its modern successors, this cult-building enterprise reflected the failure of the antecedent model of government, the need for a new focus of legitimacy, and, at the same time, a way of confirming the position of a new ruling class. Over the course of centuries, the state developed various institutions—the examination system and the civil service in particular—to buttress this cult and confirm the legitimacy of scholar-officials. It may well be, as C. K. Yang argues, that there was a need for "supernatural sanction to the Confucian values" and that even "rational" Confucianism depended upon sacred components for its ultimate authority.[74]

Nonetheless, the cultist, religious aspects of Confucianism remained in subordination to its secular, rationalistic, and political functions. Though temples were built and ceremonies conducted in his honor, Confucius remained a remote figure, of little functional importance in the social order. The cult, writes D. Howard Smith, "was encour-

[73] Franz Schurmann, "The Attack of the Cultural Revolution on Ideology and Organization," in Ho and Tsou (eds.), *China in Crisis,* Vol. I: *China's Heritage and the Communist Political System,* Bk. 2, p. 543.
[74] Yang, "The Functional Relationship between Confucian Thought and Chinese Religion," in John K. Fairbank (ed.), *Chinese Thought and Institutions* (Chicago: University of Chicago Press, 1957), p. 279.

aged by the state as a buttress to public morality, and in order to
sustain the power and authority of the scholar-class." [75] As a result,
participants in its observances were limited to that class. Furthermore, the cult of Confucius never occupied an exclusivistic role vis-à-
vis other allegiances. The teachings of Confucius were venerated of
course, but there was no such thing as the "thought of Confucius,"
not even an entity known as "Confucianism." Such an overlay of
commentaries and subcommentaries, interpretive essays, and scholarly
controversy developed around the canon of books that the Master
had presumably composed and edited that only radical fundamental-
ists—often reformers of an extremist bent—dared to cut through this
intricate web in search of the original Confucius.

Such a man was K'ang Yu-wei. By the late nineteenth century, the
cult of Confucius had little more than formalistic functions. The institutions of government seemed self-perpetuating, and the official ideology only a convenient instrument for defending *raison d'état*. The
emperor himself was the chief victim of this, reigning but not ruling,
while the shrewd and corrupt empress dowager controlled the levers of
power. The problem was twofold: how to change and how to legitima-
tize change. K'ang's response was: (1) a restoration of the emperor to
a central position in the political order, and (2) a restoration of Confucius to a central place in the ideological order. The Confucius restored was a Confucius who had never been: a radical reformer whose
teaching stressed the necessity of change and pointed toward a future
utopia that, in fact, borrowed heavily from the West. The cult that
K'ang sought to create was, likewise, a cult that had never been, for
now there would be a monotheistic state religion in which the Sage
would have the position of a god and in which the Sage's teachings,
"properly" understood, would have the function of holy writ. In the
monopolistic pretensions of a faith designed to justify radical change,
we find a phenomenon much closer to the cult of Mao than to the traditional cult of Confucius.

K'ang's machinations failed, the emperor was effectively deposed,
and reformers were executed or, like K'ang, driven into exile. Faced
with this crisis, K'ang organized the *Pao-huang hui* (Society to Defend
the Emperor). Impeccably conservative in nomenclature, this organization was dangerously radical in political implications. "Defending the
emperor" implied the release of the incarcerated emperor and the over-

---

[75] Smith, *Chinese Religions* (New York: Holt, Rinehart & Winston, 1968), p. 147.

throw of the empress dowager, hence the destruction of the existing ruling group. Nonetheless, K'ang refused to advocate overthrow of the ruling *system,* for monarchy, he felt, was an essential matrix for carrying out change within tradition. Etymologically, echoes of the *Pao-huang hui* may be found in Mao's Red Guards, whose *raison d'être* was to "defend Chairman Mao." This too meant the ouster of the effective ruling group, though Mao, like K'ang, refused to go so far as to challenge the basic institutions of Party and state, much as he felt they needed overhauling.

The Revolution of 1911 destroyed the Manchu dynasty, but the monarchial idea sputtered on. Yüan Shih-k'ai's attempt to found a new dynasty in 1916 involved another attempt to establish a cult. Since Yüan himself provided the inspiration for this radically reactionary move, the cult was more particularistic than the revitalized emperorship envisioned by K'ang. Yüan's charismatic appeal—such as it was—stemmed from his personal qualities and relationships and not from any offices he held or hoped to hold. This proved a grave weakness of his plan, for his own political and personal strength would have to compensate for the discredited state of the monarchial ideal. This is a danger that Mao also has courted insofar as his charisma, too, is noninstitutional. But, as the leader of his party for nearly three decades and of China for over two, Mao is in a much stronger position. The fact that the cult is built more around his thought than around his person also enhances its chances of surviving his death.

The origins of the cult of Sun Yat-sen may be traced back to the early years of the twentieth century when Sun came to symbolize the Chinese revolution. As Harold Z. Schiffrin has pointed out, it was Sun's presumed capacity for "entrepreneurial leadership" and not his ideological pre-eminence that overcame the skepticism of China's overseas students who once had scorned him as a common adventurer-intriguer.[76] Sun's charisma arose from personal attributes which were immediately communicated to those who came into contact with him: his obvious sincerity, his total identification with his cause, and his unshakable conviction that he was the man destined to lead China into a revolutionary future. Since his appeal rested on his qualities as an individual, Sun readily developed rivalries with men whose talents lay in more mundane areas. Spurning the parliamentary path proposed

---

[76] Schiffrin, *Sun Yat-sen and the Origins of the Chinese Revolution* (Berkeley and Los Angeles: University of California Press, 1968), p. 365.

by the assassinated Sung Chiao-jen, Sun founded a new party to be held together by pledges of fealty to himself. While he lived, the most volatile rivalries within KMT ranks were kept under control.

Despite efforts to create a cult of Sun during his own lifetime (efforts in which Sun himself took the lead), it was his death that prepared the way for apotheosis. As John McCook Roots noted in 1927, "factions that had opposed him in life now honored him in death. His name became a national watchword, his 'Will' a sacred document. Loyalty to the party that he had founded became inseparable from loyalty to the country. . . ." [77] The Sun cult borrowed elements from earlier examples. His portrait, like tablets of departed ancestors, was honored by bows of respect. Like the sacred edicts of great emperors, his "will" was read before reverent gatherings of officials and common people. His bier was deposited in a magnificent mausoleum near the Ming tombs overlooking Nanking. Like the last months of Yüan Shih-k'ai's life, the period after Sun's death witnessed the immortalization of the cultal object in prose and verse, portraiture and coin.

In the cult of Sun, however, one element that had played a lesser role in previous cults became vitally important: the ideology of the sage-hero. The *San-min chu-i* (Three People's Principles), Sun's catchy and catch-all lectures on government, became as sacred as the memory of the man himself. For all the *Chung-shan* (Sun Yat-sen) villages, streets, and buildings, there are likewise *San-min chu-i* constitutions, model provinces, and projects for national construction. Since the Three People's Principles were very general, they lent themselves to broad interpretations. J. O. P. Bland, a harsh critic of the Sun cult, wrote in 1929:

> The leaders of the Kuomintang have adroitly exploited the nation's instinctive need of some object of veneration, some rallying point to take the place of the Dragon Throne and the Confucian sages. To conform to Chinese ideals of what is expected of rulers, they must discover and invoke some moral authority higher than their own. Moreover, . . . in claiming this moral authority for a "political Bible"—which is wholly unintelligible to the masses and inexplicable by its commentators, [the KMT leaders] are observing the continuity of mandarin tradition. For Sun Yat-sen's "Three Principles," as a guide to political wisdom and morality, has this in common with the Book of Changes, venerated for centuries by every Chinese scholar, including Confucius, that none has ever fathomed its meaning and everyone is, therefore, entitled to interpret it as he chooses. . . .
> The Sun legend will endure so long as the political elements which created it

[77] Roots, "The Canton Idea: How Chinese Nationalists Are Carrying Out Sun Yat-sen's 'Three Stages' Formula," *Asia,* XXVII, No. 4 (April, 1927), 285.

hold together. But it can never become a permanent national cult, for the reason that it conveys to the mind of the masses nothing which can inspire them with that respect for their rulers, based on understanding, which makes for permanence of authority.[78]

Judging from recent reverberations of the Sun cult on the mainland as well as its survival on Taiwan, it might seem that Bland's prognostications were overly dour. Nonetheless, his negative assessment of the *San-min chu-i*'s ideological authority for the masses was well taken. The stature of the Three People's Principles failed to exceed that of the men who championed them. These were not tenets that could readily be applied to specific problems. The irrelevance of Sun's theories to China's realities is ironical considering Sun's highly programmatic bent. As James Hsiung has observed, the *chu-i* of Sun is etymologically at least as close to the world of action as the *ssu-hsiang* of Mao.[79] Etymology, however, fries no fish.[80]

The *San-min chu-i* fell short both as science and as religion. The ideological vacuum that resulted provides at least a partial explanation for Chiang Kai-shek's initiation of the New Life Movement in 1934. Hoping to capitalize upon the residual emotional appeals of traditional Confucian moral virtues, he sought, simultaneously, to address himself to the specifics—or minutiae, as critics have charged—of daily life. However, the New Life Movement, like the *San-min chu-i*, related neither to the intellectual and emotional needs of the elite nor to the pressing economic concerns of the common people.

Close upon the heels of the New Life Movement came the creation of another personal cult, that of Chiang Kai-shek. Even more than the cult of Sun, this was the plaything of political fortune. It came closest to viability when Chiang personified the anti-Japanese united front, between his release from Sian in December, 1936, and the New Fourth Army incident of January, 1941. The cult of Chiang, like the cult of Mao, found an organizational base in the army and attempted, albeit less successfully, to create a mass student following through the Three People's Principles Youth Corps. The cult enjoyed a brief renaissance in the months following V-J Day, but was soon buried in the rubble of the Nationalist debacle. By that time, the cult of Sun had been reduced to Monday morning rituals, and the New Life Movement was little more than a bad joke. Though some might find

[78] Bland, "The Cult of Sun Yat-sen," *The English Review,* No. 49 (August, 1929), pp. 175, 180.
[79] Hsiung, *Ideology and Practice,* p. 130.
[80] An ancient saying of uncertain origins.

the survival of these cults on Taiwan analogous to the survival of Celtic Christianity during the "Dark Ages," less sanguine observers would liken this exotic phenomenon to the last spastic movements of a chicken after the head is cut off.

How does the Mao cult compare to the impressive list of failures that preceded it? Structurally it shares some formal similarities with C. K. Yang's "diffused" religion of the cult of Heaven, which had "no independent organizational existence" and in which ethical values drew support from, but did not derive from, the religion.[81] However, it is a long way from the cult of a long-dead Confucius that actively involved but a tiny minority of Chinese to the adulation of a living god by a nation of some 800 million. And, unlike the cult of Sun, the Mao cult has broken into full flower during the lifetime of the cult-head. This should discourage, at least temporarily, the kind of imaginative reinterpretation of Sun that has occurred since his death at the hands of both the KMT and CCP.

Because only the ideas of Sun have been cultified in a way comparable to those of Mao, the two ideologies merit further comparison. Sun as a man continues to receive veneration, but the ideological part of his cult has not fared well. In spite of numerous interpretations and commentaries, or perhaps abetted by them, it has assumed a dependent relationship to the figure of Sun himself. Mao's cult, on the other hand, relies squarely on the thought of Mao for continued vitality. Sun's ideas were incohesive and visionary, but in a materialistic realm. He made too many demands on the limited economic and material resources that China would have at her disposal, and his plans depended too much upon outside assistance. Mao's ideas are visionary in quite a different sense. They make demands upon men. Thus, to the extent that man is a malleable, unpredictable element, these precepts are less capable of being outdated by the vagaries of international diplomacy or the financial situation. Mao's ideas, unlike Sun's, have been extensively tested in practice during his own lifetime. The Maoist package, moreover, includes techniques to assure the continual readjustment and reassessment of ideas in a working situation. If the Maoist techniques—small group discussions, criticism and self-criticism, and the mass line—prevail, there is a good chance that the thought of Mao Tse-tung can avoid the fate of the theories of Sun Yat-sen.

As a revolutionary leader, Sun remains honored, even during the Cultural Revolution that excoriated other remnants of the bourgeois

[81] Yang, "The Functional Relationship," p. 279.

past. Mao apparently gave his personal blessing to the celebration of the hundredth anniversary of Sun's birth on November 12, 1966.[82] He could well afford the gesture. Speakers took pains to emphasize the subordination of Sun to Mao. Sun was the "great revolutionary predecessor," according to Chou En-lai; but, as Tung Pi-wu expressed it: "No other revolutionary movement in history can compare with this Great Proletarian Cultural Revolution. What we have done and are doing has greatly surpassed our predecessors'. However, we are historical materialists; we have founded our own cause on the basis of endeavors made by our predecessors, and we are the successors to the revolutionary cause of Dr. Sun Yat-sen." [83]

Safely relegated to a position of "merely historical significance" (*vide* Levenson), Sun's ideas could be praised as "advanced" for their day. In spite of the Sino-Soviet split, his "New Three People's Principles" or "Three Cardinal Principles," which included alliance with the USSR, were praised by speaker after speaker. His refusal to compromise with the reformers K'ang Yu-wei and Liang Ch'i-ch'ao was cited as the mark of a true revolutionary. However, little effort was made to devise broader contemporary applications for Sun's ideas. This is not surprising since his philosophy was constructed upon an amalgam of Western liberalism, democratic socialism, and traditional Chinese thought—all of which were anathematized in the Cultural Revolution. Other elements of Sun's thinking that deviate from the spirit of the GPCR are his programmatic approach to political and economic problems, his emphasis upon forms and structures (three historical stages, five-part government), and his heavy emphasis upon Western-style, foreign-financed modernization, with little understanding of the problems, or the potentialities, of China's rural masses.

Mao's personal stature, like Sun's, seems indestructible because Mao, like Sun, embodies the revolution. Each in his own day has become synonymous with China. Of course, Mao is the most powerful figure in China, or at least the most authoritative, whereas Sun never controlled more than a portion of a single province. Yet Mao's cult, like Sun's, does not really depend upon the Leader's presence. The death of Sun, whose faults (vanity, capriciousness, opportunism, bombast) were well known, certainly facilitated his apotheosis. Mao, whose

---

[82] "Speech at a Report Meeting" (October 24, 1966), in "Selections from Chairman Mao," *JPRS*, No. 49826, p. 11.

[83] "Chou En-lai's Speech," *Peking Review*, No. 47 (November 18, 1966), p. 9; "Vice-Chairman Tung Pi-wu's Opening Speech," *ibid.*

personal foibles are well known mainly to his closest associates, has been deified in his own lifetime.

Strangely enough, the fact that Mao still lives has not made a great deal of difference. This man of the masses plays a less active role in the Mao cult than the aloof Chiang once played in his own. We have no reason to doubt that the reissues and re-editions of Mao's works bear the author's personal stamp of approval, but he has chosen to add little to their volume. Though his secret speeches and off-the-cuff remarks were reported by Red Guard publications of undetermined reliability, his public declamations during the Cultural Revolution were so sparse that his followers had to make much of mangoes for lack of more specific verbal indications of his wishes.

Venerated for his historic accomplishments and his eternal ideas, Mao now finds it unnecessary to "earn" adulation. The emperor's charismatic appeal was a charisma of office. Chiang's was based upon his military leadership during the Northern Expedition and the War of Resistance. Hitler mesmerized mass rallies. Franklin D. Roosevelt had homey fireside chats. But Mao? Mao need only stand on the platform of the T'ien-an men. Even when it is dark and the ancient gate is visible only in its lighted outlines, the air is electric: Mao is there. If Mao is China's supreme helmsman, there is scant evidence to prove it. In terms of his past record, he may resemble a wall-building legalist despot or a Confucian emperor who attracts loyalty by setting an edifying example. But at present, he seems to be working toward the dream of Lao Tzu: to accomplish everything by doing nothing.

When Mao dies, he, like Sun, will leave behind the challenge of an ongoing and unfinished revolution. This idea—the unfinished character of a great man's work—may similarly become a clarion call to inspire men to struggle and sacrifice. Meanwhile, the cult of Mao rests upon two seemingly ethereal but truly potent phenomena: the thought of Mao's reality and the reality of Mao's thought. Like the smile of the Cheshire Cat and the cult of Sun Yat-sen, the Thought of Mao may well survive after its namesake has passed from view.

"A SINGLE STEP CAN LEAD TO A 10,000-MILE JOURNEY
—SO YOU MIGHT AS WELL STAY HOME" [84]

Though the ideology of the Cultural Revolution has been termed "extreme," it does in fact move toward reconciliation of some polarities that have plagued modern Chinese thinkers. It is Chinese yet of

[84] Ancient Taoist saying.

universal applicability; revolutionary yet practical; scientific yet populist; modern yet antibourgeois. Most important it is Chinese. As James Hsiung writes, "It may be that the Cultural Revolution is an aging Mao's last campaign to Sinify Communist ideology and to create . . . a new proletarian culture . . . that the Maoist-Chinese could accept as their own and regard as superior to Soviet 'revisionism.' " [85] And, we might add, superior to bourgeois modernization as well.

The Sinifying function of the Cultural Revolution has nothing to do with whether its ideology supports or rejects traditional values. In fact, if we examine a list of ten pervasive ideas in Chinese philosophy, concepts that Wing-tsit Chan contends are unlikely to be rejected by "any philosophical system that hopes to enjoy a permanent place in China," we find that the GPCR rejects almost all of them. Take the first six: (1) "central harmony or cordial relationship between Nature and man"; (2) "the 'both-and' attitude"; (3) "Golden Mean"; (4) "humanism"; (5) "the preservation of one's life and the full realization of one's nature"; (6) "mental tranquillity." [86] We are stunned by the decisive break that the GPCR has made with so many of the "permanent" ideals of Chinese philosophy. Man no longer is to enjoy a "cordial relationship" with Nature via the "central harmony," but to conquer it via contradiction and struggle. In place of "both-and," we have a militant "either or" to divide one into two. To practice the "Golden Mean" would mean capitulation to the class enemy. Man remains central, but scarcely in a traditional "humanistic" sense. To die for the people is superior to preservation of life, and to serve the masses more important than the fulfillment of one's nature. Mental tranquillity may be purchased only at the price of criminal indifference to right and wrong.

Since Mao is identical to China, no iconoclasm that spares him can be deemed un-Chinese. During the early stages of the Red Guard movement, Joseph Levenson observed that Maoists had (literally and figuratively) ransacked museums where they had hoped "to keep the past passé." [87] The alternative to the "demuseumification" of the dead Confucius was deemed to be the "museumification" of the living Mao. GPCR ideology also Sinifies China's world view by restoring

[85] Hsiung, *Ideology and Practice*, p. 81.

[86] Chan, "The Story of Chinese Philosophy," in Charles A. Moore (ed.), *The Chinese Mind* (Honolulu: East-West Center Press, 1967), p. 67.

[87] Levenson, "An Exchange on China," *New York Review of Books*, January 7, 1967, p. 31.

China to her centrist position. What is Chinese is the insistence that the values for China will derive from Chinese experience, that they will be sanctified by a Chinese ruler of exemplary intelligence and virtue, and that they will eventually transform men from afar by their inherent reason and correctness. Whether the rest of the contemporary world confirms or denies these ideas is quite secondary.

What is the role of the foreign scholar standing beyond the fringe and looking in? Interesting as it may be to seek out continuities and discontinuities, I remain unconvinced that this kind of analysis will provide instant enlightenment. If we want to know something about the ideology of the Cultural Revolution, let us start with contemporary China. If we desire sharper perspective, let us study other ideologies and other societies. If we want to understand the minds of contemporary Chinese, by all means let us study their lives, the environment in which they grew up, and their cultural and intellectual heritage. But let us not expect too much. The Chinese have enough problems with the "heavy hand of the past." We need not allow the weight of Chinese history to burden us as well. It may be more important to understand how the Chinese think they relate to their past than to speculate about how we think they relate to it.

There are severe limitations to historical study. History is one route to understanding, and not necessarily the most important one. Our present task is to break through the barriers of culture, politics, values, language (including our own jargon), and sheer distance to seek a human understanding of China. A proper interest in China's past will enhance this endeavor by placing current problems and solutions in the context of earlier ones, making us aware of how Chinese resemble, and how they differ from, various peoples. To become excessively absorbed in the continuity or discontinuity of China's past would only reinforce our sense of otherness, which is one form of abstraction that has kept us from understanding the Chinese as fellow human beings.

RICHARD H. SOLOMON

From Commitment to Cant: The Evolving Functions of Ideology in the Revolutionary Process

Where do correct ideas come from? . . . They come from three kinds of social practice: the struggle for production; the class struggle; and scientific experimentation. . . . Generally speaking, those [ideas] that succeed are correct and those that fail are incorrect. . . . Such is the Marxist theory of knowledge, the dialectical materialist theory of knowledge. Among our comrades [however] there are many who do not understand this theory of knowledge. When asked the source of their ideas, opinions, policies, methods, plans and conclusions, eloquent speeches and long articles, they consider the question strange and cannot answer it.

MAO TSE-TUNG, "Where Do Correct Ideas Come From?" (1963)

Ideas shape men's action in their struggle for social change; yet an ideology is more the product than the precursor of a revolution. As one explores the role played by new concepts of society, social change, and political action in the formation and growth of the Chinese Communist movement, it becomes evident that a fully developed ideology—in the sense of an explicit, relatively systematic and comprehensive idea system, closely related to the assertion of political authority and capable of mobilizing intense involvement on the part of its adherents [1]—is

---

[1] In developing this analysis I have found particularly suggestive the following works: David E. Apter (ed.), *Ideology and Discontent* (New York: Free Press, 1964); Harry Johnson, "Ideology and the Social System," in David L. Sills (ed.), *International Encyclopedia of the Social Sciences* (New York: Macmillan and The Free Press, 1968), VII, 76–85; Lucian W. Pye, "Personal Identity and Political Ideology," *Behavioral*

something that evolved as the movement grew and attained state control. The ideas of Party leaders were shaped by the struggle for power, and their thinking—as expressed in the written media of the movement—served different functions at each stage of the revolutionary process. Their Marxist concepts, first acquired in partial, unsystematic form during the May Fourth era, were elaborated, modified, and codified as an association of intellectuals grew into a mass political movement. The ideology which today is termed "Marxism–Leninism–Mao Tsetung Thought" thus was "built up" as ideas interplayed with reality and were adapted to the functional demands of the struggle for power.

This paper is an exploration of the changing functions of ideology in the course of the Chinese revolution based on interpretation of the autobiographical statements and political writings of Party leaders, and on analysis of the content of the various Party periodicals which have grown with the movement. These materials indicate that an ideology serves a variety of functions for a political movement, although a given function seems to have particular salience at a given stage of the revolution.[2] As the Communist movement in China grew and attained state power, these various functions were reflected in the evolution of the movement's idea system, which "accreted" new qualities while retaining the old, much as an evolving personality, in epigenetic fashion, acquires new dimensions as it matures.[3]

In this analysis we shall explore six functions of ideology as it shapes political action: legitimacy; identity; solidarity; agitation; communication; and goal-specification. These functions, in practice, are not always clearly differentiated. A number of them usually are operative at one time, just as a political movement must cope with a

Science, VI, No. 3 (July, 1961), 205–21; Giovani Sartori, "Politics, Ideology, and Belief Systems," *American Political Science Review,* LXIII, No. 2 (June, 1969), 398–411; Franz Schurmann, *Ideology and Organization in Communist China* (2nd ed.; Berkeley and Los Angeles: University of California Press, 1968); and Edward Shils, "The Concept and Function of Ideology," in Sills (ed.), *International Encyclopedia of the Social Sciences,* VII, 66–76.

2 In relating this interpretation to concepts of stages of revolution, I have relied heavily on the notion of crises of political development, as has been suggested by members of the Social Science Research Council's Committee on Comparative Politics. See Lucian W. Pye, *Aspects of Political Development* (Boston: Little, Brown, 1966), pp. 62–67. This analysis has been further developed in the volume edited by Pye and Sidney Verba, *Crises of Development* (forthcoming), especially Chap. vii by Sidney Verba, "Sequences and Development." I find this conception of stages supported by Anthony Wallace's analysis of "revitalization movements" as detailed in his article of that title in *The American Anthropologist,* LVIII (1956), 264–81.

3 Erik H. Erikson, *Identity: Youth and Crisis* (New York: W. W. Norton, 1968), pp. 92–93.

variety of real problems at any given time. Our objective in this analysis, however, is to separate out these functions for purposes of analytical clarity, and to show how they relate to the practical requirements of political action.

Research indicates, moreover, that just as a given function may predominate at any given stage of the revolution, so at each stage there are contradictory choices or problems associated with the use of a formal idea system in shaping action. In the formative years of a political movement, the problem may be a matter of choice between differing idea systems. In the case of China's revolution, this was a matter of conflict between an internationalist doctrine and the demands of a national political struggle. In the years after the attainment of power, the "contradictions" inherent in the use of an ideology seem related to conflicting goals which the idea system cannot resolve, and to the tension between revolutionary ideals and the practical measures required to attain them—the conflict between "Redness" and expertise.

For the purposes of presentation, the various functions of ideology, their relation to the organizational and functional problems which predominate at each stage of the revolution, and the contradictions which seem to be associated with them are summarized in Table 1.

LEGITIMACY

In most general terms, an ideology legitimates political action. To the degree that human behavior is shaped by cognitive mental processes, as opposed to internal emotional drives (the equivalent of animal instincts) or the pressures of social or natural environments, an idea system identifies collective goals and rationalizes operative procedures for attaining them. As justification for (future) action, an ideology draws its sense of authoritativeness from past successes. Such was certainly the case with the Chinese intellectuals' turn to Marxist socialism, shaped by the success of the Bolshevik Revolution in Russia which, as Mao Tse-tung recalled, "helped progressives in China, as throughout the world, to adopt the proletarian world outlook as the instrument for studying a nation's destiny and considering anew their own problems." [4]

While a revolutionary idea system draws its meaningfulness from demonstrated efficacy, it remains vulnerable to erosion in the face of

[4] Mao Tse-tung, "On the People's Democratic Dictatorship" (1949), *Selected Works of Mao Tse-tung* (Peking: Foreign Languages Press, 1961), IV, 413.

TABLE 1

THE FUNCTIONS OF IDEOLOGY IN THE REVOLUTIONARY PROCESS

Crises of Political Development	Phases of Institution-building	Functions of Ideology	Contradictions in the Development of Ideology
Legitimacy	(Common to all phases)	Legitimacy	Ideals vs. reality
Identity	Party leadership formation	Identity ("conscious-ness")	Tradition vs. images of the future
Participation	Party-building	Solidarity ("study" and "rectification")	Competitive images of the future (socialism vs. nationalism)
Penetration	Developing a mass following (united front organizations, army recruit-ment)	Agitation (mass mobiliza-tion, "the mass line")	Elitism vs. mass appeals; Party loyalty vs. paro-chial commitments (to family, clan, etc.)
Integration	State-building	Communication	Bureaucratization; "Redness" vs. expertise (policy–operations gap)
Distribution	Economic and social con-struction	Goal-specification	Revolutionary goals vs. the functional re-quirements of rule (institutional interests)

failure on the part of the action it shapes. There thus is a delicate in-terplay between ideals and reality which can both impel men to strive for a utopia in a context of social turmoil, and yet lead them to reject the utopian vision when actions taken in its name prove ineffective.

It is this interplay between ideal and reality which occupies so ob-vious a part of the past century of political turmoil in China: the dis-crediting of the Confucian world-view in the face of a reality of foreign pressures and domestic rebellion with which it could not cope; the struggle to attain socialist ideals, and the transformation of Marx-ism-Leninism under the impact of setbacks to the Communist movement in its struggle for power; and the eventual (if perhaps temporary) discrediting of Mao Tse-tung's political "thought" under the combined influences of Khrushchev's revelations of Stalin's errors and the hardships created by Maoist policies applied within China.

The need to justify action in terms of an authoritative idea system, while to some degree a common human quality, is an aspect of political behavior strongly influenced by cultural values. As is indicated by research into Chinese political attitudes, "the power of the word" has been a dominant theme in the Confucian political culture. The socialization practices of this society gave a growing child a sense that authority was associated with the right to express opinions, and that power lay in the ability to invoke an official literature. In their perceptions of political authority, Chinese reveal an intuitive assumption that a leader asserts his power through an "ism" (*chu-i*), and seeks signs of submission on the part of subordinates through their willingness to "study" his words. Command of language has constituted a basic political skill in the Chinese social context.[5] As this association of words and power was expressed by an assertive young Mao Tse-tung: "When I was thirteen I discovered a powerful argument of my own for debating with my father on his own grounds, by quoting the [Confucian] Classics. My father's favorite accusations against me were of unfilial conduct and laziness. I quoted, in exchange, passages from the Classics saying that the elder must be kind and affectionate."[6]

Mao's perception of the authority that could be attained even by an exploited subordinate through invoking the words of the Sage in time became adapted to his rebellion against Chinese society. In the "Hunan Report," Mao described how the slogans of a revolutionary movement could legitimate for the peasants their resistance to the established social order:

> Some of the peasants can . . . recite Dr. Sun Yat-sen's Testament. They pick out the terms "freedom," "equality," "the Three People's Principles" and "unequal treaties" and apply them, if rather crudely, in their daily life. When somebody who looks like one of the gentry encounters a peasant and stands on his dignity, refusing to make way along the pathway, the peasant will say angrily, "Hey, you local tyrant, don't you know the Three People's Principles?" Formerly when the peasants from the vegetable farms on the outskirts of Changsha entered the city to sell their produce, they used to be pushed around by the police.

[5] These aspects of the Chinese political culture are analyzed on the basis of interview and documentary data in the author's study, *Mao's Revolution and the Chinese Political Culture* (Berkeley and Los Angeles: University of California Press, 1971), esp. pp. 48–49, 87, 145–46.

[6] Edgar Snow, *Red Star over China* (New York: Grove Press, 1961), pp. 125–26.

Now they have found a weapon, which is none other than the Three People's Principles. When a policeman strikes or swears at a peasant selling vegetables, the peasant immediately answers back by invoking the Three People's Principles and that shuts the policeman up.[7]

In time Mao's own words, verbalizing his *ssu-hsiang* or "thoughts," were to convey the sense of legitimacy of the political movement that he led from near defeat in the mountains of south China to the strength of the Yenan-based Party and army, which reconstituted itself in the struggle against Japan. The Party *cheng-feng* (rectification) of 1942–44 was Mao's first systematic effort to have his ideas serve as the basis for training a new generation of Party cadres; and his consolidation of leadership within the Party was symbolized in 1945 by inclusion of the phrase "the thought of Mao Tse-tung" in the Party's Seventh Constitution as one of the Chinese Communist movement's theoretical guides to action.

In the mid-1950's loss of support for Mao's policies within the Party leadership was to be signaled by removal of the phrase "the thought of Mao Tse-tung" from the Eighth Party Constitution; and in the 1960's the deepening conflict within the leadership between competing visions of China's path to national development was to be expressed by certain leaders proclaiming their allegiance to "Marxism-Leninism" with others asserting the continuing correctness of Mao's "thought" as a guide to action.[8] In the Cultural Revolution Mao was to seek to reassert the legitimacy of his authority through mass study of his "word," as embodied in the little red book of quotations from his writings.

In the Chinese political context, then, a formal idea system has been —and remains—a basic vehicle for conveying the aura of legitimacy of political authority.

IDENTITY

If there is one quality that differentiates the great ideologically based revolutions of our time from the periodic dynastic revolts of China's tradition, it is their profound and purposeful challenging of entire cultural systems. The Bolshevik effort to transform the diverse national cultures of the Soviet Union into a proletarian civilization is the carrying to conclusion—under the justification of an ideology

[7] Mao, "Report on an Investigation of the Peasant Movement in Hunan" (1927), *Selected Works*, I, 48.

[8] This use of the symbols "the thought of Mao Tse-tung" and "Marxism-Leninism" to signal political loyalties is documented in Solomon, *Mao's Revolution*, pp. 431–32, 458–59.

of historical change—of Peter the Great's desire to have "backward" Russia keep up with the developing societies of Europe.[9]

Such a clash of cultural systems has been no more profound than in the case of China's confrontation with assertive Western traders and missionaries, educators, and militarists. The failure of nineteenth-century efforts to strengthen the Chinese self (*t'i*) through adoption of Western material culture (*yung*), so sharply revealed by China's defeat at the hands of the Japanese in 1894–95, the inability to reform Confucianism and the imperial political order in 1898, and the final, punctuating humiliation of the Boxer episode, precipitated a collective crisis of cultural identity. Indeed, Mao Tse-tung may only now be helping his compatriots to resolve the humiliations and self-doubts which were so much a part of the May Fourth era and the anti-Japanese war through contemporary claims that the Soviets have betrayed the lofty goals of the October Revolution and that his thought has made China the center of the world revolution.

For Mao and other young intellectuals coming to maturity in the early years of this century, however, the demonstrated inefficacy of China's political institutions, and the ideology that asserted their legitimacy, constituted a profound *personal* crisis. Their basic education had begun in the age-old pattern of parents pressing sons into the severities of Confucian learning. The pain of the "stern treatment school" was justified, as it had been for centuries, in terms of the potential official career, material wealth, and status that would accrue to those who successfully passed the imperial examinations.[10] With the abolition of the examination system in 1905, however, an entire generation already grounded in the classical literature found itself cut off from the avenues of career for which they had been so harshly trained. A new generation of would-be intellectual leaders suddenly found themselves in a confusing world where long-established paths of career mobility and patterns of social service no longer existed. Thus a crisis of society and culture intersected with crises of personal identity and career, compounding the receptivity of the May Fourth generation to ideological solutions to the personal and social uncertainties of their lives. If the old words had lost their power, at least one had the alternative of a search for the new.

[9] See Leopold H. Haimson, *The Russian Marxists and the Origins of Bolshevism* (Cambridge, Mass.: Harvard University Press, 1967), p. 4 and *passim*.

[10] The phrase, "stern treatment school," is Mao's, as recorded by Snow in *Red Star over China*, p. 124. The harshness of the traditional Confucian curriculum, and its relation to career mobility, is explored further in Solomon, *Mao's Revolution*, Chap. v.

As one reads the personal accounts of youths of this period who were to emerge as political leaders, and the histories of their early revolutionary struggles, it is apparent how uncertain were their strivings for a meaningful career and social commitment. Mao Tse-tung's experience in his student years is probably common to many of his generation. Mao recalled for Edgar Snow his late teens, when he alternately decided to become a soldier, policeman, soapmaker, lawyer, businessman, and teacher.[11] Mao finally dealt with the confusion of a welter of career choices of uncertain relevance through what Erik Erikson has termed a psychosocial "moratorium," a voluntary withdrawal from society by which the maturing individual seeks to gain some perspective on himself and his relation to society.[12] "I [came] to the conclusion that it would be better for me to read and study alone . . . which consisted of reading every day in the Hunan Provincial Library. I was very regular and conscientious about it, and the half-year I spent in this way I consider to have been extremely valuable to me." [13]

Other youths sought to deal with the confusion of the times through a withdrawal into scholarship (from which some, like the philosopher Hu Shih, were never fully to emerge), while some sought after mystical values through Buddhist practices.[14] A few, like the early feminist leader Ch'iu Chin, placed their lives on the altar of their troubled society through the personal political sacrifice of an insurrectionary act against the injustices of imperial rule.[15] In all, the manner in which individuals coped with the uncertainties of China's time of troubles has a strong element of randomness, of chance personal encounters which were to shape entire careers. The early Party leader Ch'ü Ch'iu-pai, for example, went to Peking in search of a university education. Although Ch'ü passed the entrance examinations at Peking University, his inability to pay tuition eventually led him to the government-sub-

[11] Snow, *Red Star over China*, pp. 138–41.
[12] Erikson, *Identity*, pp. 156–57.
[13] Snow, *Red Star over China*, p. 141.
[14] See Jerome B. Grieder, *Hu Shih and the Chinese Renaissance: Liberalism in the Chinese Revolution, 1917–1937* (Cambridge, Mass.: Harvard University Press, 1970), Chap. x. The appeal of Buddhism is noted in the early careers of such subsequent political activists as Ch'ü Ch'iu-pai and Kuo Mo-jo. See Bernadette Yu-ning Li, "A Biography of Ch'ü Ch'iu-pai: From Youth to Party Leadership (1899–1928)" (Ph.D. dissertation, Columbia University, 1967), p. 22; David T. Roy, *Kuo Mo-jo: The Early Years* (Cambridge, Mass.: Harvard University Press, 1971), pp. 58–60.
[15] Mary B. Rankin, *Early Chinese Revolutionaries: Radical Intellectuals in Shanghai and Chekiang, 1902–1911* (Cambridge, Mass.: Harvard University Press, 1971), pp. 41–44.

sidized Russian Language Institute. This choice under financial duress was to lead to a career in journalism, study in the Soviet Union, and, eventually, a prominent role in the Chinese Communist movement.[16]

In a social context which heightened personal insecurity, political events that threatened China's security—Japan's "Twenty-one Demands" of 1915, the injustice of the Versailles Treaty settlement of World War I, and the foreign economic penetration of China brought to public attention in the May Thirtieth demonstrations of 1925—established points of identity between individual and nation. Such events became catalysts in the formation of a revolutionary leadership, precipitating the coalescence of anxious young intellectuals out of a society that could assure them no future. In such circumstances, doctrines which accounted for China's trouble in political terms, as well as the individual's misery in personal terms, had powerful emotional grounds for claiming allegiance.[17] The ability of an ideology to provide that sense of identity which a society beset by chaos and injustice can no longer claim—its capacity to focus the anxieties of youth in search of a future—was clearly expressed by the radical writer Pa Chin, as he recalled reading in his teens *An Appeal to the Young* by the Russian anarchosocialist Peter Kropotkin: "I put this book under my pillow. I read it every night with a trembling heart. I cried and laughed reading it. . . . From that time I understood the meaning of justice, and the Idea of justice helped me to reconcile [my] feelings of love and hatred."[18]

The ability of a formal idea system to resolve the anxieties of young people at the critical "identity formation" stage of psychosocial growth can have all the dramatic qualities of a religious conversion. In the early 1920's the writer Kuo Mo-jo searched for a career, torn between the practical contribution he could make to China through medical training, yet lured by an instinctive attraction to the world of literature. His efforts were rendered all the more uncertain by estrangement from his Japanese wife and children, and dissolution of the Creation Society, founded by Kuo with student companions in 1921 as a vehicle for their literary efforts. In this context Kuo neared a nervous breakdown. His writings of the moment revealed "feelings of inferiority, in-

[16] Li, "Biography of Ch'ü Ch'iu-pai," p. 19.

[17] Lenin's theory of imperialism seems to have had a strong appeal to China's intellectuals in the May Fourth era for precisely these reasons. See a more detailed development of this view in the chapter by Sullivan and Solomon in this volume.

[18] Olga Lang, *Pa Chin and His Writings: Chinese Youth between the Two Revolutions* (Cambridge, Mass.: Harvard University Press, 1967), pp. 44–45.

adequacy, guilt, depression, resentment, and paranoia." [19] As he explicitly (if at the distance of the third person) observed of this period of his life in a letter to a friend: "Our internal demands cannot be brought into harmony with the external conditions. No longer finding any signposts along our path, we have sunk into inactivity, and even think frequently of suicide." [20]

For Kuo, the practical toil of translating a Marxist text by the Japanese Socialist Kawakami Hajime finally brought meaning to his uncertain personal life: "The translation of this book constitutes a turning point in my life. It has awakened me from my semisomnolent state, it has delivered me from my uncertainty before the crossroads, it has rescued me from the shadow of death. I am deeply grateful to the author and profoundly grateful to Marx and Lenin. . . ." And he concluded, "I now have a dream which is sustaining my life." [21]

The reasons for such personal crises have all the variety of the individual life experience: disgust with the hypocrisy of established social institutions; parental harshness, usually brought to a point of conflict over an arranged marriage or career choice; even personal profligacy, and the desire to purify a corrupt self through social sacrifice.[22] It is only at the level of individual biography that one can begin to account for the powerful claim which Marxism had for many youths of the May Fourth era, as well as for the zeal with which some who early flirted with Marxism, such as the Nationalist ideologue Tai Chi-t'ao, and even the "Red General" himself, Chiang Kai-shek, were to be led back to a reaffirmation of the values of Confucian

[19] Roy, *Kuo Mo-jo,* p. 156.

[20] *Ibid.,* p. 167.

[21] *Ibid.,* pp. 159, 158.

[22] For a particularly revealing personal statement of the disgust with which Ch'en Tu-hsiu viewed the imperial examination system, even as he complied with family wishes to seek an official degree, see Ch'en's "Autobiography," as translated in Richard C. Kagan, "The Chinese Trotskyist Movement and Ch'en Tu-hsiu: Culture, Revolution, and Polity" (Ph.D. dissertation, University of Pennsylvania, 1969), esp. pp. 193–96.

Conflict over arranged marriages seems to have been a particularly common point of parent-child conflict for the May Fourth generation, indicating the depth of breakdown of the traditional value system and the institutions which sustained it. See, for example, the autobiographical statements in Nym Wales, *Red Dust: Autobiographies of Chinese Communists* (Stanford, Calif.: Stanford University Press, 1952), esp. pp. 49, 78, 114. See also Mao Tse-tung's writing on this subject of the injustices of arranged marriages in Mao Tse-tung, *The Political Thought of Mao Tse-tung,* ed. and trans. Stuart R. Schram (New York: Praeger, 1963), pp. 226–29.

The desire for self-purification seems to have been an element in Chu Teh's turn from opium addiction to the revolutionary movement. See Agnes Smedley, *The Great Road: The Life and Times of Chu Te* (New York: Monthly Review Press, 1956), pp. 130–31.

society.[23] The depth of ideological commitment, however, can be said to reflect the degree of personal anxiety which found resolution through commitment to a doctrine which had the capacity to relate personal torment to matters of social evil and salvation.

In this regard, it is also worth noting here the eventual discrepancy between the depth of psychic commitment to a doctrine by the formative generation of a revolutionary movement, and the very different set of personal needs which postrevolutionary generations bring to established "revolutionary" institutions. In a time of social order and personal security, the founding fathers who guided a movement to power sense in the involvement of those "youngsters" professing faith in their goals an air of opportunism, or uncertain commitment to the ideals for which they risked their lives. Those who found personal salvation in a revolutionary doctrine fear with some reason that their "sons" may not be dependable "revolutionary successors."

In viewing individual political awakenings of the May Fourth generation through periodicals of the era and the personal accounts of those who came to "consciousness," two qualities of their search for new identities are evident. First is the confusing diversity of ideological debate, evidenced by the proliferation of more than four hundred new intellectual journals and student newspapers in the year after the May Fourth incident.[24] Second, one is struck by the sparse content of their early doctrinal commitments, as apart from the intensity of their emotional involvement with the symbols ("myths") of a new era.

Intellectual historians of China have documented the search for new social visions which evolved with the increasingly evident failures of Confucianism in the nineteenth century. Debate initially centered on how to resolve Chinese values with the unwanted pressures brought on by Western technological superiority. In the *t'i-yung* controversy of the 1870's and 1880's, the leaders of the Self Strengthening Movement asserted that China's ancient social values could be defended by adopting the very Western material culture which had humiliated the dynasty.[25] The failure of this effort to resolve the contradiction

23 For Tai Chi-t'ao, see Howard L. Boorman and Richard C. Howard (eds.), *Biographical Dictionary of Republican China*, 4 vols. (New York: Columbia University Press, 1970), III, 201. Chiang's return to advocacy of Confucian values is documented in Mary C. Wright, *The Last Stand of Chinese Conservatism: The T'ung-Chih Restoration, 1862–1874* (New York: Atheneum, 1966), pp. 300–12.

24 See Chow Tse-tsung, *The May Fourth Movement: Intellectual Revolution in Modern China* (2nd ed.; Cambridge, Mass.: Harvard University Press, 1964), pp. 176–82.

25 See Joseph R. Levenson, *Modern China and Its Confucian Past: The Problem of Intellectual Continuity* (Garden City, N.Y.: Doubleday Anchor Books, 1954), pp. 81–83.

between tradition and contemporary political pressures, made evident by defeat at the hands of the Japanese in 1894–95, created the political context for K'ang Yu-wei's attempt to bring about more substantial reforms, justified by the reinterpretation of Confucius as himself a reformer.[26] The conflicts inherent in this effort were soon manifest in the conservative reaction to the reform movement, as those whose life style and institutional interests were sustained by Confucian values lashed back at K'ang's effort to give new meaning to those values through institutional change.

The tension between tradition and future seems to have been felt most keenly by those whose early lives straddled the historical boundary between a traditional upbringing and the onset of political change. K'ang Yu-wei (1858–1927) was never to propose a revolutionary future for China, moving instead to support the imperial restoration attempt of Chang Hsün in 1917. It was K'ang's disciple Liang Ch'i-ch'ao (1873–1927) who intellectually made the transition from reformer to revolutionary through his advocacy of constitutional monarchy. Liang, however, was to see this relatively moderate conception of change challenged by his contemporary Sun Yat-sen and a subsequent generation advocating massive social revolution. Liang himself rejected a more radical position with the assertion that China's traditional "well field" system of land ownership already embodied the values of those seeking socialism.[27]

Maurice Meisner has suggested that the intellectual leader of the May Fourth era, Ch'en Tu-hsiu—originally trained as a classical scholar, active in the anti-Manchu Revolution of 1911, progressively a Francophile and advocate of Western science and liberalism, Marxist-Leninist, and ultimately a supporter of the Trotskyite position—felt the conflict between China's traditional values and alternative images of the future more forcefully than his younger cohort Li Ta-chao. This appears to reflect the fact that Li had come to social maturity when tradition had been fully discredited by the failure of the self-strengthening effort.[28] Yet one sees in Ch'en's own shifting political advocacy the confusion of a search for alternatives to tradition. (Further discussion of the evolution of Ch'en's political views, based on

[26] John K. Fairbank, Edwin O. Reischauer, and Albert M. Craig, *East Asia: The Modern Transformation* (Boston: Houghton Mifflin, 1965), pp. 388–89.

[27] See Li Yu-ning, *The Introduction of Socialism into China* (New York: Columbia University Press, 1971), pp. 18, 32–33.

[28] Maurice Meisner, *Li Ta-chao and the Origins of Chinese Marxism* (New York: Atheneum, 1970), pp. 4–5.

a content analysis of his journal, *Hsin ch'ing nien* [New Youth], is presented in the essay by Lawrence Sullivan and the present author in this volume.) While the contradiction between old values and the future was ultimately resolved for many Chinese by the collapse of the imperial order, the conflict between contending images of the future was confronted in a context of the interplay between the success or failure of alternative conceptions of social change and the struggle between those who committed themselves to organizations dedicated to realizing given social visions.

For those who did make a personal commitment to a revolutionary doctrine, one finds that in the formative stage of a political movement this commitment is largely symbolic or "mythic" in quality, rather than representing highly intellectualized consideration of the intricacies of an idea system which comes to characterize ideological debate in a postrevolutionary era. The onset of revolution is the era of the political slogan—"Down with the Manchus," support "Mr. Science and Mr. Democracy," "Long Live the Three People's Principles," "Down with Imperialism," "Long Live the Bolshevik Revolution"—a time characterized by the intense emotionalism of personal efforts to deal with insecurity and injustice. The practical measures needed to attain utopian goals, and their consequences, are scarcely considered, and the dimensions of the future are hardly perceived.

This largely symbolic commitment to the revolution was revealed consistently in the personal accounts of first-generation Communist leaders as they recalled their initial involvement in the revolution. In the words of the early Party "theoretician," Ch'ü Ch'iu-pai:

In China during the year of 1923, there were very few who had studied Marxism or the social sciences in general. Thus, simply for this reason, after I became a professor of sociology at Shanghai University, I gradually gained the title of a so-called "Marxist theoretician," which I did not deserve. In reality, what I knew was very superficial. At that time I compiled my lecture notes by translating several foreign books. Now [1935] I find them extremely naive and full of mistakes.[29]

In a similar vein, Liu Shao-ch'i recalled his understanding of the goals of the Socialist Youth League, which he joined in 1920: "At that time I only knew that Socialism was good. I had heard about Marx and Lenin and the October Revolution and the Bolshevik Party, but I was not clear what Socialism was or how it could be realized."[30]

[29] Li, "Biography of Ch'ü Ch'iu-pai," p. 140.
[30] "Chairman Liu Shao-ch'i's Speech at the Moscow Meeting" (December 7, 1960), as translated in *SCMP*, No. 2398 (December 15, 1960), p. 29.

SOLIDARITY

The personal uncertainties of an era of social upheaval almost in-
stinctively lead a generation alienated from discredited or ineffectual social organizations to establish associations of their own, through
which they seek personal meaning in collective action. Describing this
impulse, Mao Tse-tung recalled of his student days: "Feeling expan-
sive and the need for a few intimate companions, I one day inserted
an advertisement in a Changsha paper, inviting young men interested in
patriotic work to make contact with me. I specified youths who were
hardened and determined, and ready to make sacrifices for their
country. . . . Gradually I built up a group of students around myself, and the nucleus was formed of what later was to become a society
[the Hsin Min Hsüeh Hui (New People's Study Society)] that was
to have a widespread influence on the affairs and destiny of China." [31]

The "solidarizing" function of an idea system is inherent in this
search of the intellectual for companionship in the face of an uncertain world and discredited tradition.[32] Mao observed that his
Changsha cohorts "were a serious-minded little group of men . . .
[who had] no time for love or 'romance' and considered the times too
critical and the need for knowledge too urgent to discuss women or
trivialities. . . . [We] preferred to talk only of large matters—the
nature of man, of human society, of China, the world, and the universe!" [33]

Mao's group was but one of a profusion of associations of young
intellectuals which coalesced in the era of transition from opposition to
the discredited Ch'ing dynasty to advocacy of alternatives to ineffectual parliamentary politics and warlordism. At first these associations, like Sun Yat-sen's Hsing Chung Hui (Revive China Society) of
1894, were established in the clandestine manner of the traditional
secret societies. As Chinese students in increasing numbers traveled
abroad to study, associations were openly created in indifferent or
supportive foreign settings such as Japan (where Sun's T'ung Meng
Hui [Alliance Society] was founded in 1905) and France, where students advocating anarchism became active before the fall of the

---

[31] Snow, *Red Star over China*, pp. 144–45.

[32] The term "solidarize" is developed by Franz Schurmann in a discussion of how
cadres use the Party's ideology in their organizational work. See *Ideology and Organization*, p. 167.

[33] Snow, *Red Star over China*, pp. 145–46.

dynasty.[34] With the collapse of imperial authority within China, the fragmentation of power in the early republic enabled such associations to grow with only sporadic and ineffectual harassment from regional authorities or the police in foreign concessions such as Shanghai's International Settlement, where the Chinese Communist Party (CCP) held its first national congress in the summer of 1921. These notable organizations, as well as more short-lived associations such as the Restoration Society of Shanghai, the Social Welfare Society of Hupeh, and Tientsin's Awakening Society, brought together those who were to be the leaders of China's major political movements of the early twentieth century. As Mao Tse-tung noted, the intellectual debate of the times shaped the formation of these leadership nuclei: "Most of these societies were organized more or less under the influence of *New Youth (Hsin Ch'ing Nien)*, the famous magazine of the Literary Renaissance, edited by Ch'en Tu-hsiu." [35]

While this search by China's young intellectuals for solutions to their country's problems had the capacity to unite them, the debate over alternative visions of the future was to be a highly divisive process. In part this fragmentation reflected the factiousness of all intellectual exchanges, accentuated by the considerations of status and personal loyalty which for so long have been a part of Chinese social relations.[36] Yet the debate was founded on genuine differences of opinion over how to revitalize Chinese society; and in time the partisan uses of ideological commitment were to further enhance divisiveness as the May Fourth generation made the transition from polemic and protest to the organized struggle for power.

The search for solutions to China's problems was not confined only to consideration of the alternatives of anarchism, socialism, pragmatism, democracy, and Bolshevism; debate also confronted the basic question of whether an ideology would be a help or hindrance in dealing with the social crisis. The debate over "problems or isms," initiated by Hu Shih—a student of the pragmatist philosopher John Dewey—and published in *Mei-chou p'ing-lun* (The Weekly Critic) during the

[34] See Robert A. Scalapino and George T. Yu, *The Chinese Anarchist Movement* (Berkeley: University of California, Center for Chinese Studies, 1961), pp. 2–5.

[35] Snow, *Red Star over China*, p. 147.

[36] For example, efforts to establish a political alliance between K'ang Yu-wei and Sun Yat-sen in 1898 foundered on K'ang's insistence that Sun become his disciple. Subsequent moves to have Sun and Liang Ch'i-ch'ao join forces were thwarted by K'ang's claim of loyalty on his follower Liang. See Fairbank, Reischauer, and Craig, *East Asia*, p. 633.

summer of 1919, is a remarkably self-conscious evaluation of the role of ideology in a period of cultural criticism and political change. Hu Shih reflected the views of his mentor when he attacked "fundamental solutions" advocated by socialist-inclined political activists, which he claimed would make men "satisfied and complacent" in the belief that they had found a panacea.[37] China's problems, he claimed, had to be dealt with in a practical manner, "by inches and drops," rather than through invocation of "fanciful, good-sounding isms" which could easily be utilized by unprincipled politicians.[38]

Hu received a politically more astute reply from a man who within two years was to become a founder of the CCP. Li Ta-chao ridiculed the intellectual aloofness inherent in Hu's position:

In order to solve the problems of a society, you must rely upon the concerted action of a majority of the people of that society. Hence, if we want to think of solving a given problem, we must establish methods which will cause [the problem] to become the common concern of a majority of the people. . . . Otherwise, even if you exert all your efforts researching your social problems a majority of the people in society will not develop the slightest relationship [to your efforts]. They will never develop any striving to solve the social problem; and your research will not have any influence on reality.[39]

Li's own position stressed both the "solidarizing" function of an idea system ("We must enable a majority of people who want to solve together this or that social problem to first have the common direction of an ideal ism [*chu-i*]"), and its instrumental qualities:

We can use this or that ism, adopt it for use as a tool (*kung-chü*), use it in practical movements. Depending on the nature of the times, the location, or the issue, [an ism] can produce a transformation suitable to the environment. In the Ch'ing era democracy was used as a tool to overthrow the imperial rule of Aisin-gioro. Today we can use it as an instrument for overthrowing the power of the warlords. In other countries where capitalism is developing, socialism can be used as an instrument for striking down the capitalist class. . . . This goes to prove the essential quality of an ism, its basic possibilities of being applicable to any circumstances.[40]

Li's views came to be accepted by Ch'en Tu-hsiu, who within the year was to become a convert to Marxism. Ch'en also understood the

[37] Grieder, *Hu Shih*, p. 183.

[38] Meisner, *Li Ta-chao*, p. 105.

[39] Li Ta-chao, "Tsai lun wen-t'i yü chu-i" (More on Problems and Isms), *Mei-chou p'ing-lun* (The Weekly Critic), August 17, 1919, as reproduced in Shih Chün, *Chung-kuo chin-tai ssu-hsiang shih t'san-k'ao tzu-liao chien-pien* (Collection of Reference Materials on the History of Contemporary Chinese Thought) (Peking: San-lien shu-tien, 1957), pp. 1256–57.

[40] *Ibid.*, pp. 1256, 1258.

unifying function of his newly adopted "ism," for when the Comintern in 1922 urged the just-formed CCP to establish a united front with the Kuomintang (KMT), Ch'en objected to the alliance, in part on the grounds that Party members would become "confused" about their organizational loyalty and political goals in a situation of dual affiliation.[41] Indeed, when the first KMT-CCP united front broke down, in 1927, many lower-level cadres *were* unsure about whether their basic commitment was to the Nationalist or Communist movement.[42]

The role of an ideology in enhancing the solidarity of a political movement is evident in the evolution of the content of the most influential intellectual journal of the May Fourth era, *Hsin ch'ing nien*. Analysis of its articles from the first issue of 1915 to its final number in 1926 reveals its transformation from an instrument of search for a new cultural identity to partisan political advocate.[43] With deep emotional commitment, the formative generation of the Chinese Communist movement used its newly adopted world view to gain support for its cause. Yet in the process of asserting the correctness of its political identity, the Party began to build up strains with nonbelievers, and more importantly, with "other-believers."

In the growth of the CCP this paradox between the need to define the boundaries of the movement and the requirement of gaining popular support was initially dealt with under Comintern direction—by defining the Party's goal as completing the "bourgeois-democratic" stage of the revolution. This was to be achieved by working within the more broadly based Nationalist movement. With the collapse of the first united front in 1927, the leadership adopted a series of "sectarian" political lines which, according to subsequent Maoist interpretations, cut the Party off from popular support, destroyed the unity of the leadership through factional struggles, and led to defeat in the KMT's

[41] Donald W. Klein and Anne B. Clark, *Biographic Dictionary of Chinese Communism, 1921–1965*, 2 vols. (Cambridge, Mass.: Harvard University Press, 1971), I, 141; Thomas C. T. Kuo, "Ch'en Tu-hsiu and the Chinese Communist Movement" (Ph.D. dissertation, University of Pittsburgh, 1969), p. 191.

[42] This phenomenon was described by the Party leader Ch'ü Ch'iu-pai: "Most of the Kuomintang with the exception of its leading organs had become [by 1927] in fact a Communist appendage. This proved to be embarrassing after the final rupture: how was this tightly knit alliance to be disentangled? Many local Party units fell into confusion: which party was it that was theirs? From which should they take orders? Even in 1928, such units still existed: in name, part of the Kuomintang; in outlook, vaguely Communist." Cited from Ch'ü's *Chung-kuo ti ko-ming yü kung-ch'an-tang* (China's Revolution and the Communist Party), as translated in Conrad Brandt, *Stalin's Failure in China* (New York: W. W. Norton, 1966), p. 132.

[43] See the article by Lawrence Sullivan and the present author in this volume.

fifth "encirclement and extermination" campaign.[44] It was only after the Tsunyi meeting that a correct balance was struck between measures to sustain organizational unity (through political "study" and "criticism–self-criticism") and the need to rally mass support (through nationalistic appeals to resist the Japanese invaders, and the formation of a second "united front" with the KMT) which enabled the movement to grow both in discipline and popular support.

It is from this historical experience that the CCP institutionalized the "solidarizing" uses of ideology, both for Party members and the population at large. The ability of political study (*hsüeh-hsi*) to sustain organization discipline was utilized in the Party "rectification" (*cheng-feng*) of 1942–44, a period of great privation and uncertainty for the movement. After the assumption of state power, the ability of ideological education to convey a common sense of purpose was to become a basic element of teaching curricula from elementary schools through universities. And in the "Mao's thought propaganda teams" of the Cultural Revolution era the disciplinary aspects of study were to become evident in the use of Mao's "little red book" to assert control over factious Red Guards.

AGITATION

The leadership core of a social movement such as Chinese communism is characteristically formed by distraught young intellectuals. However, the growth of such a movement—spurred on by its confrontation with rivals for power—requires an expansion of organized strength through recruitment beyond intellectual circles. The leadership thus must seek to transmit its own sense of agitation over social or political issues to less "conscious" sectors of the population through organized appeals for support. In the case of Chinese communism, this effort to penetrate and draw support from society began with the formation of labor unions in the urban areas and rural peasant associations, and with the concomitant establishment in 1921 of the Party's first "nonintellectual" media of communication, *Lao-tung chou-k'an* (Labor Weekly), and *Ch'ih-hsin chou-pao* (Red Heart Weekly), which was begun by the peasant organizer P'eng P'ai.[45]

---

[44] See "Resolution on Certain Questions in the History of Our Party" (adopted on April 20, 1945, by the Enlarged Plenary Session of the Sixth Central Committee of the CCP), *Selected Works*, III, esp. 180–94.

[45] See Chang Ching-lu (ed.), *Chung-kuo hsien-tai ch'u-pan shih tzu-liao* (Historical Materials on Publishing in Contemporary China), 4 vols. (Peking: Chung-hua shu-chü, 1954–59), I, 87, 103.

This effort to expand the political movement by appealing to new social groups brings with it the need to adapt the abstract theories of the intellectual world to the earthy perceptions and daily concerns of those who work with their hands. P'eng P'ai, for example, analyzed the difficulties he encountered in rallying support from peasants in his native province of Kwangtung: "What we had been saying to the peasants . . . was much too cultured; much of what we had been saying the peasants didn't understand. . . . [Our] bookish terminology had to be translated into plain talk." [46] Such practical problems force modification of the ideology, and its media of expression, to the requirements of gaining popular support.[47]

In China the adaptation of Party doctrine to the tasks of mass mobilization encountered two particular problems: the reluctance of the (intellectual) cadre of the movement to communicate with the masses on their own terms; and the need to adapt an internationalist doctrine of imperialism and class warfare to the parochial concerns of China's workers and peasants. Mao Tse-tung's political writings reveal a preoccupation with problems of communication between intellectuals and the laboring classes. In his 1930 tract, "Oppose Book Worship," Mao lashed out at the time-honored Mandarin habit of the intellectual to assume that it was his possession of some understanding of official doctrine which gave him the right to wield power. As Mao phrased his complaint, Party cadres "eat their fill and sit dozing in their offices all day long without ever moving a step and going out among the masses to investigate." [48] His conclusion was, "no investigation, no right to speak," a new style of leadership in the context of China's elitist political tradition that Mao has sought to propagate throughout his career.

A related problem was the traditional use of doctrine as an artistic form, a language of the elite, rather than of mass communication. In the 1942 article, "Oppose Stereotyped Party Writing," Mao ridiculed a Party propagandist who wrote the characters for an anti-Japanese slogan in elaborate classical form. "Perhaps he had taken a vow that

---

[46] P'eng P'ai, "Hai-feng nung-min yün-tung" (The Hai-feng Peasant Movement), in *Ti-yi-tzu kuo-nei ko-ming chan-cheng shih-ch'i ti nung-min yün-tung* (The Peasant Movement during the First Period of Domestic Revolutionary War) (Peking: Jen-min ch'u-pan-she, 1953), p. 54.

[47] The importance of face-to-face, oral media in Party relations with the peasantry is discussed in Allan P. L. Liu, *Communications and National Integration in Communist China* (Berkeley and Los Angeles: University of California Press, 1971).

[48] Mao, "Oppose Book Worship" (1930), *Selected Readings from the Works of Mao Tse-tung* (Peking: Foreign Languages Press, 1967), p. 39.

the common people should not read them," jibed Mao.[49] He urged propagandists and artistic workers to learn the rich vernacular of the peasantry, for without such "popularization" of its political vocabulary the Party would not be able to use its ideology as an instrument of mass mobilization.[50]

In practice, the adaptation of Marxism and the Party's leadership style to the demands of building widespread popular support occurred in the context of the war of resistance against Japan. The symbols of nationalism and economic reform provided the basis for a united front against the invader, while the problems of overcoming peasant resistance to political involvement were dealt with through increasing use of the "speak bitterness" rally, enabling those with little experience in intellectualizing problems to "emotionalize" their commitment to the revolution.[51] Such modifications of the Party's ideological appeals, however, again raised the problem of sustaining a sense of political identity in the context of an unresolved struggle for power with the Nationalists. In this light, the *cheng-feng* of 1942–44 can be seen, in part, as an effort to sustain for the Party's leadership cadre its sense of organizational identity as an internationalist, revolutionary movement even while waging a national struggle with "conservative" popular appeals.

From the vantage point of those to whom the Party directed its appeals, calls to resistance and revolution posed difficult choices between the existing social commitments of peasant life and an uncertain future of opposition to economic exploitation and military violence that long had been endured as a "natural" and inescapable aspect of rural life. In the 1920's the Party found its greatest successes in building mass support among a small urban working class which was to some degree unburdened of the traditional commitments of rural life. Efforts to elicit peasant support were most effective where traditional clan associations or secret societies had been weakened through social dislocation or warlordism.[52]

After the Long March the Party found larger numbers of the rural population "freed" for new social commitments as a result of the mas-

---

[49] Mao, "Oppose Stereotyped Party Writing" (1942), *Selected Works,* III, 59.

[50] See Mao, "Talks at the Yenan Forum on Literature and Art" (1942), *ibid.,* pp. 69–97.

[51] The role of the *su-k'u,* or "speak bitterness," technique in mobilizing peasant support for the Party is discussed in Solomon, *Mao's Revolution,* pp. 194–200.

[52] See Roy Hofheinz, Jr., "The Peasant Movement and Rural Revolution: Chinese Communists in the Countryside 1923–1927" (Ph.D. dissertation, Harvard University, 1966), pp. 218–20, 365.

sive Japanese military disruption of life in north China. Yet Jan
Myrdal's interviews with Shensi peasants affirm the powerful hold of
established social relations on the rural population. Where peasants
feared the return of the landlord, or sustained their obligations to
family, the Party encountered strong resistance to its appeals.[53] The
power of the Red Army and the brutality of the Japanese were to be
powerful aids in building widespread support for the movement.

While it would be wrong to ignore the ability of the Party's doctrine
to rally support for its cause, it is notable how restricted were the
numbers of people even within the Party who derived their basic sense
of involvement in the movement from its ideology. As Mao noted in
a revealing comment of 1936: "So far as shouldering the main responsibility of leadership is concerned, our Party's fighting capacity will be
much greater and our task of defeating Japanese imperialism will be
more quickly accomplished *if there are one or two hundred* comrades
with a grasp of Marxism-Leninism which is systematic and not fragmentary, genuine and not hollow." [54]

COMMUNICATION

A fifth function of ideology, its role as a communications medium,
is inherent in the use of an idea system from the moment young intellectuals begin to debate among themselves about the problems of their
society and the methods to be used in solving them. The salience of
ideology as a language of policy debate, however, and the ability of
ideologically couched policies to give coherence to political action—
that is, to integrate—grows as the movement expands in size and degree of organization.[55]

At the level of leadership policy debate, ideological categories become a stylized set of concepts for interpreting and describing the
world. To an outsider this use of the ideology appears to be an "esoteric" or obfuscating form of notation masking real intentions.[56] To
"decode" the communications system, "the investigator must know the

---

[53] Jan Myrdal, *Report from a Chinese Village* (London: Heinemann, 1965), esp. pp.
66–67, 78–80, 136–38, 143–45.

[54] Mao, "The Role of the Chinese Communist Party in the National War" (1938),
Selected Works, II, 209 (emphasis added).

[55] For an insightful discussion of the communications functions of ideology, see
Schurmann, *Ideology and Organization*, pp. 58–68.

[56] See Myron Rush, "The Role of Esoteric Communication in Soviet Politics," in his
Rise of Khrushchev (Washington, D.C.: Public Affairs Press, 1958), pp. 88–94; and
William E. Griffith, *Communist Esoteric Communications: Explication de Texte* (Cam-
bridge, Mass.: M.I.T., Center for International Studies, 1967).

history and content of numberless Party controversies in the past as thoroughly as a learned theologian would [understand] the countless disputes that marked the course of Christian dogma. He must know the [verbal] formulas used by the various parties in these controversies, and the historical situations for which they were devised." [57] In the interpretation of Chinese Communist political communications, analysts have noted Party use of such "standard" Marxist-Leninist categories as "the nature of the historical epoch," "the balance of class forces," and the politically most salient "contradictions" in formulating and articulating a Party "line." [58] Party leaders convey a sense of the degree to which others are challenging their policies through oblique public references to the mistaken views of "some [unnamed] comrades," and through warnings of the dangers of "right" or "left" opportunistic deviations from their "correct" policy line.

Such linguistic usage reflects the strong Soviet and Comintern influences over the development of the Chinese Communist Party. Yet, as the political movement has become increasingly "Sinified," as the "universal truths of Marxism-Leninism have been integrated with the practice of the Chinese revolution," Soviet ideological categories have acquired new meanings and the Chinese now have a distinctive political vocabulary reflecting their own problems and history. This process, obviously intensified by the Sino-Soviet conflict, is now formally expressed in Chinese claims that "Mao Tse-tung thought" *is* Marxism-Leninism in the present historical epoch.

The inability of a common ideology to bind together the international Communist movement, however, as with Stalin's earlier liberties in interpreting Marxism-Leninism according to his own purposes, raises the question of the degree to which an ideology is a *guide* to action as opposed to merely a *rationalization* for policies arrived at through other processes of analysis. Our earlier discussion of the identity-formation capacities of an idea system indicates that doctrine *can* represent a "genuine" world view; yet even given such an assumption, there is ample evidence in the history of Chinese communism that ideological categories are sufficiently abstract, or ambiguous, to allow contentious leaders to interpret policy "lines" very differently even

---

[57] Franz Borkenau, "Getting at the Facts behind the Soviet Façade," *Commentary,* XVII, No. 4 (April, 1954), 398.

[58] See, as examples, William E. Griffith, "The November 1960 Moscow Meeting: A Preliminary Reconstruction," *CQ,* No. 11 (July-September, 1962), pp. 38–57; and Benjamin I. Schwartz, *Chinese Communism and the Rise of Mao* (Cambridge, Mass.: Harvard University Press, 1964).

within a shared commitment to the Marxist view of society.[59] Such variations in political judgment seem to reflect the personal idiosyncrasies of different leaders, and perhaps an unstated "operational code" of policy determination shaped by cultural and historical factors as much as by ideology.

Yet ideological categories *do* serve as a formalized set of concepts for articulating what the dominant leadership comes to feel is correct policy, no matter by what means it is determined. Consequently, one may find one leadership group claiming the existence of "phoney" Marxist-Leninists as it seeks to assert a new "line" over a defeated rival. As Mao Tse-tung and his supporters asserted as they consolidated their control over the Party in the mid-1940's:

Cloaking themselves in "Marxist-Leninist theory" and relying on the political and organizational prestige and influence built up by the Fourth Plenary Session, those comrades who were guilty of dogmatist errors were responsible for the domination of the third "Left" line in the Party for four long years, gave it the fullest and and most systematic expression ideologically, politically, militarily, and organizationally, and enabled it to exercise the most profound influence in the Party and consequently to do the greatest damage.[60]

While Mao's ability to establish a position of Party leadership over Wang Ming and other supporters of the disastrous "third 'Left'" line was based on defeats suffered in the KMT's fifth "encirclement and extermination" campaign and the Long March retreat, Party cadres would have learned of the consolidation of Maoist control at "Central" by the Chairman's ability in the early 1940's to shape the terms of debate and study within the Party—what cadres term "the power to make pronouncements" (*fa-yen ch'uan*): "Since 1942, under the leadership of Comrade Mao Tse-tung, the Party-wide rectification of subjectivism, sectarianism, and stereotyped Party writing and also for the study of Party history has corrected, at their very ideological roots, the various 'Left' and Right errors that have arisen in the history of the Party." [61]

Mao's ultimate opportunity to consolidate power came with victory in the Civil War. In order to establish control fully over what to this time had been a remarkably decentralized guerrilla movement, Mao

[59] A particularly good example of policy dispute within commonly accepted ideological categories is Li Li-san's assertion of policy in the CCP during 1929-30, and his subsequent fall from leadership. See Schwartz, *Chinese Communism*, pp. 127–63.

[60] Mao, "Resolution on Certain Questions in the History of Our Party" (1945), p. 192.

[61] *Ibid.*, p. 193.

utilized the ability of a communications system to integrate by establishing a regular system of political reporting by the Party's regional
bureaus and subbureaus to the center, in order "to overcome certain
manifestations of indiscipline or anarchy existing in many places." [62]
Through this technique Mao sought to heighten Party organizational
unity for the coming phase of state-construction. By its very terms,
however, this effort was to embody the danger of "bureaucratism,"
the consolidation of a Party and state system of such a level of integration that it would become an organization communicating largely
within itself, responsive to its increasingly institutionalized procedures
and interests rather than to the people who supported the movement
in its struggle for power—or to the leader who directed the struggle.

Such a phenomenon, of course, was exactly what was to lead Mao to
the Cultural Revolution. As early as 1956 the Chairman complained
of the way in which bureaucratic communications were turning the
Party-state system in upon itself:

> Now there are dozens of hands interfering with local administration, making
> things difficult for the regions. Although neither the Center nor the State Council
> knows anything about it, the Departments [of the central government] issue or-
> ders to the offices of the provincial and municipal governments. . . . Forms and
> reports are like floods. This situation must change and we must find a way to deal
> with it.[63]

The Party initially blocked Mao's efforts at administrative simplification, but out of the Hundred Flowers episode the Chairman was to
acquire the political leverage to bring about the decentralization of the
Great Leap Forward. However, continuing Party resistance to Mao's
pressures, which the Great Leap crisis enhanced, led to Mao's political
isolation by the bureaucracy in the 1960's—a thwarting of his political
influence which Mao ultimately dealt with by using the Cultural Revolution to purge recalcitrants in the Party-state system.

For those who experience the political bureaucracy in a more passive
manner at the lower levels of the system, Party communications are
read for clues to shifts in political "line." Interviews with Party cadres
who joined the movement after liberation indicate that their exposure
to the ideology results not so much in the establishment of an identity
(which is provided by the context of stable social institutions that the

---

[62] Mao, "On Setting up a System of Reports" (1948), *Selected Works,* IV, 177–79. See
also Mao, "The Work of Land Reform and of Party Consolidation in 1948" (1948), *ibid.,*
pp. 253–59.

[63] Mao, "On the Ten Great Relationships" (1956), in Jerome Ch'en, *Mao* (Englewood Cliffs, N.J.: Prentice-Hall, 1969), p. 75.

revolutionary generation did not enjoy in its youth), but in the learning of a "language of politics." Former cadres have described Party efforts in the early 1950's to transmit Marxism-Leninism through formal study of (translated) original works by Marx, Lenin, Stalin, and certain Chinese leaders; but this effort foundered on the low cultural level of most of the cadres.[64]

About the time of the onset of the first five-year plan, efforts were made to raise cadre ideological levels through study of simplified interpretations of Marxist theories authored by Chinese writers. The effort to regularize the ideological training of cadres reached its height in the years 1956–57, only to be disrupted by the radicalization of the Great Leap Forward. Since that time, cadres assert, their ability to interpret the political signals emanating from the Party leadership has come through participation in "class struggle"—the series of political campaigns that was to grow into the Cultural Revolution.

Skill in interpreting communications of the political system is in no small measure shaped by exposure to ideological study. Cadres, caught up in a regular routine of administration, political *hsüeh-hsi*, and "criticism–self-criticism" meetings, learn to read the signals through daily practice, or else they commit such "deviations" that they are removed from positions of authority. Intellectuals, by all accounts, acquire greater skill in interpreting political communications than workers or peasants because of their relatively systematic exposure to Marxist-Leninist doctrine in the educational experience. This sensitivity to shifts in political line was described by a young intellectual as he and a friend searched the Party press for policy changes in the period of crisis after the Great Leap Forward:

"Listen to this," Hu said. He picked up a newspaper and read aloud. "There have been quite a few shortcomings in our work which, together with the natural calamities of the [past] two years, have given rise to difficulties." Hu put down the paper and looked at me for a moment in silence. "That statement was buried in a speech on July 1 by Liu Shao-ch'i, the Chairman of the Republic," he said, and added, "It is the most important policy announcement made by the regime in six years. Your survival and mine depends upon our knowing what the new policy is." . . . For several days, Hu and I went over the speech sentence by sentence. . . . Hu's conclusion was that a short period of leniency was coming. We should take advantage of the situation by studying hard. For a while, most students would be

[64] An interesting example of how the Party sought to transmit its own sense of political identity to a new generation of cadres at the time of liberation is the study pamphlet *Lun ssu-hsiang* (On Thought) (Peking: Ch'ün-chung shu-tien, 1949). Articles by Mao, Liu Shao-ch'i, Wu Chih-p'u, and Chu Teh, among others, attacked the old "work styles" of "liberalism," "individual heroism," "warlordism," and "bureaucratism."

confused by the sudden change [in policy]; they would be slow to readjust. Those who had little scholastic ability . . . would be at a disadvantage. Temporarily we would be out in front.[65]

As younger generations come to know the language of their leaders through the impersonal media of the press, and in the passive manner of "subjects" (or "objects"—*tui-hsiang*) of the political process, their perception of the ideology becomes itself that of an "object." It comes to be seen as a manipulative vehicle of communication and career advancement rather than an intellectual tool for evaluating the world. It was such a transformation that Mao Tse-tung seems to have resisted through the Red Guard movement, by which he sought to have China's youth, who were unexposed to the deprivations and struggles which made Marxism-Leninism a living system of political thought for the May Fourth generation, "steel" themselves in a conflict which would give enduring vitality to the ideological legacy of the revolution.

GOAL-SPECIFICATION

Ideological politics has its roots in the search for new social goals and values; yet as the social movement enters its phase of struggle for power, ultimate objectives are set aside under the tactical pressures of political combat. In such a situation there evolves the distinction between "pure" and "practical" levels of ideology, or what others have termed the leadership's "operational code," as apart from its explicit and consciously held doctrine.[66] It is only in the period of social and economic reconstruction which follows the attainment of power that the leadership can begin to relate its new-found security and growing resource base to the goals for which the revolutionary struggle had originally been undertaken.

As has been so evident in the conflict within China between "Redness" and expertise, the effort to realize revolutionary goals is hampered by the creation of the bureaucratic organizations of "socialist transformation." Industrialization, intended to improve the material welfare of "the masses," requires the creation of administrative bu-

[65] Tung Chi-ping and Humphrey Evans, *The Thought Revolution* (New York: Coward-McCann, 1966), pp. 127–29.

[66] The distinction between "pure" and "practical" levels of ideology is developed by Schurmann in *Ideology and Organization*, pp. 21–38. For discussion of the "operational code," see Alexander L. George, *The "Operational Code": A Neglected Approach to the Study of Political Leaders and Decision-making* (Santa Monica, Calif.: The Rand Corporation, 1967); and Nathan Leites, *The Operational Code of the Politburo* (New York: McGraw-Hill, 1951).

reaucracies and specialized skill groups. Yet these very groups, in the process of nation-building, acquire power and vested interests which may subvert their striving for goals of mass welfare or for the elimination of elitism and rural-urban differences. In the contradiction between policy and operations lies ground for political conflict between "radical" or "ideological" leaders and those of a more practical or "pragmatic" orientation.

In China such tensions have been evident in policy conflicts over the role of intellectuals in developing a peasant society, in military policy, and in conflicting strategies of economic development. If there is one quality which has characterized Mao Tse-tung's leadership style, in contrast to those now reviled as "revisionists," it is his unwillingness to see revolutionary goals subverted by bureaucratization. In the Great Leap Forward Mao sought an organizational instrument of social change which would not transfer power to a specialized elite of managers and technical workers, and which would eliminate social distinctions based on property ownership, intellectual level, and/or urban and rural life styles. As justification for the people's communes, the Chairman and his supporters invoked the ultimate goals of their revolution: the attainment of a utopia where each person would contribute to the development of Chinese society according to his abilities and be remunerated according to his needs. As Ch'en Po-ta phrased it in June, 1958, in the newly formed Party journal *Hung-ch'i* (Red Flag): "Under the leadership of [Mao Tse-tung] the Chinese people, in the not-distant future, will steadily and victoriously advance to the great Communist society." [67]

The foundering of the Great Leap, however, only increased the political contradictions between those leaders seeking cautious social advance and a Mao determined that the revolution's ultimate goals not be compromised in the process of development. Where the people's communes had been designed to sustain the economic objectives of the revolution, the Cultural Revolution came to be an effort to insure commitment to its political goals. In purging the Party, Mao attempted not only to remove from leadership those of uncertain commitment to his conception of the "transition to socialism," but also to institute the Paris Commune ideal of popular political participation.[68]

[67] Ch'en Po-ta, "Under the Flag of Comrade Mao Tse-tung," *Hung-ch'i* (Red Flag), No. 4 (July 16, 1958), p. 9.

[68] See Solomon, *Mao's Revolution*, pp. 499–500, 504.

IDEOLOGICAL EROSION: THE ENDURING QUESTION OF LEGITIMACY

The Cultural Revolution brings us back to the issue with which we began this essay, the role of an ideology in legitimating political action. From the perspective of two decades of Party rule of Chinese society which culminated in the open political warfare of the late 1960's, it is evident that initially the ideology was flexible enough to encompass significant variations in policy. Only gradually did differences among various leaders evolve into a "two-road" struggle between fundamentally different approaches to national development. This divergency grew from the insistence with which Mao Tse-tung pressed a reluctant Party organization to institute his policies for economic development and social change, and the difficulties created by those policies in the Hundred Flowers Campaign, the Great Leap Forward, and the dispute with the Soviet Union.[69]

In the context of the Great Leap crisis, the willing cooperation which Mao could elicit from long-time comrades within the Party leadership eroded as doubts increased about the efficacy of his policies. In the playing out of the political conflict, however, the relationship between failures in the application of Mao's political "line" and erosion of his stature as leader of China's revolution was not to be a matter of simple decline. During the early 1960's the Chairman was to invoke his residual authority first to rally the army and then the student population to his side in a struggle against "revisionism."

One sees an inverse relationship between Mao's loss of political authority at the Party center and public claims made for the efficacy of "the thought of Mao Tse-tung." By 1964 Mao had made commitment to his thought the test of loyalty in a sharpening confrontation between "revolutionary" and "revisionist" styles of leadership in China's national development. This policy was expressed in a *Chieh-fang-chün pao* (Liberation Army Daily) editorial of June, 1964:

To study Chairman Mao's works is a shortcut to the study of Marxism-Leninism. Chairman Mao is a great standard-bearer of Marxism-Leninism in the contemporary era, and Mao Tse-tung's thought is an important development of Marxism-Leninism. At present many revolutionary people are studying Chairman Mao's works. . . . [But] not every comrade understands clearly what must be done before success can be made of the study [of Chairman Mao's works]. Some comrades

[69] The evolution of differences between Mao and other Party leaders is documented in Part IV, *ibid.*

hold that the mentality of a person and his ideological cultivation [*hsiu-yang*] have something to do with whether or not he is able to study Chairman Mao's works well. This view is incorrect.[70]

Ideological banners were being unfurled for political combat between those content with "cultivating" cadres for the Party's bureaucracy and Mao's effort to "steel" a new generation of "revolutionary successors" in class struggle.

In the open political warfare of the Cultural Revolution one sees manifestations of the varied uses of ideology which we have explored in this analysis. In the Red Guard movement Mao sought to give renewed life to his thought as a personal identity for China's younger generation. Study of "the thought of Mao Tse-tung" was both the sign of solidarity with Mao's cause and a ritual of discipline for the factious Red Guards in their combat with Party "revisionists." Mao's interpretation of the essence of Marxism—"Rebellion is justified"—was the agitational war-cry for rousing the students to battle, while Mao's quotations became the medium by which the Red Guards communicated with each other and attacked the Chairman's opposition.[71] And in propagating the "little red book" of his quotations as the distilled wisdom of a career of struggle to revolutionize Chinese society, Mao was seeking to sustain the Party's commitment to the goals of his life's work.

The Cultural Revolution, however, was also a struggle reflecting the eroded legitimacy of Mao's thought. In that interplay between ideals and reality, thought and practice, from which the aura of legitimacy is derived, many Party leaders had come to feel that the Chairman's political "line" had to be revised if it was to cope effectively with the problems of China's "socialist construction." From Mao's perspective, however, the Cultural Revolution was an effort to prevent (his) ideology from becoming mere cant, a bureaucratic doctrine divorced from reality by a new generation of "book worshipers" who in the age-old Confucian pattern would institutionalize their power through a monopoly of doctrine.

---

[70] "Study Chairman Mao's Works with a Profound Class Feeling," *Chieh-fang-chün pao* (Liberation Army Daily), June 8, 1964, as translated in *CB*, No. 739 (August 24, 1964), p. 60.

[71] As an example of how Red Guards communicated by quoting from Mao's "little red book," rather than using their own words, see the delightful chapter, "Mao Says So Too," in Alberto Moravia, *The Red Book and the Great Wall: An Impression of Mao's China* (New York: Farrar, Straus & Giroux, 1968), pp. 53–55.

In such conflicting purposes lay the breakdown of the May Fourth generation of leaders who brought communism to power in China. Thus far the outcome of the Cultural Revolution holds an uncertain set of prospects for the ideology which, for Mao at least, sums up the lessons of a half-century of struggle for social change. At the Ninth National Congress of the CCP, held in the spring of 1969, Mao's chosen successor Lin Piao observed that "the Party Constitution has clearly reaffirmed that Marxism-Leninism-Mao Tsetung Thought is the theoretical basis guiding the Party's thinking." [72] Lin's disappearance from the political scene in the fall of 1971, however, and subsequent measures to vilify his use of "idealist metaphors" and to downgrade the propagation of Mao's thought indicate that the Chairman's influence on China's political life remains vulnerable to the vagaries of factional conflict.

It is possible that "the thought of Mao Tse-tung" will shape future policies designed to sustain the Chinese revolution according to the Chairman's design; yet given the controversy that has surrounded Mao's policies in the past, a Maoist political line will have to regain a sense of legitimacy through effective "practice." A more likely prospect is that Mao's successors will continue to invoke the Chairman's thought as justification for policies which in fact go against the spirit of his doctrine. In such circumstances, either the increasing disparity between words and actions will undermine the sense of relevance of Mao's concepts, or—as is the Soviet pattern—subsequent generations of Party leaders will revise Mao's thought, claiming that such revisions are "creative applications" of the Chairman's ideological legacy.[73]

There does remain, however, the possibility that a successor to Party leadership, in Khrushchevian fashion, will denounce Mao's thought for the difficulties it brought to the Party and people. This was one eventuality which Mao sought to prevent through the Cultural Revolu-

[72] Lin Piao, "Report to the Ninth National Congress of the Communist Party of China," *CB*, No. 880 (May 9, 1969), pp. 41–52.

[73] William Zimmerman has described this phenomenon in a study of changing Soviet attitudes toward international relations: "Both for the ruling group and the specialist, ideology continued to serve a major legitimating function [during the late 1950's and 1960's]. Specialists throughout this period analyzed, continued generally to invoke the proper authorities when they introduced new facts and concepts, thereby minimizing the personal risks of innovation. They and the generalists continued to follow the time-honored Soviet practice of pronouncing the legitimating symbols 'creative Marxism-Leninism' when discarding *specific,* awkward Leninist dictums." *Soviet Perspectives on International Relations, 1956–1967* (Princeton, N.J.: Princeton University Press, 1969), p. 290.

tion attacks on "China's Khrushchev." In sum, one can only say that the future of Mao's ideas has all the uncertainty of political struggles and the interplay between ideals and an evolving reality. As students of ideology in the Chinese revolution, our studies are hardly over.

JEROME CH'EN

The Development and Logic of Mao Tse-tung's Thought, 1928-49

Ts'ai Ho-sen, a close friend of Mao, wrote to him from Paris in 1920: "Some say that there is no class distinction in China; this I cannot accept."[1] It was at this time that China's search for the solutions to her problems was entering into a new period. The Darwinian analysis, which had led to severe self-criticism and a rejection of much of Chinese tradition, had already lost its self-confidence. This change of opinion, which was largely a result of World War I, seemed to demonstrate to the Chinese intellectuals the dangers, even meaninglessness, inherent in Western European civilization.[2] Within a quarter-century China then passed through her second ideological crisis: with Confucianism having been discarded as the guiding doctrine of state and society, Social Darwinism was found fallacious. In the previous crisis the intellectuals felt the need to design a new social order and to find their own niches in it; now they had to do it all over again.

Social Darwinism was the doctrinal source of China's ethnic nationalism of the first twenty years of the twentieth century. It subscribed to a hierarchical view of fit and unfit nations, and exhorted the unfit to emulate the fit so that "those Chinese who have never lived like men

---

[1] *Hsin-min-hsüeh-hui hui-yüan t'ung-hsün chi* (Correspondence of the Members of the New Citizen's Study Society), No. 3, quoted from *Hunan li-shih tzu-liao* (Historical Material of Hunan), No. 4 (1959), p. 80.

[2] Joseph R. Levenson, *Liang Ch'i-ch'ao and the Mind of Modern China* (Berkeley and Los Angeles: University of California Press, 1967), pp. 199–204; and Jerome B. Grieder, *Hu Shih and the Chinese Renaissance: Liberalism in the Chinese Revolution, 1917–1937* (Cambridge, Mass.: Harvard University Press, 1970), Chap. v. Both authors give accounts of Liang's impression of the postwar Europe, its squalor and disappointment.

will do so like men." [3] Within their own country, it enabled the
Chinese to distinguish themselves from the "inferior" Manchus and to
overthrow the regime of the "inferior" race. When this doctrine failed
to put China on her feet and when Marxism-Leninism guided the Russians through a successful revolution, the racial analysis of Social
Darwinism gave way to the class analysis of Marx. Throughout the
1920's all those who sought to make either China a better country or
the Chinese a better people had to choose between the acceptance or
rejection of the class analysis. The choice was made more difficult by a
fact that even Stalin had observed: "In the oppressed nations, 90 per
cent are peasants and urban small workers." [4] However attractive it
may have appeared, class analysis was by no means easy to apply to a
country like China. Some, like Sun Yat-sen, Hu Shih, even Lu Hsün,
rejected a class analysis on the grounds that all the Chinese were poor
people, or that the poor and ignorant were as stupid as Ah Q, waiting
passively for the advent of a savior.[5] Some others, like Li Ta-chao, Ch'en
Tu-hsiu, and Mao Tse-tung, accepted class analysis, and by doing so
were able to ascribe China's miseries to both internal and external op-
pressor classes, thereby giving the Chinese revolution an international
significance. Between this rejection and this acceptance of a class
analysis lay the fundamental difference between the Kuomintang
(KMT) and the Chinese Communist Party (CCP).

MAO AND CLASS ANALYSIS

More than any other Marxian theory, class analysis gave Mao and
many others who had begun their nationalist orientation prior to World
War I a new vista of Chinese state and society. Ts'ai Ho-sen's correspondence, Li Ta-chao and Ch'en Tu-hsiu's writings, and the translations of works by Marx and Marxists were responsible for this. However, it would be an oversimplification to say that Mao's conversion
was entirely due to reading. Principally a man of action even as far
back as 1911 and 1915, Mao had always drawn knowledge both from
book learning and from actual experience, theory, and practice, as he

---

[3] Ch'en Tu-hsiu, "Kuan-yu she-hui-chu-i ti t'ao-lun" (The Discussion on Socialism),
HCN, VIII, No. 4 (December 1, 1920).

[4] "Lun shih-yüeh ke-ming yü pei-ya-p'o min-tsu chieh-fang tou-cheng" (On the October Revolution and the Liberation Struggles of the Oppressed Nations, 1923), in *Lieh-
ning ssu-ta-lin lun chung-kuo* (Lenin and Stalin on China) (Peking: Jen-min ch'u-pan-
she, 1965), p. 67.

[5] Sun's rejection of class analysis can be found in his second lecture on the "Principle
of People's Livelihood" (1924), quoted from *Kuo-fu ch'uan-shu* (Complete Works of
the Father of the Republic) (Taipei: Kuo-fang yen-chiu-yuan, 1960), p. 266.

confessed in 1965: "I did not read any book on strategy either. I read
Tso's Commentary, The Mirror of Administration, and *The Romance
of the Three Kingdoms* which recorded how battles were fought. But
they did not influence me when I was actually fighting. When we
fought, we did not take any book with us. We just analysed the war
situation between ourselves and the enemy, the concrete situation." [6]

Naturally, Mao's views on the social classes of China changed as
the revolution developed. But class analysis remained a constant aspect of his thought. Take his report on the Hunan peasant movement,
for instance. While it is true that it is "almost completely bare of
Marxist trappings," it was nonetheless inspired by Marxian class
analysis. It could not conceivably have been written by a Chinese
before 1919. From 1926 to 1939 Mao had published essays on the
classes of Chinese society, and he also urged his comrades to apply
class analysis. [7]

By using class analysis Mao could come to the Leninist conclusion
that the majority of the people were always revolutionary and progressive, only a minority being reactionary and opportunistic. [8] From this
Leninistic stance Mao came to regard the reaction, which had neither
numerical superiority nor mass support, as a "paper tiger," hence always weak. Still, this minority would never gracefully withdraw from
positions of power; it had to be driven from them by means of a
violent revolution. The strength of reaction, like that of revolution,
fluctuated metaphysically in Mao's mind. For instance, in 1958 the exploiting classes seemed to have been reduced to "mere drops in the
ocean," but in 1964, and especially in 1966, their bogey seemed to grow
to enormous dimensions again. [9] Vagueness of distinction between some
classes may have been responsible for this fluctuation, and thus an erst-
while comrade like Wang Ming or Liu Shao-ch'i, in a similar manner to
Trotsky or Bukharin, might become a class enemy overnight. Although
Mao generally adhered to the Marxist-Leninist criterion for class dif-

---

[6] Jerome Ch'en, *Mao* (Englewood Cliffs, N.J.: Prentice-Hall, 1969), p. 108.

[7] See Benjamin I. Schwartz, *Chinese Communism and the Rise of Mao* (Cambridge,
Mass.: Harvard University Press, 1951), p. 75; and the text of the Ku-tien conference
in *Mao Tse-tung hsüan-chi* (Selected Works of Mao Tse-tung), Supplement IV (n.p.:
Chin-ch'a-chi jih-pao, 1944), p. 146.

[8] "One Step Forward, Two Steps Back" (1904), in V. I. Lenin, *Collected Works*
(hereafter *CW*) (London: Lawrence and Wishart, 1961), VII, 206; "Two Tactics of
Social Democracy" (1905), *ibid.,* IX, 56; Jerome Ch'en, *Mao Papers* (London: Oxford
University Press, 1970), p. 53.

[9] See *Hung-ch'i* (Red Flag), No. 1 (June 1, 1958), p. 3; and Mao Tse-tung, *The
Political Thought of Mao Tse-tung,* ed. and trans. Stuart R. Schram (Middlesex, Eng.:
Penguin Books, 1969), p. 351.

ferentiation, which was the ownership of the means of production and exploitation, in his classification of individuals he attached more importance than his predecessors to the person's ideology.[10]

This tendency is clearly shown in his three attempts at defining the class in Chinese society in 1926, 1933, and 1939. He seems to have regarded such criteria as the ownership of land and other means of production and the role one played in the productive relations as theoretical, academic, even esoteric; his interest was undoubtedly concentrated on the attitudes of the different classes toward the national, the agrarian, and eventually the socialist revolutions. To ascertain these attitudes was to differentiate friends from foes, to lay the foundation of a strategy for the revolution.

Among Mao's class enemies, the most numerous and tenacious were the landlords—a "feudal" class in his judgment. The views of the Communists in China and the USSR about the nature of this class and the way it should be handled were almost identical. Their class analysis differed from Mao's mainly in regard to the other major classes.

As to the Chinese "grande bourgeoisie," Marx's description of the German capitalists in 1848 seems to fit rather well: "Without faith in itself, without faith in the people, grumbling at those above, trembling before those below, . . . no energy in any respect, plagiarism in every respect, . . . without initiative, . . . an execrable old man who saw himself doomed to guide and defloot the first youthful impulses of a robust people in their own senile interests." [11] Lenin shared this view and thought the Russian bourgeoisie just as weak and fickle.[12] The national bourgeoisie was therefore excluded from the people who formed the revolutionary alliance in 1848, 1905, or 1917. As to the Asian bourgeoisie, Lenin felt it "still sides with the people against reaction." [13] From this observation, Stalin formulated the theory of the two sections of the Chinese national bourgeoisie—the revolutionary and the compromising.[14]

[10] *Mao Tse-tung hsüan-chi* (Selected Works of Mao Tse-tung) (hereafter *HC*) (Peking: Jen-min ch'u-pan-she, 1961), III, 892; or Mao, *Selected Works of Mao Tse-tung* (hereafter *SW*) (Peking: Foreign Languages Press, 1964), III, 90–91. For a fuller exposition on this extreme view, see Ch'en Po-ta, *Jen-hsing, ke-hsing, tang-hsing* (Personality, Individuality, and Party Attributes) (Hong Kong, 1947), pp. 2–3.

[11] *Neue Rheinische Zeitung* (1848), quoted in Lenin, "Karl Marx" (1914), *CW*, XXI, 77.

[12] "Two Tactics of the Social Democracy," p. 58; "What to Fight For?" (1910), *CW*, XVI, 167.

[13] "Backward Europe and Advanced Asia" (1913), quoted in H. C. d'Encausse and Stuart R. Schram, *Marxism and Asia* (Middlesex, Eng.: Penguin Press, 1969) p. 139.

[14] *Ibid.*, p. 226; Stalin maintained this view until 1927. See *Lieh-ning ssu-ta-lin lun chung-kuo*, pp. 113–14.

Like Ch'ü Ch'iu-pai, Mao drew a parallel between the weakness and fickleness of the Chinese national bourgeoisie and its Russian counterpart. The root of these characteristics lay in the lack of economic robustness of a class which depended heavily on the imperialists for its survival, and whose economic interests were closely bound up with those of the landlords. The Chinese bourgeoisie was often caught in a love-hate relationship with the imperialists on the one hand and the landlords on the other. The section (to use Stalin's terminology) that was readier to surrender to the imperialists and landlords was described by Mao as the "comprador bourgeoisie." According to Stalin, this section fell out of the Chinese revolution in 1927,[15] thus further weakening the grande bourgeoisie's leadership capacity in the democratic revolution.

In the views of Ch'ü Ch'iu-pai, Wang Ming, and Mao, the comprador bourgeoisie was represented by the KMT of Chiang Kai-shek, which was weak in the presence of the imperialists but admittedly strong compared with the CCP. The failure of the land revolution and the soviet movement between 1927 and 1936 served to prove this view. Therefore, in 1935, while the defeated CCP was still itinerant, this class and Chiang came to be regarded in an unfavorable light. The turning point was recorded in the Wa-yao-pao resolutions in December, 1935, which made no reference to the comprador class.[16] The puzzling thing is that Mao still used the term in his speech delivered a few days thereafter and once more singled out Chiang as a class enemy. The inclusion and exclusion of the comprador bourgeoisie on the side of the democratic revolution depended therefore not so much on the inherent characteristics of the class as on the current intensity of the "national contradiction" vis-à-vis a foreign aggressor. At some point, the national contradiction would overshadow that of the class contradiction between the comprador bourgeoisie and the revolutionary classes. When that point was reached, the comprador capitalists could conceivably drop back into the ranks of the revolution, as it did in 1936. In 1945, as the national contradiction was resolved, the class

[15] *Lieh-ning ssu-ta-lin lun chung-kuo,* p. 115; and Hu Ch'iao-mu, *Chung-kuo kung-ch'an-tang ti san-shih-nien* (Thirty Years of the Chinese Communist Party, 1951), p. 19.

[16] See Lyman P. Van Slyke, *Enemies and Friends: The United Front in Chinese Communist History* (Stanford, Calif.: Stanford University Press, 1967), pp. 58–59. The text in the *K'ang-jih chiu-kuo chih-nan* used by Van Slyke, as noted in his book on page 59, is the original text of the resolutions, which can be collated with that included in the *Chung-kuo ke-ming-shih ts'an-k'ao tzu-liao* (Reference Material on the History of the Chinese Revolution), manuscript (Peking: Chung-kuo jen-min ta-hsüeh, 1957), III, marked 145–65 (no actual pagination).

Chiang represented once more became the object of the democratic revolution. The grande bourgeoisie split again into two sections, with the national bourgeoisie in the revolutionary alliance. The revolutionary character of the national bourgeoisie ceased to exist, according to Mao, as soon as the democratic revolution faded into its socialist successor. In this final transformation, the national bourgeoisie must change itself into a working class and disappear forever.

It is interesting to note that in the discussion of the Chinese capitalists, the Communist theorists consistently ignored or played down the beneficial effect of bourgeois ideology to the class itself, as if the physical weakness of the bourgeoisie had caused its ideological barrenness. In their view, the bourgeois wing of the KMT, having betrayed Sun Yat-sen's Three People's Principles, seemed to have neither an adequate long-term policy nor the rudimentary ideas of a suitable culture for China. The weakness of the Chinese bourgeoisie cannot be denied, for its economic feebleness was combined with the intellectual confusion which characterized Western Europe and China after 1919. By then the old confidence in progress and evolution was gone in Europe, while the most important experiment in Westernization, parliamentary democracy, foundered in China.

In the discussion of the other major classes, however, the ideological factors were to play an active role. The "petite bourgeoisie," especially the intellectuals—to which both Lenin and Mao belonged—was not particularly liked by either. The emasculated emancipation of the serfs in Russia led Russian intellectuals into a commitment to revolution. In a comparable way, the failure of the reform of 1898 turned a large number of Chinese intellectuals toward revolution. As reform continued to demonstrate its inefficacy during the republican period, revolution became firmly established in the minds of many intellectuals as the only road to China's salvation, although the patterns conceived for revolution may have been widely different. However, Lenin strongly warned against the Russian intelligentsia as a class, characterizing it by its individualism and incapacity for discipline and organization. As a stratum, it might be good at theory, planning, and reasoning, but it needed the proletariat to translate its drab theory into living reality. Because the intellectuals lived like capitalists, or aspired to do so, and thus shared the bourgeois outlook, they had to be considered wavering and unreliable as revolutionary allies.[17]

[17] Lenin, "One Step Forward, Two Steps Back," p. 269; and M. M. Drachkovitch, *Marxism in the Modern World* (Stanford, Calif.: Stanford University Press, 1965), p.

What Lenin described as "individualism" and "incapacity for discipline and organization" was what Mao called "liberalism." All "liberalist" defects should be eliminated in the process of the proletarianization of the intellectuals. But on the whole, Mao had a slightly more favorable impression of the intelligentsia than Lenin. He felt that the intellectuals in a colonial or semicolonial country, like its bourgeoisie, were more progressive than their counterparts in a capitalist or imperialist country because, like workers and peasants, they were under imperialist and feudalist oppression and hence developed an antiimperialist and antifeudal orientation. Their knowledge and sensitivity made them the first to be aware of the class interests and revolutionary possibilities, and their participation in the revolution was therefore necessary for success.

The fact that the majority of the CCP leaders came from an intellectual or petite bourgeoisie background, albeit a declining one in most cases, may explain why their attitude toward their own class was more congenial than Lenin's. Also, proletarianization was of greater importance to the CCP than to the Bolsheviks, and proletarianization through propaganda and education required that a considerable number of intellectuals join the ranks of the CCP and dedicate themselves to the proletarian cause.[18] Ironically, the intellectual leaders of the CCP seemed to be extremely jealous of the Marxist "truth" they had acquired and were unusually hostile to those who had rejected it. Their hostility was directed not only at such politically less active scholars as Hu Shih but particularly at the small groups of intellectual politicians led by Wang Ching-wei, Teng Yen-ta, and the social democrats.[19] It was this prejudice that determined their attitude toward, say, the Fukien Uprising at the end of 1933.

The CCP accepted the historical mission, the revolutionary character, and the internationalism of the proletariat as defined by Marx.[20]

---

83. Also see Lenin, "The Reorganization of the Party" (1905), *CW,* X, 38; Lenin, "Tasks of the Proletariat in Our Revolution" (1917), *ibid.,* XXIV, 62.

　18 The Sixth Congress of the CCP showed an exceptional anti-intellectualism, but it was short-lived. See *Liu-tz'u ta-hui chüeh-i-an* (Resolutions of the Sixth Congress) (1928), on microfilm, pp. 67–68; or Conrad Brandt, Benjamin Schwartz, and John K. Fairbank, *A Documentary History of Chinese Communism* (Cambridge, Mass.: Harvard University Press, 1952), p. 135.

　19 *Liu-tz'u ta-hui chüeh-i-an,* pp. 58–59; Wang Chien-min, *Chung-kuo kung-ch'antang shih-kao* (A Draft History of the Chinese Communist Party) (Taipei, 1965), II, 46–47, 528–29.

　20 "The Manifesto," in *Selected Works of Marx and Engels* (London: Lawrence and Wishart, 1968), p. 44; and in A. B. Ulam, *The Unfinished Revolution* (New York: Random House, 1960), pp. 39–40.

The goal of the revolution was the emancipation of man, but in a country where even the bourgeois democratic revolution was yet to be accomplished, the fulfillment of the goal had to go through two stages. In both stages the consistent and resolute proletariat would have to lead and claim the hegemony of the revolutionary coalition.[21]

To those revolutionary characteristics attributed to all working classes in general, Mao added some specific qualities to the Chinese proletariat to make it even more eligible for the leadership of the Chinese revolution. In his view, the Chinese urban workers were under the threefold oppression of imperialism, the bourgeoisie, and the feudal forces; were led by their own party, the CCP; and were actually bankrupt peasants, who thus retained natural ties with the vast peasantry, their ally.

The alliance with the peasantry was vital to the revolution in view of the smallness of the Chinese proletariat. Both the Li Li-san leadership after the Sixth Congress and the Wang Ming leadership were conscious of this fact, which was thrown in sharp relief when the CCP was driven from the cities to the remote countryside of mountain fastnesses, lakelands, and townships.

Marx in his analysis of the French and Engels in his study of the German peasant wars recognized that the peasants were "the natural allies of the urban proletariat." [22] Both, however, adopted a contemptuous attitude toward the peasants and neither had ever entertained the thought of proletarianizing them. It remained for Lenin to formulate the following point of view: ". . . the small peasant, who is being oppressed and ruined by all modern capitalism, should desert *his* own class standpoint and place himself at the standpoint of the proletariat." [23] Lenin was also responsible for diagnosing the peasant revolution against medievalism, under conditions of a bourgeois economy, as being itself a bourgeois revolution. Nonetheless, the peasants still had to be supported, incited, and won over by the proletariat.[24] On the whole, Lenin ascribed a rather passive role to the peasantry during the Russian revolution and afterward minimized their role in shaping history. Their proletarianization might eventually eradicate the differences between them and the urban workers, at some future date

[21] Lenin, "Two Tactics of Social Democracy," p. 60; "The Lessons of the Revolution" (1910), *CW*, XVI, 301–2; Robert V. Daniels, *A Documentary History of Communism* (New York: Random House, 1960), p. 41.

[22] "The Peasant War in Germany," in *Selected Works of Marx and Engels,* pp. 243–44.

[23] "The Agrarian Programme of Russian Social Democracy," *CW*, VI, 125.

[24] "Agrarian Programme of Social Democracy" (1907), *ibid.*, XIII, 351; for instance, "The Proletariat and the Peasantry" (1905), *ibid.*, VIII, 233.

when agricultural productive relations were completely altered by mechanization; but such a change would take a long time to accomplish.[25]

To Marx, Engels, and Lenin, the revolution was largely *for* the peasants rather than *by* the peasants. In other words, as Chalmers Johnson has indicated, the proletariat or its political organization should act for the sake of the peasantry—but not quite on the side of the peasantry, for the peasantry might not even have a side of its own.[26]

It is well known that Mao attributed a much more active role to the Chinese peasantry in the revolution. This was possible because he posited a Leninistic type of change in class standpoint through proletarianization. Even in a peaceful context, Mao regarded the Chinese peasantry as the source of industrial workers, suppliers of food and industrial raw materials and consumers of industrial goods, the source of the Chinese army, the main force for democracy, and the main beneficiaries of all cultural movements. In Mao's scheme of things, the peasants in peace and war played a far more decisive part.

As conceptualized by Stalin, the division of the Chinese bourgeoisie into two sections—the revolutionary and the compromising—was a useful tool when the intensities of the national and class contradictions were delicately balanced. At such a juncture the CCP could use it to tip the balance and redirect the revolution from or to a national war. As for the other classes, the petite bourgeoisie was more important than the proletariat in the Communist movement, and this fact alone should have revealed to the CCP leaders before Mao that proletarianization by political indoctrination and education would be more of a determining factor than Marxian productive relations. Numerically, the peasants overwhelmed all the others. After decades of agricultural depression through civil wars and ruthless extortion by warlords, landlords, and miscellaneous governments, the mood of the Chinese poor peasants was expectedly explosive. To ignite this mood and to instill the full political significance into the minds of the peasants in action, proletarianization was also a process of the highest import.

---

[25] "Economics and Politics in the Era of the Dictatorship of the Proletariat" (1919), *ibid.*, XXX, 112–13.

[26] See Conrad Brandt, *Stalin's Failure in China, 1924–1927* (Cambridge, Mass.: Harvard University Press, 1958), p. 109; and Chalmers Johnson, *Peasant Nationalism and Communist Power: The Emergence of Revolutionary China, 1937–1945* (Stanford, Calif.: Stanford University Press, 1962), p. 19.

CLASS ANALYSIS IN PRACTICE

What has been said above constitutes the more outstanding features of Mao's class analysis as it was applied to the Chinese revolutionary situation. The application itself can be conveniently and neatly divided into two periods: the period of the land revolution (the Kiangsi Soviet period) from 1927 to 1937, and the period of the anti-Japanese united front (the Yenan period) approximately from 1937 to 1947. In each there was a crucial theoretical innovation, conditioned and induced by the circumstances in which the CCP fought. The movement was no longer centered on any big city of China, and the importance of the small proletariat to the movement was greatly reduced. For its survival alone, the peasantry now had to constitute the class base of the Party in place of the proletariat. Now that the movement existed only in the remote countryside of central China, it would take the Communists a long time to fight their way back to the well-defended cities. The pattern of the revolutionary war became therefore less Marxist-Leninist and more traditionally Chinese; its protractedness was imagined by neither Marx nor Lenin under any circumstance.

The substitution of the peasantry for the proletariat in China meant the substitution of a great, tangible mass of people for an almost non-existent class. From this mass, the CCP was to draw both human and material resources for the needs of the revolution as well as for the Party's own survival. Consequently, there followed the vital problems of political arousal and organization: first, how to fan the peasants' revolutionary fervor and, second, how to give that fervor a shape and consolidate it. As the struggle was not to be accomplished in a matter of one or two months—not even in one or two years—it was essential to sustain such revolutionary fervor in order to prevent the revolution's premature demise. One technique was to allow the masses themselves to participate in decision-making over critical issues, to involve them in the survival of the movement. At length this class substitution and the protractedness of the revolution made it clear to the Chinese revolutionaries that the CCP could not and, in the final analysis, should not be a Leninist elitist party, and that the strategy could not be one of proletarian hegemony or of the city leading the countryside.

In 1937 the period of the anti-Japanese united front arrived. In Communist parlance, the formation of the united front represented a change in the relative positions of the class and national contradictions.

Now the national contradiction overshadowed the class contradiction; the Civil War gave way to the anti-Japanese struggle. This change was already noticeable after the battle of Kuang-chang in April, 1934. Later, in the name of the Party, Wang Ming issued the well-known Manifesto of August 1, 1935, to be followed by this theoretical formulation:

The proletariat and its Communist Party belong to the Chinese people, and therefore their fate and the fate of the Chinese people as a whole are inseparably bound together. The proletariat and the Communist Party are the vanguard of the Chinese people, and so they have the deepest concern and the greatest responsibility for the fate of China. Apart from the interests of the Chinese people, the Chinese proletariat and the Communist Party have no other interest.[27]

This was what the Wa-yao-pao resolutions of December, 1935, meant by "the political situation has had a fundamental change." At Wa-yao-pao, the enemies of the CCP were narrowed down to the Japanese imperialists and "the archtraitor," Chiang Kai-shek. Early in 1937 even Chiang became an ally. It was in this period of a rising anti-Japanese tide that class analysis was almost completely replaced by a populist approach so that the greatest majority of the nation would take part in the patriotic war. An outstanding example of this change was Mao's report to the Sixth Plenum of the Central Committee in 1938, "On the New Stage," which seldom applied the class analysis. The KMT was described in this report as a national coalition, broader even than what Stalin had once envisaged as a bloc of only four classes.[28]

In the Shen-Kan-Ning Border Region and the anti-Japanese base areas, the same wide alliance policy was pursued. The widest possible support from the inhabitants became indispensable especially after 1940 when on the one hand the Japanese initiated the "three all" (*san-kuang*) policy of persecution, and on the other the KMT tightened its encirclement of the border region. The struggle might not have been a class war; but it was just as protracted. For the CCP, the tasks were still twofold: arousal of the masses and sustenance of their support. The first part, consisting of the resistance war and unity (*k'ang-chan, t'uan-chieh*), was nationalistic; the second part, consisting of democratic political reform and the amelioration of the peasants' living standard (*chin-pu*), was mildly socialistic. The war was sustained on

[27] Wang Ming, "Hsin hsin-shih yü hsin cheng ts'e" (New Situation and New Policies), *Wang Ming hsüan-chi* (Selected Works of Wang Ming) (Tokyo, 1970), I, 83.

[28] See d'Encausse and Schram, *Marxism and Asia*, p. 228, and Mao, "Lun hsin-chieh-tuan" (On the New Stage), in *Wen-hsien* (Documents) (Shanghai, January, 1939), pp. E. 16–17, 34.

unity and progress. When unity became nominal and progress was off-set by retrogression in China at large, the resistance war was gradually transformed into a stalemate of little action. It was a long wait, in fact, for the defeat of the enemy by China's allies, while the class struggle between the KMT and the CCP reasserted itself.

As the relative positions of national and class contradictions shifted, the political reality of China changed, also. Most important, perhaps, was the loss of the KMT's monopoly in nationalism; the CCP, now cut off from the Communist International and Sinocized, was able to challenge the KMT's leadership in nationalism. With no credit to claim in the introduction of democracy or economic reform, the KMT's position in Chinese politics now became precarious.

ORGANIZATIONS

The proletariat was represented and led by its vanguard, the Party,[29] which was organized in accordance to the Leninist principles of democratic centralism. Since the adoption of the Party's constitution in 1928, the CCP had been working under conditions of either police persecution or army attack, so it is understandable that the Party practiced centralism more for the sake of security than democracy. The danger was that the Party might become infested with commandism, routinism, blind obedience, and a lack of incentives altogether.[30] The safety mechanism upon which the party relied to protect itself against these faults seemed to be criticism and self-criticism. In a country of long and deep-seated authoritarian tradition, the efficacy of this device was open to doubt. But in the Yenan period, the Party operated with more security within the border region and the anti-Japanese base areas than it had ever had since 1927. Even in the KMT areas, the united front, however nominal it might have been since 1940, enabled the CCP to enjoy a measure of security. Therefore, there should have been a greater measure of democracy. Inside the Party, this principle meant the obedience of the minority to the majority, the lower grade to the higher grade, the branch to the whole Party, and the whole Party to the center. Outside the Party, in the Communist-dominated governments and front organizations, Mao tended to regard democracy exclusively as a matter of decision-making, while he regarded centralism exclusively as a matter of decision imple-

29 Lenin, "What Is to Be Done?" (1902), *CW*, V, *passim*, esp. pp. 464 ff.
30 Wang Chia-hsiang's article of February 5, 1931, summarized in Tso-liang Hsiao, *Power Relations within the Chinese Communist Movement, 1930–1934: A Study of Documents* (Seattle: University of Washington Press, 1961), pp. 141–42.

mentation or administration. Neither the choice of administrators nor the vigilance over the implementation of decisions received much attention from Mao as integral parts of democracy. This omission may have been due to his unfamiliarity with democratic practice, or it may have been due to his dislike of constant interruptions from the people and their representatives to a degree that might impair administrative efficiency.

There remain two other problems relating to the principle of democratic centralism. First, for the CCP to function under ideal conditions, should democracy procedurally come before centralism? Mao's answer was affirmative.[31] The scope of democracy under such conditions could become so broad as to make the principle of democracy identical with Mao's mass line. In this sense, the institution designed to prevent the leadership from persistently going wrong must be democracy, or the mass line. Twice in the history of the CCP—once in the *cheng-feng* (rectification) movement of the early 1940's and once again in the Cultural Revolution—Mao extended the principle of democracy or applied the mass line as a technique for rectifying the mistakes of the Party. In so doing he contravened the Party's iron discipline and made a mockery of the Party's status as the vanguard of the class.

The second problem concerned the actual control of CCP branches and members during the land revolution and the anti-Japanese war. There was an astonishing degree of difference in organization, attitudes, and even manners of address between the First Front Army from Kiangsi and the Fourth Front Army from Oyüwan and later from northern Szechwan. This difference, which the armies themselves noticed when they met in Mou-kung in 1935, showed a lack of centralism or control in the Chinese Communist movement in spite of the bureaus of the center that had been set up in the major soviets.[32] With the branches and members so widely scattered and constantly dodging and hiding from the spies, police, and soldiers of either Chiang Kai-shek or Japan, how could the center of the Party control them? Physically, it was impossible; administratively, there was nothing better than periodic inspections; institutionally, it could hardly be effective in a large region, not to speak of the Party as a whole. The point on autonomy Mao was making then was addressed not only to

[31] *Mao chu-hsi wen-hsüan* (Selected Essays by Chairman Mao) (n.p. [China], n.d. [1967?]), p. 64.

[32] Chang Kuo-t'ao, "Wo-ti hui-i" (Memoirs), *Ming-pao yüeh-k'an* (Ming-pao Monthly), No. 36, p. 83.

Chiang but also to the Party center. These conditions left ideological control as the easiest and most effective control the center had at its disposal. Unity in thought, in order to achieve unity in action, was the only extreme centralism the CCP could hope for. This was the counter-part of the mass line. The mass line and ideological unity therefore constituted the two essential aspects of Mao's organization line, which in turn corresponded perfectly with his political line.

If the CCP was to be organized in this way, could it claim to be a Bolshevik Party? Two points must be clarified before answering this question. First, to the CCP, Bolshevization was a reality as well as an ideal. Both the reality and the ideal changed with the passage of time; so did the divergence between them. Second, we must consider what Lenin meant by a Bolshevik Party.

The Bolshevik Party was a politically articulated and behaviorally disciplined corps of cadres which served to fill a hierarchy of leading positions in the revolution. The double requirement for this cadre corps was a firm grasp of the current, correct political line and an un-questioned obedience to iron discipline.[33] Lenin had used such an or-ganization in the class struggle for power. After the struggle ended and power was won by the proletariat, the Party was supposed to be trans-formed from a political into an administrative organization.[34] In this transformation, the Party might not as a whole become administrative or bureaucratic. Only those professional revolutionaries, who had com-prised the Party's core before the seizure of power and who had no other training by which to claim continuing leadership positions under the new circumstances, would become such.[35]

In the USSR, the transformation of the Bolshevik Party into an administrative organization took place when the intra-Party struggles were going Stalin's way. This change in the USSR was specifically sig-nificant because it was precisely at this time that the Chinese Com-munist Party began to think of itself as a Bolshevik party. To be sure, there is no generally acknowledged periodization for the CCP's Bol-shevization. The Sixth Congress spoke of the conference held on August 7, 1927, as the *terminus a quo* of the CCP's Bolshevization, and neither Li Li-san nor Wang Ming disputed this dating. To Hsiang

[33] Lenin, "Left-wing Communism: An Infantile Disorder" (1920), in Daniels, *Documentary History of Communism*, p. 190.

[34] Lenin, "State and Revolution," in *Selected Works* (Moscow: Foreign Languages Publishing House, 1967), II, 314.

[35] Milovan Djilas, *The New Class: An Analysis of the Communist System* (1957), quoted in Daniels, *Documentary History of Communism*, p. 261.

Chung-fa, Bolshevization seemed to be no more than a waging of intra-Party struggles against all deviations; there was not yet any coherent conceptualization of Bolshevization. To Wang Ming, the term meant fidelity to the political line of the Communist International and its implementation in spite of all conceivable hardships.[36] The concept of Bolshevization became clearer at the Wa-yao-pao conference, whose resolutions stipulated both the Bolshevik political line and iron discipline as the two requisites. Up to this point, the Party had consistently regarded itself as an elitist party, the vanguard of the working class, led by a core of professional revolutionaries.

Mao had his own views on this matter, and they were considerably different. In his estimate, the Bolshevization of the CCP did not begin until the Tsunyi conference of 1935.[37] Never had he stated simply that the Bolshevized CCP was the vanguard of the working class; he did not even insist that the CCP must be an elitist party. Instead, he emphasized that the Party must be national in scale, have a broad mass character, and be fully consolidated ideologically, politically, and organizationally. During wartime, when the Party was under Mao's leadership, this broad outline was translated into more specific terms, in which Bolshevization was defined in the following concrete ways: (1) the correct handling of the relationship between the Party and the bourgeoisie (the united front with the KMT) and between the Party and the peasants (the peasant war); and (2) the consolidation and expansion of the Party in the meantime.[38] By 1939 this was still an ideal, but Mao then tried to materialize it during the *cheng-feng* campaign of 1942–44.

Mao's periodization raises a couple of questions. First, how would Mao explain the claim that Bolshevization began prior to his leadership—namely, from August, 1927, to January, 1935, when all the time the CCP had been under the tutelage of the Communist International? We must bear in mind that Wang Ming even went so far as to make fidelity to the Comintern the cardinal condition of Bolshevization. On this question, Liu Shao-ch'i—at that time still Mao's faithful aide—gave a rather unoriginal answer by drawing a parallel with the devel-

[36] Wang Ming and K'ang Sheng, *Chung-kuo hsien-chuang yü chung-kung jen-wu* (The Present Situation of China and the Tasks of the Chinese Communist Party), speeches at the thirteenth plenum of the Executive Committee of the Communist International, Moscow, 1934, pp. 73–74. Wang, more than any other CCP leader, was a true internationalist who consistently regarded the Chinese revolution as a part of the world revolution.

[37] Mao, *HC*, II, 602; or *SW*, II, 293.

[38] *Mao Tse-tung hsüan-chi,* supplement 1947 edition, pp. 43–44.

opment of the Russian party. In Liu's view, from January, 1931, to January, 1935, the Party leadership, while acting in the name of Bolshevism, Leninism, and the International line, had actually based their decisions on dogmatic and bookish knowledge. Far from being Bolshevik, it had been Menshevik! [39] The *cheng-feng* was consequently an intra-Party struggle against this Chinese Menshevism.

Second, at a time when the Party was still under the influence of the elitist tradition and its structure was still in the hands of the elitist leadership, Mao may have had to wage the intra-Party struggle not strictly according to the rules of the game. Fidelity to rules and regulations did not seem to be a strong point of the Chinese in general or the CCP in particular; Chang Kuo-t'ao's observation on the lack of democratic (in terms of institution and practice) tradition in the CCP may have been well taken.[40] After all, even the Moscow-trained leaders themselves violated the rules and set up a bad example by bringing nonmembers into Politburo meetings after the fourth plenum of the sixth session.[41] This example was in turn copied at Tsunyi and then Mao-erh-kai, rebounding to the detriment of the Moscow-trained leaders. In the *cheng-feng*, Mao carried his defiance of rules a step further by appealing to the masses and the army to help rectify the ills of the Party. Since Mao had to initiate these steps himself in order to win the struggle, his understanding of fidelity to the Party did not mean obedience merely to rules and regulations; it meant, as Stuart Schram has pointed out, first and foremost an obedience to the author of the Party line (Mao) or the correct ideology (Mao's thought).[42]

In by-passing the hierarchy of the Party to link up the leader and the membership directly, Mao showed his distrust of, and indeed an aversion to, the Party bureaucracy. The long and retardatory bureaucratic tradition of China and the fact that the one-party hegemony of the KMT amounted to little more than a useless second bureaucracy were a strong warning to Mao that the CCP should never be allowed to tread the same path of decline as the KMT.

But a revolution without a revolutionary cadre was unthinkable, as unthinkable as an organized society without an elite. Lenin's motive in

---

[39] "Ch'ing-suan men-hsi-wei-k'e" (Liquidate the Mensheviks), in *Liu Shao-ch'i hsüan-chi* (Selected Works of Liu Shao-ch'i) (Tokyo: Chung-kuo wen-hua fu-wu ch'u-pan-she, 1967), pp. 122–23.

[40] *Ming-pao yüeh-k'an*, No. 49, p. 81.

[41] *Ibid.*, No. 34, p. 83.

[42] Stuart R. Schram, "The Party in Chinese Communist Ideology," in John W. Lewis (ed.), *Party Leadership and Revolutionary Power in China* (Cambridge: Cambridge University Press, 1970), p. 172.

designing an elitist party was to provide leadership for the proletarian power struggle.[43] Without such a party, it would be difficult to translate the ideological unity of Marxism into effective action. Its effectiveness came from the substitution of a strong party for a weak class. This substitution, unfortunately, went on during and after Lenin's lifetime and eventually led to the substitution of the party by a personal dictatorship, as predicted by Leon Trotsky.[44]

Mao also acknowledged the indispensability of the cadre as he accepted Stalin's dictum that cadre determined everything.[45] But to him the cadre was not a collective of "deployable personnel" but leaders in various mass organizations or members of the Party who performed leadership roles and were responsible to higher authorities.[46] To Lenin and his successors in the USSR, the task of the Party was to raise the standard of the masses to that of the cadre; [47] to Mao, it was to learn from the masses before teaching the masses. With his emphasis on men rather than on the collective, on masses rather than on the cadre elite, it is debatable whether Mao, like Lenin, attached as much weight to organization as he did to propaganda and indoctrination.

We shall return to the discussion on the masses and mass line, but let us now turn our attention to the most important mass organization—the government. In the early soviet areas of China, the CCP was the only party, all the other political groups having been suppressed. Obviously, this followed the example of the one-party dictatorship established in the USSR on June 14, 1918. Theoretically, the Soviet government was a proletarian dictatorship whose apparatus for rule was, among other things, the Russian Communist Party. The Chinese governments in the soviet areas were those of the democratic dictatorship of both workers and peasants; but the curious thing was that the peasants were not allowed a party of their own, not to mention having a party organized for them by the petite bourgeoisie. The mandate of representing the peasants belonged to the CCP. By this mandate, as we have mentioned before, the Party conducted a revolution *for* the peasants, not *by* the peasants. The Party now existed among a great rural population, and its membership came to consist overwhelmingly

---

[43] Lenin, "One Step Forward, Two Steps Back," quoted in Daniels, *Documentary History of Communism,* pp. 26–27.

[44] Trotsky, "Our Political Tasks" (1904), *ibid.,* pp. 26–27.

[45] Mao Tse-tung, *Ching-chi wen-t'i yü ts'ai-cheng wen-t'i* (Economic Problems and Financial Problems) (Hong Kong, 1949), p. 210.

[46] Franz Schurmann, *Ideology and Organization in Communist China* (Berkeley and Los Angeles: University of California Press, 1966), p. 162.

[47] "What Is to Be Done?" p. 470.

uf peasants. The fear that rural conservatism would prevail over proletarian progressiveness was therefore real, and the task of proletarianization was urgent.

The conditions of an absence of a peasant party in the Chinese
soviet areas and of the proletarian representation of the peasantry con-
formed to the Marxist-Leninist principle of the town leading the country.[48] Incidentally, it also transformed the CCP from a proletarian
party into a bloc of two classes. As long as the principle of the town
leading the country remained unchallenged, the success of the Chinese
revolution depended upon the proletarian revolutionary movement in
the West in general, and the guidance and strength of the Soviet Union
in particular. The Chinese revolutionaries had then to understand the
revolutionary situations in Europe and North America, in addition to
that in their own country. Contrariwise, if the country led the town, the
Chinese revolutionaries could act with a greater measure of autonomy
and less care for the world at large.

At a stage when the Communist movements in all countries other
than the USSR, especially the backward ones, were considered so im-
mature as to need Soviet tutelage or help, the principle of the town
leading the country was useful. It was not just that the heart and brains
of the reaction lay in the towns; the towns were also the seats of the
Communist International, the ultimate authority of the world Communist movement. A defeat of the Chinese soviets in the countryside
was not thought to be capable of shaking the authority structure of the
whole movement; the movement could still go on.

Within the Chinese context, a proletarian hegemony in the rural
soviets was a fiction. Nevertheless, this fiction was maintained, even
by Mao, while the process of proletarianization was set in motion. And
eventually this process led to Mao's ideological domination. The fiction
remained even in the Yenan period, when the land revolution gave way
to the united front and the democratic dictatorship of workers and
peasants was replaced by the new democracy of four revolutionary
classes. Although the new democracy provided accommodation for other
parties representing the national bourgeoisie and petite bourgeoisie,
there was still no peasant party in the border region and the anti-
Japanese base areas. The CCP still acted as the guardian of the interests of the peasants.

During both the periods of the soviet dictatorship of workers and

[48] Ulam, *Unfinished Revolution*, p. 63; and d'Encausse and Schram, *Marxism and Asia*, pp. 58, 242.

peasants and the Yenan democratic dictatorship, "dictatorship" meant a system of special rights to the ruling classes. "Democracy," however, had an institutional meaning of varying breadth: it was narrower under conditions of war or siege and wider under a united front. This variation was not considered a question of choice, for the political goals at each stage were seen as fixed by the inevitability of history and by the leadership. Under both soviet and united front governments, it was desired that China should have a constitutional rule. According to Mao's understanding, a constitution would be based on democratic practice following the success of the revolution. Consequently, a constitution was the recognition of the practice; it was equated to democracy. Mao did not seem concerned about whether a Chinese constitution, be it soviet or new democratic, was or was not coupled with constitutionalism. Never in his long and distinguished career did he make it clear that the government, the Party, or himself as supreme leader could not under any circumstance act against the constitution.

Lenin had urged colonial and semicolonial countries to establish a soviet form of democracy after the Second Congress of the Communist International.[49] He adopted the soviet as a means for leaping over the capitalist stage of socioeconomic development. Stalin regarded the soviet as the most adequate organization for carrying out class struggles.[50] In China, soviets were to be set up only when there was a revolutionary upsurge. Under such conditions, or at places where peasant associations had existed or were still functioning, a transitional form of government—the revolutionary committee—should be adopted before the inauguration of a soviet. In either case, as Mao argued against Lin Piao in January, 1930,[51] the establishment of a regime must precede the winning over of the masses. The unspoken reason for this procedure was of course a question of legitimacy: to set up a Red regime on even a small piece of land was to deny legitimacy on the same piece of land to any other government. With itself as the only government, the Red regime or the CCP did not have to plunder as a means for survival and expansion. Instead, it could collect taxes and conscript soldiers.

The only CCP leader who argued against the soviet form of government at a time when the land revolution reached its nadir in August, 1935, was Chang Kuo-t'ao. From reading his memoirs, one gets the

[49] D'Encausse and Schram, *Marxism and Asia,* pp. 149–50.

[50] *Ibid.,* p. 29, and *Lieh-ning ssu-ta-lin lun chung-kuo,* p. 117.

[51] Mao Tse-tung, "Ke Lin Piao t'ung-chih ti hsin" (A Letter to Comrade Lin Piao), *Mao Tse-tung hsüan-chi,* supplement 1947 edition, p. 95.

unmistakable impression that, in spite of his long years of education
and research in Moscow, Chang's command of Marxism-Leninism
was surprisingly shallow. In debates on theory or basic Party lines,
his tendency was to compromise, to strike what might be called a
"golden mean" (*chung-jung*). He was never a sharp debater. In
August, 1935, he proposed abandoning the soviet form of government
in favor of a federal union with the minority nations in west China.
Chang's failure on that occasion to carry his comrades with him and
the manner in which he failed have not yet been cogently explained by
anyone, not even by Chang himself. At a time when Chang's military
strength surpassed that of Mao and there was a leadership crisis in the
wake of the disastrous defeats in 1934, the acceptance of Chang's proposal could have meant the establishment of a Chang Kuo-t'ao line,
hence a Chang Kuo-t'ao leadership. The development of the CCP would
have taken an entirely different course. Seen in this light, Chang Kuo-
t'ao's attack on the soviet system can be interpreted as his opening gam-
bit in the game for power in August, 1935. It failed because the course
mapped out by the proposal was a dismal one and its author was essentially a mediator rather than an advocate.

The soviet form of government was abandoned soon afterward, but
not for the reasons Chang Kuo-t'ao put forward. At the Wa-yao-pao
conference, "the Soviet Workers' and Peasants' Republic" was
changed to "the Soviet People's Republic" so that the new political
form could represent the interests of the nation in its war for freedom
and independence against Japanese imperialism.[52] Anti-imperialism
could not have claimed a high priority in Chang Kuo-t'ao's proposal
since his federal union government, if it had been set up, would have
been situated between Szechwan and Tibet, thousands of miles from
the nearest Japanese army unit. Furthermore, Chang himself claimed
that when he made his proposal, no one had yet thought of forming an
anti-Japanese united front either with or without Chiang Kai-shek.

The rural soviets were designed to win over the peasants during the
land revolution and to keep them on the side of revolution. Land was
the central problem of the whole movement. The redistribution of land
could on the one hand dismantle "feudal" productive relationships in
rural China and on the other mobilize the fervor of the peasant masses
to participate in the revolution and administration of the soviet areas.[53]

[52] See the text of the Wa-yao-pao resolutions quoted in *Chung-kuo ke-ming-shih ts'an-
k'ao tzu-liao*, III, 145–65, or Mao, *HC*, I, 153, or *SW*, I, 168.
[53] See Ilpyong J. Kim, "Mass Mobilization Policies and Techniques Developed in the
Period of the Chinese Soviet Republic," in A. Doak Barnett (ed.), *Chinese Communist*

This was what Lenin had called "land fever" in a colonial or semi-colonial country.[54] With redistribution of ownership, rather than land utilization, as its principal goal, the CCP's land policy thus remained essentially a political and short-term policy throughout the land revolution and united front periods, and even several years after 1949.

Broadly speaking, all the factions of the CCP agreed to classify the rural population according to criteria of land ownership and degrees of dependence on exploitation for income. They also agreed that the poor (the exploited) and the middle (neither exploiting nor exploited) peasants were the firm allies of the proletariat or the CCP. They advocated that the land of the landlords (the exploiters who did no manual work) should be confiscated and redistributed. The only bone of contention was whether to confiscate the land of rich peasants (the half-laboring and half-exploiting class).

Following confiscation there came the questions of redistribution: whether to redistribute the ownership or only the right to use land; whether to redistribute land equally on the basis of size or on purely economic considerations. The sixth Congress of the CCP resolved to confiscate only the land of landlords and to redistribute land economically, not equally, with only the rights of use.[55] It is well known that during the Li Li-san period, the toughening of the CCP's attitude toward the rich peasants partially corresponded to the Stalin-Bukharin power struggle. Even so, Li Li-san did not go beyond depriving the rich peasants of only that portion of their land which they leased to others to farm.[56]

The ways in which rich peasants were treated varied from soviet to soviet. We know almost nothing of Ho Lung's land policy either in Hung-hu or west Hunan. In the Oyüwan soviet, the land of the middle peasants remained intact, the poor and hired peasants were given fertile land, but the landlords and rich peasants shared only lean land. Land was generally redistributed in terms of the value of the crops.[57] Later, in north Szechwan, the rich and even the middle peasants were treated harshly; it is probable that their land was taken away. Mao Tse-tung confiscated all land in his Chingkangshan soviet in 1928, but

---

Politics in Action (Seattle and London: University of Washington Press, 1969), p. 81; and Mao, *HC*, III, 994, or *SW*, III, 195.

[54] "On Our Agrarian Programme" (1905), *CW*, VIII, 250. See also *Lieh-ning ssu-ta-lin lun chung-kuo*, pp. 68, 154.

[55] *Liu-tz'u ta-hui chüeh-i-an*, pp. 5–6; and Wang, *Chung-kuo kung-ch'an-tang shih-kao*, II, 22.

[56] Hsiao, *Power Relations*, p. 21.

[57] *Ming-pao yüeh-k'an*, No. 40, p. 98.

confiscated only public and landlords' land at Hsing-kuo county in 1929. In the soviet, the ownership of land was nationalized; no private transaction of land was permitted.[58] Mao made further concessions to the rich peasants in the land law of February, 1930, whereby the only land to be confiscated, besides the landlords', was that which the rich peasants leased to others to farm. The rich peasants were entitled during redistribution to a fair share of land, not just a piece of inferior land. Land was to be twice redistributed: first, equally on a per capita basis and second, justly according to the quality of the soil. From this action was derived the slogan of taking from those who had too much to give to those who had too little and taking from those who had superior land to give to those who had only inferior land.[59] Mao's purpose was not the optimum utilization of land, but to rally as many peasants as possible to the soviet movement.

In the eyes of the International faction led by Wang Ming and Ch'in Pang-hsien, Mao's concessions to the rich peasants were a violation of the Marxian class standpoint. The rich peasants had even infiltrated into and dominated the organizations of the poor and hired peasants.[60] From 1931 onward the anti–rich peasant line was introduced and intensified steadily. The rich peasant, having lost his land and surplus farming tools, was to be given only poor plots to farm. As the Civil War situation deteriorated during the long, drawn-out fifth encirclement campaign, Mao, having succumbed to the authority of the "twenty-eight Bolsheviks" in the Party center, launched his land investigation movement (*ch'a-t'ien yun-tung*) in order to ferret out the remnants of "feudal" and reactionary elements and confiscate their land.[61] This, too, was a design to mobilize the peasants for an intensified war effort, and it was coupled with a "red terror" against the counterrevolutionaries, landlords, and rich peasants.[62]

---

[58] Ho Kan-chih, *Chung-kuo hsien-tai ke-ming-shih* (A History of the Modern Chinese Revolution) (Peking: Kao-teng chiao-yü ch'u-pan-she, 1957), pp. 143–44; Tso-liang Hsiao, *The Land Revolution in China, 1930–1934: A Study of Documents* (Seattle and London: University of Washington Press, 1969), pp. 19–20.

[59] Ho Kan-chih, *Chung-kuo hsien-tai ke-ming-shih*, pp. 142–43; and John E. Rue, *Mao Tse-tung in Opposition, 1927–1935* (Stanford, Calif.: Stanford University Press, 1966), Appendix D, p. 300.

[60] Directive from the center to the soviet areas, in Wang Chien-min, *Chung-kuo kung-ch'an-tang shih-kao*, II, 508; and Hsiao, *Power Relations*, p. 161, or *Land Revolution*, p. 49.

[61] Mao Tse-tung, "Ch'a-t'ien yun-tung ti ch'u-pu tsung-chieh" (A Preliminary Summing Up of the Land Investigation Campaign), in *Tou-cheng* (Struggle), No. 24, reproduced in Takeuchi Minoru (ed.), *Collected Writings of Mao Tse-tung* (Tokyo: Hokubosha, 1970), Vol. III.

[62] Chang Wen-t'ien's article of June 25, 1934, in Hsiao, *Land Revolution*, p. 285.

The alienation of the peasants through the harsh land policy of the early 1930's caused a drastic change in the CCP's land policy and rich peasant policy in 1935. Wang Ming advocated the confiscation of land-lords' land only, while leaving the land and tools of the rich peasants alone.[63] Rich peasants and the others were treated alike by being given an equal share of land. In other words, Wang finally came to terms with Mao's earlier "rich peasant line." In fact, as the united front was being formed, even the confiscation of landlords' land was discontinued while rent and interest reduction became the center of the CCP's agrarian policy. Rent reduction, however, was not to be effected by decrees from above, but by mass struggles from below.[64]

Thus it was also a form of political education to arouse the peasants' fervor in production. By relying on this fervor, the border region could successfully lead a massive production drive to raise the standard of living of the people and to lessen their tax burden when the region was undergoing enormous economic difficulties caused by the conditions of siege in the early 1940's. A new rich peasant class, with members like Wu Man-yu, grew in the process.[65] Even during the Civil War after 1945 the Party center still counseled caution in the treatment of the rich peasants, who were distinguished from traitors, bad gentry, and local ruffians. In the "old" liberated areas where land had been redistributed already, there would be no need to do it all over again; in the "new" liberated areas, the policy was to neutralize the rich peasants in the Civil War. Under Mao, the rich peasants were more charitably treated so that the landlords and other reactionary elements would be isolated and the revolution would be brought to an early conclusion.

OPERATIONAL STRATEGIES

But it is in its operational aspects that Mao's thought is most controversial and most Chinese. Here his differences from his colleagues become most noticeable. The basic assumptions of the unevenness of

---

[63] Wang Ming, "Hsin hsing-shih yü hsin jen-wu," *Wang Ming hsüan-chi*, I, 97–98.

[64] Mao, *HC*, III, 933, or *SW*, III, 131. See also "Cheng-chih-chü kuan-yü chien-tsu sheng-ch'an yung-cheng ai-min chi hsüan-ch'uan shih-ta cheng-ts'e ti chih-shih" (The Politburo's Instruction on Rent Reduction, Production, Supporting the Government, Cherishing the People, and the Propaganda on the Ten Great Policies), in Wang Ping (ed.), *Sheng-ch'an wen-hsien* (Documents on the Production Drive) (Shantung, 1946), p. 2.

[65] *Ibid.*, p. 92.

the revolutionary situation and the malleability of man helped Mao develop his own thought in a peculiarly Chinese fashion.

The unevenness of revolutionary conditions in China was easily observable. References to it may have been developed as extensions of the metaphor "tide" (*ch'ao*). The tides of revolution rose and ebbed one after another; they also came one beside another. It seems to be a Russian metaphor that took root in the Chinese language; but it is a vague metaphor, inviting various interpretations as to when and how the next upsurge would come. On the eve of the Sixth Congress of the CCP, it was generally agreed that the high tide of the Chinese revolution was over: the workers and peasants, as Bukharin stated at the ninth plenum of the Executive Committee of the Comintern, had suffered heavy defeats. But there was always a psychological reluctance for the professional revolutionaries to admit that the "sea" had become calm and the "crew" could take a rest. The use of this metaphor had something like an inherent tendency to impetuosity and leftist adventurism. That was probably why, having admitted defeat, Bukharin hastened to add: "Numerous symptoms indicate that the workers' and peasants' revolution is approaching a new surge."

The judgment of Bukharin and the spirit of the ninth plenum were reflected in the resolutions of the Sixth Congress of the CCP. The short-term tasks of the Party were to set up local revolutionary regimes (soviets), aiming at victories in one or several provinces. Toward the end of 1928, however, CCP leaders in Moscow began to show signs of impatience over the lack of spectacular actions. The leftists, represented by Ch'ü Ch'iu-pai, thought a new upsurge had arrived, while the rightists, represented by Chang Kuo-t'ao, thought not.[66] The controversy between them went on for two months. In Shanghai, closer to the scene of action, the center of the Party was shrouded in pessimism. Accepting the judgment of an uneven revolutionary situation, Li Li-san confined himself to the task of consolidating the soviets and the center's control over them.[67]

The Comintern's directive on October 26, 1929, pointed out that a national crisis was then evolving in China between the autumn of 1929 and the autumn of 1930. This situation deteriorated into confused civil wars between Chiang Kai-shek and various factions of militarists.

[66] *Ming-pao yüeh-k'an*, No. 32, pp. 96–97.
[67] *San chung-ch'uan-hui ts'ai-liao shih-hao* (No. 10 of the Material concerning the Third Plenum), on microfilm.

These wars took place in North and Central China where the soviets seized the opportunity to expand. Li Li-san read the situation as a firm indication of the arrival of the general upsurge, in spite of Chou En-lai's more cautious assessment.[68]

In the context of 1930, to deny the unevenness of the revolutionary situation was to overlook the weakness of the working class movement in the cities and a lack of revolutionary enthusiasm on the part of the peasants in North China. Only by such a denial could the cities logically continue their claim to leadership over the much stronger rural soviets. The cities could probably have aid, even military aid, from the Soviet Union, if the Communist International and the Russian party regarded the Chinese revolution as sufficiently important to the world Communist movement.[69] It was with such a denial and such a supposition about Russian aid that Li Li-san cast the dice. His evanescent triumph was actually hailed by the official organ of the Communist International, the *Inprecor*, on August 7, 1930.

As a soviet leader, Mao held the view that the revolution in China was at a low ebb and that its unevenness necessitated the more advanced to lead the relatively backward.[70] Under Li Li-san, and even later under the twenty-eight Bolsheviks, Mao insisted: "The result of subordinating rural work to city work, instead of the other way round, was that after the work in the cities failed, most of the rural work failed too." [71] To imply that the country was actually more advanced than the city reminds one of Lenin's dictum of the East being more advanced than the West. But to maintain the view that the urban working class movement lagged behind the peasant movement constituted one of the chief characteristics of "right opportunism," according to the twenty-eight Bolsheviks.[72] Their main task was after all to reassert the proletarian leadership by repudiating the idea that Chinese peasants had some special revolutionary attributes, and by invalidating the observation that the proletarian movement in the cities was less advanced than the Chinese peasant movement.[73]

As long as the cities maintained their superior position, their capture remained a high priority in the Communist agenda of action. The experiences of 1930 showed that the better defended cities could not be

---

[68] See Wang Chien-min, *Chung-kuo kung-ch'an-tang shih-kao,* II, 44, for the resolutions of the Politburo on June 11, 1930. See also Hsiao, *Power Relations,* p. 62.

[69] Wang Chien-min, *Chung-kuo kung-ch'an-tang shih-kao,* p. 43.

[70] Takeuchi (ed.), *Collected Writings of Mao Tse-tung,* III, 249–50.

[71] *HC,* III, 998, or *SW,* III, 200.

[72] Ho Kan-chih, *Chung-kuo hsien-tai ke-ming-shih,* I, 163.

[73] Hsiao, *Power Relations,* pp. 206–7.

taken without well-equipped troops. The anxiety to capture them led the twenty-eight Bolsheviks to overestimate the capabilities of the Red Army and to belittle Chiang Kai-shek's achievement in the encirclement campaigns.[74] Nevertheless, the twenty-eight Bolsheviks accepted the concept of the unevenness of the revolution; they did not make any adventurist attempt like the Autumn Harvest Uprising initiated by Ch'ü Ch'iu-pai or the attacks on Changsha ordered by Li Li-san. Within the limits of the soviet movement, they thought the Red Army strong enough to fight positional warfare in both offense and defense. Their appraisal of the situation and the strategy to be adopted had the acquiescence even of Mao.[75] But after the military disasters of 1934 Mao was able to turn the table against them at the Tsunyi conference by relentlessly criticizing their strategy and their mistakes in the conduct of the war.

The second basic assumption upon which Mao built his revolutionary strategy concerned man himself. It must be remembered that the first modern systematic view of man introduced to the Chinese intellectuals was Social Darwinism, under whose influence Mao and his contemporaries grew up. For some decades, Chinese scholars actually had feared that the Chinese race might be obliterated from the face of the earth in the way that some of the American Indian tribes and Australian aborigines had been. The Malthusian theory of population had never managed to convince or impress many Chinese. Their theoretical dilemma lay not with the number but with the quality of the Chinese, a people who were admittedly inferior in Darwinian terms and yet had scaled great heights of cultural attainment in the past.

An obvious solution to this dilemma was to cite past glories for proof that the Chinese were in no sense inferior, thus treating their present incompetence as temporary. Consequently, there was the anxiety to reassert China's "rightful place" under the sun, and this anxiety ran through the thoughts of Li Li-san, Wang Ming, and Mao. For them, there was no doctrinal difficulty in refuting Malthus, as Marx himself had already done so. By rejecting Malthus, they also accepted the nineteenth-century belief in the miraculous power of science and in the prodigious growth of the productivity of labor.[76] In the long run, science and higher productivity would help China reassert her rightful place, for this was a predetermined law of develop-

[74] Wang and K'ang, *Chung-kuo hsien-chuang yü chung-kung jen-wu*, pp. 9–15, 27–29.
[75] Hsiao, *Power Relations*, pp. 241–42.
[76] Ulam, *Unfinished Revolution*, p. 19.

ment. Thus, in the end China would be regarded as an equal to any nation.

But in the short run, only the Communists in other countries were prepared in theory to treat the Chinese as their equals. For the sake of revolution, however, the CCP still had to accept instructions from the Communist International, though the readiness with which CCP leaders did so differed. Li Li-san was not the only one who thought that the Comintern leaders specially dealing with Chinese affairs had a scanty knowledge and understanding of China. It was this attitude of the Chinese which Dimitri Manuilsky complained about at Li's trial in Moscow.[77] Li also regarded the Chinese Communist movement as next in importance only to its counterpart in Russia.[78] His temerity in challenging the Comintern leadership in 1930 was partly due to this kind of sinocentric thinking. Even Wang Ming, perhaps the most faithful supporter of the Comintern, was not free from such proud thoughts as, "The Chinese Soviet Republic is the only other soviet republic outside the USSR." He went on:

The destruction of this revolutionary base on the Pacific would be the prerequisite for world imperialists to prepare and launch a world war on the Pacific, especially to launch a war of intervention against the USSR from the East. The destruction of the Chinese Soviet Republic would deal a crippling blow to the world proletarian revolution. The destruction of the Chinese Soviet Republic would be the necessary step toward rendering the Chinese stateless and enslaving them.[79]

As long as the revolutionaries held to the assumption that the Communists were the vanguard of the working class and that the Party consisted of the most advanced elements of the revolutionary classes, there would be no need to learn from the masses, although the Party had to know the wishes and views of the masses. But these advanced elements had to learn from their even more advanced comrades in the Soviet Union. The relationship between them and their Russian comrades was not radically different from American-trained Chinese scholars and their American professors of the same period.

Mao's stance and attitude on this matter were basically different. His ideal Communist learned only selectively and critically from the Soviet Union, but wholeheartedly (*kan*) from the masses. When it came to a choice between the Russians and the Chinese masses, the Maoist knew perfectly what to do.

[77] Hsiao, *Power Relations*, p. 86.
[78] Wang Chien-min, *Chung-kuo kung-ch'an-tang shih-kao*, II, 43.
[79] Wang, *Chung-kuo hsien-chuang yü chung-kung jen-wu*, pp. 51–52.

The dilemma of the superiority and inferiority of the Chinese is reflected in Mao's dictum of "poverty and blankness" (*i-ch'iung erh-pai*)—the attribute being at once good and bad. In 1956 he was not sure whether "poverty and blankness" was a good thing; nor was he sure that the Chinese were truly blank in the sense of being ignorant. In 1958 he was more positive.

[1956:] I have said before that we are very poor and not very knowledgeable. [We are] "poor and blank." Poverty means underdeveloped industries and agriculture; "blankness" is like the blankness of a piece of paper—a low standard of culture and science. Poverty [or an impasse, *ch'iung*] urged us to change, to revolt, and to search for strength. A piece of blank paper is just the thing for writing [or for making impressions on]. Of course I am speaking only in general terms. I do not imply that we are ignorant, in view of the wisdom of our laboring people and the existence of a contingent of good scientists.

Poverty and blankness have kept our tail down. Even if in the future our industries are greatly expanded and our scientific and cultural standards greatly raised, we shall continue to be modest and considerate and refuse to stick our tail up. We shall keep on learning from others, for thousands of years to come. What is wrong with that?

[1958:] Apart from their other characteristics, the outstanding thing about China's 600 million people is that they are "poor and blank." This may seem a bad thing, but in reality it is a good thing. Poverty gives rise to the desire for change, the desire for action and the desire for revolution. On a blank sheet of paper free from any mark, the freshest and most beautiful characters can be written, the freshest and most beautiful pictures can be painted.[80]

One has to have incorrigible optimism, indomitable spirit, and combativeness to see the cheerful side of "poverty and blankness." Neither Hu Shih with his view of the "five demons" that were plaguing China nor James Yen with his view on "poverty, stupidity, weakness, and selfishness" shared Mao's attitude. Ever since his article, "The Great Union of the Popular Masses," published in 1919, Mao does not seem for a moment to have lost his faith in the people as a source of energy and power. Above all he had unquestioned faith in the revolutionary potentials of the Chinese masses. It was this kind of faith that deprived Marxism of most of its empirical content, making many of Mao's policy proposals hard for his more theoretical comrades to accept.

Since man could by his will power change himself and determine the

---

[80] The 1956 quotation is from Ch'en, *Mao*, p. 84. The 1958 quotation is in Mao Tse-tung, *Mao Tse-tung chu-tso hsüan-tu* (Peking: Jen-min ch'u-pan-she, 1964) II, 519, or *Selected Readings from the Works of Mao Tse-tung* (Peking: Foreign Languages Press, 1967), p. 403.

course of history, a counterrevolutionary could become a revolutionary, a "poor and blank" nation could transform itself into a rich and knowledgeable nation, a diffident people could gain confidence. Man is perfectly malleable. He could "Reach the ninth heaven high to embrace the moon/Or the five oceans deep to capture a turtle: either is possible."

Under preindustrial conditions, voluntarism ran common to all great social reforms, economic progresses, and social rebellions. The Confucianization of China and Japan, the Christianization of Europe, and such primitive rebellions as the Tong Hak of Korea and the Boxers of China were all examples of voluntarism of different content and degree. A rebel had to feel that he was larger than life-size so as to have the courage to challenge the existing order of things and to assign himself the task of reform and progress. How else could Mao boast that he and his comrades won the revolution on "millet and rifles." Deficiencies in the strength of the rebellion vis-à-vis the status quo were made up for by a voluntarism justified by an ideology.

Unevenness in the temporal as well as the geographic sense determined the protractedness of the Chinese revolution. During this long process both the military strategy and the political approach of the Party had to differ vastly from the revolutionary precedents of France and Russia. Let us consider the military strategy before coming to the political approach, which was designed to support the Party's military efforts for the final victory.

Li Li-san began his strategic thinking from a peculiar hypothesis: the nature of a revolution was not determined by its political forces (or class structure), but by its objective tasks.[81] In other words, what was most important was what *should* be achieved, not what *could* be achieved. When the two goals diverged, he was not prepared to wait too long before taking action. For this reason, Mao in 1945 accused him of inadequate preparation: "This wrong line [the Li Li-san line] arose for a number of reasons. It arose because Li Li-san and other comrades failed to recognize that the revolution required adequate preparation by the building up of its own organizational strength."[82]

With the revolutionary upsurge as Li saw it early in 1930, the success of the CCP was dependent on the proletariat:

[81] [Li] Li-san, "Fan t'o-lo-ssu-chi-chu-i ho chung-kuo ti chi-hui-chu-i" (Against Trotskyism and Chinese Opportunism), in *Chung-kuo ke-ming wen-t'i yü fan-tui-p'ai* (Problems of the Chinese Revolution and the Opposition) (n.p., 1929), p. 9.

[82] *HC*, III, 982, or *SW*, III, 183.

The great struggle of the proletariat is the decisive force in the winning of preliminary successes in one or more provinces. Without an upsurge of strikes of the working class, without armed insurrection in key cities, there can be no successes in one or more provinces. It is a highly erroneous concept to pay no special attention to urban work, and to plan "to use village [forces] to besiege the cities" and "to rely on the Red Army alone to occupy the cities." Henceforth, the organization of political strikes and their expansion into a general strike, as well as the strengthening of the organization and training of the workers' militia to set up a central force for armed insurrection, are major tactics in preparing for preliminary successes in one or more provinces.[83]

In his view, it would be wrong to rely on the Red Army, essentially a peasant force, for these revolutionary tasks, for that would be tantamount to the abdication of the proletariat from its hegemony. To carry this to the extreme, it might even lead to a denial of proletarian participation in the revolution. Without proletarian leadership in the cities, the revolutionary forces could only attack "the limbs of the ruling class, instead of its brains and heart."[84] In consequence the revolution would last until Li Li-san's hair turned gray.

From the Ku-tien conference in December, 1929, and his famous letter to Lin Piao in January, 1930, onward, Mao had consistently defied Li Li-san. He differed from Li on almost every point of strategy. For Mao, the important task was still the build-up and consolidation of the soviets. (The soviets were discontentedly referred to by Li Li-san as "local regimes" or "regional governments.") For the fulfillment of this task, the Party would have to rely on the peasants and the Red Army, not on the nonexistent urban proletariat and its local and general strikes. As there was still no steady upsurge according to Mao's judgment, the Party and army should take only small, not big, actions. He hoped the expansion of the soviets would one day lead to the encirclement of the cities from the countryside. But Mao still lacked a cogent answer as to how this would be done. The distant vision remained vague to him as well as to his comrades in the Chingkangshan base. Li Li-san may have been justified in describing Mao's strategic thought at this stage as "localism and conservatism characteristic of peasant mentality."[85]

The military strategy adopted by the twenty-eight Bolsheviks differed from Li Li-san's since it was applied to quite different conditions.

[83] Brandt *et al., Documentary History of Chinese Communism*, pp. 190–91.
[84] *Hung-ch'i*, No. 88 (March 29, 1930), p. 2.
[85] *HC*, III, 982, or *SW*, III, 184.

If we accept August, 1932, as the date of Mao's loss of military power in the central soviet, and early 1933 as the date of the removal of the Party center from Shanghai to Juichin, then the strategy of the twenty-eight Bolsheviks did not take effect till the end of the fourth encirclement campaign. In other words, they took over the command at a point when the Red Army had successfully beaten back four of Chiang's encirclements, when the central government in Nanking was thrown into utter chaos in the wake of the Japanese invasion of Shanghai, and when the impact of the world depression was acutely felt in China. In the resolution adopted on January 9, 1932, the CCP judged the situation ripe for a struggle for victory in one or more provinces.[86] This strategic goal was reiterated in another resolution adopted in August, 1933, which also called for the defense of every inch of the soviet territory.[87]

During all this time the initiative remained in the hands of the Red Army; it was not lost until just before the battle of Kuang-chang in April, 1934. Before that, the Red Army was regarded as proficient in both mobile and defensive warfare, for it was a regular army in offensive as well as defensive operations.[88] Hence voluntarily or involuntarily the Army fought more positional than guerrilla engagements.[89] It is in this light that one should appreciate the plausibility of the Party declaration that the fifth campaign was the decisive battle between soviet China and colonial China.[90] Partly owing to this strategy of the CCP and partly owing to the astute maneuvering of Chiang's troops, small gains to the government troops culminated in the decisive battle of Kuang-chang, followed by the rapid collapse of the Communist defense.

We have no means of knowing Mao's strategic proposals at this precise point of time. Later he told Edgar Snow that he was not in charge of the military campaign. The earliest systematic exposition of his strategic thought available to us is the resolution of the Tsunyi conference. This was to be further developed in his conversation with Snow and his later military writings such as "Problems of Strategy in China's Revolutionary War" in December, 1936, and "Problems of

[86] *Shih-hua* (Honest Words), No. 3 (April 20, 1932).

[87] *Tou-cheng*, No. 21 (August 21, 1933).

[88] *Ibid.*, No. 46 (February 9, 1934), and *Hung-hsing* (Red Star), No. 29 (February 18, 1934).

[89] *Hung-hsing*, No. 4 (August 27, 1933).

[90] See the resolutions of the fifth plenum of the center, January 18, 1934, in *Tou-cheng*, No. 47 (February 16, 1934).

Strategy in Guerrilla War against Japan" and "On Protracted War" in May, 1938.

In essence, Mao's strategy presupposed a protracted war for the Communists to carry the revolution from the countryside to the cities. This pattern differed completely from the orthodox Franco-Russian pattern which consisted of a series of urban uprisings before the seizure of power. Following this pattern, the war was conducted most of the time under conditions unfavorable to the Red Army. Not only was the Red Army numerically inferior but its equipment and supplies were also below the standard of its enemy. It had therefore to depend on mobility and secrecy, on iron discipline and good relations with the masses. In other words, it had to depend on superior human qualities to compensate for material deficiencies. No revolutionary army could win without these qualities.

Mao's way of making the Red soldiers better fighting men was to give them technical skills and to instill a new ideology in them. Instead of keeping soldiers from politics, Mao's army was to be thoroughly politicized. The more adverse the conditions, the harder the tasks of revolution, the greater would be the demand for the soldiers' politicization. This may be what Lenin meant by "barracks . . . becoming hot beds of revolution." [91] This was certainly what Lenin had in mind when he proposed that "the standing army be abolished and that a militia be established in its stead, that all the people be armed. A standing army is an army that is divorced from the people and trained to shoot down the people. . . . A standing army is not needed in the least to protect the country from attack by an enemy; a people's militia is sufficient. If every citizen is armed, Russia need fear no enemy." [92]

As indicated above, Mao may have developed his military strategy rather late, probably some time early in the 1930's when the war situation became unfavorable to the Communists. His mass line, however, can be traced back a long way. Faith in the great union of the popular masses, an influence coming from Li Ta-chao in 1919, found an echo in Mao's report on the Hunan peasant movement: "To talk about 'arousing the masses of the people' day in and day out and then to be scared to death when the masses do rise—what difference is there between this and Lord Sheh's love of dragons?" [93]

[91] "The Armed Forces and the Revolution" (1905), *CW*, X, 54–55.
[92] "To the Rural Poor" (1903), *ibid.*, VI, 401.
[93] *HC*, I, 44, or *SW*, I, 56.

If Mao's populist traits sometimes offend the more stringent class point of view of a Marxist-Leninist, we can quote from Lenin himself to show that Mao was not all that heretical. In his essay, "Better Fewer, but Better," of 1923 Lenin wrote:

The issue of the struggle depends ultimately on the fact that Russia, India, China etc. form the immense majority of the earth's population. And it is just this majority which, for the last few years, has been drawn into the struggle for its freedom with unbelievable rapidity. In this light, there can be no doubt as to the final outcome of the universal struggle. In this sense, the victory of socialism is absolutely and fully assured.

Here, on a larger scale, the final outcome of the revolution also depended on arousing the popular masses; class analysis did not seem to dominate Lenin's considerations in this passage. Earlier in his life, Lenin held different views. He had no patience with "wretched amateurs"; he found that "it is more difficult to unearth a dozen wise men than a hundred fools." [94] (Perhaps the type of fools Mao had in mind who could move mountains?)

Following the orthodox Leninist line, the Sixth Congress of the CCP regarded the masses as consisting of the workers, peasants, and soldiers, whose participation in armed uprisings was essential. The Chinese revolution was conceived of as following a pattern similar to those in France and Russia, that is, a series of urban uprisings leading to the seizure of power in a relatively short time and followed by a war against reaction. Thus the need for mass participation would be temporary—at most a matter of a year or two. The vanguard of the masses would play a more decisive role than the masses themselves; the organization and discipline of the vanguard would be more important than the arousal and consolidation of the support of the masses. Even as late as January, 1934, the twenty-eight Bolsheviks still spoke of the masses in this way: "The victory of the revolution depends on the party, the bolshevized line and work, the unity of thought and action, discipline and ability to lead the masses, and the repudiation of any line that deviates from the line of the International and the CCP." [95]

To regard the masses in this manner was to conform to the concepts of an elitist party and the hegemony of the proletariat. But after the battle of Kuang-chang, Chang Wen-t'ien, one of the twenty-eight Bolsheviks, remarked on mobilizing, working through, and relying on the masses: "The problem is rather one of how to promote the activism of

<hr/>

[94] "What Is to Be Done?" pp. 464, 466.
[95] The resolutions of the fifth plenum in *Tou-cheng*, No. 47 (February 16, 1934).

the masses, raise the degree of the consciousness of the masses, and rally and organize the masses around the soviet regime when we carry out a clear and definite class line." [96] Chang was surely moving closer to Mao's view on the masses—a view Mao reiterated at the fifth plenum of the sixth session, January, 1934. Mao was against arousing the masses only, and he pointed out two questions which his comrades had failed to stress: the well-being of the masses and the CCP's methods of work. "We are the leaders and organizers of the revolutionary war as well as leaders and organizers of the life of the masses." [97]

Concern over the well-being of the masses and the CCP's styles of work were the main content of the *cheng-feng* campaign of 1942–44, during which Mao's mass line was worked out in detail. In 1943, half-way through the rectification, Mao defined his mass line in the often quoted passage which follows:

In all the practical work of our Party, all correct leadership is necessarily "from the masses, to the masses." This means: take the ideas of the masses (scattered and unsystematic ideas) and concentrate them (through study form them into concentrated and systematic ideas), then go to the masses and propagate and explain these ideas until the masses embrace them as their own, hold fast to them and translate them into action. Then once again concentrate ideas from the masses and once again go to the masses so that the ideas are preserved in and carried through. And so on, over and over again in an endless spiral, with the ideas becoming more correct, more vital and richer each time. Such is the Marxist theory of knowledge.[98]

To carry his line through, it was vital that the Party and masses should have this kind of relationship:

Hence communists have the duty to co-operate democratically with non-Party people and have no right to exclude them and monopolize everything. The Communist Party is a political party which works in the interests of the nation and people and which has absolutely no private ends to pursue. It should be supervised by the people and must never go against their will. Its members should be among the people and with them and must not set themselves above them.[99]

The objective of the whole exercise was to prevent the Party from becoming unrealistic and bureaucratic—in other words, to go against the wishes and practices of the masses. The implication was that the masses must themselves be a real entity, not simply the elusive Chinese proletariat. To identify with the broad masses was by definition to rid oneself of bureaucratism, to bridge the gap between the leaders and the

---

[96] Hsiao, *Land Revolution*, p. 289.
[97] *HC*, I, 134, or *SW*, I, 150.
[98] *HC*, III, 921, or *SW*, III, 119.
[99] *HC*, III, 831, or *SW*, III, 33–34.

led. In these two respects the masses could never be wrong, and this was why the vanguard must learn from them. Hence the real heroes were not the Party vanguard but the masses.[100] Neither Liu Shao-ch'i nor Kao Kang, both of whom supported Mao's mass line, was prepared to go as far as this in his praise of the masses.[101]

In the scheme of his mass line, did Mao ever allow the masses to be wrong sometimes and the minority or the few to be right? After all, Marx, Engels, and Lenin had spent long periods of their lives in the minority against the majority, and Mao himself had been continuously in a minority opposition to the majority of his Party from 1927 to 1934 and again more recently. Was he right then? In 1962 he admitted once that the truth was often in the hands of the few.[102] In such a case, it seems that the few should use persuasion to purge the majority of its errors. It can still be argued that the few, though opposed to the majority, had nevertheless the masses on their side. The process of the successful persuasion of the majority by the few was the process of establishing their ideological authority.

In Mao's dialectics, the masses must not be assumed to be incoherent, inarticulate, or forever confused; nor must the vanguard be assumed to be always politically more advanced than the masses. Through the processes of political education, the masses would grow increasingly aware of political problems and the way to tackle them. The "endless spiral" would lead to the optimum politicization of the masses, a point at which the difference between the vanguard and the masses would disappear. But in such an event, what would be the role of the Party among the thoroughly politicized masses? Should the Party transform its functions from political to simple administrative ones as prophesized by Lenin? Was this the first step toward the withering away of the Party?

There is another consideration. Since the few could use persuasion to convert the majority to the correct view, it would be possible to establish a direct relationship between the few and the masses without going through the vanguard or the Party organization. In this sense, the Party could transform itself as Lenin predicted or simply wither away.

The application of the mass line is neatly summed up by John W.

100 *HC*, III, 810, or *SW*, III, 12. See also Ch'en, *Mao Papers,* p. 25.

101 Ch'en, *Mao,* p. 25; and Kao Kang, "Shih-shih k'e-k'e wei lao-pai-hsing hsing-li ch'u-pi" (Always Work for the Interests of the People), a speech delivered on December 22, 1944, in *Sheng-ch'an wen-hsien,* pp. 71–72.

102 *Mao Tse-tung wen-hsüan,* p. 76.

Lewis into four processes: perception, summarization, authorization, implementation.[103] This, incidentally, corresponds with Mao's theory of knowledge. As to the practical significance of the mass line when it is implemented, we must first of all bear in mind that it is designed to solve the contradiction between the state and society, or the problem of the alienation of the state from society. For this, such nauseating styles of political action as commandism, dogmatism, and so on should be eliminated through rectification campaigns. Here we witness a curious "unification of contradiction"—the identification of the in- fallible Mao with the infallible masses. This is also the unification of extreme centralism (cult of Mao) and extreme democracy (the mass line). Between these two extremes—Mao and the masses—everyone and everything can be wrong and is jettisonable in order to preserve the infallible authority (no longer the Comintern, of course, but Mao and the masses) of the revolution (and the socialist construction), so that the revolution (and the construction) can go on.

Second, the identification of the infallible Mao with the infallible masses enabled Mao to use the masses legitimately in his efforts to rectify the Party or a mass organization. The masses, like himself, have become the criterion of realism and correctness.

But all this presupposes that the Chinese masses would do what Mao expected them to do. They would speak up in their criticism of the authorities; they would have a full sense of responsibility in politics and administration instead of pragmatical cynicism; they would be interested in Chinese and world politics as Mao had been all his life. If these assumptions do not hold good and if the masses could not articu- late sincerely, the mass line might fail in its attempt to "unify the contradiction" between the state and society. It could become perfunc- tory and even "bureaucratic." Worse still, the masses might be manip- ulated by their leaders—a distinct possibility in the context of the institutional weakness of Chinese politics.[104]

In his long career as a revolutionary, Mao pointed out many prob- lems of the Chinese revolution and proceeded to find solutions to them in the light of some knowledge of Marxism-Leninism, but chiefly by his penetrating understanding of Chinese history and society. His in- tellectual development and his way of handling problems seem to sug- gest that he is more often stimulated by practical problems than in-

[103] John W. Lewis, *Leadership in Communist China* (Ithaca, N.Y.: Cornell University Press, 1963), p. 72.
[104] Richard H. Solomon, "Communication Patterns and the Chinese Revolution," *CQ*, No. 32 (October-December, 1967), p. 110.

spired by theory. He even acted sometimes intuitively with only his Chinese background as his guide.

After the victory of the revolution Mao went on to discover many other problems, problems of socialist construction. His speeches, "On the Ten Great Relationships," "On the Correct Handling of Contradictions among the People," and the "Sixty Points on Working Methods," abound with such problems. More of them were pointed out by Mao during the Cultural Revolution. But he has solved almost none of these.

One major contradiction which has been there all the time but lies dormant is the contradiction between the collective and the individual. To assume its nonexistence is to assume away a great part of Chinese politics; to repress it by shifting the people's focus of attention to the collective has been the outstanding success of Maoism. Will Mao's masses one day become aware of their individual existence? Will they become conscious of the contradiction between their individual interests and those of the collective when the more urgent collective interests such as the honor of the nation and the irrigation of a commune are satisfied and fade into the background? Usually it is at such a juncture that individual interests come to the fore.

PART II

Ideology and the Intellectuals

LAWRENCE SULLIVAN and
RICHARD H. SOLOMON

The Formation of Chinese Communist Ideology in the May Fourth Era: A Content Analysis of Hsin ch'ing nien*

The ideology of a revolutionary political movement is not a fixed set of ideas or a rigid and unchanging doctrine. As is emphasized in Richard H. Solomon's study in this volume, the idea system which shapes the action of a political elite grows in relation to the needs and insights of individuals who assume leadership roles, and in response to the functional demands of the struggle for power.

This analysis explores the process by which a revolutionary elite establishes an ideological position in the formative period of political action. The Chinese Communist Party (CCP) traces its origins to the 1910's, when large numbers of intellectuals, alienated by the ineffectiveness of their society's social and political institutions in the face of foreign intrusion, searched for ways to transform China into a strong and modern nation. A New Culture Movement which began at mid-decade initiated a period in which foreign cultural values and political institutions were explored as alternatives to a discredited Chinese tradition. The May Fourth incident of 1919, in which urban intellectuals became enraged at the compromising of Chinese interests

* The authors wish to express their indebtedness to Professors Richard Kagan, Harriet Mills, and Herbert Weisberg for their assistance in matters of data analysis and documentary interpretation. The interpretations, and any errors, in this paper, however, are the responsibility of the authors.

by Western powers at the Versailles peace conference, transformed this cultural search into a political struggle. By the mid-1920's one section of the May Fourth generation of intellectuals had become firmly committed to Marxism-Leninism as a doctrinal solution to China's problems.

The apparent success of Lenin's Bolsheviks in coping with the problems of political chaos and poverty which plagued Russia, as well as China, at the end of World War I stimulated the more activist of China's intellectuals to begin what was to prove to be a decades-long process of adapting a foreign doctrine of proletarian revolution to the conditions of a peasant society. The contemporary Chinese Communist ideology termed "Marxism-Leninism-Mao Tsetung Thought" bears only partial resemblance to the idea system that inspired Mao Tsetung and other political activists in the early 1920's to begin the struggle for power. As is revealed in some measure by the ideological dimensions of the continuing Sino-Soviet dispute, the evolution of the leadership doctrine of the CCP in the context of Chinese society was to occur to such an extent that at present there are only limited grounds on which the now-aged May Fourth generation leaders—men who in their youth had been stimulated by the theories of Marx and Lenin—can relate to Lenin's political heirs.

The founders of the Chinese Communist movement were by no means organizational specialists, but rather students and their professors. In consequence, they began their political activities in the May Fourth era guided by concepts that had been formed largely out of study and debate rather than revolutionary action. By virtue of several excellent interpretations of this period, we have a general understanding of why Marxism-Leninism appealed to some members of this generation.[1] Less attention has been paid, however, to the question of how initial interpretations of that ideology related to the philosophical debates, intellectual themes, and political events which structured liberal and radical thought prior to and immediately following the formation of the CCP.

What was the nature of intellectual developments from 1915 to 1920 which presaged the adoption of Marxism-Leninism? How did non-Marxist cultural and political ideas, such as conceptions of science and

[1] For a comprehensive treatment of the May Fourth Movement and the appeal of Marxism to this generation, see Chow Tse-tsung, *The May Fourth Movement: Intellectual Revolution in Modern China* (Stanford, Calif.: Stanford University Press, 1960); and Maurice Meisner, *Li Ta-chao and the Origins of Chinese Marxism* (New York: Atheneum, 1970).

education, interact with each other to establish the intellectual foundations for early Chinese interpretations of Marxism-Leninism? Did the
adoption of this European doctrine by China's revolutionaries radically
alter existing concepts of politics and social change, or merely give
established intellectual positions a new framework for expression?
Our approach to exploring such questions is structured around a content analysis of the most influential intellectual journal of this period,
Hsin ch'ing nien (New Youth).[2]

Hsin ch'ing nien (*HCN*) was first published in September, 1915.
At the time, Western-influenced members of China's intellectual circles
were just beginning to emerge from several years of political seclusion
brought on by the repressive policies of the president of the newly
founded Republic of China, Yüan Shih-k'ai. The journal, radically
transformed into a CCP organ in 1920, eventually ceased publication
in July, 1926, in the context of the anti-Communist suppression carried out by Chiang Kai-shek's Kuomintang. Within the eleven-year
period of its publication, however, *HCN* served as an influential forum
for the translation, discussion, and propagation of new artistic forms,
social values, and eventually, political doctrines.

The value of a study of the content of this journal as an approach
to analysis of the process of ideological formation lies partly in the
prominence of its influence, and partly in the fact that its publication
spans the critical period of time when alternative social and political

[2] *Hsin ch'ing nien* was actually three separate journals published between 1915 and
1926. The original *HCN* was first published by Ch'en Tu-hsiu from 1915 to May, 1919,
and then by the New Youth Society from September, 1919, to July, 1922. The second *HCN* was published by Ch'ü Ch'iu-pai between June, 1923, and December, 1924.
The third was published from April, 1925, to July, 1926. The original *HCN* was converted from a journal of the Westernized intelligentsia to a medium of the Chinese
Communist Party. The second and third versions were both established by the CCP.
In terms of both editorial staff and writers, the latter two versions, especially the
third, were very different from the first and most famous edition of *HCN*. Thus the
justification for grouping all three publications in one analysis might be questioned.
While recognizing the critical differences between these journals, the authors believe
that the following content analysis is a viable research method for exploring the organic
linkages between patterns of thought developed during the May Fourth Movement and
interpretations of Marxism-Leninism espoused by Chinese intellectuals in the 1920's. As
well, intellectual continuity was provided by the carry-over of some writers between
the non-Communist and Communist editions—particularly the leading figure Ch'en
Tu-hsiu. The latter two versions of the journal inherited an intellectual tradition and
image from the former which carried over conceptual themes even as a more rigorous
ideology related to the formation of the CCP developed.
Hereafter, issues cited from the first *HCN* will be followed by "(1)," those from the
second by "(2)," and those from the third by "(3)." Page numbers cited are from the
English paginal system used in the reproduction of *HCN* published by the Daian Co. of
Tokyo, Japan. For further information on the publication of *HCN*, see Chow, *May
Fourth Movement*, p. 44, note d.

ideas were being explored and then advocated as solutions to China's problems. The founder of *HCN* was the Peking University professor Ch'en Tu-hsiu. A man initially committed to the transformation of Chinese society through the application of science and democratic political processes, Ch'en was to become a founder and early leader of the Chinese Communist Party. The evolution of the content of the journal in no small measure reflects Ch'en Tu-hsiu's own intellectual transformation as it was influenced by the political and social context of early Republican China.

A further justification for focusing on *HCN* lies in the prominent role Chinese intellectuals traditionally have played in politics, and their conscious reliance on ideology in the process of governance. While students in the May Fourth period explicitly renounced China's Confucian political culture, in style they continued to be shaped by its influence. The importance of a "correct" doctrine and the leading role of intellectuals in politics were two traditional assumptions that were not challenged by the *HCN* group.[3]

HCN attained an immediate prominence in China's intellectual circles as a result of the pre-eminent position of Peking University (known in Chinese by its acronym, Peita) as a national educational institution. Spurred on by the policy of Peita's rector, Ts'ai Yüan-p'ei, of promoting educational freedom, *HCN* played an important role in heightening among radicalized young intellectuals an awareness of Western civilization.[4] In 1917 university circles were incensed by an attempted imperial restoration by Anhwei Governor Chang Hsün. In response, the *HCN* group used its magazine as a medium for leading a campaign to discredit once and for all the cultural basis of China's traditional political system.[5] From 1917 to 1919, this so-called New Culture Movement was the focus of a search through a myriad of Western and Japanese philosophies and cultural forms in an effort to identify a viable alternative to what many young intellectuals saw as their own society's anachronistic and moribund tradition. Although each member of *HCN*'s editorial board identified with a unique configuration of these ideas and cultural forms, the unanimous rejection

[3] Such assumptions did come to be challenged by Mao Tse-tung, however, in the later periods of the Chinese Communist movement, and became issues in the Cultural Revolution which culminated Mao's political career. See p. 160 below.

[4] Jerome B. Grieder, *Hu Shih and the Chinese Renaissance: Liberalism in the Chinese Revolution, 1917-1937* (Cambridge, Mass.: Harvard University Press, 1970), p. 78.

[5] Professor Harriet Mills of the University of Michigan drew our attention to the relationship between the restoration attempt and the intellecual activities of the *HCN* group.

of Confucianism combined with a felt need for cultural regeneration produced a sense of common purpose among this group of intellectual leaders.

Beginning in the summer of 1919, however, this unity began to crack.[6] Political events such as the May Fourth demonstrations generated conflicting reactions within the group over such questions as the propriety of the intellectuals' participation in politics, and the value of piecemeal reform versus revolutionary change. In 1920–21, what initially had been a disparity of opinion within the New Culture Movement culminated in a split between liberal and revolutionary factions. The former group abandoned *HCN* in protest against its growing radicalization; the latter, which was instrumental in organizing the CCP, converted *HCN* into a Party organ. From 1921 until the journal's suppression, Marxism-Leninism was discussed in *HCN* from both theoretical and operational perspectives, and was reinterpreted to fit in with the trends of ideological development previously expressed on its pages.

A formal content analysis of the complete run of *HCN*, to be presented below, enables us to identify a pattern in the evolution of the journal's focus of attention and form of presentation. This pattern seems to reflect the process of ideological formation of *HCN*'s editors. An initial period emphasizing cultural search and critical analysis of China's tradition was followed by an evident increase in the level of politicization of the journal's contents, culminating in the use of *HCN* as a medium for advocacy of Marxism-Leninism and as an instrument for building a political movement. This process of ideological formation will be detailed below and placed in the context of the political events and personal rivalries which were part of the period of formation and early growth of the Communist movement in China.

STAGES OF IDEOLOGICAL FORMATION IN THE NEW YOUTH PERIOD

The period of political and social change in China from 1915 to 1926 was characterized more by cultural search and intellectual experimentation than by the development of a rigid ideology geared to organized political action. Individuals distraught by a sense of cultural alienation entered the arena of politics primarily to fulfill deep-seated intellectual and emotional needs.[7] The creators of the New Cul-

---

[6] Grieder, *Hu Shih,* p. 183.

[7] Mary B. Rankin, *Early Chinese Revolutionaries: Radical Intellectuals in Shanghai and Chekiang, 1902–1911* (Cambridge, Mass.: Harvard University Press, 1971), pp. 225–35.

ture Movement and its various political successors were more concerned with linking personal values to the abstract goal of a rejuvenated China than with sacrificing their individuality to a tightly organized political movement. Accordingly, they showed little penchant for organizational discipline and action during these early years. Associations formally established to find solutions and strategies for China's salvation were often little more than personal cliques and discussion groups. For example, *HCN* was initially the personal publication of its founder, Ch'en Tu-hsiu, and to a lesser extent of his friend, Hu Shih. Even the CCP, at its founding in 1921, was more an extension of Peita professor-student relationships than a Leninist organizational weapon.[8]

In such circumstances is it really possible to speak of ideology during this period of time? Since they lacked a tightly knit organizational base and a full commitment to political action, can it be stated that the advocates of the New Culture Movement or even the founding members of the CCP were in the process of developing an ideology? One can respond affirmatively to this question if ideology is defined in terms of formative stages of development. For intellectual leaders in the May Fourth era, ideology was not primarily a code for political action, nor as Franz Schurmann has defined it, "the manner of thinking characteristic of an organization."[9] Although these aspects of the concept emerge in later periods of the Chinese Communist movement, ideology for the period of this study is best defined as an evolving pattern of thought serving to link individual philosophies, values, and needs to the general political and cultural environment of Chinese society. Conceived in these terms, the apparently disparate articles published in *HCN* indicate some degree of common purpose and ideological growth. In this analysis we shall trace the course of ideological development through its various formative stages by documenting shifts in the general content of articles published in the journal and by relating these shifts to changes in the ideas of important contributors who shaped the New Culture Movement and ultimately came to establish the CCP.

The notion of stages developed in this study is an analytical conclusion derived from a coding of *HCN* articles; it is an interpretive device which reveals a degree of structure to a process of intellectual

---

[8] Meisner, *Li Ta-chao,* p. 117.

[9] Franz Schurmann, *Ideology and Organization in Communist China* (2nd ed.; Berkeley and Los Angeles: University of California Press, 1968), p. 18.

debate and discussion that evolved in an additive and incremental fashion.[10] For the eleven years of ideological development contained in *HCN*, six stages can be constructed from the journal's contents. In the first stage, which we term "search," the incipient New Culture Movement set out to discover and promulgate new ideas and cultural forms imported from other societies. Intellectuals such as Ch'en Tu-hsiu, Lu Hsün, and Hu Shih, having consciously dichotomized Chinese "tradition" with "modernity," rejected that tradition completely.[11] A concomitant aspect of their iconoclasm was the tendency to look to the West for cultural models which could provide completely new alternatives to their demoralized society. Politics, literature, philosophy, and language were discussed in terms of their relationship to complete cultural systems. That is, ideas and their institutional frameworks were consistently treated as expressions of particular cultural traditions, especially the French, English, and German. Consistent with the university environment of most members of the *HCN* group, articles written in this stage were almost exclusively exercises in intellectual exploration. The focus of most writers was the internal logic of a particular culture's philosophies and the structure of its social and political institutions. For instance, the images of politics developed during this stage of search focused on political philosophy and the form of governmental organizations. Because most intellectuals were fearful of entering a political system dominated by the northern warlords, the more activist concept of politics as an arena for the playing out of con-

---

[10] The categories and stages employed in this article were developed by Lawrence Sullivan on the basis of a reading of the contents of *HCN* in Chinese. First, several issues were selected from various years of publication during which significant political events had occurred, such as the Chang Hsün Restoration Attempt (1917), the May Fourth Movement (1919), and the formation of the Chinese Communist Party (1921). After each article in these issues had been read, a preliminary set of eleven categories of ideological development was formulated. These categories were then employed in the classification of each article appearing in *HCN* during the eleven years of its publication, with the exceptions noted below. Throughout the analysis, the eleven categories were refined in order to make them as accurate and analytically distinct as possible. The categorization of each article according to this scheme was based on thematic content. Many articles—especially those in translation—required only a reading of the title, the introduction, the conclusion, and a skimming of the central portion, to be coded. Other more sophisticated and complex articles, especially those by Chinese writers, required a complete reading in order to be classified. When this operation was completed, the six stages were decided upon as seeming to provide a useful description of the cohesion of the various categories. The sequence of categories and stages was then subject to statistical tests, to be discussed below, in order to measure the strength of the various patterns of sequential ideological growth.

[11] Lin Yu-sheng, "The Crisis of Chinese Consciousness: Iconoclasm in the May Fourth Era" (Ph.D. dissertation, University of Chicago, 1970), p. 5.

flicts through organized power was not yet a part of the *HCN* message.

The initial stage of search gradually gave way to a tendency to synthesize the various strands of foreign idea systems and employ them as tools for the analysis of China's social and political problems. Whereas the first stage was characterized by a rather random selection of ideas and institutional models from Western societies,[12] this second stage, which we term "analysis," is notable for a greater emphasis on critical evaluation of specific philosophies and an attempt to relate abstract ideas to their institutional expressions. In addition, there is a new trend toward discussion of social and political problems in the context of Chinese society, rather than in European society alone. Although during this stage of analysis ideas were still explored largely at an abstract level, there began to develop a trend toward the examination of political ideas in terms of their relevance for immediate social issues and action.

Following the stage of analysis, ideas became more explicitly related to practical political action; hence we term the third stage "politicization." This phase was characterized by a major shift in journalistic style from the intellectualized discussion of philosophies and institutional forms to advocacy of complete social programs and doctrines embodying specific goals and methods for their realization. As will be discussed in a subsequent section, this politicization of the New Culture Movement marked one of the major turning points in pre-Communist ideological development.

Just as the stage of analysis laid the basis for the acceptance of political ideas and strategies, politicization opened the door for the introduction of Marxism-Leninism. Beginning in 1918 with the publication of Li Ta-chao's messianic article, "The Victory of Bolshevism," Marxism-Leninism was rapidly adopted by many intellectuals of the *HCN* group as the most appealing framework for expressing their ideas and guiding their political actions.[13]

Marxist philosophy was not new to the Chinese political and intellectual scene in the late 1910's. Earlier in the century, from 1905 to 1907, Marxism had been received favorably by Chinese students in Japan and imported into China as part of the overall appeal which

---

[12] Early in 1916 Hu Shih criticized some of the articles Ch'en Tu-hsiu had chosen for translation as being irrelevant to the Chinese situation. Prime examples of the articles he attacked were the song "America," Oscar Wilde's *An Ideal Husband,* and parts of Benjamin Franklin's *Autobiography*. See Grieder, *Hu Shih*, p. 90.

[13] Li Ta-chao, "Bolshevism ti sheng-li" (The Victory of Bolshevism), *HCN* (1), V, No. 5 (October, 1918), 473–79.

European philosophies of social democracy held for Chinese revolutionary groups.[14] Influenced by Sun Yat-sen's call for a program of public welfare (*min-sheng*), Chinese radicals interpreted Marxism primarily as a philosophy of reformist socialism. In this early period it was not considered a doctrinal prescription for political revolution. For this reason, Marxism's initial appeal was eclipsed by Russian nihilism and anarchism, which gained prominence in Chinese intellectual circles during 1906 as a result of their influence in the Russian Revolution of 1905.[15]

When Marxism was reintroduced into Chinese intellectual circles in late 1919, once again it was discussed in *HCN* primarily in the philosophical terms of a theory of socialism. In our general scheme of analysis, this fourth stage of ideological development is termed "theory building." This continued philosophical orientation illustrates the importance given to scholarly methods throughout the entire early period of ideological formation. Yet in a context where foreign interference in China's internal affairs was brought home to intellectuals through such events as the May Fourth demonstrations, and later the May Thirtieth incident of 1925, Leninism found a receptive audience and gave increasingly concrete focus to philosophical discussions. Thus the phase of theory building, in which some members of the *HCN* group adopted a systematic Marxist-Leninist philosophy, was transformed into the fifth stage of ideological development, which we term "internalization."

In the stage of internalization the philosophy of Marxism-Leninism was integrated with the previous ideological phases of analysis and politicization to form an integral pattern of political perceptions and goals. In this phase, attitudes and emotional currents which already were influential in intellectual circles were given systematic expression through political theory, and they began to shape practical revolutionary activity. The adaptation of Marxist-Leninist concepts to the concrete problems of Chinese society in the stage of internalization was revealed in new analytical approaches used by contributors to *HCN*. They began to focus their discussions on the problems of building a political movement around the Chinese working class. They reinterpreted political and historical developments in China within a Marxist framework. And they began to express their growing awareness of

---

[14] Martin Bernal, "The Triumph of Anarchism over Marxism," in Mary Wright (ed.), *China in Revolution* (New Haven, Conn.: Yale University Press, 1970), pp. 97–142.
[15] *Ibid.*, p. 128.

China's vulnerability to the machinations of international power politics in the terms of Lenin's theory of imperialism. These intellectual developments transformed Marxism-Leninism from just another political philosophy to an internalized system of political beliefs.

Following the stage of internalization, the formation of the CCP in 1921 and its turn to China's workers as the social base for revolutionary activities placed new demands on the ideology. Although the Party in its first few years of existence was an intellectual rather than an agitational organization, the adoption of Marxism-Leninism represented a conscious decision by the early Communists to improve their potential for building a powerful political movement. Where the methods and goals of liberalism, anarchism, and other competing philosophies apparently had failed to produce any meaningful changes in Chinese society, Marxism-Leninism appeared to point the way to a successful revolutionary struggle. This shift toward practical political activity created a need for knowledge of organizational and leadership techniques which could implement a strategy of mass action. This development in the conception of the revolutionary process created the conditions for a further stage of ideological growth oriented to the problems of organization and tactical political in-fighting.

This sixth stage of ideological development, which we call "movement building," became evident in *HCN* during the last three years of its publication. Strategies and tactics for operating within the immediate context of Chinese politics began to be dealt with in a Marxist-Leninist framework, along with discussions of the internal problems facing the CCP as a revolutionary organization. At this point, Marxism-Leninism was no longer just a set of individualized political beliefs, but an embryonic operational code for collective action. The full evolution of this phase of ideological formation is not revealed in the pages of *HCN*, however. Not only was the journal suppressed as the Communist movement began to grow in strength, but new leaders more oriented toward practical action than the academic Ch'en Tu-hsiu began to make their influence felt through other Party publications.

The evolution of the *HCN* group's idea system from the initial stages of search, analysis, and politicization into the phases of Marxist-Leninist advocacy which we term theory building, internalization, and movement building in practice did not occur in fully discrete steps. Each stage of ideological development laid the basis for subsequent phases by generating new problems and questions which could not be dealt with adequately in the existing intellectual framework. This interaction of stages is evident in the overlap of the various phases as new issues were confronted even before older ones had been fully laid aside. Yet as will become evident in the following content analysis of *HCN*, there is a clear pattern of thematic development in the journal which reveals an underlying process of ideological formation.

The general trend of ideological development is illustrated in Table 2. The larger units of categorization are the stages described above, each of which is broken down into two categories (except for the first stage of search) and cross-tabulated with the twelve years of *HCN*'s publication. The operational definitions of the twelve categories are given in a footnote to the table. The number in each cell represents the percentage of all articles published in any given year which falls into the specific category.[16] This handling of the data in percentage terms was necessitated by variations in the number of issues—and consequently the total number of articles—appearing in any one year of publication.

The data do not include "Letters to the Editor," nor the famous "Sui kan-lu" (Random Thoughts), which frequently appeared in *HCN*. Although publication of the former undoubtedly is some reflection of the moods and concerns of the editors, such materials were eliminated from the data set because of the problem of weighting them relative to regular articles and the uncertainty about the extent of serious editorial control which may have been exercised over their publication. The "Sui kan-lu" column was also excluded because even though it did come under the scrutiny of editorial decisions, its format created serious problems of categorization.

The figures in the cells thus represent the relative frequencies in any given year of various types of articles written by Chinese authors and of translations of foreign works selected by the editors for publication. In view of the fact that this study focuses on the formation of ideology among Chinese intellectuals associated with the New Culture Movement, separate categories were set up for these two different types of articles. The content of the translations published in *HCN* reflects, to some extent, the foreign cultural themes and models of thought which *influenced* the thinking of May Fourth era intellectuals. The content of articles written by Chinese authors, however, reveals the manner in which intellectuals were integrating relevant political events

---

16 In order to add a measure of verification to these categories, an inter-coder reliability test was carried out independently by a research assistant. The result of this test was an 84 per cent level of reproducibility.

TABLE 2

Stages of Ideological Formation as Revealed in a Content Analysis of Hsin ch'ing nien *

Year of Publication	Cultural Search		Analysis				Politicization			Marxist Theory Building				Ideological Internalization				Political Movement Building		Total Number of Articles Coded
	1	1 tr.†	2	2 tr.	3	3 tr.	4	5	5 tr.	6	6 tr.	7	7 tr.	8	8 tr.	9	9 tr.	10	11	
1915	32	38	12		18		10	7												44
1916	12	32	18	1	18	1	14	9	2											53
1917	12	17	30	4	12		7	12												79
1918	12	21	28	1	17	1	9	17	1							2				90
1919	4	14	27		14	5	1	8	1			8								74
1920	8	10	15	2	15	6		11		26	5	5		1	2		1			115
1921	7	10	13		7	1		11		23	5	55	11		7	5	2	3		64
1922															11	11				9
1923									4	8	4	8	4	8	18	25	21			24
1924												16	12	12	12	25	20	12	4	25
1925														14	10	40	9	22	5	22
1926										6		6	3	19	6	39	13	10	3	31

* Definitions for the eleven categories of content analysis used in this study are as follows.

Stage of search for a new cultural identity: (1) Enunciation of European, Japanese, or American ideas in a descriptive manner, with little or no explicit reference to China, and no common theme other than search for modern cultural forms and models of personal behavior.

Stage of analysis: (2) Informative discussions of modern social, educational, literary, philosophical, and scientific subjects relevant to China, but with no overt political or agitational purpose. Many of these ideas are used here to criticize traditional Chinese philosophers. This category contains modern Chinese plays and poems, and articles presenting various views on language reform. (3) Analytical writings on the social and political problems of contemporary Chinese society. This category includes discussions of current world politics, political theory and analysis, and youth in politics. Two major themes in this category are the concern for an activist role for Chinese youth and the need to institutionalize scientific thought in Chinese society. This level of ideological development does not involve the propagation of a specific ideology or deal with immediate political issues.

Stage of politicization: (4) Systematic attacks on traditional Chinese society, with some sense of promoting an alternative social and political system, including attacks on those individuals and groups attempting to resurrect the Confucian system. (5) Articles with a focus on specific political, economic, and/or social subjects as major issues of Chinese society. The primary focus of articles in this category is propagation of an ideology or program (excluding Marxism-Leninism) and development of embryonic ideas of political organization, leadership, and mobilization. In this category language reform is advocated and discussed in political and social terms.

Stage of theory building: (6) Writings which emphasize Marxism or other socialist philosophies as the basis for promoting national economic development and mass welfare, especially for the benefit of the working class. Translations of articles on Soviet economic development are included in this category. (7) Discussions of Marxism primarily from a theoretical or philosophical point of view.

Stage of internalization: (8) Articles which analyze political and historical developments in China within a Marxist-Leninist framework, including attacks on people who oppose this point of view. This category includes translations on contemporary Soviet politics. (9) Discussion of Marxism-Leninism in terms of the international Communist movement and the policies of the Third International. Much of this material is presented without direct reference to China. A number of articles included in this category, however, contain analyses of European political developments and their effects on China from a Marxist-Leninist perspective.

Stage of movement building: (10) Discussion of immediate problems of political strategy and/or tactics using a Marxist-Leninist framework as the guide to action. (11) Discussion of internal politics of the CCP, or the Party's role in the Chinese revolution (as distinct from other political organizations).

† "Tr." indicates translations from foreign language articles coded according to the given category.

and foreign ideas with their own philosophies to form an evolving ideology. For these reasons, our analysis preserves the distinction between articles and translations.

Coding the articles naturally presented a number of problems of interpretation and procedure. Most of the articles contain elements found in several of the categories, thus raising the question of whether to categorize each major theme raised in one article or simply to come to a decision on the one central theme in each article.[17] Due to the fact that the basic purpose of the content analysis was to determine the general thrust of ideological development, each article was placed into the *one* category that most closely characterizes its central theme. The high level of reproducibility of our content analysis categories, as noted in footnote 16, increases our confidence that this approach is justified.

With these various points in mind, we can now evaluate the statistical fit between the data and the model of ideological formation introduced above. In light of the need to handle our data in percentage form, the most appropriate statistical technique for measuring the association between our model and reality as illustrated in *HCN* is the Goodmand and Kruskal Gamma.[18] The highest value this statistic can achieve is 1, which indicates that each category (or stage) is completely developed or "unfolded" before a single frequency appears in any of the succeeding categories. As the value of Gamma approaches 0, the unfolding process assumes an increasing random character. A value of 0 indicates there is no separation of categories into different stages.

Our first calculation of the Gamma is based on the twelve categories of articles, including the translations. The result is a value of .78 for the complete period of publication between 1915 and 1926. This relationship seems to indicate a relatively strong degree of association between an evolutionary model of ideological formation and the reality of this process as expressed in the pages of *HCN*.

If we make our calculation according to the six stages (again including the translations), we can measure the strength of association on a

---

[17] For a treatment of these different methods of content categorization, see O. R. Holsti, *Content Analysis for the Social Sciences and Humanities* (London: Addison-Wesley, 1969), pp. 5–8.

[18] The Goodmand and Kruskal Gamma statistic was chosen because it measures the sequential process which seems to characterize the development of an ideology, and because it is not adversely affected by data formulated in percentage terms. See William L. Hays, *Statistics* (New York: Holt, Rinehart & Winston, 1963), pp. 655–56.

more general level. The result of this calculation is a higher Gamma value of .82. This indicates that the unfolding model of ideological formation is a better description of reality when viewed from the general perspective of the six stages.

Both of these Gamma values leave unexplained, however, a significant amount of variance in the data, indicating that as the *HCN* group evolved its ideological position, there were a number of deviations from our six-stage conceptualization of this process. The primary sources of these deviations lie in the stages of search, analysis, and movement building. The first two stages have an impact on the entire process of ideology formation that endures well beyond the discrete phases prescribed by our model; the latter stage, on the other hand, plays a much weaker role in the process than our model would suggest. One purpose of the following sections of this paper is to examine the articles in *HCN* in order to explain these "deviations" from a fully regular process. In addition, other concepts promulgated by *HCN* relevant to the formation of ideology will be analyzed below, along with discussion of the relation of the journal's editors to the establishment of the Chinese Communist movement. By proceeding in this fashion we hope to gain a greater understanding of how a political ideology evolved from the social concerns and practical revolutionary actions of those who initiated the search for a new Chinese culture.

The Search for a New China: Cultural or Political Change?

The inordinate strength of the stage of cultural search—in the form of articles and translations from foreign works—is one of the three notable characteristics of the *HCN* data that depart from our unfolding model of ideological formation. Instead of diminishing after two or three years of publication, as our model suggests, the cultural search pattern remains a strong component of *HCN* up until the magazine was transformed into an organ of the Communist Party.[19] When seen in combination with certain political trends to be discussed below, this fact highlights the important role played by cultural themes in the

[19] Beginning in 1922, nearly all translations contained in *HCN* were taken from Soviet and Comintern publications. Although both sources were foreign, they were not placed in category 1 of the search stage because we felt that the use of this type of translation reflected a qualitatively different decision on the part of the editors than the earlier selection of foreign materials. The difference seems to be between an open-minded search for new ideas and the selection of materials to reinforce an established ideological commitment.

first three stages of ideological formation. Even as the *HCN* group shifted its emphasis from search to analytical and political modes of thought, the striving for new cultural forms and philosophies remained a major concern of the magazine's editors. Thus, as illustrated in Table 2, there is considerable overlap in frequencies between the first stage of search and the two succeeding stages of analysis and politicization. Issues of the journal published in 1921, for example, contained translations of Italian plays, Hungarian literature, and English innovations in modern drama juxtaposed against articles on the Comintern, Marxist political theory, and international politics. Although the percentage of articles classified in the category of search drops significantly after 1918, the pattern of cultural search does not fully conclude until 1922.

This pattern is clearly illustrated when a more detailed statistical analysis is made of the data. If a Gamma is calculated for stages 1 and 2 alone, we get a value of .37. When compared with the Gamma of .82 for all six stages of ideological growth, this value indicates that there is considerable overlap between the search for new cultural forms and values, and the development of analytical modes of thought. The *HCN* group did not, of course, make a clear distinction between search and analysis as they attempted to construct a new world view. Understandably, the search process was conducted in a highly critical spirit. If we add the third stage of politicization to our calculation, we get only a moderately larger figure of .44, which illustrates the continuing influence of the cultural search pattern even into the phase of politicized thinking.

There are two probable explanations for this pattern. The first is a function of the persisting differences in perspective taken by the liberal faction of the *HCN* group, headed by Hu Shih, and the revolutionary faction, led by Ch'en Tu-hsiu, toward the relative importance of political action versus cultural reform in transforming China into a new society. The second seems related to the belief of even the more politicized members of the May Fourth generation that the revitalization of Chinese society, while necessitating political action, required most basically a "cultural revolution."

Hu Shih believed that cultural change, developed through intense individual effort in the realms of literature, language, and science, was the key to the construction of a new China. This opinion was clearly reflected in his contributions to *HCN*. Of the approximately twenty-five articles that appeared in the magazine under his name from 1916 to 1920, nearly three-quarters dealt with these subjects.[20] Even as his old friends Ch'en Tu-hsiu and Li Ta-chao became immersed in politics, Hu persisted in his efforts to use the magazine as an organ for promoting cultural change. For example, when Ch'en and Li began to talk about a workers' revolution in highly politicized Marxist terms, Hu restricted his interest in the working class movement to the apolitical goal of setting up an Association for the Education of Workers.[21] In a similar vein, in the May, 1919, edition dedicated to an examination of Marxist philosophy, Hu contributed an article entitled "Why I Want to Write Vernacular [*pai-hua*] Poetry." [22]

Ch'en Tu-hsiu, on the other hand, developed a positive view of politics soon after his initiative in setting up *HCN*. As early as February, 1916, in an article entitled "Our Most Recent Political Awakening," which discussed how the Western intrusion had exacerbated conflict between the old and new in Chinese society, Ch'en came to the conclusion that a "political solution" was required to deal with China's problems.[23] Where Hu felt that politics was a minor or even negative aspect of a society's culture, Ch'en considered the "modern" forms of political action characteristic of the West the critical mechanism for changing China.

By accepting modern politics as the essential method for achieving his goal of a new China, Ch'en came to challenge the traditional linkage between culture and politics in the realm of political organization and action; that is, he attacked the Confucian view that politics was the domain of cultured men who used their education to govern less "cultivated" souls. Ch'en did not consider the state as the guardian of culture. Contrary to Chinese tradition, he believed that political issues should not be defined in terms of basic cultural precepts or of the individual's moral inadequacies.[24] Thus Ch'en, unlike Hu Shih, advocated a complete transformation of politics by promoting a movement of mass-based political parties headed by political leaders and organized on the basis of issues and ideology rather than on ascriptive

---

[20] The actual figure on this calculation is 18/25 or 72 per cent.

[21] Hu Shih, "Kung-tu chu-i shih-hsing ti kuan-ch'a" (Views on the Experiments in Education for Workers), *HCN* (1), VII, No. 5 (April, 1920), 817–20.

[22] Hu Shih, "Wo wei-shen-ma yao tso pai-hua shih," *HCN* (1), VI, No. 5 (May, 1919), 549–60.

[23] Ch'en Tu-hsiu, "Wu-jen tsui-hou chih chüeh-wu," *HCN* (1), I, No. 6 (February, 1916), 457–60.

[24] Richard Kagan, "The Chinese Trotskyist Movement and Ch'en Tu-hsiu: Culture, Revolution, and Polity" (Ph.D. dissertation, University of Pennsylvania, 1969), pp. 33–37.

personal relationships. Political action should emerge from common social interests among the people rather than ascriptive kinship or regional ties. Similarly, Ch'en believed that attacks on political enemies should be restricted to their ideas and behavior. If China was to become a modern polity, the traditional practice of attacking an opponent's personality and morals would have to cease. In contrast, Hu Shih retained his emphasis on cultural action to the exclusion of politics. Just as Liang Ch'i-ch'ao at an earlier date had tried to break away from culturalism to political nationalism,[25] Ch'en Tu-hsiu attempted to shift from a sole reliance on cultural reform into a political framework.

Looking at a second explanation, the fact that many articles categorized as search appeared after 1919, when Hu Shih played almost no role in editorial decisions,[26] indicates that there was more to the enduring pattern of cultural exploration than just the liberal opposition's abhorrence of political in-fighting. For the most part, once the traditional cultural domination of politics was challenged, it became even more apparent to the revolutionaries that Chinese culture had to undergo a radical transformation as the political revolution progressed. Politicization seemed to intensify, rather than weaken, the early belief that Chinese culture had to be changed in its entirety. Thus, even though the liberal and revolutionary groups did reach the point of an irreconcilable split in 1920, the line of cleavage between them was not one of politics versus culture. On the contrary, as is vividly illustrated in the famous "Problems versus Isms" controversy of 1919–20, the crux of their conflict was the *method* by which intellectuals should attempt to change society. The liberal belief was that the improvement of individual character and morality primarily through education was the key to undermining traditional Chinese culture. The revolutionaries called for a radical change of strategy by asserting that a new form of political action was needed to overthrow those warlords and puppets of imperialism who sustained the traditional culture. In short, transformation of the cultural superstructure—literature, language, art, personal mores, social values, and so on—was considered both the antecedent to and the primary object of revolutionary political action.

This intertwining of cultural and political themes is made evident by a more thorough qualitative analysis of articles appearing in *HCN*.

---

[25] Joseph R. Levenson, *Liang Ch'i-ch'ao and the Mind of Modern China* (Berkeley and Los Angeles: University of California Press, 1967), pp. 122–24.

[26] Grieder, *Hu Shih,* p. 184.

In the first stage of search, politics was treated as a cultural expression, inseparable from individual mores, philosophical traditions, and the structure of a society's institutions. In the translations and discussions of material from the "advanced" societies of Europe, politics was delineated as just one aspect of these foreign cultural forms. For instance, in the first issue of September, 1915, Ch'en Tu-hsiu related his conception of politics to an overall fascination with French culture.[27] As a self-proclaimed Francophile, Ch'en idealized the political thought and governmental institutions of France as the manifestation of that society's modern culture. France was an advanced polity *because* of its culture.

As a corollary of the above conception, politics in the early stage of search was not promulgated as an independent force for changing society; it was subsumed under the broader category of cultural development. Political change would come about as a part of the larger process of restructuring social institutions, developing new philosophies, and remolding individual behavior, rather than through building an organized mass movement which would struggle for power. For example, in the only article written by Mao Tse-tung prior to the May Fourth Movement that is completely available in the West, "A Study of Physical Education," Mao did not focus on the problems of building a mass political movement.[28] Rather, in a manner similar to the concern of other *HCN* writers in the late 1910's, he dwelt on the problem of promoting cultural change through the remolding of individual character. For Mao, China would become a strong nation only after the Chinese people conscientiously reshaped their values so as to develop physical self-reliance, a strong sense of individual will, and a greater degree of assertiveness as complements to the traditional emphasis on cultivating individual morality and knowledge. At this point in the formation of ideology, Mao and the *HCN* group interpreted political change *as* cultural change.

With the shift to analysis there was a gradual separation of politics from cultural themes. Political ideas were no longer presented as just one aspect of the cultural totality, but were developed and synthesized

27 Ch'en Tu-hsiu, "Fa-lan-hsi jen yü chin-tai wen-ming" (The French People and Modern Civilization), *HCN* (1), I, No. 1 (September, 1915), 27–30.

28 For a partial English translation of this work, see Mao Tse-tung, *The Political Thought of Mao Tse-tung*, ed. and trans. Stuart R. Schram (2nd ed.; New York: Praeger, 1969), pp. 152–60. Within two months of the May Fourth demonstrations, however, Mao revealed a new awareness of the possibilities of organized mass political action in his article, "The Great Union of the Popular Masses." See Stuart Schram, *Mao Tse-tung* (Baltimore: Penguin Books, 1966), p. 65.

by *HCN* writers as a tool for the analysis of their society. Political ideas acquired a dynamic of their own, independent of specific cultural traditions. For example, Ch'en Tu-hsiu analyzed the role of politics as a device for handling the contradictions in Chinese society between the old and the new, weighed the relationship between practical action and political theory, and formulated a conception of patriotism.[29]

Even here, however, the conceptions of political and cultural change remained closely tied. This is evident in the image of youth promulgated by *HCN* in the stage of analysis.[30] Although Ch'en Tu-hsiu, Kao I-han, and other contributors were by no means young when they started publishing the journal,[31] the theme of youth received a great deal of their attention. Even prior to the May Fourth Movement, the young people of China were perceived as the first "constituency" of the *HCN* group's efforts to reshape Chinese society, as the title of their publication implies. In many of the articles categorized in this stage, the young were portrayed as the dynamic force which would revitalize Chinese society.[32] The rationale for this analysis was that whereas the old and the middle-aged in China were too ingrained in the old culture to create a milieu in which modern institutions could thrive, the young, because of their malleability, were able to make the kind of totalistic changes in personal behavior, values, and ideas necessary to form the cultural basis for a modern Chinese polity. Such a view, one might add, was to have renewed prominence in the Red Guard movement of Mao Tse-tung's Cultural Revolution of the 1960's.

In the shift from the stage of analysis to politicization, politics and culture interacted once again, but at a higher level of ideological sophistication. Cultural themes in the stage of politicization gave structure and direction to the intellectuals' new belief in the efficacy of political organization and agitation. If we consider the essence of this stage—as compared to search and analysis—to be an orientation to the immediate political issues of Chinese life and advocacy of specific methods needed to effect solutions to those issues, culture served to define the major targets and goals of political action. That is, cultural concerns still constituted the major category of analysis through which

[29] See Ch'en, "Wu-jen tsui-hou chih chüeh-wu"; Ch'en, "Wo chih ai-kuo-chu-i" (My Patriotism), *HCN* (1), II, No. 2 (October, 1916), 107–12.

[30] See the operational definition of category 3 in the asterisked footnote to Table 2.

[31] In 1915, the year *HCN* was established, Ch'en Tu-hsiu was thirty-seven years old.

[32] For example, see Ch'en Tu-hsiu, "Hsin ch'ing nien" (New Youth), *HCN* (1) II, No. 1 (September, 1916), 5–8.

the *HCN* group entered the political arena. Modern political organization and action was the new method; cultural change remained the primary target.

The enduring role of cultural concerns in the May Fourth generation's ideology is apparent from even a cursory glance at the articles that marked the beginning of the politicization stage. In 1916, the first year in which political themes were discussed in an issue-oriented context, the dominant subject was the need to bring an end to the cultural grip of Confucianism by defeating those political forces which were trying to bring about an imperial restoration. Of the eight articles classified as politicized in that year, six dealt with Confucianism primarily in political terms. In the following year this pattern continued, with more than half of the politicized articles focusing on the necessity of ridding China of this anachronistic cultural force and its contemporary supporters. Ch'en Tu-hsiu led the political attack in his article, "The Constitution and the Confucian Creed," published in 1916.[33] Here Ch'en berated all attempts to reconcile Confucianism with a modern state structure: "My people must come to believe that Chinese law and Confucian morals are no longer sufficient to organize our state and control our society while [we are] competing for existence in the contemporary world." [34] If China was to build viable republican institutions, then Confucianism would have to be destroyed. Allowing Confucianism to remain as a dominant cultural force would make it inevitable that China's political system would revert to the traditional bureaucratic monarchy.[35] In July 1917, Ch'en's prognosis came to a painful realization as the Peiyang warlord Chang Hsün entered Peking with his troops and restored to the throne the child emperor, Hsuan-t'ung.

Monarchy was also linked to the most basic institution of Chinese society, the family. In an article entitled "The Family and the Clan System Are the Basis for Despotism," Wu Yü, a frequent contributor to the pages of *HCN*, cited the European experience to prove that China must radically change its family and clan structure in order to achieve political (and economic) progress.[36] Family and clan life in China, he argued, were based on the social standards of the Confucian

33 Ch'en Tu-hsiu, "Hsien-fa yü k'ung chiao," *HCN* (1), II, No. 3 (November, 1916), 199–203.

34 *Ibid.*, p. 201.

35 Ch'en Tu-hsiu, "Chiu ssu-hsiang yü kuo-t'i wen-t'i" (The Old Thought and the Question of the Form of the State), *HCN* (1), III, No. 3 (May, 1917), 207–9.

36 Wu Yü, "Chia-tsu chih-tu wei chuan-chih-chu-i chih ken-chü lun," *HCN* (1), II, No. 6 (February, 1917), 491–94.

classics and thus perpetuated such archaic political behavior as "having the people blindly follow the lord, and the lord blindly follow heaven." [37] Therefore, Wu asserted in a subsequent article, the family in its present form had to be eliminated because along with Confucianism and monarchy it comprised part of an integral political-cultural system: "The family, the clan system, and monarchical political bodies are mutually dependent. . . . Therefore, Confucianism and the family are primarily what the monarchical system relies on and uses." [38]

In a similar vein, China's educational system was severely attacked for continuing to inculcate attitudes and values based on Confucian philosophy, which were perceived as inimical to the interests of a modern society.[39] If the assumption was correct that there was a direct link between Confucianism and monarchy, then it naturally followed that Confucian practices and teachings in the schools—the traditional source of China's political elite—had to be terminated. A generation of students could not be educated in Confucian cultural precepts and then be expected to support republican institutions.

The strong linkage developed between cultural and political change is also revealed in the efforts to modernize China's classical language. The *pai-hua,* or literary reform, movement initiated by Hu Shih in January, 1917, was accepted by most contributors to *HCN* as a critical element in the changes they were trying to achieve in Chinese society.[40] This is clearly illustrated by the large number of articles which appear in category 3 under analysis (see Table 2), the classification into which almost all articles on literary reform fall. From 1917 to 1920, a primary goal of *HCN* writers was to generate a radical transformation in the Chinese language. This concern extends the impact of the analysis stage beyond the level implied by our model of ideological growth. Even as articles using a political mode of thought appeared in *HCN,* the persistence of the literary reform movement diluted the sharpness of the shift from analysis to politicization. The Gamma value of .32 for these two stages is indicative of this phenomenon. Analysis did not diminish once the stage of politicization took hold.

[37] *Ibid.,* p. 491.

[38] Wu Yü, "Tu Hsün-tzu shu hou" (After Reading Hsün-tzu), *HCN* (1), III, No. 1 (March, 1917), 9–10.

[39] Kao I-han, "I chiu i ch'i nien yü-hsiang chih ko-ming" (Premonitions in 1917 of Revolution), *HCN* (1), II, No. 5 (January, 1917), 401–5.

[40] Hu Shih, "Wen-hsüeh kai-liang ch'u-i" (Tentative Proposals for the Improvement of Literature), *HCN* (1), II, No. 5 (January, 1917), 407–17.

Instead, literary reform and political thinking coexisted during these years as primary components of the ideological message of *HCN*. Ch'en Tu-hsiu, who made major contributions to creating a new literature while developing a more sophisticated concept of politics, was the personification of this close relationship.

The thrust of the *pai-hua* movement, especially for the liberal faction, was not political, but literary and linguistic. For the more politicized members of the *HCN* group, however, the overall effect of literary reform contributed both to the specific stage of politicization and to the entire process of ideological formation. In the first place, the literary reform movement was never intended solely as a device for improving and popularizing Chinese literature. Even Hu Shih, who bitterly opposed personal involvement in what he perceived as the dirty game of politics, recognized that the new literature must perform social as well as literary functions. He felt that the new literature must focus on China's pressing social and cultural problems, such as poverty, the living conditions of industrial workers and ricksha coolies, and the emancipation of women.[41]

For the revolutionary faction of the *HCN* group, Hu's concept of the literary movement was consciously integrated into their political perspective as another aspect of the overall effort to undermine the traditional culture. The classical literature not only glorified the attitudes and values of Confucianism, but, more importantly, restricted literacy to the upper classes, thereby isolating the intellectuals from the rest of Chinese society. Thus, as Ch'en Tu-hsiu and the more politicized members of the *HCN* group became sensitive to politics as a process of organization building, and the construction of communication linkages with groups beyond the isolated world of the intellectuals, the literary revolution assumed significant political import. Accordingly, several articles on literary reform written by this group of authors were more political than literary in content. Hence, in our content analysis they were classified in category 6 under the stage of politicization.

The politicization of the *pai-hua* movement was evident in Ch'en Tu-hsiu's first article on this subject. Whereas in the January, 1917, issue of *HCN* Hu Shih had launched the movement primarily in terms of Chinese literature, Ch'en in the February issue labeled Hu's proposals a "literary revolution" and immediately infused the whole

41 Grieder, *Hu Shih*, p. 87.

process with political and ideological overtones.[42] "Of my three great principles of the [literary] revolution, one is that we must eliminate the literature which, like polished gems, flatters the nobility, and in its place establish an egalitarian and flexible national literature."

To be sure, Ch'en and his revolutionary colleagues interpreted the *pai-hua* movement as primarily a literary rather than a political effort. Nevertheless, the great interest shown in developing a more popular literature, which as Ch'en stressed could "create the plain, simple, and expressive literature of the common people," [43] facilitated the shift from a narrow, intellectual conception of politics to an embryonic strategy for building a mass political movement. New concepts of popular participation, organization, and activism were heavily influenced by radical ideas on expanding the audience of literature and other forms of written communication. Writing in the vernacular style was seen as a powerful political tool for making contact with the people of China. In sum, the literary revolution was another example of how cultural change was considered an inseparable part of political change. Politics as a depersonalized, issue-oriented process was an extremely appealing concept to politicized members of the May Fourth generation in light of their alienation from traditional society. But they all realized that in establishing a modern polity in a China just emerging from a long "feudal era," the creation of a new culture would have to be an enduring objective in their efforts.

SCIENCE, EDUCATION, AND THE REVOLUTION IN THOUGHT

The strong link between culture and politics in the evolving ideology of the May Fourth generation produced a unique concept of revolution. Even as the movement began to interpret politics in terms of organized popular action based on specific issues as a mechanism for changing society, intellectuals felt that political action would succeed only if carried out in a larger context of cultural change. From this aspect of ideological development emerged a concept of revolution which, unlike Leninism, interpreted the essence of revolutionary change as a restructuring of thought rather than just the capturing of state power and subsequent efforts to transform China's largely agricultural economy.

---

42 Hu Shih, "Chien-she-ti wen-hsüeh kuan-nien lun" (On the Constructive Concept of Literature), *Collected Essays of Hu Shih*, IV, 1153–72, cited in Grieder, *Hu Shih*, p. 87. Ch'en Tu-hsiu, "Wen-hsüeh ko-ming lun" (On the Literary Revolution), *HCN* (1), II, No. 6 (February, 1917), 487–90.

43 Ch'en, "Wen-hsüeh ko-ming lun," p. 490.

Competition for political power became a salient issue for the *HCN* writers by late 1916, as is evident in the onset of the politicization stage of ideological formation summarized in Table 2. Nonetheless, the intellectuals still seemed to believe that a radical change in popular thinking on a broad scale was needed prior to a political takeover in order to translate that takeover into a true social revolution. This concept permeates articles throughout the stages of analysis and, especially, politicization. As early as 1916, Ch'en Tu-hsiu wrote of the continuing threat of Confucianism to the Chinese revolution. He advocated a fundamental change in people's thinking before political matters could be settled.[44] Otherwise, Ch'en argued, traditional forms of political rule would be resurrected even though the political institutions had been changed. Kao I-han, another major contributor to *HCN*, made much the same point in January, 1917, when he commented on the failures of the 1911 Revolution:

The past revolution was one of form while the present revolution must be spiritual. The revolution in the political system is already quite well known by our countrymen and it is being continually carried out. The revolution in political spirit and methods of education, however, has not yet been implemented. This is the goal of the "revolution of 1917."[45]

Even in late 1919, when *HCN* took on a greater political role, as stated in an editorial entitled "Our Manifesto," this concept was still very much a part of the group's thinking. "We feel that to seek social progress, we must smash the old ideology of 'unalterable principles' and 'continuity from the old' . . . create new political, economic, and moral viewpoints, and establish a modern spirit which will conform to the needs of a new society."[46]

The concept of transforming thought as a central part of the revolutionary process was reflected in the concern shown by *HCN* writers for education and science. If the social thinking of the Chinese people had to be restructured, then, as in traditional China, the educational system would have to play a crucial role. This emphasis on the role of education in social change derived in no small measure from Hu Shih's identification with John Dewey's educational philosophy, which Hu embraced as the most appealing guideline for remolding Chinese society.[47] Nevertheless, politicization and the eventual advocacy of Marxism-Leninism did not alter the revolutionaries' belief in the im-

44 Ch'en Tu-hsiu, "Hsien-fa yü k'ung chiao," p. 199.
45 Kao I-han, "I chiu i ch'i nien yü-hsiang chih ko-ming."
46 "Pen-chih hsüan-yen" (Our Manifesto), *HCN* (1), VII, No. 1 (December, 1919), 2.
47 Grieder, *Hu Shih*, pp. 111–21.

portance of education. For example, in April of 1921, Ch'en Tu-hsiu—
already a committed Communist—still showed a deep concern for developing a new educational system in his lead article, "What Is the
New Education?"[48] In 1925, despite his day-to-day involvement in
political activities, Ch'en took the time to publish a high school text-
book.[49] The Communists may have disagreed with Hu Shih's emphasis
on pragmatic educational methods as the primary mechanism for
creating a new China, but they still considered education as a key
social process capable of revolutionizing society.

If education was to be a major method for changing Chinese thinking, then science was seen as the primary component of the new mode
of thought. To replace traditional attitudes with scientific thought
represented a major goal of the *HCN* group. From the first issue of
the journal, in which Ch'en Tu-hsiu characterized science as one of the
major contributions of French civilization,[50] the integration of scientific thought into Chinese life was perceived as a critical step in building a new culture. Science was not just considered a methodology or
technique for understanding physical processes, but as a radically new
perspective for viewing social and political life.[51] Hu Shih described
science as the core of the new thought then "sweeping" across China:
"The spirit of the new thought is a kind of critical attitude. The tools
of the new thought are the research of problems and the utilization of
scientific theory."[52]

The importance of science for the formation of ideology was twofold. First, the prominent influence it achieved among Chinese intellectuals reinforced the concept of "revolution" as meaning a changed
manner of thinking. Second, modern science was one of the major
strands of thought imported from the West which served to shape the
intellectuals' basic concepts of politics and revolution—as was to be
most explicitly revealed in the popularity of the doctrines of "scientific
socialism."

Articles on the theory of science and scientific subjects did not disappear from the pages of *HCN* as the journal became increasingly

[48] Ch'en Tu-hsiu, "Hsin chiao-yü shih shen-ma," *HCN* (1), VIII, No. 6 (April, 1921),
785–93.
[49] The title of this volume is not available to the authors. According to Richard Kagan,
however, Ch'en's book is accessible in the library of Kyoto University.
[50] Ch'en Tu-hsiu, "Fa-lan-hsi jen yü chin-tai wen-ming," pp. 27–30.
[51] D. W. Y. Kwok, *Scientism in Chinese Thought 1900–1950* (New Haven, Conn.:
Yale University Press, 1965), p. 17.
[52] Hu Shih, "Hsin ssu-hsiang ti i-i" (The Meaning of the New Thought), *HCN* (1),
VII, No. 1 (December, 1919), 11.

politicized. In 1920, at a time when the major writers were engaged in a debate over the centrality of politics, all of the March issue was devoted to discussions and translations on scientific theories of population growth.[53] Once again, part of this persistence of scientific themes could be explained by the influence of Hu Shih, who was one of the earliest proponents of introducing science into Chinese life. On the other hand, Ch'en Tu-hsiu, Kao I-han, and other politicized members of the *HCN* group also recognized the supreme importance of science to their concept of modern society. Thus, we find Ch'en in September, 1920, discussing the value of scientific thought at the same time that he was criticizing Hu Shih for ignoring politics.[54]

The primary reason science linked up with the formation of ideology was that it provided an intellectual basis for gaining a sense of certainty and prediction about social and political phenomena. The fact that at this time Chinese society was fragmented by political chaos contributed to the appeal of scientific thought. The major proponents of science took the idea that it gave man power over the physical world and—with the help of Western writers—grafted it on to the complexity of human affairs, most notably politics. Science seemed to infuse life with a rationality which made it amenable to control by man. Bertrand Russell, for instance, was revered in *HCN* because he was able to use science "to throw light on society's basic ills and then advocate the proper course for change."[55] Although our understanding of the process of ideological formation remains rudimentary, a critical "intellectual step" in coming to rely on a formal idea system seems to be perception of the world as comprehensible through theory, and hence controllable. The doctrines of science gave the editors of *HCN* this sense of comprehensibility. The success of Lenin's Bolsheviks, guided by a "scientific" theory of society and revolution, gave them the hope of attaining political power.

A viable ideology must also fulfill related functions of providing a justification for rejection of the past, and, in similar conceptual terms, establishing guidelines for building a new future. For the *HCN* group, science acted as the crucial intellectual link, tying together the alienation these men felt from the traditional culture with their desire to create a new China. Science was perceived as a conceptual tool for discrediting the influence of Confucian ideas and the primitive beliefs

[53] *HCN* (1), VII, No. 4 (March, 1920).
[54] Ch'en Tu-hsiu, "T'an cheng-chih" (On Politics), *HCN* (1), VIII, No. 1 (September, 1920), 3–11.
[55] Chang Sung-nien, "Lo-su" (Russell), *HCN* (1), VIII, No. 2 (October 1920), 182.

which dominated popular thinking, and then constructing an alternative cultural system. *HCN* writers described logic and experimentation as the essence of the scientific method and as constituting an irresistible force capable of exposing the lethargy of Confucianism as a way of thinking and living. The spirit behind the scientific method contained the élan necessary to bring about a fundamental change in Chinese culture in a short period of time. Science seemed to provide a totalistic solution to what was seen as a totalistic problem.

The use of science as a tool for discrediting the traditional culture is well illustrated by the way it was used to combat the persisting influence of Confucianism. In 1916, when K'ang Yu-wei made a last-ditch effort to restore the doctrine of the Sage by petitioning the government to make Confucianism a state religion, the entire concept of religion was attacked in the journal as being antithetical to modern scientific thought.[56] In later issues, Hu Shih invoked the prestige of the critical attitude and open-mindedness of scientific inquiry as he encouraged an end to the Confucian practice of rites.[57] Further, Ch'en Tu-hsiu stressed the importance of science as a way of liberating the Chinese people from their debilitating belief in ghosts and other forms of superstition: "We believe that the most important condition for advancing modern society is for us to venerate natural science and a realistic philosophy, and use them to eliminate superstition." [58] In sum, advocacy of science was a primary expression of the strong alienation felt by the *HCN* group toward China's tradition. The universality and critical spirit of scientific inquiry seemed a powerful weapon for ending the two-thousand-year monopoly of Confucian concepts on Chinese social and political thinking.

The same mode of thought that was used to justify rejection of the traditional culture also helped shape *HCN*'s approach to the problem of how to build a political movement that could create a new China. Most of the intellectuals who constituted the *HCN* group had just emerged from several years of withdrawal from the political conflicts that were rending Chinese society. It is not surprising that many felt ambivalent about leaving the relatively secure world of ideas to par-

---

56 K'ang's attempt at restoration is described in Chow, *May Fourth Movement*, p. 292. It was attacked by Ch'en Tu-hsiu in "Po K'ang Yu-wei chih tsung-t'ung tsung-li shu" (Refuting K'ang Yu-wei's Petition to the President and the Premier), *HCN* (1), II, No. 2 (October, 1916), 127-33.

57 Hu Shih, "Wo tui-yü sang-li ti kai-ko" (My Views on the Reform of Funeral Rites), *HCN* (1), VI, No. 6 (November, 1919), 641-50.

58 Ch'en Tu-hsiu, "Yu kuei lun chih-i" (Doubts concerning the Theory of the Existence of Ghosts), *HCN* (1), IV, No. 5 (May, 1918), 443.

ticipate in the risky and uncertain arena of political struggle. Anxieties about involvement in the world of warlord intrigue were reinforced by the widely respected opinion of Hu Shih, who felt that politics was a dirty business and, thus, unsuitable as a process for generating mean- ingful social change.[59] The reluctance of the aforementioned 1919 *HCN* editorial, "Our Manifesto," to commit the journal fully to a role in party politics was indicative of the appealing influence Hu Shih's view held for many of his colleagues. Although a variety of fac- tors contributed to convincing the group that they should commit themselves to the task of building an independent political movement, scientific thought facilitated their transition from the intellectual to the political world. It gave these men a feeling that they could manipu- late complex human affairs in their own interests. Ch'en explained this well: "From now on our duty toward learning and thought must be the analysis of human affairs and circumstances so as to establish the basic facts." [60] For Ch'en and his supporters, science made the affairs of society susceptible to the kind of understanding and manipulation which China's traditional Confucian-trained literati had long enjoyed through intellectual manipulation of the classical literature. As a re- sult, they found it easier to plunge themselves into China's political turmoil.

Another dimension of science relevant to the growth of politicization was the idea that the scientific method provided a form of predicta bility and control over a future which for years had appeared to these intellectuals as chaotic and hopeless. The adoption of any ideology by a group bent on capturing political power requires a firm precon- ception that one's objectives are both just and attainable. Science seems to have fulfilled this need for a sense of attainable goals, as is evident in the interpretation of the scientific method advanced by *HCN* writers, which contained a strong strain of determinism.[61] This made the intellectuals feel that the future of their movement did not lie with chance, but would inevitably be victorious because it was guided by a powerful theory. Even though the *HCN* group was small in number, scientific rationality provided its members with what seemed a superior analytical weapon for understanding the trend of social events, thus making their political and cultural goals appear attainable. It was also this concept of science as a superior conceptual

[59] Grieder, *Hu Shih*, p. 178.
[60] Ch'en Tu-hsiu, *Collected Essays of Ch'en Tu-hsiu*, III, 273, cited in Kwok, *Scientism in Chinese Thought*, p. 81.
[61] Kwok, *Scientism in Chinese Thought*, p. 77.

system with deterministic powers that prepared some members of the group for the adoption of Marxism-Leninism.

POLITICS, SCIENCE, AND THE ADVOCACY OF MARXISM-LENINISM

As is evident from a glance at Table 2, the transition from politicization to the various stages where *HCN* became an advocate of Marxism-Leninism represents a major shift in the process of ideological development. Except for the two years of 1920 and 1921, when the magazine had not yet been officially converted into a medium of the just-forming CCP, there is no appreciable overlap between the early non-Marxist period and the last three Marxist-Leninist stages. Statistically, this can be expressed by calculating the Gamma value for the two stages of politicization and theory building. The substantial figure of .87 for this pair indicates that the unfolding pattern is not only much stronger than the average of .82 for the complete run of all stages, but also that it is stronger between these two categories than any other pair of stages in the data set. The fit between the data and all three Marxist-Leninist stages of theory building, internalization, and movement building is also strong. The Gamma calculations for the Marxist-Leninist period are .66 with translations, .69 without, both figures being higher than their counterparts in the first three stages (.32 and .33, respectively). The adoption of Marxism-Leninism thus represents a "tightening up" of the world view of *HCN*'s editors, and a narrowing of their modes of thought after several years of search for new values and approaches to promoting social change.

There are several questions that must be asked of these data. Does the break between politicization and the succeeding Marxist-Leninist stages represent a real shift in the ideological orientation of China's intellectuals, or were concerns and commitments from earlier stages of the movement carried over to shape initial interpretations of Marxism-Leninism? Was the ideology of Lenin's Bolshevik Party interpreted in terms of the success of the October Revolution of 1917, or did more parochial Chinese conditions lead the May Fourth intellectuals to a selective commitment to the doctrines of social-democratic politics?

There is no doubt that some unmeasurable portion of the strong break between the first three and the last three stages was due to developments within China which shaped the intellectuals' perceptions of the world. The most important of these was the physical move of *HCN* from its base in Peking to new quarters in Shanghai in the winter of 1920, followed in April of the next year by another move to Canton.[62] In both cities, *HCN* articles were authored by a number of new writers who had been intellectually reared in an environment much different from that of Peking. Neither Shanghai nor Canton was equivalent to Peking as a center of literary and cultural ferment; neither city had an intellectual institution to compare with Peita. On the contrary, Shanghai was a highly Westernized city which had been deeply affected by the intrusions of Western commercialism and foreign rule while Canton was the center of revolutionary agitation against the Northern warlord government.

Many of the contributors to *HCN* from Canton and Shanghai had very different intellectual backgrounds and interests than their Peking counterparts. For example, after 1921 the editors of *HCN* cleared its pages of poetry, except for occasional revolutionary verses or poems written by Soviet authors. Combined with the final exit of Hu Shih from the magazine's editorial staff in the winter of 1920, the shift in location and personnel helps to explain some of the transformations in ideological themes that appeared in the magazine from 1920. Yet, as we will now note, many earlier themes continued to endure.

Studies of the early Marxist-Leninist period in China have tended to characterize the decision by Ch'en Tu-hsiu, Li Ta-chao, and other Westernized intellectuals to adopt Marxism-Leninism as a major watershed in their intellectual and political development. For instance, Benjamin Schwartz argues that Ch'en's rapid conversion to the new doctrine was a clear indication that in Ch'en's eyes " 'Democracy and Science' had failed" and that his adoption of Marxism-Leninism seemed to mark a manifest rejection of his previous identification with republicanism and scientific thought as key components of modern society.[63]

To be sure, Marxism Leninism did fundamentally transform the ideology of men like Ch'en. However, many intellectual themes bridged the gap between the non-Marxist and Marxist-Leninist periods of ideological development. The superficial components of political philosophies, such as republicanism, were advocated and then abandoned in rather rapid fashion, but many of the basic social and political concepts developed in the earlier stages of ideological formation endured to shape initial interpretations of Marxism-Leninism. In this

---

62 Chow, *May Fourth Movement*, p. 44, note d.
63 Benjamin I. Schwartz, *Chinese Communism and the Rise of Mao* (New York: Harper & Row, 1951), p. 23.

sense, Marxism-Leninism provided a new intellectual framework for reinterpreting old themes and giving them meaning in terms of evolving political interests and realities. Its adoption was organically linked to previous patterns of thought. Ch'en Tu-hsiu did not adopt Marxism-Leninism because he felt science had failed to have any beneficial effect on Chinese society; on the contrary, he believed that the doctrine of Marxism-Leninism embodied the most advanced development of scientific thought. Marx, and his disciple Lenin, had achieved the ultimate intellectual feat of applying the rationality and determinism of physical science to the problems of human social development. This interpretation was apparent even in the earliest articles on Marxist philosophy appearing in *HCN*. In the May, 1919, issue, dedicated to an examination of Marxist theories, the article by the writer Ling Shuang, "A Criticism of Marxist Philosophy," emphasized that "the theories of Karl Marx occupy an important position in the scientific world of today." [64]

Four years later, in June, 1923, when the new editor of *HCN*, Ch'ü Ch'iu-pai, published yet another manifesto—this time dedicating the journal to revolution, the proletariat, and Marxism-Leninism—the scientific theme was even more prominent. Ch'ü declared that *"Hsin ch'ing nien* will be the guiding light of the science of society." [65] Thus, Marxism-Leninism was not yet seen so much as a guide to political action as the ultimate expression of the scientific method. Such a view was revealed in the new manifesto by a rather strange characterization of the Communist International as "the most progressive *social science group* which has a close relationship with the proletarian world revolutionary movement" (emphasis added). [66]

The essential link between the Chinese interpretation of Marxism-Leninism and the intellectuals' previous views of science was centered on the idea of environmental manipulation. In the earlier stage of analysis, the conception had developed that modern ideas must be used by intellectuals to analyze and then consciously change their society. This was the essence of the appeal of science to the *HCN* intellectuals which was given a definite form by Marxism-Leninism. It was felt that the theories of Marx and Lenin had delineated the structure of society and forecast the direction of future social development. This

---

[64] Ling Shuang, "Ma-k'o-ssu hsüeh-shuo ti p'i-p'ing," *HCN* (1), VI, No. 5 (May, 1919), 526.

[65] "Hsin ch'ing nien chih hsin hsüan-yen" (The New Manifesto of *New Youth*), *HCN* (2), I (June, 1923), 9.

[66] *Ibid.*, p. 12.

seemed to provide avowed Marxist Leninists with manipulative powers over society analogous to that which the scientists held over physical processes. This interpretation is apparent in Li Ta-chao's early exploratory article, "My Marxist Views," where the author takes issue with the orthodox Marxist theory of economic determinism and argues that throughout the course of history ideas have had an independent causal effect on society.[67] For Li, Marxism-Leninism was deterministic not so much because it presupposed unalterable and impersonal economic processes which shape social development, but because it gave enlightened men power to mold the destiny of their society in line with their own interests and values.

It can be argued that Li's interpretation was not a function of scientific thought, but an adaptation of Lenin's activist interpretation of the role of intellectuals in a society. After all, as ideology evolved in the final three years of *HCN*'s publication, Leninism exercised great influence over China's intellectuals. However, from 1919 to 1923 Leninist ideas did not noticeably shape the inchoate ideology of Chinese communism. One reason for this statement is that in his writings of this crucial period, including the article "My Marxist Views," Li Ta-chao did not quote from Lenin or make use of any explicitly Leninist formulations.[68] Similarly, in the first two years of heavy Marxist emphasis in the journal, during 1920 and 1921, the Marxian concept of socialism was pre-eminent, while virtually nothing was published on Lenin. Yet even here the conception of the creative and manipulative role of ideas is well expressed in Li Ta-chao's interpretation of socialism: "We must understand socialism's true meaning and use it to acquire an understanding of a new kind of life. All of our past history which we want to understand is something which we depended on our strength to create and was not something which was created for us by a noble sage. . . . Our future must also be like this."[69] In short, Marxian socialism, even apart from its Leninist development, was a revolutionary idea system capable of transforming China's economic and social life when employed by an intellectual elite.

From a purely political perspective, Marxism-Leninism strengthened the link established at an earlier stage between science and po-

---

[67] Li Ta-chao, "Wo ti ma-k'o-ssu-chu-i kuan" (Part 1), *HCN* (1), VI, No. 5 (May, 1919), 583–99.

[68] Meisner, *Li Ta-chao*, p. 139.

[69] Li Ta-chao, "Wei-wu shih-kuan tsai hsien-tai shih-hsüeh-shang ti chia-chih" (The Value of a Materialist Historical Viewpoint for the Study of Modern History), *HCN* (1), VIII, No. 4 (December, 1920), 516.

litical action, as discussed above. Science provided the *HCN* group with a sense of control over human affairs, which, in turn, reduced their ambivalence about involvement in immediate political conflicts. Marxism-Leninism, as the culmination of the scientific method, increased this sense of political efficacy. The new manifesto of 1923 is instructive on this point:

Hsin ch'ing nien's revolutionary characteristic does not exist because *Hsin ch'ing nien* is in itself especially revolutionary. . . . Rather, it is because modern-day science already possesses the material base for solving social problems. Therefore, we must produce a science of society, and then based on the objectivity of science, we will study, investigate, and learn the conditions under which revolution can be advanced. . . . Of even more importance, the proletariat cannot depend upon the old society's idea of the individual resigning himself to his destiny. They must carry out an intense struggle. Therefore, we must help them acquire a basic knowledge of the science of society.[70]

Two years later, the linkage between science and politics was described as an integral part of Lenin's appeal as a revolutionary. Ch'ü Ch'iu-pai commented, "As to Lenin's theory of proletarian revolution . . . the element we should emphasize most is [its ability] to determine a plan for promoting revolution on the basis of the objective, natural conditions of a society's productive capacity." [71] As in the earlier period of ideological formation, a basic transformation of thought was regarded as the prerequisite of revolution rather than its consequence. If the new Marxist-Leninist science of society could be transmitted to the proletariat, as proposed in the new manifesto, then without question revolution would occur.

The emphasis placed upon cultural themes served as another important link between the non-Marxist and Marxist phases of ideological development. While *HCN*'s early preoccupation with cultural refinement—as expressed in the publication of plays, literature, and poetry—diminished once the magazine had committed itself to Marxism-Leninism, cultural perspectives nevertheless continued to structure political ideas and identified major targets for political action. From 1920 to 1921, during the first two years of heavy Marxist influence in *HCN* that comprised the stage of theory building, cultural themes were muted. Most articles dealt with Marxism as a philosophy of socialism and history. Internalization of the theory, however, linked Marxist-Leninist concepts with the intellectuals' world view, reinforc-

---

[70] "Hsin ch'ing nien chih hsin hsüan-yen," p. 9.

[71] Ch'ü Ch'iu-pai, "Lieh-ning-chu-i kai-lun" (A Summary of Leninism), *HCN* (3), I (April, 1925), 40.

ing the linkage between cultural transformation and revolutionary change. Marxism-Leninism no longer was conceived of simply as a philosophy of economics and history, but as a major part of the intellectuals' conceptual framework for the analysis of society. The 1923 manifesto, for example, takes a strong stand against the old culture, using a Marxist-Leninist perspective: "Regarding the inevitable collapse [of traditional society], *Hsin ch'ing nien* will become the representative of revolutionary thought, and in regard to the conservative culture which has repeatedly oppressed the Chinese laboring people, we will initiate the first general attack." [72]

Although in its European form Marxism-Leninism had singled out the bourgeoisie as the prime target for class warfare, certain Chinese interpretations of the doctrine stressed that the vestiges of the old culture took precedence over capitalism as the chief impediments to revolution. Thus, *HCN* writers began to attack in Marxist-Leninist terms the same cultural problems they had been criticizing for years:

Hsin ch'ing nien has already become the motive force of proletarian class thought. Not only have we taken up a violent struggle against the thought of clan society, we have at the same time attacked bourgeois thought. The truth is, if we want to liberate Chinese society, we must first eliminate all kinds of obstacles—the dictatorship of clan society, the opposition to science, and the belief in superstition, which are obstacles to revolution. Moreover, the commercialism of the capitalists . . . is also a major obstacle to revolution. [73]

Cultural themes not only influenced the nature of political ideas, but, in some respects, pre-empted them as separate subject matter even after the adoption of Marxism-Leninism. A prime example of this was the "science versus metaphysics" debate on the proper mode of thought for Chinese society, which dominated the Chinese intellectual scene in 1923 and in which Ch'en Tu-hsiu and *HCN* played a leading role. [74] Ch'en, Hu Shih, and Ting Wen-chiang of the proscience group took issue with Carsun Chang and others of the metaphysics school in order to discredit the latter intellectually and steer China toward the development of a truly modern culture.

Although there were political undertones to this debate, the issues under discussion—religion, a philosophy of life, the nature of knowledge, and so on—were predominantly cultural. In fact, many of the issues were defined in the cultural terms of a "spiritual" Eastern civili-

---

[72] "Hsin ch'ing nien chih hsin hsüan-yen," p. 9.
[73] *Ibid.*, p. 10.
[74] See " 'Science' versus 'Metaphysics' in the Debate of 1923," in Kwok, *Scientism in Chinese Thought*, pp. 135–60.

zation versus "materialistic" Western social values.[75] Marxism-Leninism, as well as the many immediate political issues which faced China, was hardly touched upon in these arguments. Hence, despite the fact that Ch'en Tu-hsiu and Hu Shih had split two years earlier over the political question of "Problems versus Isms," in this debate the two men found themselves on the same side. The need to infuse Chinese society with a modern, scientific mode of thought was more important to Ch'en and Hu than their political differences. The belief which had emerged in the earlier stages of ideological development that transformation of thought and culture constituted the essence of China's revolution thus remained salient even two years after the adoption of Marxism-Leninism.

The continuity in the cultural and scientific themes of the non-Marxist and Marxist-Leninist stages must not obscure, however, the important changes in ideological development generated by Marxism-Leninism. Marxism-Leninism took general ideas developed in the stage of politicization and placed them in a more explicit political framework, facilitating their implementation. It increased the saliency of the practical political concepts of mass mobilization, propaganda work, power politics, and organization, and related these to the role played by social classes, political elites, and international politics in the process of revolution. As was mentioned earlier, Marxism-Leninism provided Chinese revolutionaries with a new target for political action (the Chinese working class), with a major theoretical justification for a socialist revolution in China (Lenin's theory of imperialism), and with a revolutionary hero to serve as a model of behavior (Lenin). Together, these concepts brought about a significant transformation in the ideology promulgated by *HCN*.

Prior to the introduction of Marxism-Leninism, political action in China was usually structured about one man and his immediate entourage or around a small, oligarchical body of men, thereby perpetuating an elitist conception of politics. This orientation seems to have been shared by *HCN* writers. The popular outbursts of the May Fourth Movement, however, sensitized many intellectuals to the possibilities of mass political action. Further reinforced by the image of popular participation in the October Revolution, Marxism-Leninism provided these intellectuals with a new class focus for such political action—the Chinese proletariat.

Perception of the working class as a new revolutionary force, as

[75] *Ibid.*

stressed by Marxism-Leninism, had an immediate effect on the Communist Party's strategy and tactics. After the formation of the CCP in 1921, the Party became engaged in a flurry of organizational and propaganda activities aimed at establishing a strong working class movement under Communist control. The Chinese Labor Organization Secretariat was established by the Communist Party for the purpose of stirring up labor unrest and encouraging the formation of trade unions.[76] Beyond its organizational tasks, the secretariat published *Lao-tung chou-k'an* (Labor Weekly), the first nonintellectual journal aimed specifically at mobilizing the working class. In addition, it appears that Marxism-Leninism made the eager labor cadre aware of the political and economic advantages of unions organized on industrial lines, in contrast to China's traditional *pang,* or mutual aid associations.[77] In this manner, the acceptance of Marxism-Leninism as a political doctrine had an immediate structural influence on the building of the Chinese Communist Party and its affiliated organizations such as the Socialist Youth League and Labor Organization Secretariat.

It is apparent that the editors of *HCN* were strongly influenced by the Marxist emphasis on the proletariat as the primary social force for transforming "feudal" China: "Ever since the creation of *Hsin ch'ing nien,* we have fought against clan society and the warlord system. Our revolutionary commitment has always been unmistakably clear. . . . Now in regard to the concept of revolution we have acquired a genuine understanding. . . . We know that it is the working class which is revolutionary." [78] In order to win over the intellectuals to the idea of a workers' revolution, *HCN* initiated a campaign to educate its largely academic readership in the revolutionary potential of the proletariat. Beginning in 1920, a plethora of articles appeared on the working class movement in China and Europe. Initially, the content of these articles was largely descriptive of the economic conditions oppressing the workers and the events surrounding their participation in strikes and demonstrations. Once the realities of class struggle in China were brought home to the writers by the February Seventh and May Thirtieth incidents (1923 and 1925, respectively), their articles began explicitly to link the working class movement to the CCP's policies, tactics, and leadership.

---

[76] Jean Chesneaux, *The Chinese Labor Movement, 1919–1927* (Stanford, Calif.: Stanford University Press, 1968), p. 178.

[77] *Ibid.*

[78] "Hsin ch'ing nien chih hsin hsüan-yen," p. 10.

In contrast to early articles on the labor movement, in which the role of the CCP was hardly mentioned, by the latter part of 1925 *HCN* writers were consciously integrating the CCP's policies into their over-all analyses of class struggle: "The Chinese Communist Party must strengthen itself organizationally and plant a foundation among the masses. All educated Party personnel must be able to serve as leaders of the proletariat. . . . We must agitate the National Government and the Assembly." [79] Similar ideas, expressed in such articles as "The Question of Armed Conflict in the Chinese Revolution," "A Concise History of the Labor Movement before and after 'February 7,' " and "What We Can Learn from the Twenty-seven Years of National Revolution," indicate that a rudimentary linkage between theory and practice had been made.[80] What began as a romanticized treatment of the Chinese proletariat's revolutionary potential was transformed by these political events into a more realistic conception of the relationship between ideas, organization, and political action. The selection of an entire social class as a revolutionary base, in combination with the political events of the mid-1920's, forced the intellectuals to transform their Marxist-Leninist ideology from an internalized component of a personal world view to an incipient operational code for building a mass-based movement.

The second major shift in the formation of ideology following the adoption of Marxism-Leninism derived from Lenin's theory of imperialism. This theory dominated the pages of *HCN* from 1921 to 1926. Of the approximately 175 articles published in the magazine during this period, 45 per cent concerned the theory of imperialism in one form or another. Lenin's thesis was discussed in purely theoretical terms as a contribution to general Marxist theory and was seen as the most appealing framework for analysis of world politics. The May Fourth demonstrations of 1919 had made the *HCN* intellectuals aware of the realities of international politics and their effects on China. Lenin's theoretical statement served to crystallize these strands of thought and place them in an overall perspective consistent with the world view of the intellectuals. This made the confusion of world

79 Liu Jen-ching, "Shih-chieh ko-ming yü shih-chieh ching-chi" (World Revolution and the World Economy), *HCN* (3), V (July, 1926), 648.
80 Ch'ü Ch'iu-pai, "Chung-kuo ko-ming chung chih wu-chuang tou-cheng wen-t'i," *HCN* (3), IV (April, 1926), 428–38; Chang T'e-li, " 'Erh-ch'i' ch'ien hou kung-hui yün-tung lüeh-shih," *HCN* (3), II (June, 1925), 178–96; Ch'en Tu-hsiu, "Erh-shih ch'i nien i-lai kuo-min yün-tung chung-so ti chiao-hsün," *HCN* (2), IV (December, 1924), 469–76.

events more understandable and, most importantly, linked China's national struggle with the world revolution: "Lenin considers the anti-imperialist movement of the Eastern peoples to be one of the most important conditions for the victory of all laboring peoples." [81]

HCN articles made it clear that the Chinese Communist conception of revolution was now inextricably bound up with their view of world revolution. Under the influence of Ch'en Tu-hsiu's cosmopolitan search for a path to China's modernization, the magazine began to publish more articles on the Communist International than on the internal political situation in China. Many of these articles implied that the success of the Chinese revolution was more a function of world politics than of the domestic activities of the CCP.

Lenin's theory of imperialism undoubtedly contributed to the development of CCP ideology. Not only was it internalized as a major element in the revolutionaries' world view, but its very popularity among Chinese intellectuals helped to provide the ideational cement necessary to hold the Party and movement together as an organization committed to political action. The preoccupation with the theory of imperialism, however, inhibited the full-scale development of the stage of movement building. Ch'ü Ch'iu-pai warned against this preoccupation when he stated, "We should recognize that our country's problem is a Chinese problem and not an international problem. That it is a problem which should be solved by our Chinese people, and not a problem in which we should join with the one class of the whole world to smash another class, must be understood. . . ." [82]

The strong emphasis on international politics continued, however, leading *HCN* to neglect the organizational and strategic problems of domestic revolutionary action. In this sense, there developed a serious "contradiction" between the requisites of political power and the internationalist doctrines of Leninism. This effect is well illustrated by the magazine's treatment of Lenin, in which the Soviet revolutionary's ideas on party and organization were almost totally overlooked in favor of his writings on internationalism. A year after his death, in April, 1925, Lenin was eulogized in a memorial edition of *HCN*. The emphasis in the majority of articles was on Lenin's theory of imperi-

---

81 Wei Ch'in, "Lieh-ning, chih-min-ti min-tsu yü ti-kuo chu-i" (Lenin, Colonial Peoples, and Imperialism), *HCN* (3), I (April, 1925), 97–102.

82 Ch'ü Ch'iu-pai, "Pei-ching t'u-sha yü kuo-min ko-ming chih ch'ien-t'u" (The Peking Massacre and the Future of the National Revolution), *HCN* (3), IV (March, 1926), 409–22.

alism. In the first essay almost no concern was shown for Leninism as an inspiration and guide to organization building.[83] In the following article, the author listed thirteen qualities that Chinese revolutionaries should learn from Lenin. The role of the Party was placed tenth in the list and given little elaboration in the final sections of the article.[84] In the same edition, Ch'ü Ch'iu-pai summed up his perception of Lenin in the following way:

Leninism naturally is Marxism. However, after Marxism reached Lenin, he made it more understandable, completed it, and enlarged it. Of the points which Lenin cleared up, completed, and enlarged, the most important were the two ideas of the proletarian dictatorship coming between the capitalist system and the communist system, and the anti-imperialist, international people's movement. The latter especially has a relationship to China's current people's revolution. . . .[85]

To be sure, Lenin's reputation as the architect of the Soviet Communist Party did have a definite impact on China's intellectuals. But the image of Lenin projected in *HCN* was not that of an organizational specialist and supreme disciplinarian, but of a political genius and revolutionary hero who used intellect and courage to manipulate political struggles to his advantage. This muting of the organizational aspect of Lenin's theories undoubtedly accounts for the limited shift from internalization to movement building in the general process of ideological formation as revealed in the pages of *HCN*.

To what extent this minimal concern with organizational and tactical matters reflects the state of the entire Chinese Communist movement in this period cannot be stated on the basis of this analysis alone. It seems evident, however, that other less intellectual Party publications such as P'eng P'ai's peasant journal *Ch'ih hsin chou-pao* (Red Heart Weekly), the official CCP organ *Hsiang-tao chou-pao* (The Guide Weekly), and *Lao-tung chou-k'an* began to show a greater concern for these matters in the mid-1920's. Thus, there developed in the movement a tendency for certain groups, organized around different publications, to approach Marxism-Leninism from very different perspectives. Most of the contributors to *HCN* were intellectuals with an academic background. Men who were to become organizational specialists, such as P'eng P'ai, Chang Kuo-t'ao, Mao Tse-tung, and Liu

83 "Chung-kuo kung-ch'an-tang ti ssu-t'su ta-hui tui-yü Lieh-ning shih-shih i-chou chi-nien hsüan-yen" (The Chinese Communist Party's Commemorative Resolution of the Fourth Party Congress regarding the First Anniversary of Lenin's Death), *HCN* (3), I (April, 1925), 7–8.

84 "Lieh-ning shih-shih ti ti-i chou-nien" (The First Anniversary of Lenin's Death), *ibid.*, p. 11.

85 Ch'ü Ch'iu-pai, "Lieh-ning-chu-i kai-lun," p. 39.

Shao-ch'i, contributed next to nothing to its pages. It might even be said that the magazines and newspapers which grew with the Chinese Communist Party functioned in part as focal centers for differing views on the revolutionary process, thus contributing to incipient factionalism.

To the extent that the weak interest in problems of organization and mass mobilization shown by *HCN* writers was indicative of the orientation of early Party leaders, we also gain some sense of the ideological roots of the political failures of the mid and late 1920's. The Nanchang Uprising, Autumn Harvest Uprising, and Canton Soviet were all marked by demonstrated organizational chaos, inept leadership, and tactical blunders. The fact that the journal did not prepare its readers for such operations by investigating problems of intraorganizational communication, command relationships, and Party leadership of mass political action may have contributed to these failures. Only through a comparative study of early Communist Party communication media, however, can we acquire a more detailed understanding of these issues.

CONCLUSION

This study of *Hsin ch'ing nien* develops two interpretive themes which go beyond a mere content categorization of one journal in a specific historical period. The first is a case study of the intellectual process involved in the formation of an ideology (and, parenthetically, some perspective on the difficulty with which academic intellectuals make the shift to practical politics). Second, the findings of this study give some sense of political concepts developed in the May Fourth era which have shaped the perceptions and policies of the Chinese Communist elite down to the present day.

The thrust of our model illustrated in Table 2 is that the formation of ideology for the *HCN* group involved a sequential development of certain intellectual trends—cultural search, analysis, and politicization —which culminated in the adoption, reinterpretation, and advocacy of Marxism-Leninism. In *HCN*'s pre-Marxist stages, intellectual themes were an amalgamation of certain concepts handed down from Chinese tradition, ostentatious rejection of some other traditional concepts, and selective adoption of new ideas imported from the West. Ch'en Tu-hsiu, Li Ta-chao, Hu Shih, and other prominent contributors to the journal were among modern China's most brilliant intellects, combining a profound knowledge of their own cultural tradition with a hunger for new ideas that would point the way to their country's rejuvenation. Although they explicitly rejected Chinese tradition as being unsuited to the problems of their time, they were well within the bounds of classical Chinese thought when they defined their political goals largely in cultural terms, and accepted the leading role of intellectuals in political affairs.

On the other hand, these men revered "Western science" as a tool for destroying China's backwardness and overcoming its vulnerable international position. Intertwined with the intellectuals' growing politicization following the May Fourth demonstrations, science in its Marxist variant of "scientific socialism" gave the leaders of the New Culture Movement a conceptual approach to understanding processes of social change and a theoretical basis for justifying revolutionary goals. In a similar manner, Western concepts of the nation and political participation convinced many radicals that they should reject the tradition of personalized and elitist bureaucratic politics and mobilize for social change by building a political movement on the basis of a revolutionary program and popular support.

Marxism-Leninism came to be accepted by some members of the May Fourth generation as an appealing theoretical framework because it crystallized many of the above themes. The logic of its ideas seemed to satisfy their desire to understand and manipulate social and political reality. Marxist-Leninist concepts served as new forms of political communication for expressing basically the same issues and modes of social action which had appeared in the pre-Marxist period of *HCN*.

This continuity of basic themes left most intellectuals tied to the world of ideas rather than the hard reality of political struggle. In the years 1921 through 1926, when *HCN* was made an organ of the newly formed Chinese Communist Party, the ideology was more of a philosophy than an operational code for political action. To be sure, the adoption of Marxism-Leninism marked the first attempt by these intellectuals to find new social forces (that is, the working class) outside their own narrow circle to help them promote revolution. Yet in terms of developing the organization and tactical mechanisms for achieving their general objective of a strong and modern China, *HCN* writers remained hampered by their intellectual backgrounds. The best available source of ideas on revolutionary political action—Leninism—was received by the *HCN* group in theoretical rather than action-oriented terms. Writers in the journal focused on Lenin's theory of imperialism as an explanation of China's contemporary political difficulties, while ignoring the Russian revolutionary's writings on organization-building and political struggle.

In all, the formation of ideology as revealed in the pages of *HCN* is more characterized by the reinterpretation of existing intellectual themes than by a sharp breakthrough to new perceptions. In this initial period of commitment to Marxism-Leninism as an approach to social revolution, ideology served as a new source of identity for intellectuals alienated from their society's traditions. The more practical dimensions of ideological growth were to be confronted as the Communist movement began to cope with the hard realities of political action.

The second major perspective that emerges from this study is the identification of certain ideological themes that have shaped Chinese Communist action down to the present day. The conception developed by *HCN* writers of the need to undermine the cultural constraints hindering social and political change emerges as a basic tenet of the ideology of the political elite that formed out of the New Culture Movement, including Mao Tse-tung. As with Ch'en Tu-hsiu and his *HCN* colleagues, Mao has never perceived state power in the hands of Communist revolutionaries as the ultimate goal of the political struggle.[86] He has consistently tried to break the grip of China's traditional culture over his contemporaries and to institutionalize a new style of political participation for the Chinese people.

Beginning with his 1917 *HCN* article, "A Study of Physical Education," Mao emphasized the cultural goals of China's revolution. In his famous "Talks at the Yenan Forum on Literature and Art" (1942), he stressed the necessity of radically altering the uses of language, literature, and art in order to reduce "the domain of China's feudal culture and of the comprador culture which serves imperialist aggression." [87] Consistent with views developed by other *HCN* writers, Mao has considered the transformation of thought to be an integral component of revolutionary change: "To put things in order organizationally requires our first doing so ideologically, [requires] our launching a struggle of proletarian ideology against nonproletarian

[86] Mao told Edgar Snow in 1936 that "I began to read this magazine [*HCN*] while I was a student in the normal college and admired the articles of Hu Shih and Ch'en Tu-hsiu very much." Later in the same interview, Mao commented, "When I was at Peking University, . . . he [Ch'en Tu-hsiu] influenced me perhaps more than any one else." See Edgar Snow, *Red Star over China* (New York: Grove Press, 1961), pp. 147, 154.

[87] Mao Tse-tung, "Talks at the Yenan Forum on Literature and Art," in *Selected Works of Mao Tse-tung* (Peking: Foreign Languages Press, 1961–65), III, 69.

ideology." [88] And just as with the *HCN* group, Mao has stressed dissemination of scientific ideas as an important aspect of "ideological remolding." In 1942 he placed science in the same category as the nation, the masses, and the Communist Party as a concept fundamental to the Chinese revolution.[89] Mao's sayings contain a strong strain of popularized scientific method expressed for mass consumption. The contemporary Maoist models of the Tachai production brigade and the Tach'ing oil field represent the Chairman's efforts to institutionalize scientific thought and method at a practical level.

Where Mao seems to part company with many of those who emerged as leaders of the Chinese Communist movement is in his commitment to practical political action and in his enduring sensitivity to the problem of the resurgence of traditional cultural patterns. While Ch'en Tu-hsiu, through *HCN,* played a key role in disseminating the idea of a cultural revolution as the goal of the May Fourth generation, he—even in his role as the first leader of the Chinese Communist Party—was never able to make the transition to practical political struggles. The contemporary Maoist stress on the unity of theory and practice derives from Mao's early frustrations at seeing intellectuals debate solutions to China's problems without involving themselves in the political activities required to attain them. Mao came to ridicule Ch'en Tu-hsiu after his fall from Party leadership in 1927 for his "panic" at the thought of an armed revolutionary struggle by China's workers and peasants.[90]

The depth of Mao's commitment to the goal of a cultural revolution as the basis of China's modernization was to be revealed only at the end of his career. Apparently convinced that the institutionalization of the Chinese Communist Party in the decades after the attainment of state power was leading to a resurgence of traditional political and social practices, Mao launched the Great Proletarian Cultural Revolution to repudiate manifestations of the "Four Olds" of China's traditional culture. At the end of his career Mao thus seemed to return to the student struggles of his youth in an effort to keep the Chinese revolution on the course that *Hsin ch'ing nien* had plotted in the May Fourth era.

[88] *Ibid.,* p. 72.
[89] *Ibid.,* p. 89.
[90] Snow, *Red Star over China,* p. 165.

◈◈◈ ◈◈◈◈◈◈◈◈◈◈◈◈◈◈◈◈◈◈◈◈◈◈◈◈◈◈◈◈

SUZANNE PEPPER

Socialism, Democracy, and Chinese Communism: A Problem of Choice for the Intelligentsia, 1945-49

Ideology, it is said, is a pattern of ideas that provides for its adherents both a definition of the self and a description of the current social environment, including its background and the way it is likely or ought to develop in the future.[1] Ideology is also a system of beliefs about the economic, political, and social arrangements of a society which can serve to transform ideas into levers for social action.[2] An ideology may help to bind the community together and to establish the identity of the individual within it.[3] Among the most insightful commentaries on the subject is one by Clifford Geertz, who suggests that ideologies are schematic images or symbols of social order which function to make politics possible by providing the authoritative concepts that make it meaningful. Ideologies are thus sources of information and points of reference for the organization of social and psychological processes on the part of individuals and groups within a given society. More specifically, Geertz suggests that these processes include the motivation, perseverance, and moral strength necessary for the effective conduct of public affairs. If such qualities and others like them do not exist by force of habit or tradition, then if they are to

[1] Mary Matossian, "Ideologies of Delayed Industrialization," reprinted in Jason L. Finkle and Richard W. Gable (eds.), *Political Development and Social Change* (New York: John Wiley & Sons, 1966), p. 174.

[2] Daniel Bell, *The End of Ideology: On the Exhaustion of Political Ideas in the Fifties* (rev. ed.; New York: The Free Press, 1960), p. 400.

[3] David E. Apter, *The Politics of Modernization* (Chicago: University of Chicago Press, 1965), p. 328.

exist at all, they must be developed on the basis of some more self-conscious vision of public purpose. The weaker or the more unsatisfactory are the existing guides for social behavior, the greater is the potential scope for explicit ideological formulations which can define or redefine the social environment and indicate a meaningful direction for future development.[4]

Despite the beneficial functions that ideology may perform, however, adherence to any particular ideology is not without cost.[5] This is particularly true if the ideology has not been uniformly accepted as a common source of values and guide for social conduct by all groups within a given society. The costs are felt, for example, in the strains that may develop within a political party or movement which may have to choose between maintaining its ideological purity on the one hand and mobilizing enough support from various sectors of the population to win political power on the other. In such a situation, the political leader might feel obliged to alienate certain groups for which he has no ideological affinity, such as the bourgeoisie or the intelligentsia, even though they might then become a considerable obstacle to his political ambitions. Or he might choose to downplay or modify, even if only temporarily, the content of his ideology and thus risk being labeled an opportunist by members of his own party or being coopted by the groups whose support he needs.

Conversely, adherence to a particular ideology may result in considerable cost, both psychological and otherwise, for the group whose beliefs about the social environment do not happen to coincide with those of the society's dominant elites. It is apparent that such strains were felt both by political leaders and by at least one social group in China during the late 1940's when the country was in the midst of an all-out civil war. What follows here is an effort to examine primarily how these strains developed for one particular group of people, the urban intellectuals, and how they reacted to the problems created by adherence to a set of political commitments that did not happen to coincide with those of either of the society's two dominant political elites. A secondary theme has to do with the pressures that developed for the

4 Clifford Geertz, "Ideology as a Cultural System," in David E. Apter (ed.), *Ideology and Discontent* (New York: Free Press, 1964), pp. 63–64. On the functions of ideology in China specifically, see Richard H. Solomon, "From Commitment to Cant: The Evolving Functions of Ideology in the Revolutionary Process," this volume.

5 This problem is discussed briefly in Warren E. Ilchman and Norman Thomas Uphoff, *The Political Economy of Change* (Berkeley and Los Angeles: University of California Press, 1969), pp. 240–41.

Chinese Communists as they acted to win over these same urban intellectuals.[6]

The Ideological Commitments of the Urban Intelligentsia

In his farewell statement issued as he was about to return home after the failure of the United States mediation effort between the Nationalist government and the Communists, General George Marshall suggested that the situation in China might be saved if only the liberals could somehow gain power within the government. However well-meaning, the suggestion was politically unsound, for the liberal community was made up primarily of intellectuals. Being intellectuals first and politicians at best only second, they lacked the kinds of resources necessary to survive in the political environment of Kuomintang (KMT) China where, as one writer put it, the most essential forms of political capital were money and soldiers.[7] Yet there is little doubt that liberalism was the dominant political current among intellectuals and that these intellectuals were among the most highly politicized elements within the KMT-controlled areas. Their liberal commitments thus inspired a critique of the Nationalist government as devastating as anything the Communists themselves were able to offer.

It has been suggested that a Chinese tradition of humanism, Western missionary education, and the large proportion of teachers and professors who had received advanced training abroad, particularly in the United States and western Europe, all contributed to the Chinese intelligentsia's acceptance of what were essentially Western concepts of political liberalism.[8] Whatever factors may have been responsible, by the late 1940's the growth of a modern liberal climate was quite firmly established among the intelligentsia, if not among political leaders.

[6] In Chinese Communist usage during this period, an intellectual was anyone who was receiving or had received anything above and including a middle-school education or the equivalent. Thus, where Communist sources and views about intellectuals are cited, this is the definition that must be applied. In non-Communist sources, however, the term tended to have a somewhat narrower meaning. Throughout most of this study, therefore, the term "intellectual" refers more specifically to persons such as writers, journalists, college professors, and teachers who were directly contributing to the intellectual life of the nation.

[7] *Kuan-ch'a* special correspondent (Nanking), "Ho-ch'u shih kuei ch'eng?" (Where Will the Journey End?), *Kuan-ch'a* (The Observer) (Shanghai), IV, No. 20 (July 17, 1948), 12.

[8] John K. Fairbank, *The United States and China* (Cambridge, Mass.: Harvard University Press, 1959), pp. 196–200.

This was the intellectual milieu in which the student movement against the Civil War developed on a scale almost unprecedented in modern China, where students had created a tradition of political activism.[9] But the students took to the streets in spontaneous bursts of opposition to the policies of the KMT government and left to their elders the task of spelling out the intellectual arguments in finer detail. This the older generation did in a profusion of editorials and political essays which in the persistence and intensity of the criticism they contained were clearly the middle-aged equivalent of the students' activism. The Civil War and the strains it created seemed to inspire a degree of intellectual ferment that had not existed since at least the start of the Sino-Japanese War.

During the late 1940's, intellectuals publicized their views in a number of newspapers and periodicals which enjoyed varying degrees of popularity as well as attention from the KMT authorities and the secret police. Despite the harassment, however, the two most widely read liberal publications of the Civil War years survived more or less unscathed until the end of 1948. These were the *Ta kung pao* (Impartial Daily), a newspaper with editions in Shanghai, Tientsin, and Chungking (the Hong Kong edition was not revived until 1948); and *Kuan-ch'a* (The Observer), a weekly journal published in Shanghai. It was popularly assumed that the *Ta kung pao* enjoyed political immunity not only because of its prestigious position as one of the nation's leading newspapers but also because of its close association with the Political Study Clique of the KMT. The secret of *Kuan-ch'a*'s success, on the other hand, remained something of a mystery. Despite periodic attacks from both the right and the left, *Kuan-ch'a* generally succeeded in maintaining its credibility as an independent journal of liberal political commentary beholden to no political group. It was also reputed to be the most popular journal of its kind in the late 1940's. For these reasons, and because it was primarily a journal of political opinion with the majority of its articles contributed by college professors, *Kuan-ch'a* has been used here as the basic source of information on the political liberalism of the intelligentsia during the Civil War years.[10]

[9] See Suzanne Pepper, "The Student Movement and the Chinese Civil War," CQ, No. 48 (October-December, 1971), pp. 698–735.

[10] As will become apparent, other sources have also been used. A second major source was the journal *Shih-tai p'i-p'ing* (Modern Critique) published by Chou Ching-wen in Hong Kong. Unlike *Kuan-ch'a*, this journal contained articles and statements by Communist and Democratic League spokesmen. But despite Mr. Chou's reputed leftist sympathies at this time and the fact that the journal was published in the British Col-

The founder and editor-in-chief of *Kuan-ch'a* was Ch'u An-p'ing, a professor at Futan University in Shanghai. The journal first appeared on September 1, 1946, and was published weekly thereafter until December 24, 1948, when it was banned by the central government on charges of aiding and abetting the Communists. During the two years and four months of its existence, the journal's popularity grew steadily. By the end of 1948 its circulation had reached 60,000. It circulated nationwide, the four cities of Peiping, Tientsin, Nanking, and Shanghai accounting for only about 20 per cent of its subscriptions. According to its own statistics, its readership was divided about evenly among three groups: the academic community, students as well as teachers; government employees, including middle- and lower-level civil servants and military officers; and industrial, business, and banking circles. Commenting on the success of his journal, Professor Ch'u related proudly how the great majority of those taking the entrance examinations for Ch'inghua, Nankai, and Peking universities in the summer of 1948 had discussed *Kuan-ch'a* in response to a civics question asking for a critique of a newspaper or journal that they read regularly.[11] And when it was banned some months later, one of the few commentators still left to write the journal's obituary suggested that the more than 100,000 faithful readers of *Kuan-ch'a* would now have even greater conviction that the KMT regime had no future before it. The commentator declared, "The Age of Professor Ch'u An-p'ing cannot be allowed to exist any longer, and the periodical may be considered to have fulfilled its mission. . . . The present moment appears to be the last five minute period in the existing order of things, and so more talking seems unnecessary." [12]

But in September, 1946, talking seemed far from unnecessary. Issue number one of *Kuan-ch'a* contained a declaration of purpose in which the editor explained the orientation of the new journal and why he had undertaken the task of publishing it. Noting the growing sense of public demoralization, he recalled how the nation had been able to unite against a foreign aggressor not too many years before. But today, he wrote, people seem to be more concerned with their own interests than with the welfare of the nation as a whole. The purpose

---

ony, beyond the reach of the KMT police, *Shih-tai p'i-p'ing* (hereafter *STPP*) did not differ markedly in the tone of its editorials and much of its political commentary from *Kuan-ch'a*.

11 Ch'u An-p'ing, "Ch'ih chung, k'u tou, chin hsin" (Heavy Burdens, Bitter Struggle, Determined Effort), *Kuan-ch'a* (Shanghai), IV, No. 23–24 (August 7, 1948), 4.

12 *Chien hsien jih-pao* (Shanghai), December 28, 1948, translated in U.S. Consulate-General (Shanghai), *Chinese Press Review*, December 31, 1948.

of his enterprise, therefore, was to arouse the people "in order to save the nation from disaster." [13]

Inherent in all the liberal writings of this period, and in the student demonstrations as well, was the belief (or at least the hope) that if only the arguments were compelling enough, the public would become sufficiently aroused and the government would somehow be obliged to respond to popular demands for peace, economic reconstruction, and social reforms. This belief in the efficacy of popular opinion seems to have been maintained until about the middle of 1948, by which time it was becoming fairly obvious that the government was not going to respond and indeed that it would soon not even be in a position to do so. Prior to that time, however, the students sought actively to mobilize public opinion through their parades, petitions, and various propaganda activities, while the older generation of intellectuals emphasized "public reflection and serious discussion." Toward this end, *Kuan-ch'a* was dedicated to the presentation of political opinions and arguments containing positive suggestions for improvement as well as critical evaluations of the government, the KMT, and the opposition parties. These opinions and arguments were based on the liberal view of politics and society, which held that the interests of the nation and of its people would best be served through the realization of democracy, freedom, progress, and rationality in political and economic life.

The ideals and expectations which this view encompassed were clearly drawn. Of democracy, the editor wrote:

We cannot agree that any group which represents the interest of a minority should dictate national affairs. . . . We cannot agree that all of the government's measures should serve only the power and interests of a minority. . . . The government's actions must be in accordance with the decisions of the people and in all that it does the government must be responsible to the people. Democratic government exists for the welfare of the people: to guarantee their freedom and promote their happiness. . . .

[13] Although his meaning is not entirely clear, it is unlikely that by "disaster" Ch'u was referring here to a Communist victory. For one thing, he never wrote of the Communists in that vein and, for another, few people at this time seemed seriously to believe that the Communists could actually defeat the forces of the Nationalist government. The real disaster that everyone feared in mid-1946 was the Civil War itself. The mediation effort of General Marshall was still in progress, but it was becoming increasingly apparent that a peace settlement between the Communists and the government was not going to materialize. At this time, and for at least a year and a half thereafter, writers and journalists in nonofficial circles within the KMT-controlled areas seemed to be almost unanimous in their evaluation of the Civil War as a costly and hopeless venture which was likely to drag on indefinitely since neither side had sufficient strength to defeat the other.

Of freedom:

We demand freedom, demand the various basic human rights. Freedom is not license, freedom must be law-abiding. But the law must first guarantee the freedoms of the people and must make everyone equal before the law. . . .

Of progress:

We demand democratic politics and industrialization, but for democratic politics and industrialization to succeed, everyone must first have a scientific spirit and a modern mind. We demand full modernization in politics, economics, society, education, and military affairs. . . . For only with modernization can we seek greater and faster progress and only then can we advance on equal terms with the various nations of the world and exist together with them. . . .

And of rationality:

Without rationality society cannot be secure and culture cannot progress. Today in China, everywhere there is a reliance on force to resolve disorder, even young people presently receiving an education are repeatedly using force. . . . In the past ten years or so education in China has failed completely in this area. We demand that government and the various sectors of society pay full attention to this point. Only with the development of rationality will society begin to be able to differentiate between right and wrong and begin to have peace and public morality. . . .[14]

THE LIBERAL CRITIQUE OF THE NATIONAL GOVERNMENT

These ideals were given most forceful expression in the liberal critique of the Nationalist government. This criticism by writers and journalists had begun to gather momentum almost immediately after the Japanese surrender and was therefore already well developed by the time *Kuan-ch'a* made its appearance upon the literary scene. As a strategy of attack, the liberals began by accusing the KMT of having betrayed the political mandate that in principle legitimated its right to govern. It was not that liberal intellectuals subscribed to Sun Yat-sen's Three People's Principles as an act of political faith, or even that they had any particular respect for Sun's program as a guide for the conduct of modern government. But as it happened, the three principles of "Nationalism," "Democracy," and the "People's Livelihood," while meaning different things to different people, nevertheless summed up in a general way the three most basic political concerns of the intellectual community. By officially adopting as its political creed Sun's program, including the concept of tutelage as a preparatory stage

[14] Editorial, "Wo-men te chih-ch'ü ho t'ai-tu" (Our Purpose and Attitude), *Kuan-ch'a* (Shanghai), I, No. 1 (September 1, 1946), 3–4.

leading to constitutional government, the KMT clearly intended to preserve for itself the mantle of Sun's prestige and authority as the founder of modern China. But in so doing, the KMT of Chiang Kai-shek had pledged itself to the implementation of a program which it was in practice either unwilling or unable to pursue. The party's nationalist credentials and the fund of prestige derived therefrom during the Sino-Japanese War were all but obscured in the postwar period by the KMT's inability to fulfill in any meaningful sense popular aspirations for peace, economic reconstruction, and some form of responsive government.

The liberal indictment of the KMT therefore contained two major charges. One had to do with the form and the other with the output of KMT rule.

Form. The belief that government should exist not only for the people but of and by them as well was reiterated time and again. The only possible justification for twenty years of KMT tutelage was, as Sun Yat-sen had indicated, to prepare the way for a constitutional form of government. The consensus was that the KMT had failed utterly in this task. Few writers could pass up a chance to score the KMT for its failure to live up to the democratic principles it ostensibly espoused. Ch'u An-p'ing treated his readers to some cynical comments in this regard on the occasion of a peddlers' riot involving several thousand people which occurred in Shanghai on November 30 and December 1, 1946:

Big shops were attacked as were dance halls and movie theaters and automobiles passing on the street. All of these brought forth the hatred of the poor for the rich. The unjust conditions between rich and poor are beginning to be understood by the poor and they are expressing their will, which shows the progress of Chinese society. We have felt that there has been little achievement to speak of during the past twenty years of KMT tutelage, but now the people are daring to protest and to ask openly, "Why don't you give us food?" The KMT authorities should be proud because the objective of tutelage is to raise the people's political knowledge and to give them political power. . . . Perhaps, after all, twenty years of KMT tutelage has not been without result. . . .[15]

Professor Wu Shih-ch'ang was equally blunt. The KMT one-party dictatorship was just like that of the Soviet Union, he declared. The only difference was that KMT tutelage was supposedly nothing more than a transitional stage in the process of building a genuinely demo-

[15] Ch'u An-p'ing, "Lun Shang-hai min luan" (On the Disorders in Shanghai), *ibid.*, I, No. 16 (December 14, 1946), 4.

cratic polity. But the stage had lasted too long in his opinion, and in the process the original objective seemed to have been forgotten.[16]

Held up for particular criticism were the institutions and procedures being established in the name of representative government.[17] Indicative of this mood were the responses of some seven hundred Chinese students studying in the United States to the question, "Do you feel that the recent elections held in China and the promulgation of a constitution indicate that the country is truly moving in the direction of a democratic government?" Close to 80 per cent of those responding to this question answered either "no" or "not necessarily." [18]

The same negative attitude was also reflected in the letters-to-the-editor columns of *Kuan-ch'a* and other publications. One disillusioned young lawyer just out of law school wrote that the promulgation of the constitution was something that should have pleased those in the legal profession; instead, the words "rule of law" had become a mockery for them. He remarked that the judiciary may have been independent in the early years of the republic, but under the tutelage of the KMT it was no longer.[19]

Another letter described the process whereby a certain *hsien* (county) had elected its representative to the First National Assembly. The KMT had nominated one T'ung Hsiu-ming as its candidate

[16] Wu Shih-ch'ang, "Lun tang te chih-yeh hua" (On the Professionalization of the Party), *ibid.*, II, No. 2 (March 8, 1947), 10. Wu Shih-ch'ang was a professor at National Central University in Nanking.

[17] These included the revision of the 1936 draft constitution and the convening of a National Assembly on November 15, 1946, to adopt the revised draft. The draft was adopted on December 25 and the new constitution promulgated on January 1, 1947. Both the Chinese Communist Party (CCP) and the Democratic League (DL) charged that the government had violated the terms of the agreements relating to these constitutional matters that had been concluded at the Political Consultative Conference, a multi-party gathering which met in January, 1946 (see below, note 57). The CCP and DL therefore refused to attend the National Assembly, criticizing it as a one-party KMT affair. Elections were then held in 1947 to choose delegates to the First National Assembly, which met between March 29 and May 1, 1948, for the purpose of electing the nation's president and vice-president.

[18] This survey was sponsored by the North American Chinese Students Christian Association and was conducted in March and April, 1948, among Chinese students in United States colleges and universities. Two thousand questionnaires were sent out, to which 714 students responded. Of that number, 48 per cent had come to the United States in the autumn of 1947 or later; 33 per cent had arrived between 1944 and 1947. The survey was designed to canvass Chinese students' attitudes on a variety of questions, including proposals for reform of the land system in China, public as opposed to private ownership of industry, the political role of Chinese liberals, and the Civil War. The results of the survey were reprinted in *Kuan-ch'a* (Shanghai), IV, No. 20 (July 17, 1948), 8–9.

[19] Unsigned letter, dated February 8, 1948, at Shanghai, *ibid.*, IV, No. 2 (March 6, 1948), 2.

in that district. At an election rally the county magistrate reportedly addressed the audience: "I order you to vote for Mr. T'ung Hsiu-ming. This order is the same as an order telling you that you must do repair work on the town's defense installations. It is wrong for anyone to disobey. . . ." Afterward, the local officials went around to every household telling the people that Magistrate Wang had said that whoever did not vote for T'ung would be responsible for the work on the defense installations the next time they needed repairs. The result, of course, was that T'ung was elected.[20]

The meeting of the First National Assembly itself aroused equally critical comment. From Nanking, where the assembly met in April, 1948, a *Kuan-ch'a* reader described the scene as one of confusion and disorder. The Three People's Principles have become nothing but slogans which everyone shouts but about which no one does anything, he wrote. He also declared that the government's greatest failure had been in the promotion of democracy: because there had been no achievement whatsoever in this area, the Communists had broken out in rebellion—and people everywhere were responding to them.[21] Of the National Assembly meeting, Ch'u An-p'ing himself could only write: "The pandemonium was such that I could think of nothing else to do except laugh." He questioned why the quality of the elected representatives was so low, why the elections themselves had in so many cases been conducted in such a way as to make a mockery of the election process, and why in all of KMT-controlled China there was no other leader of national stature either within the KMT or without to compete with Chiang Kai-shek for the office of president. For all these shortcomings, he placed blame directly on the KMT and asserted that "the past twenty years of KMT tutelage have been a complete failure." Yet even at this late date, he still seemed to retain the hope that the KMT leaders could learn from past mistakes. He therefore called on the party to "come forward with good intentions and a courageous spirit to change completely its style of work and do something meaningful for the country." [22]

[20] Letter signed by Ting K'e-shan, March 30, 1948, at Hsüan-hua *hsien, ibid.,* IV, No. 7 (April 10, 1948), 2. Liberal publications printed many commentaries on this election. For another, see Tu Jen, "This Kind of Election," *Tsai sheng* (Rebirth Weekly [a Democratic Socialist Party organ]) (Shanghai), No. 177 (August 16, 1947), as translated in U.S. Consulate-General (Shanghai), *Chinese Press Review,* August 26, 1947.

[21] Letter signed Hsü Shao-fu, at Nanking, April 3, 1948, *Kuan-ch'a* (Shanghai), IV, No. 7 (April 10, 1948), 2.

[22] Ch'u An-p'ing, "Kuo ta p'ing-lun" (Commentary on the National Assembly), *ibid.,* IV, No. 9 (April 24, 1948), 3.

Perhaps even more important to the intellectual community than the mockery made of representative government were the official transgressions against civil liberties. These had been guaranteed by the constitution as well as in numerous official statements and declarations. But in practice these liberties were all too often honored only in the breach, either arbitrarily ignored by local political and security authorities or held officially in abeyance by a declaration of martial law or some similar emergency proclamation. Such measures, often carried out at the hands of the secret police, were used specifically to silence those who criticized the government, its policies, and the Civil War. Since students and intellectuals in the KMT areas continued to be the most persistent and articulate in this regard, they naturally bore the brunt of the government's repressive measures. This interference with freedom of the press, freedom of assembly, and the right to petition and protest thus became itself a major object of liberal criticism. Such criticism grew intense on a number of occasions.

One such occasion was the arrest of over 2,000 persons within the space of a few days in the course of a so-called census investigation conducted by some 8,000 military police in Peiping. Those taken into custody included professors, teachers, doctors, publishers, some shop clerks, and a few students. Among the first to issue a public protest were thirteen professors who released a statement demanding a guarantee of human rights. The statement wondered at the duplicity of a government that could promulgate a constitution guaranteeing civil liberties and release 1,000 prisoners from Peiping jails in January, and then within two months instigate a wave of arbitrary mass arrests.[23] A few days later, 192 members of the faculties of Peking, Ch'inghua, Sino-French, Yenching, and Normal universities made public the text of their "Declaration of Human Rights" in which they called the "census investigation" and the arrests a betrayal of President Chiang's announcement of January, 1946, and of the government's repeated proclamations over the years guaranteeing civil liberties, and also of the recently promulgated constitution.[24]

Another event that aroused widespread criticism in 1947 was the government's promulgation in May of the "Provisional Measures for the Maintenance of Public Order," which banned striking, parading, and petitioning by more than ten persons. Local law enforcement au-

[23] Chu Tzu-ch'ing *et al.,* "Pao-chang jen-ch'üan" (Guarantee Human Rights), reprinted *ibid.,* II, No. 2 (March 8, 1947), 21.

[24] "Our Special Correspondent" (Peiping), "Hsin wu ssu yün-tung chih ch'ien-hsi" (The Eve of a New May Fourth Movement), *ibid.,* II, No. 3 (March 15, 1947), 16–17.

thorities were empowered to use all means necessary to enforce the ban, which was issued in an effort to bring a halt to a nationwide series of student demonstrations against the Civil War.[25] There was widespread support among the older generation for this particular student tide, as it was called, which had in fact been precipitated by the demand of professors at National Central University in Nanking for higher pay to meet the rising cost of living. Opinion in liberal circles was therefore outraged at the measures used to suppress the student demonstrations. The comments of Chou Shou-chang, editor of the Nanking *Hsin min pao* (New People's News), were typical: he claimed that the methods used to suppress the student demonstrations were even worse than those used by the Peiyang government. And besides killing students, banning newspapers, and arresting journalists, he continued, the government must also accuse all of them of being Communist "traitors and bandits." What sort of government is it, he queried, that dares to speak of law and rationality and then in practice violates both reason and the constitution? [26] The general practice of arresting students, which culminated in the special tribunals set up in August, 1948, for the purpose of investigating and prosecuting student activists, was angrily denounced as undemocratic and illegal. The Hong Kong journal, *Shih-tai p'i-p'ing* (Modern Critique), was particularly vehement in its criticism of the KMT government in this

[25] This was known as the Anti-Hunger, Anti-Civil War Movement, which began in Nanking in late April and continued until the first of June, by which time student demonstrations had taken place in most major cities throughout the KMT-controlled areas. After the provisional measures were announced, hundreds of students were arrested. Some were simply abducted off the streets by plainclothesmen while others were apprehended in night raids on school dormitories. In one such raid at Wuhan University, three students were shot and killed. Also at this time, three liberal Shanghai newspapers, the *Hsin min wan pao* (New People's Evening News), the *Lien-ho wan pao* (United Evening News), and the *Wen-hui pao* (Cultural Exchange Daily), were banned and a large number of journalists arrested, apparently because of their sympathetic reporting of the student movement.

[26] Chou Shou-chang, "Feng-k'uang le te chung-kuo" (China Gone Mad), *Kuan-ch'a* (Shanghai), II, No. 16 (June 14, 1947), 7. In two strongly worded editorials, Ch'u An-p'ing also denounced the measures being used by the government to suppress the student protests and declared that any other position would be contrary to the feelings of the general public. In addition, Ch'u took the Shanghai edition of the *TKP* severely to task for not having come out unequivocally in support of the students. He suggested that if the editor-in-chief, Wang Yün-sheng, had not been out of town and the editorial writing had not fallen into other hands, the paper would not have fallen into such an error. Ch'u An-p'ing, "Hsüeh-sheng ch'e ch'i-i ch'i, li-shih cheng tsai ch'uang-tsao" (The Students Are Raising the Flag of Rebellion, History Is in the Making), *ibid.*, II, No. 14 (May 31, 1947), 3–4; and "Lun *wen hui, hsin min, lien-ho* san pao pei feng chi *ta kung pao* tsai che ts'u hsüeh ch'ao chung suo piao-shih te t'ai-tu" (On the Closing of the *Wen-hui pao,* the *Hsin min wan pao,* and the *Lien-ho wan pao,* and the Attitude Expressed by the *TKP* in This Student Tide), *ibid.*, pp. 5–7.

regard and accused it of carrying out a "bandit extermination campaign" against the student community.[27]

The harassment of the press aroused as much resentment as did the measures used against the students. In May, 1947, 130 journalists belonging to the North China Correspondents Association met in Peiping. The slogans adopted by the conference were "Freedom of the Press" and "Guarantee Civil Liberties." Even the official coordinator of the conference, who was himself a manager of the government's Central News Agency, felt obliged to respond to the prevailing mood. In an address, he deplored the recurrent attacks on newspaper offices and incidents such as that on May 1, when a newspaperman, Chang Chin-wu, was arrested. "We should concentrate all our strength," he continued, "on the struggle for freedom and the guaranty of civil liberties. The arrest of Mr. Chang of the *North China Daily News* is an illegal measure and all newspaper circles throughout the country should protest it. . . ."[28] The correspondents' protest may have been instrumental in securing Chang's release, but it was not sufficient to keep similar incidents from occurring throughout the country. Within a month after this meeting of the North China Correspondents Association, three newspapers had been banned, a fourth had been ordered to suspend publication temporarily, censorship had been temporarily declared in Tientsin, and about sixty journalists had been arbitrarily arrested in the cities of Chungking and Chengtu. Countless appeals and protests were made, to which officials invariably replied that the freedom of the press would be maintained and the security of newspapermen guaranteed. But the harassment continued, and criticism of the government not surprisingly grew apace.

One of the most extreme attempts to silence critics of the government was the assassination of Wen I-to, a popular professor of Chinese literature at Southwest Associated University in Kunming. Outspoken

[27] Among the many editorials and articles in *STPP* on the student movement, see "K'u tou chung te ching hu ta hsüeh-sheng" (The Bitter Struggle of University Students in Nanking and Shanghai), V, No. 98 (February 15, 1948), 27–28; "Tuan p'ing" (Short Comment), V, No. 100 (April 15, 1948), 15–16; T'u Chin, "Chao ling chih ch'un" (Bright Spring), *ibid.*, p. 30; "Tuan p'ing: ch'üan kuo hsüeh-sheng shou-tao hsin te p'o-hai" (Short Comment: The Nation's Students Are Suffering New Persecution), V, No. 105 (September 15, 1948), 2.

[28] Quoted by "Special Correspondent" (Peiping), "Ts'ung mei chün hsia ch'i tao Chang Chin-wu pei shih" (From the Withdrawal of the American Military to the Release of Chang Chin-wu), *Kuan-ch'a* (Shanghai), II, No. 13 (May 24, 1947), 17–18. Chang Chin-wu was arrested on May 1, 1947, and held as a military criminal on suspicion of being a "Communist and a traitor." The correspondents sent an open letter to General Li Tsung-jen, head of Chiang Kai-shek's Peiping headquarters, and Chang was subsequently released on bail. No specific charges were brought against him.

(as were many of his colleagues) in his demands for reform, Wen was gunned down in front of the faculty dormitory as he was returning from a Democratic League [DL] press conference on July 15, 1946. Four days earlier, Li Kung-p'u, another prominent member of the DL, had been shot and killed on a Kunming street. After their painstaking investigation of the murders on behalf of the DL, which the local authorities obstructed at every turn, Liang Sou-ming and Chou Hsin-min came to the conclusion that the assassinations had been planned and carried out either by or with the knowledge and consent of the headquarters of the Yunnan Garrison Command.[29] It was an incident which the academic community never forgot. Almost two years later, in April, 1948, the head of the Peiping Municipal KMT Committee, Wu Chu-jen, issued a public warning to "three professors" accusing them of being used by the CCP to incite the students. Everyone knew that the three referred to were Hsü Te-heng, Fan Hung, and Yüan Han-ch'ing, who had addressed a student rally at Peita the previous month. Ninety of their colleagues from Peking, Ch'inghua, Yenching, and Normal universities immediately published an open letter of protest addressed to Chairman Wu, in which they wrote: "We want to inquire further: is a second Wen I-to incident being planned? Because we would like to enlighten the authorities. Wen I-to was killed, but not only did it not eliminate dissatisfaction with the situation among academicians, it instead only deepened further their alarm and anger. . . ."[30]

Output. There were, of course, many causes for alarm and anger. The liberal creed held that government existed not only of and by the people but for them as well. This second major charge in the liberal indictment of the Nationalist government tended to be stated in even harsher terms than the first. Few in the late 1940's were willing to argue that the government was even concerned with, let alone actually acting to promote, the interests and well-being of the majority of the population. The case against the government's policies and perfor-

[29] Liang Sou-ming and Chou Hsin-min, *Li Wen an tiao-ch'a pao-kao shu* (Report on the Investigation of the Li-Wen Case) (Nanking: Chung-kuo min-chu t'ung-meng tsung-pu, 1946).

[30] The letter was published in *Kuan-ch'a* together with a list of the ninety professors who had signed it (IV, No. 10 [May 1, 1948], 2). *STPP* printed the speech that Professor Yüan Han-ch'ing had made at the Peita student meeting in March: "Chih-shih ch'ing-nien te tao-lu" (The Way for Intellectual Youth), V, No. 101 (May 15, 1948), 6. This also provided the occasion for one of Ch'u An-p'ing's harshest attacks on the government: "Ti-erh-ko Wen I-to shih-chien wan wan chih-tsao pu te" (A Second Wen I-to Incident Absolutely Must Not Be Created), *Kuan-ch'a* (Shanghai), IV, No. 10 (May 1, 1948), 4.

mance was usually argued in terms of one or more of three interrelated issues: corruption, incompetence, and the Civil War.

It is difficult to ascertain which of these three may have occupied the most central position. Except for the first months of the take-over period following the Japanese surrender (when official peculation in the newly reoccupied areas reached truly unprecedented proportions), corruption seemed to inspire relatively less critical comment than did the other two issues. But this is not necessarily indicative of the position it occupied in the liberal critique of the political system. One writer summed up what he felt to be the prevailing attitude when he suggested: "We have already heard so much of the sounds of corruption that we have become numbed by it and neglect it as the source of all inadequacies. . . ."[31] Ch'u An-p'ing set forth his own feelings when he wrote that of all the government's faults, the greatest must surely be its "lack of virtue" which had infected and demoralized the entire society. "Under this sort of government," he continued, "living is much easier for those who do not observe the law, who are immoral, and lacking in goodwill as compared with clean, law-abiding citizens. . . . Except for a minority who have been able to maintain their own ideals, most people have already turned toward speculation, are not to be trusted, will not take responsibility, and commit evil deeds. . . ."[32]

In keeping with their humanist concerns, liberal writers tended to focus on the consequences of official corruption in terms of those who suffered most from it. The most glaring examples in this regard were generally reported from the provinces and rural areas.[33] There was nevertheless a tendency to concentrate not so much on corruption itself as on its causes. This did not place the government in any better light; it only shifted somewhat the emphasis of responsibility. Morality, it

[31] Yang Jen-keng, "Kuo-min-tang wang ho ch'u ch'ü?" (Where Is the Kuomintang Headed?), *Kuan-ch'a* (Shanghai), II, No. 3 (March 15, 1947), 6. Yang Jen-keng was a professor at Peita.

[32] Ch'u An-p'ing, "P'ing P'u-li-t'e te p'ien-ssu te pu chien-k'ang te fang hua pao-kao" (A Critique of Bullitt's Biased Unhealthy Report on His Visit to China), *ibid.*, III, No. 9 (October 25, 1947), 5.

[33] Among the more detailed reports of this kind were the following three stories concerning conditions in Shansi, Kansu, and Kiangsi, respectively: "Our Special Correspondent" (Chin-nan), "Fa wai t'ien-ti, jen chien hsüeh lei" (Heaven and Earth without Law, Tears of Blood among the People), *ibid.*, I, No. 20 (January 11, 1947), 20–21; "Our Special Correspondent" (Lan-chou), "Yu huan chung chung te hsi-pei chiao" (Manifold Troubles in the Northwest), *ibid.*, I, No. 17 (December 21, 1946), 14–16; and Wang K'e-lang (*Kuan-ch'a* dispatch from Nanchang), "Ts'ung shu-tzu k'an chiang-hsi" (Looking at Figures in Kiangsi), *ibid.*, III, No. 8 (October 18, 1947), 17–18.

was said, followed the economy. Thus a major reason for the marked increase of official graft and corruption over the pre-1937 period was the economic impoverishment caused by the Japanese War and intensified by the Civil War which followed.[34] It was a fact that the nation's public servants, together with teachers in all public institutions and the military, bore the main burden of the government's reliance on inflation to finance its war effort. By the latter half of the 1940's, the real wages of all public employees had been reduced to only a fraction of their pre-1937 levels. In urban areas middle- and lower-level civil servants with no other source of income often suffered genuine hardship even in terms of such basic necessities as food, clothing, and shelter. This economic hardship argument therefore tended to shift the focus of attention onto the Civil War itself as a basic cause of everyone's misfortunes.

The Civil War actually became a political liability for the central government on a number of grounds. For their part, liberals generally opposed the government's war policy because they reasoned that a prolonged war was too high a price to pay to keep the KMT regime, as then constituted, in power. This reasoning was based on a view, widely held in 1946 and 1947 and even during the first half of 1948, that the war was likely to continue indefinitely since neither side had the capacity to defeat the other. However much he may have overstated the case, there seemed to be a good deal of truth in Professor Wu Shih-ch'ang's statement:

If the Communist armies could really be destroyed within three or five months, everyone would tolerate the hardships and support the government's "suppression of disorders." We believe that the majority of the people truly would not oppose the war if by the next New Year, they could see the nation united, reconstruction begun, an end to the conscripting of soldiers, requisitioning of grain, and collection of miscellaneous taxes, and also if there could be freedom and democracy. . . .[35]

But it was clear to everyone that the war would not be over in five months, and there were increasing doubts that freedom and democracy would indeed be realized even if KMT troops could defeat the Communists. As for the costs of the war itself, these were calculated both in terms of the inflation which had completely disrupted the urban

[34] One of the most thoughtful presentations of this argument was Hao Jan, "Lun cheng-chih shang te hsin ping t'ai" (On the New Malaise in Politics), originally in *Shih-chi p'ing-lun* (Century Critic) (Nanking), III, No. 14, and reprinted in *Kuan-ch'a* (Shanghai), IV, No. 7 (April 10, 1948), 18–19.

[35] Wu Shih-ch'ang, "Lun ho-p'ing wen-t'i" (On the Problem of Peace), *Kuan-ch'a* (Shanghai), II, No. 16 (June 14, 1947), 4.

economy, and of the further impoverishment of the rural areas. The printing press may have been the government's chief source of revenue. But the government depended also on a land tax, on the forced purchase of grain at lower than market prices, and on the collection of grain on loan. Together with the abuses associated with conscription, and the support of an undisciplined and underpaid army, these exactions created an insupportable burden for the peasantry. In addition, an increasingly militaristic government and increased political alienation among the populace were also condemned as direct results of the war. Finally, some argued that these wartime conditions, which were making it possible for a minority to enrich themselves even as the majority were becoming poorer, were creating conditions most appropriate for the further growth of the Chinese Communist Party. For all of these reasons, then, the government's insistence on fighting the Civil War provided yet another piece of evidence to support the charges that KMT leaders cared for nothing but the preservation of their own power and were willing to sacrifice the interests of the nation as a whole in pursuit of their own selfish aims.

The manner in which the CCP managed to avoid sharing full responsibility with the KMT for the war is interesting and, contrary to what at least one observer has suggested, seems to have had little to do with the Communists' expressions of support for the peace movement in the KMT areas.[36] For one thing, the Communists did not emerge entirely unscathed. There were many who suggested that both the CCP and the KMT were responsible for the war and that the Communists probably did not want peace any more than did the KMT. And there were many bitter comments condemning both parties for pursuing their own selfish interests at the expense of the nation as a whole.[37] Nevertheless, the main thrust of the antiwar movement was directed against the Nationalist government, for a number of reasons. As Wu Shih-ch'ang suggested specifically with respect to the student antiwar protestors, the reason they took their petitions to the government and not to the CCP was that they were not yet ready to go over

[36] Jack Belden, *China Shakes the World* (New York: Harper and Brothers, 1949), p. 398.

[37] For example, Chou Shou-chang, "Feng-k'uang le te chung-kuo"; Yang Jen-keng, "Lun nei chan" (On the Civil War), *Kuan-ch'a* (Shanghai), IV, No. 4 (March 20, 1948), 5–6; Fu T'ung-hsien, "I chiao-yü chiu chung-kuo" (Save China through Education), *ibid.*, II, No. 12 (May 17, 1947), 6. Fu T'ung-hsien was a professor at St. John's University in Shanghai. See also Wu Shih-ch'ang, "Ts'ung mei su shuo-tao kuo nei" (A Discussion about the U.S., the USSR, and Internal Affairs), *ibid.*, II, No. 6 (April 5, 1947), 5; and editorial, *STPP* (Hong Kong), IV, No. 85 (June 16, 1947), 2–3.

to the Communist side. They still recognized the Nationalist government as the legitimate ruler of China with the power to make peace as well as war. Petitions, noted Professor Wu, are only presented to recognized governments, not to opposition parties.

Secondly, there was a tendency to believe that the Communists had been sincere at the Political Consultative Conference in January, 1946, when they agreed along with representatives of the KMT to a number of compromises aimed at resolving the differences between them and avoiding civil war. Unfortunately for its case, the KMT managed almost immediately to destroy belief in its own sincerity by unilaterally breaking a number of the agreements at a KMT Central Executive Committee meeting within a few months after they had been concluded.[38]

But perhaps most important was the knowledge that the strength of the CCP was being built on the weaknesses and shortcomings of the KMT. The government was held responsible for not having acted to remedy these defects during its years in power. And because of that failure, the liberals argued, the government also had to bear the main burden of responsibility for the growth of the Communists and therefore for the Civil War as well. This theme was strongly emphasized by the economist Wu Ch'i-yüan. "If we want to understand the nature of the Civil War," he wrote, "we must turn to the government's economic policies and measures during the past nine years." He continued:

The result has been nine years of currency inflation, price fluctuations, and the division of wealth so that the Chinese economy has been changed into a condition of sharp contrast, with the rich getting richer and the poor poorer. Even before the [civil] war, the middle classes except for cliques of corrupt officials were almost all impoverished under the pressure of inflation and low wages. The peasantry which occupied over 85 per cent of the population was already in a state of hunger and was threatening to rise up due to the depredations caused by soldiers, bandits, grain requisitions, conscription, natural disasters, and all kinds of oppression. While the majority of our countrymen had no way of living, the policies of currency inflation were expanded, which increased the power and wealth of a privileged group. . . . With society in such a state, would there not be a civil war whether or not there was a CCP? The expansion of the power of the Communists can be attributed directly to such economic policies.[39]

38 Ch'ang Ming, "Fan-lun chung-chien p'ai te cheng-chih lu-hsien" (Talking in General Terms about the Political Line of the Groups in the Center), *STPP* (Hong Kong), IV, No. 85 (June 16, 1947), 33. On the Political Consultative Conference, see note 57, below.
39 Wu Ch'i-yüan, "Ts'ung ching-chi kuan-tien lun nei-chan wen-t'i" (Talking about Civil War Problems from an Economic Viewpoint), *Kuan-ch'a* (Shanghai), I, No. 2 (September 7, 1946), 3–4. Wu was a professor at Ch'inghua University.

Ch'u An-p'ing expressed similar views in a stinging rebuke to the American envoy, William Bullitt, who visited China in 1947 and recommended that more United States aid be given to the KMT government. Ch'u wrote that Mr. Bullitt advocated such aid because the KMT government was anti-Soviet and anti-Communist; he wondered, however, whether Bullitt was aware of the circumstances under which the CCP had risen to occupy the position that it did. Ch'u went on to state that, in his own view, the corrupt control of the KMT was the major cause of the growing strength of the CCP: "If in the past twenty years politics had not been so corrupt and incompetent, how could people have been made to feel that the future is so empty that they have turned and entrusted their hopes to the CCP? I say very truthfully that I feel the corrupt control of the KMT to be the mother of the CCP; it has created the CCP and it has nurtured the CCP. . . ."[40]

Finally, on the specific charges of political, economic, and military incompetence which were leveled against the Nationalist government, several volumes could be and in some cases already have been written. A cross section of the issues in this regard which aroused the most attention and concern within the intellectual community included the government's handling of the student movement, the treatment of the tens of thousands of refugees who fled either the battle zones or the Communist areas, the complete failure of the government's performance in Manchuria, and the ineptitude with which the government went about trying to minimize the effects of its policy of inflationary wartime finance.

[40] Ch'u An-p'ing, "P'ing P'u-li-t'e . . . ," p. 5. A similar point was made in Chin Feng, "Ma-shang te chih, ma-shang shou chih, ma-shang shih chih" (Hastily Gained, Hastily Guarded, Hastily Lost), *STPP* (Hong Kong), V, No. 101 (March 15, 1948), 3–4. In a somewhat different argument, Ch'ien Tuan-sheng also suggested that the KMT must bear responsibility for the Civil War. He argued that the KMT's reliance on military means to preserve its political power had created a situation in which its opponents had no choice but to resort to arms. Once a military faction becomes dominant in politics, he wrote, then political parties have no means of opposing one another except by fighting, nor can the people be assured of their rights without resorting to force. He traced the KMT's reliance on military control back to Sun Yat-sen's original alliance with various warlords of the Peiyang government, suggesting that what was at that time strictly a marriage of convenience soon grew into a force within the party which could not easily be eliminated. Ch'ien Tuan-sheng, "Chün-jen pa-hu te chung-kuo cheng-fu" (China's Government Usurped by the Military), *STPP* (Hong Kong), V, No. 108 (December 15, 1948), 21–23.

SOCIALISM AND DEMOCRACY: THE LIBERAL IDEAL

Turning from their critique of the KMT, liberal intellectuals gave more positive expression to their ideological commitments as they debated among themselves the forms of state and society they hoped might emerge from the confusion and disorder of the Civil War. At the level of general principles, agreement was considerable. The objectives were socialism and democracy. But beyond that, diversity began to emerge. Socialism and democracy meant different things to different people; and even more controversial was the problem of the means whereby the objectives might best be achieved within the Chinese context.

Of socialism, Ch'u An-p'ing wrote: "At present the Chinese people in general and especially the intellectuals really do not oppose it but instead are positively disposed toward it." He then went on to explain how "petit bourgeois" intellectuals could espouse the same economic principles as the Communists by adding that, with the exception of a very few, all of China's intellectuals were going hungry or were in fact close to starvation and had already lost all of their property. They had therefore become one with the proletariat and had nothing to fear from socialism.[41] Indeed, many considered it the only answer for China's economic problems. Fu Ssu-nien, who tended to emphasize the need for such conventional reform measures as the elimination of privileges for the so-called favored families and equalization of the tax burden through a graduated income tax system, nevertheless stated flatly that if socialism could be effectively achieved in China, he would "approve 100 per cent." [42]

A typical view was that of Professor Cheng Lin-chuang, head of the Economics Department at Yenching University:

In a capitalist society, although there is economic freedom, there is no economic justice. But it does exist in socialist nations and only because it does are those societies secure. There are two aspects of economic justice. One is the guarantee of the right to employment and the second is the guarantee to the right of a basic

---

[41] Ch'u An-p'ing, "Chung-kuo te cheng chü" (China's Political Situation), *Kuan-ch'a* (Shanghai), II, No. 2 (March 8, 1947), 6.

[42] Fu Meng-chen [Fu Ssu-nien], "Lun hao-men tzu-pen chih pi-hsü ch'an-ch'u" (On the Necessity of Rooting Out Favored-family Capital), *ibid.*, II, No. 1 (March 1, 1947), 6. Fu was, among other things, head of the History and Language Research Section of the Academia Sinica. He created something of a sensation in Nanking political circles in early 1947 when he publicly denounced T. V. Soong and H. H. Kung by name in a series of three articles. Two of these appeared in the Nanking journal, *Shih-chi p'ing-lun;* the third was the *Kuan-ch'a* article cited here.

livelihood. The realization of these two objectives requires unceasing production and social organization for just distribution. These conditions can exist only in a planned economy. They will not be easily realized in capitalist nations unless the principle of free enterprise is changed. . . .

We believe that economic justice and social security together constitute the main direction of society's present development. At the same time, we believe even more that everything which goes against this tide will in the end be washed away by it.[43]

Socialism was also seen as an appropriate model for economic development as well as an instrument of economic justice. Thus, even as he condemned the territorial and organizational expansion of the USSR as a form of national aggrandizement which might make China its next target, Professor Ting Su of National Central University advocated that China set up a Soviet-style economic system. It would, he declared, provide the most effective form of organization for the growth of China's economy.[44]

The arguments began only when it came to the question of how best to achieve democracy and socialism in China. This was amply demonstrated in a series of exchanges between Shih Fu-liang, Yen Jen-keng, Chang Tung-sun, and Fan Hung, which took place in the pages of *Kuan-ch'a* in late 1947 and early 1948.

Shih Fu-liang's ideas always seemed to arouse a good deal of interest and response in liberal circles—perhaps because he had been one of the founding members of the CCP, from which he had withdrawn in 1927. Concerning socialism, he maintained that he had for the past twenty years been convinced that China's democratic revolution must culminate in the development of socialism, because capitalism was incompatible with the basic concept of democracy. Shih nevertheless argued that since China had not as yet achieved a material base adequate for the implementation of socialism, it would not be possible to move directly from the "feudal" stage—then in the process of being destroyed—to socialism. For the immediate future he therefore advocated a transitional stage of capital development, which he labeled the "new capitalism." New capitalism would be the economic program of a "new democratic" political regime that would be led by the laboring classes and installed after the defeat of the KMT government. The new capitalism of this labor government would

---

[43] Cheng Lin-chuang, "Ching-chi cheng-i yü she-hui an-ch'üan" (Economic Justice and Social Security), *Kuan-ch'a* (Shanghai), II, No. 3 (March 15, 1947), 9–10.

[44] Ting Su, "Su-lien chi chiang tung ku" (The Soviet Union's Imminent Concerns in the East), *ibid.*, IV, No. 19 (July 3, 1948), 7.

entail: (1) a full reform of the land system and implementation of a land-to-the-tiller program; (2) confiscation of all bureaucratic capital and the expansion of the nationalized sector to include banks, heavy industry, major communications facilities, and some light industry; (3) the protection of national business and industry, and aid for small producers; (4) the implementation of a progressive labor law to guarantee a basic standard of living for all; and (5) economic, financial, and social policies designed to discourage the accumulation of excessive personal wealth and to encourage the reinvestment of profits in productive enterprises.[45]

One would have thought that this program, similar as it was in broad outline to that spelled out by Mao Tse-tung in his "On New Democracy," would have given pause to the more radically inclined of Shih's colleagues and critics. But it did not. For example, Yen Jen-keng, a professor at Chekiang University, took him rather severely to task in one article and then in a second rebuffed Shih's attempt to minimize the differences between their two views. What Professor Yen objected to was, first, Shih's willingness to allow the continuation of exploitative relations between capital and labor, however modified for the sake of increasing production; and second, his willingness to entrust his hopes for a change in the economic system to some future type of "new democratic political regime." Yen wrote that he really had his doubts as to whether workers, peasants, rich peasants, the petite bourgeoisie, intellectuals, and national capitalists could really unite as one in the struggle for socialism, particularly if the rich peasants, petite bourgeoisie, and national capitalists were allowed to revive. They may be exploited today, he asserted, but they all contain the character of exploiters within them. He therefore advocated moving directly to socialism because, he said, "I feel that we can perhaps solve the problems of production and distribution at one and the same time." [46]

Shih Fu-liang had more in common with Chang Tung-sun and in this case was somewhat more justified in his protestations that their differences were only matters of emphasis and explanation. But dif-

---

45 Shih Fu-liang, "Fei-ch'u po-hsüeh yü tseng-chia sheng-ch'an" (Abolish Exploitation and Increase Production), *ibid.*, IV, No. 4 (March 20, 1948), 7–9.

46 Yen Jen-keng, "She-hui-chu-i? 'Hsin tzu-pen-chu-i' hu?" (Socialism? "New Capitalism?"), *ibid.*, IV, No. 17 (June 19, 1948), 5–8. Shih Fu-liang's response appeared in "Hsin chung-kuo te ching-chi ho cheng-chih" (The Economy and Politics of the New China), *ibid.*, IV, No. 21 (July 24, 1948), 4. Yen replied in "Tsai ho Shih Fu-liang hsien-sheng t'an 'hsin tzu-pen-chu-i' " (Again Discussing the "New Capitalism" with Mr. Shih Fu-liang), *ibid.*, IV, No. 23–24 (August 7, 1948), 15.

ferences there were. Chang, like Shih, insisted that developing and increasing production should be the first step China must take. Chang also dismissed socialism as an immediate solution because social reforms alone could never succeed in an impoverished nation. But he did believe—and here he differed with Shih—that liberalism and its economic equivalent, capitalism, could not ensure the development of production in China. He maintained that backward nations absolutely must not be allowed to use capitalism as a means for advancement, for it would only create new forms of injustice internally and the oppression of other nations abroad. Once the good things of Western culture entered China, he wrote, they only increased the sufferings of the people because in China there were special interests who could make use of such things to oppress the people. These oppressive forces also stood in the way of developing productivity. They included privileged bureaucratic capital, landlords, usurers, and the castoffs of a backward feudal society, such as the vagrants and wanderers, tenant farmers, and hired laborers, who could produce little and often resorted to extortion and robbery in order to live.

Chang concluded that a "progressive" planned economy was China's only hope of developing its productive capacity. He suggested also that if the economy were planned, then politics, education, and everything else would have to be planned as well. This planning should be guided by the principle that all exploitative relations which hinder production must be eliminated, while those which encourage production could be allowed to exist in the transitional period. Conversely, social reforms that benefit production should be encouraged, while those that interfere with it should not be maintained. Chang was insistent that each nation should work out its own solutions on the basis of this principle. He suggested that two models of its apparently successful application were the Soviet Union's New Economic Policy of the 1920's, which made it possible for the USSR later to move to socialism and post–World War II economic policies in Sweden.[47]

[47] Chang Tung-sun was a frequent contributor to *Kuan-ch'a* and other liberal journals. The above summary of his ideas on economic reform is based on the following articles: "Kuan-yü chung-kuo ch'u lu te k'an-fa. tsai ta Fan Hung hsien-sheng" (A View on the Way Out for China: Another Reply to Mr. Fan Hung), *Kuan-ch'a* (Shanghai), III, No. 23 (January 31, 1948), 3–4; "Cheng-chih shang te tzu-yu-chu-i yü wen-hua shang te tzu-yu-chu-i" (Liberalism in Politics and Culture), *ibid.*, IV, No. 1 (February 28, 1948), 3–5; "Ching-chi p'ing-teng yü tei-ch'u po-hsüeh" (Economic Equality and the Abolition of Exploitation), *ibid.*, IV, No. 2 (March 6, 1948), 3–5; "Tseng ch'an yü ko-ming: hsieh-li 'min-chu-chu-i yü she-hui-chu-i' i-hou" (Increasing Production and Revolution: After Writing "Democracy and Socialism"), originally in *Chung chien* (China Reconstructs), III, No. 4, reprinted in *Kuan-ch'a* (Shanghai), IV, No. 23–24 (August 7, 1948), 26–27.

Chang Tung-sun seemed to have more cause to argue with the Peita economist, Fan Hung, than with Shih Fu-liang. Professor Fan was straightforward and unequivocal in his diagnoses, as well as in his prescriptions for the realization of socialism:

> We must clearly understand that in today's world all evil is due to the exploiting of the propertyless classes by those with property. Then what remedy is there? This, of course, has to do with changes in political power.
>
> In terms of politics, I feel that China, again like other nations, has only two roads before it. One is that of revolution and the other is that of counter-revolution. The latter puts all political power in the hands of the exploiting class. But to tell these exploiters to give up voluntarily their political power or to limit their exploitation and work for the welfare of the people: this is what is called the third road and is advocated by Jesus Christ, Confucius, and contemporary professors.
>
> On the revolutionary road, the exploited classes are united with their exploiters either by peaceful or violent means. Political power is seized, the power of the exploiters is limited, and the life, health, and freedom of the exploited are protected. . . .[48]

Professor Fan's hope was that China would be transformed into "the model of a free socialist nation." But he was careful to emphasize the word "free." The fear that a socialist China might in some way become subservient to the Soviet Union was often expressed at this time. Many leftists found themselves vulnerable on this issue and went to some lengths to disavow the inevitability of any such relationship between China and the USSR—hence the common theme that China must find an approach to socialism best suited to the particular Chinese context, and that the responsibility for changing China lay entirely within China itself.[49]

Chang Tung-sun was a professor at Yenching University at this time, and a prominent member of the DL until it was banned in October, 1947.

[48] Fan Hung, "Chih yu liang t'iao lu" (There Are Only Two Roads), *Kuan-ch'a* (Shanghai), IV, No. 7 (April 10, 1948), 3–4. Professor Fan's exchange with Chang Tung-sun actually preceded this particular statement by several months and revolved around a number of related issues. The debate between the two men developed in the following articles: Chang Tung-sun, "Wo i chui-lun hsien cheng chien chi wen-hua te chen-tuan" (I Seek an Examination of Constitutional Government and Culture), *ibid.*, III, No. 7 (October 11, 1947), 3–6; Fan Hung, "Yü Liang Sou-ming Chang Tung-sun liang hsien-sheng lun chung-kuo te wen-hua yü cheng-chih" (Discussing China's Culture and Politics with Messrs. Liang Sou-ming and Chang Tung-sun), *ibid.*, III, No. 14 (November 29, 1947), 5–8; Chang, "Ching ta Fan Hung hsien-sheng" (A Respectful Reply to Mr. Fan Hung), *ibid.*, III, No. 16 (December 13, 1947), 5–6; Fan, "Wo tui-yü chung-kuo cheng-chih wen-t'i te ken-pen k'an-fa" (My Basic View of China's Political Problems), *ibid.*, III, No. 18 (December 27, 1947), 5–6; Chang, "Kuan-yü chung-kuo ch'u lu te k'an-fa."

[49] Fan Hung, "Kuan-yü 'i p'ing-teng tai-wo chih min-tsu'" (Concerning "A Nation Which Practices Equality"), *ibid.*, IV, No. 18 (June 26, 1948), 7–8. This was Fan's response to criticism of his stand on this issue by Chou Tung-chiao, "Lun 'i p'ing-teng

A more difficult problem for many of these intellectuals, however, was their simultaneous devotion to the ideals of socialism and democracy. Chang Tung-sun was one of the few to address himself directly to the complexities inherent in this dual commitment. In emphasizing the importance of a planned economy for the development of production, he suggested that both equality and freedom would have to be circumscribed and could exist only within the limits set by the plan. In a planned society which must eliminate all obstacles to production, he wrote, need one even ask whether freedom will be limited and equality harmed? Nor did he seem overly concerned about this: "As for making the plan in such a way that freedom and equality might be preserved to the greatest extent possible, that is an affair for the planner and cannot be described in detail here." But there was one point beyond which he was not willing to go. He called it cultural freedom, or absolute freedom of culture and thought, which he posited as the guarantee of a progressive political system. Once the seed of cultural freedom is sown, he concluded, its growth cannot be stopped: it will be able to nurture a tradition of freedom in China.[50]

Chang's views concerning many of the institutions conventionally associated with democracy were consistent with his treatment of the principles of freedom and equality. He argued that an Anglo-American-style constitutional form of government could not exist in China. It would, for example, be impossible to hold free elections because these would be manipulated by the existing powerful cliques to their own advantage. As for democracy itself, he maintained that the CCP, the KMT, and the DL together represented all the interests in the country so that "when such parties consult together, on the surface it may seem to be only a matter among parties, but in fact it can mean genuine democracy." Toward this end, he placed great emphasis on two concepts —compromise, and checks and balances—which he maintained were the prerequisites for the conduct of democratic politics.[51]

Another who shared some of these views was Liang Sou-ming, who argued that in view of China's cultural traditions, an Anglo-American form of government absolutely could not be established. He suggested

tai-wo te min-tsu' chien lun wo-men te tao-lu" (On "A Nation Which Practices Equality" and Our Path), *ibid.*, IV, No. 13 (May 22, 1948), 4–6.

[50] Chang Tung-sun, "Cheng-chih shang te tzu-yu-chu-i . . . ," p. 5; and "Wo i chui-lun hsien cheng . . . ," pp. 4-6.

[51] Chang Tung-sun, "Chui-shu wo-men nu-li chien-li 'lien-ho cheng-fu' te yung-i" (Reflections on Our Intention to Strive to Establish a "Coalition Government"), *Kuan-ch'a* (Shanghai), II, No. 6 (April 5, 1947), 6.

that elections, for example, were basically incompatible with the customs and behavior of the people and that a democratic constitution could never survive in China. But, like Chang, Liang was not willing to dismiss the matter entirely. He suggested that a team of experts might be able to devise some other form of democratic political system which did not entail elections or a Western-style constitution, and which would therefore be more in keeping with China's national character.[52]

This degree of pessimism concerning the future of democratic principles and institutions in China did not, however, seem to be shared by the majority of those who expressed their views on the subject in print. On the other hand, no one was willing to suggest that the obstacles were not formidable. Ku Ch'un-fan expressed a rather commonly held view when he wrote that although democratic politics had its deficiencies as a system of government for China, these could doubtless be overcome gradually and in due time.[53] Another writer, Kuo Shu-jen, agreed. Arguing specifically against the ideas of Chang and Liang, Kuo reminded them that constitutional democracy was not just a form of government but a way of life and, as such, could not be formed and developed overnight. To support his argument, he outlined the difficulties that the United States had experienced in its own political development. Many of the states had clashed with the federal constitution even after it was ratified. The development of industry had created many social injustices which the constitution was powerless to prevent. Politics and administration had often been corrupt and elections controlled. Yet remedies were gradually and sometimes painfully worked out. On the basis of the American experience he therefore concluded: "We cannot because of someone's control doubt the system itself and abandon our efforts to carry it out. . . . The ideals of this system must become a habitual part of the lives of the people so that the system can become a part of our culture. As for the deficiencies, we can continually work to overcome them. . . ."[54]

---

[52] Liang Sou-ming, "Yü-kao hsüan tsai, chui-lun hsien cheng" (A Forecast of Electoral Disaster, a Search for Constitutional Government), *ibid.*, III, No. 4 (September 20, 1947), 5–10. Part 2 of this article appeared in the next issue, No. 5, pp. 8–10.

[53] Ku Ch'un-fan, "Ts'ung min-chu tao ti-kuo" (From Democracy to Imperialism), *ibid.*, III, No. 10 (November 1, 1947), 3–5. Ku was a bank official.

[54] Kuo Shu-jen, "Hsien cheng ho chung-kuo wen-hua" (Constitutional Government and China's Culture), *ibid.*, IV, No. 3 (March 13, 1948), 6–8. The author was living in the United States at the time he wrote this article. In it he was arguing specifically against the ideas of Chang Tung-sun and Liang Sou-ming discussed above.

For some, like Ch'u An-p'ing, the British Labour Party represented the formula which was the last best hope for China. The victory of the Labour Party in 1946 provided Ch'u with an actual, real-life example to support his contention that the goals of democracy and socialism could indeed be pursued simultaneously: it was not necessary to follow the way of Moscow in order to realize socialism.[55]

Ch'u was clearly one of those "contemporary professors" scorned by Fan Hung for advocating a "third way" and expecting the exploiters to reform themselves voluntarily and abandon the system that had nurtured and enriched them. Nor was Ch'u by any means alone. Fan Hung may have been correct to deride these professors for their political naïveté, but they were at least intellectually consistent. For they seemed also to believe that the CCP could be induced, as Ch'u An-p'ing put it, "to correct its policies" and abandon its role in the Civil War.[56] These men had no illusions as to the nature of KMT rule, and, as we shall see below, they also had no illusions about the CCP. There was not one among them willing to argue that the ultimate, long-term objective of the CCP was anything but the creation of a Communist state. But what most of them did not seem to believe, at least until after about mid-1948, was that the Communists would ever be in a position to do so—a logical conclusion, since no one believed that the war could be fought to a victory by either side. Thus, to the liberal intellectual, committed to neither of the two warring parties, the perceived military stalemate was thought to provide considerable incentive for voluntary compromises on both sides and an ideal opportunity for the promotion of a centrist alternative.

Despite the seemingly endless controversy over how much socialism how fast and what kind of democracy, there was general agreement concerning the basic political structure within which all the arguments might be worked out. That structure was a coalition government to be arrived at in accordance with the general formula worked out by

---

[55] Ch'u An-p'ing, "Chung-kuo te cheng chü," p. 6.

[56] There were many who expressed this view. Among them was the economist Wu Ch'i-yüan, who wrote that the Communists "should abandon their life-and-death struggle and the attempt to set up a proletarian dictatorship by armed revolution. They should learn to become a constitutional party within a constitutional government, be willing to promote democracy, and be satisfied with this." As for the KMT, he suggested that its officials should be willing to compromise voluntarily and "in accordance with the hopes of the people of the nation and the majority of the members within the KMT itself, immediately implement democracy, and force the wealthy classes to make some sacrifices. . . ." "Ts'ung ching-chi kuan-tien lun nei-chan," pp. 4–5.

the Political Consultative Conference (PCC) at its meeting in January, 1946.[57] Wang Yün-sheng, editor-in-chief of the *Ta kung pao,* described the PCC agreements in this way:

Among them, the reorganization of the government is primary. Because all of the various political parties are to participate in the reorganization of the government, it will be coalitional in nature. This government will then be used in the convocation of a national assembly and writing of a constitution. It will be a transitional government to be replaced by democratic general elections and a constitutional government. In this way, the line of the PCC can be transformed into a democratic constitutional government.[58]

Wang added that, in his opinion, the line of the PCC represented the most attractive solution for China's problems and the best means of transforming the CCP into a constitutional political party capable of functioning within a democratic framework.

The idea of a coalition government also appealed to those who were not overly sanguine about the workability of constitutional democracy in China. Chang Tung-sun considered a coalition government the political form best suited to China's needs because it would create an environment in which there would be supervision and constraints on all sides. The KMT would then be forced out of its old pre-eminent position and would have no choice but to reform itself "voluntarily." [59]

As Professor Wu Shih-ch'ang put it, there were many reasons for reform but only one way to accomplish it. The real question was how

---

[57] The Political Consultative Conference was a multiparty gathering which met between January 11 and January 31, 1946, for the purpose of seeking a peaceful solution to the conflict between the CCP and the KMT. The conference was attended by a total of thirty-eight delegates, including nonpartisans as well as representatives of the KMT, CCP, DL, and the Youth Party. The conference reached agreement on each of five major points of disagreement that then existed between the CCP and the KMT. These included the reorganization of the national government, the reorganization of the armed forces, the revision of the 1936 draft constitution, and the membership of the National Assembly. Right-wing elements within the KMT nevertheless succeeded in revising the KMT's position on a number of issues at a meeting of the KMT's Central Executive Committee two months later. The conference had no power to enforce its decisions. Moreover, it was criticized by some liberals because only representatives of the various political parties had participated in it, whereas the people were not directly represented. But because it was a genuine multiparty gathering that had, in principle at least, resolved all of the main obstacles to the peaceful evolution of a constitutional government in which all parties would be represented, the resolutions of the PCC were held up by most liberals throughout the Civil War years as the most appropriate model on which to base a political compromise and a peace settlement. On the PCC, see Ch'ien Tuan-sheng, *The Government and Politics of China* (Cambridge, Mass.: Harvard University Press, 1950), pp. 317–19, 375–80.

[58] Wang, "Chung-kuo shih-chü ch'ien-t'u te san-ko ch'u-hsiang" (Three Directions for China's Future), *Kuan-ch'a* (Shanghai), I, No. 1 (September 1, 1946), 5.

[59] Chang, "Chui-shu wo-men nu-li . . . ," p. 6.

to induce both the KMT and the CCP to respect the resolutions of the PCC and join together in a genuine coalition government. General Marshall abandoned hope in finding an answer to that question during 1946. But liberals in the KMT areas, who had more at stake in the outcome than did General Marshall, did not give up until almost two years later. The proposals they brought forward, however, bore the mark not so much of political naïveté as of the weaknesses inherent in their own occupational roles and political commitments. They were therefore compelled to rely on their only political resources—the power of the pen and moral exhortation—as they continued to reiterate the hope that a third party or group of some kind would somehow emerge from the vast unrepresented center of the Chinese political spectrum. This was conceptualized as a genuine third force based on the support of the broad mass of the population, which deplored the war, was dissatisfied with the KMT, and allegedly did not quite trust the CCP. The reasoning was that if the strength of this hitherto un-mobilized majority could be properly channeled, the two parties would be compelled to compromise.

It was acknowledged, of course, that this might be easier said than done. And on one point there seemed to be almost universal agreement: the Democratic League and the various minor parties as they were constituted were not capable of performing the task in question. The existing parties which then made up the so-called third force were generally dismissed as weak, disorganized, and powerless. Chang Tung-sun had suggested that a truly strong and independent third force could serve as a "bridge between the CCP and the KMT, forcing each onto the right track, bringing them together, and achieving co-operation between them." Responding to him, one writer in Hong Kong wondered where such a force was to come from, and reminded Chang that the forces which then existed between the Communists and the KMT were most certainly neither strong nor independent.[60] No one quibbled with Ch'u An-p'ing when he presented his verdict on the DL, the largest of the third parties: "Our criticism of the DL can be summed up in two phrases: 'its natural endowments are weak, and it is out of tune with reality.' " He pointed out that the people in the league were mostly all "of another generation"—old scholars, thinkers, and philosophers—and that there was not a real politician among them. Having diverse educational backgrounds, political viewpoints, and historical backgrounds, they were held together only by their spirit

[60] Ch'ang Ming, "Fan-lun chung-chien p'ai te cheng-chih lu-hsien," p. 33.

of opposition to the KMT. "Really," he concluded, "the DL is hardly even worth being criticized as the tail of the CCP." [61]

What, then, was to be done? Where was a genuinely strong and independent third force to come from? This question represented the moment of truth for the liberal intellectual. In trying to answer it, the contradiction between the liberal's own ideals and the reality of the existing situation was fully exposed. It was an example of ideological commitment and intellectual insight reduced to political impotence. The most common response to the question of how a strong third force could emerge was that such a task was the responsibility and mission of the intellectuals themselves. In the words of Professor Chou Chung-ch'i:

There is only one road left to follow and that is to allow the middle parties to lead the revolution and to set up a new government. What are the third parties? They are the pro-peace elements among the intellectuals and liberals; they have intelligence, faith, and expertise; they understand the needs of the people and can get their support. If they can carry out socialism, lead the revolution, and organize a coalition government of many parties, it may take thirty years. But these are the kinds of people who must stabilize China and complete the final stage of the revolution. China today must rely on the efforts of the intellectuals.[62]

Similar views were expressed by many others, but agreement was not universal. One writer spoke derisively of the "innocence" of the so-called liberal elements who "delude themselves by believing that they have the power to reform the situation." [63] Another gave more detailed expression to such doubts while discussing a rumor that circulated for some time after Hu Shih's return to China in 1946 to the effect that he was planning to organize a political party. It is not known whether his administrative talents are as good as his intellectual capabilities, mused the writer, pointing out that politics and education were not the same. There was the case of Carsun Chang, for example, who was a very learned Ph.D. but had not been very successful at leading his Democratic Socialist Party. In terms of general ideas, Hu Shih can of course be a leader, concluded the correspondent, but a political party cannot depend solely on general inclinations and orien-

[61] Ch'u An-p'ing, "Chung-kuo te cheng chü," p. 7. For a similar but more detailed critique of the DL, see Wen Fu, "Look Out, China Democratic League," *The Weekly* (Shanghai), June 8, 1946, as translated in U.S. Consulate-General (Shanghai), *Chinese Press Review*, June 22, 1946.

[62] Chou Chung-ch'i, "Lun ko-ming" (On Revolution), *Kuan-ch'a* (Shanghai), I, No. 22 (January 25, 1947), 10. Chou was formerly a professor at Lingnan University.

[63] *Kuan-ch'a* special correspondent (Nanking), "Ho-ch'u shih kuei ch'eng?" (Where Will the Journey End?), *ibid.*, IV, No. 20 (July 17, 1948), 11-12.

tations to gain support; it must have concrete policies and administrative talent to implement them.[64]

In his ambivalence on this issue, Ch'u An-p'ing seemed to sum up the contradictory lines of thought expressed by the contributors to his and other journals. His views were developed most fully in his article, "China's Political Situation," which appeared in March, 1947. The strength of liberals is the strength of moral not political power, he wrote. It is the strength of thought and of speech, but not of political action. He recalled that General Marshall before leaving China had advocated that the greatest possible effort be exerted to encourage the truly liberal elements to organize themselves for political action. But Marshall is an American with an American point of view, wrote Ch'u, and does not seem to understand that it is not easy for Chinese liberals to form strong organizations. The reasons for this fact were partly inherent in the nature of Chinese intellectuals themselves and partly grew out of the political environment of KMT China.

Whatever their virtues, he asserted, the vices of Chinese liberals— for the most part literary men—were their narrow-mindedness and their individualism. But politics needed farsighted men who would struggle for the big things rather than quibble over the small, who could concern themselves with the whole situation and accept the principle of cooperation as the basis for political action. Such action required organization and discipline. But because liberals were more concerned with right and reason than with power, it was not easy for them to develop organizational strength. Political action also required leadership, but because of their pride and imprudence it was difficult to produce leaders among liberal elements.

The inherent political weaknesses of liberals, Ch'u went on, had been accentuated by twenty years of KMT rule. Here he listed three areas in which the KMT government had imposed restrictions that affected the liberals' strength. First were the political restrictions resulting from the government's refusal to uphold in practice such basic rights as freedoms of the press, speech, and assembly. Second were economic restrictions: the impoverished intellectual community could barely keep body and soul together, much less have the time, energy, and resources necessary for political activities. And finally, there were restrictions on the freedom of thought. But twenty years of KMT interference in education meant not only that the nation's young peo-

---

[64] Report from "Our Nanking Correspondent," "Hu Shih te t'ai-tu" (Hu Shih's Attitude), *ibid.*, I, No. 1 (September 1, 1946), 21.

ple did not become loyal followers of the KMT, but, more importantly, that they had received a poor education. Thus, instead of being able to cope in a rational manner with their dissatisfaction, many young people were simply overcome by it and turned blindly to the extremes of right or left.

Then without warning or even a paragraph of explanation, Ch'u suddenly shifted the thrust of his argument and took up almost precisely where General Marshall had left off. But whereas Marshall may have thought he was talking within the realm of realistic possibility, Ch'u An-p'ing knew better and was obliged to base his arguments instead on logical necessity and the inevitable drift of history. He wrote therefore of "historical responsibilities" and the nature of the times:

Although liberal elements have suffered from the above kinds of restrictions, their strength, objectively speaking, at present is growing daily. This growing strength is not due to their own efforts, however, but is a result of the times. From the viewpoint of morality and thought, it is not the Communists but this group of liberal intellectuals that can shake the KMT regime today. Everyone fears the CCP, fears the violence of their killing and burning, and no matter whether or not this fear is misconceived, people are still afraid of the Communists. On the other hand, it is not the KMT that can repulse the Communists, but this same group of liberals. The corruption of the KMT is already luminously displayed for every eye to see and is being recorded by every mouth. So that even if it is a question of the Three People's Principles, it is difficult for the people to maintain hope and trust in the KMT. Given these two extremes, only if the liberal elements come forward as leaders can a stable mean be achieved which is compatible with the sense of rectitude of the general population. We have said that today in China this group of liberal elements is very dispersed, and that morality is the source of their strength. The strength of morality is without form, nor can it be seen or grasped; but that strength is deep and can be long-lasting. This strength has its roots in the society and in the hearts of men. . . .

The absolute majority [of the people] hope that a new force can be produced outside the CCP and the KMT, in order to stabilize the present political situation in China. . . . Presently in China most all of the liberal elements are depressed and anxious about the nation's future. But they absolutely cannot stop there with their passive feelings of distress and anxiety. The liberal elements can and should rise up. This is not a question of whether or not they will be happy to do so, or are willing to do so; it is a question of their historical responsibilities.

Ch'u An-p'ing was correct in his assertions that China's liberals lacked both the resources and the inclination to participate effectively in the political arena, and that their strength was limited to the influence of the pen rather than of political action. Certainly the pages of his journal bore testimony to the feats of moral exhortation which the liberal intellectuals were capable of performing. But as he himself had seen so clearly, this was not enough. It might have been if they had had an unlimited period of time in which to work. But time was something else that the liberals did not have during the Civil War years. On the basis of his own assessment, then, it was almost inevitable that they should fail to have any tangible influence on the outcome of the political struggle between the KMT and the CCP, although Professor Ch'u could not yet accept that in March, 1947.

By the summer of 1948, however, he had no choice. Ch'u An-p'ing in effect conceded defeat in his lead editorial which appeared in the July 17, 1948, issue of *Kuan-ch'a*. This "farewell editorial" was prompted by apparently well-placed rumors that the journal was about to be banned. His words were a summation of all the anger and frustration that had inspired his efforts and those of his colleagues during the past two years. Ch'u wrote in part:

Finally, we are willing to say quite frankly that although the government fears our criticism, in fact we now have no more interest in criticizing this government. As for this journal, already in the past few months there have been few articles that contained heated criticism of the government because everyone is very despondent. What else is there left to say? And what use would it be? We feel that when a government has reached a stage where the people are not even interested in criticizing it, then such a government is already in tragic enough straits. Unfortunately, the government does not even have this much self-awareness, but is still there pulling at heads and ears, planning to ban journals and newspapers. How really pitiful and laughable. We want to tell all our friends who are concerned about us: ban us or don't ban us—we are past caring. And if we are banned, we ask that no one be sad. In this age of bloodshed, when untold numbers of lives have been sacrificed, buildings and property destroyed, families separated, and so many ideals and hopes have been shattered under this dark rule, what does it matter if this one small journal is banned. Friends, we should face the facts and the oppression and remain determined in our loyalty to the nation. If today this method does not work, then tomorrow try another and continue the effort. Because although methods may be dissimilar, our loyalty to the nation will never waver.

As it turned out, twenty-one more issues of *Kuan-ch'a* were published after Professor Ch'u wrote his farewell editorial. The journal was finally banned in late December. But in the intervening months, it was clear that the time for talking liberal politics in China was finished. The tones of outrage and urgency that had characterized the arguments during the past two years seemed to have dissipated. As the *Chien hsien jih-pao* was soon to comment, the "Age of Professor Ch'u An-p'ing" had indeed come to an end. In December, just before the journal was banned, Shanghai newspapers reported that both Ch'u and his friend Wang Yün-sheng of the *Ta kung pao* had left the city for an unknown destination. In January the mystery of their whereabouts was solved when the Communist radio station XNCR broadcast a report that Ch'u and Wang and many others were in Shihchiachuang attending the first National Political Consultative Conference to be held under Communist auspices.

CHINESE COMMUNISM THROUGH LIBERAL EYES

The liberal community's opinion of the Nationalist government was abundantly clear. There was, however, another dimension to the liberal dilemma. That so many liberal intellectuals ultimately decided to accept a Communist government must have been due in large part to the totality of their dissatisfaction with the KMT. But what was equally well known at this time was that they also entertained serious misgivings about the Communists—reservations as serious, in fact, as those the Communists had about them.

The liberal critique of the CCP was in many respects different from its critique, outlined above, of the KMT. For one thing, the liberals were obviously more familiar with the policies and performance of the latter. And second, since they felt that the government was in large measure responsible for the existing political situation and that it still possessed the power and authority to reform itself and end the war, they concentrated their efforts on the government in the hope of compelling such action from it. By contrast, the CCP was relegated to the position of an opposition party whose chances of participating in the national government in any capacity except that of a coalition partner appeared very slim indeed. This treatment of the CCP may of course have been due as much to the political restrictions under which the liberal press was operating in the government-controlled areas as to the political biases of the liberals themselves. Still, their critique of the CCP, although based admittedly on less than ample information, gives the impression of having been made in good faith and was in all respects consistent with their fundamental ideological commitments.

As with their treatment of the Nationalist government, the liberals' discussion of the CCP revolved around two major concerns: one had to do with the programs and performance of the Chinese Communists in the territories they controlled or occupied briefly, and the other with the forms of Communist rule as reflected both in theory and in practice. But whereas the KMT proved vulnerable on both counts, the CCP's rating on the liberal balance sheet contained only one unequivocal minus. The liberal reaction to major aspects of the Communist program ranged from positive to mixed. Communism as a form of government, however, drew an almost uniformly negative response. Ch'u An-p'ing had summed up the liberal view rather succinctly when he wrote in March, 1947, that although he had never lived in the Communist areas, he knew that much good had been said of the Communists' work in Yenan; also, in terms of its economic principles, he felt there was little to fear from the CCP. What was fearful, in his view, were Communist methods of political life. "Frankly speaking," he continued, "although the CCP is today crying out loudly about its 'democracy,' we would like to know whether in terms of its basic spirit the CCP is not really an antidemocratic political party. Because in terms of their spirit of control, there is in fact not much difference between Communist and fascist parties. Both try to control the popular will by strict organization. Today in China's political struggle, the CCP . . . is encouraging everyone to rise up and oppose the 'party rule' [*tang chu*] of the KMT. But in terms of the CCP's real spirit, what the CCP advocates is also 'party rule,' and is certainly not democracy." [65]

POLICIES AND PERFORMANCE

In terms of CCP policies and the nature of their implementation, the issues that attracted the most attention and elicited the most positive response were almost all related to the war itself. As we have seen, one of the reasons the intellectual community refused to support the government on the war was the heavy price being exacted from the

---

[65] Ch'u An-p'ing, "Chung-kuo te cheng chü," p. 6. The problem of information about the CCP was of course a real one, and disclaimers about the lack of it often prefaced essays heavy on opinion and short on fact. As Professor Yang Jen-keng put it, in trying to explain why he had not written a requested piece on the CCP: "Communist propaganda says only the good things and anti-Communist propaganda says only the bad; and it's as difficult to accept the propaganda as it is to find other materials." Ch'u An-p'ing expressed the problem somewhat more gracefully when he reminded his readers only that he had never lived in the Communist areas and that his opinions were therefore based mostly on "common sense."

A fair number of factual articles on the CCP did, however, appear in *Kuan-ch'a* and other liberal journals. These articles were either the products of interviews with people who had once lived in some Communist area, or were the reports of correspondents in the field who were able to spend short periods of time in, or in close proximity to, a Communist-controlled region. This did provide an alternative of sorts to the Central News Agency version of Communist activities. By piecing together these scattered bits of information, the interested reader in the KMT areas could get some impression, however sketchy, about what was happening in Communist-held territory. The reports of *Kuan-ch'a*'s military correspondents became famous in 1948 as the only popularly available source of accurate information on the military situation.

population because of it. That price included the burdens imposed upon the peasantry in the form of taxation, government purchase and borrowing of grain, increased opportunities for official peculation, the abuses associated with military conscription, and the depredations of a poorly disciplined army in the field. Nor did the Communists emerge entirely blameless on all of these points. But it gradually came to be recognized that however great the sufferings that the war had brought upon the people, the Communists, unlike the government, were managing to increase their strength among the peasantry in the very process of fighting that war. Whereas KMT officials and their local allies continued to use the war as a source of personal gain, the Communists were using it to broaden their base of support in the countryside.[66] The reasons for their successes in this respect were acknowledged to be their social and economic policies that centered on land reform, the relative competence and integrity with which these policies were implemented, and the discipline of the Communist armies.

One area of notable Communist success was Manchuria. The shortcomings of the KMT administration there after the end of World War II were widely known and discussed. What was also known—although not quite so intensively discussed—was how profitably the Communists were trading on the government's mistakes. A key goal of the KMT's reoccupation policy in the Northeast was to prevent the re-emergence there of the local power base dominated by the sons of the old warlord, Marshal Chang Tso-lin. Using classic divide-and-rule tactics, the central government partitioned the three northeast provinces into nine administrative units and filled virtually all important official positions with outsiders. Its local allies included primarily landlords and others who had collaborated with the Japanese, the only elements in the Northeast who could be counted on to have no loyalties either to the Communists or to the still popular Young Marshal, Chang Hsüeh-liang. Remaining suspicious of the Manchurian troops, the central government refused to allow them to participate in the takeover of the Northeast when the Russians withdrew in 1946. And finally, in late 1946 or early 1947, the Young Marshal, still under arrest for his part in the Sian Incident ten years before, was moved to a more secure exile on the island of Taiwan.

The Communists took full advantage of the widespread resentment that these measures aroused, and the government's liberal critics were

---

[66] Yang Jen-keng, "Lun nei-chan" (On the Civil War), *Kuan-ch'a* (Shanghai), IV, No. 4 (March 20, 1948), 5.

quick to point this out. Most of the former northeast troops went over to the Communists, as did Chang Hsüeh-liang's younger brother, General Chang Hsüeh-ssu. The Communists welcomed their new non-Communist allies, who together with locally organized Communist forces made up over half the Party's military strength in Manchuria by mid-1947. The Communists, it was said, understood the importance of avoiding the central government's arrogant attitude toward the northeasterners, who had lived under Japanese rule for fourteen years. The Communists used local talent and personnel in as many political and military positions as possible. Chang Hsüeh-ssu, for example, occupied a prominent position as vice-chairman of the Manchurian Administrative Committee, the highest administrative body for the Communist-controlled areas of the Northeast.[67]

Since they were not northeasterners, government troops garrisoned there soon came to be regarded as an occupying army—although they had initially been welcomed as liberators after fourteen years of Japanese occupation. A major reason for the local hostility was the behavior of the troops. The problem of military discipline, or the lack of it, became a notorious one in the Northeast and applied to the regular government armies as well as to the local self-defense forces, which were often organized by local landlords and former collaborators with the aid and encouragement of the government. Correspondents in Mukden and Changchun were fond of writing that all of the armies—meaning those of the Russians, the Chinese Communists, and the central government—were equally bad and that as a result of their activities the local people were even beginning to look back favorably on the years of the Japanese occupation.[68]

But different reports told different stories, and while there was no

[67] Ho Yung-chi, "Ts'ung yin-tu fen chih shuo-tao chung-kuo ch'ien-t'u" (Talking about the Partition of India and China's Future), *ibid.*, II, No. 20 (July 12, 1947), 4–5; *Kuan-ch'a* correspondent, "Pei wang man-chou" (Looking North to Manchuria), *ibid.*, IV, No. 3 (March 13, 1948), 15–16; Ch'ien Pang-k'ai, "Tung-pei yen-chung hsing tsen-yang ts'u-ch'eng te?" (What Has Precipitated the Grave Situation in the Northeast?), *Ch'ing-tao shih-pao* (The Tsingtao Times), February 19, 1948, reprinted in *Kuan-ch'a* (Shanghai), IV, No. 5 (March 27, 1948), 16; Kao Ch'ao (*Kuan-ch'a* Shen-yang t'ung-hsin), "Fa-pi ch'u kuan yu liu-t'ung-ch'uan pien-chih suo chi-ch'i te po-lang" (Nationalist Government Currency Enters the Northeast and the Tide of Manchurian Currency Devaluation Rises), *Kuan-ch'a* (Shanghai), IV, No. 6 (April 3, 1948), 17.

[68] "Our Special Correspondent" (Changchun), "Ling hsia san-shih tu te jen hsin" (People's Hearts Are Thirty Degrees below Zero), *Kuan-ch'a* (Shanghai), II, No. 1 (March 1, 1947), 18; "Our Special Correspondent" (Shenyang), "Shen-yang wan han" (Mukden in Late Winter), *ibid.*, I, No. 17 (December 21, 1946), 17–18; Kao Ch'ao (*Kuan-ch'a* Shen-yang t'ung-hsin), "Lei yen k'an tung-pei" (Looking at the Northeast with Tearful Eyes), *ibid.*, IV, No. 1 (February 28, 1948), 17–18.

one who had a good word for the government troops or those of the Russians, the Communists often received a somewhat better press. For example, in early 1947 one writer on a visit to the northeast spent ten days in his native village about 120 *li* distant from the city of Szepingkai. He found himself appalled at the state of apprehension and fear to which the local people, including his own family, had been reduced by marauding government troops stationed in the vicinity. The Russians had also left a bad impression, but the Chinese Communists who had occupied the area for a short time had apparently behaved rather well. Although the local people had not been aware during the Japanese occupation that there were two different kinds of Chinese troops, they had soon learned to recognize the difference. And about the Communists they now "maintained somewhat more hope" as compared with the others. The writer delivered some cynical comments about how little it took to satisfy the hopes of simple people, but he nevertheless reported that his old mother was very favorably impressed with a group of Communist soldiers who had billeted themselves in her house, because they had respected her wishes, had not bothered her sixteen-year-old granddaughter, and had taken nothing that did not belong to them when they left.[69]

There were similarly favorable reports about the Communist treatment of prisoners of war, including military officers and men as well as government personnel.[70] And the same correspondent who deplored the hardships that the war was creating for the people of the Northeast also acknowledged in April, 1948, that the government was indulging in wishful thinking if it really believed it could win popular support for a military showdown with the Communists in the Northeast because, he wrote, the Communist troops had already "entered deeply among the people." [71] Also, there were known to be many people in addition to the old Manchurian troops who had gone over to the Communists. Thus, despite the thousands of students, civil servants, businessmen, and other people of means who did not wish to live under Communist rule and had fled to KMT-held cities south of the Sungari River, there was a common saying in journalistic circles after the Taiwanese revolt in February, 1947: the reason a similar uprising did not

[69] Han Ch'i, "Tung-pei shih jih" (Ten Days in the Northeast), *STPP* (Hong Kong), IV, No. 89 (August 16, 1947), 25–28.

[70] *Kuan-ch'a* special correspondent (Shenyang), "Ha-erh-pin kuei lai" (Return from Harbin), *Kuan-ch'a* (Shanghai), III, No. 3 (September 13, 1947), 21–22; letter to the editor, signed Yüan Yün-lan, at Mukden, February 17, 1948, *ibid.*, IV, No. I (February 28, 1948), 2.

[71] Kao Ch'ao, "Fa-pi ch'u kuan . . . ," p. 17.

break out in the Northeast was that all the people who wanted to rebel had already gone over to the Communist side.[72]

Nor was Manchuria the only place where central government forces suffered by comparison with the Communists. This turned out to be a familiar story in almost every field area with which inquiring correspondents came into contact. *Kuan-ch'a* published favorable reports concerning the behavior of Communist troops in many different localities, including the Kiangsu-Chekiang-Anhwei Border Area, the T'ai-hsing area in northern Kiangsu, central Hopeh, western Shensi, Kansu, and southern Shansi.[73]

There seemed to be a general recognition, however, that the reasons for the Communist successes had to do with more than good military strategy, clever tactics, and troop discipline. Why has the KMT continued to lose, queried one writer, even when it is fully aware of its errors and weaknesses? He continued:

The KMT cannot correct its weaknesses and defeat the Communists because the KMT is limited by its social and economic organization. But because the Communist armies have changed production relations and social and economic organization in the liberated areas, they have been able to establish the new social order which they need. Grain requisitions, military conscription, and self-defense can therefore be carried out with a high degree of effectiveness and there is no need to use excessive military force to defend the villages and towns they control. . . .[74]

[72] Ho Yung-chi, "Ts'ung yin-tu . . . ," p. 4. This explanation also appeared in *STPP*. On the matter of refugees in the Northeast, see *Kuan-ch'a* special correspondent (Shenyang), "Tsung-t'an tung-pei ta chü" (Talking Freely about the General Situation in the Northeast), *Kuan-ch'a* (Shanghai), IV, No. 4 (March 20, 1948), 17–18; Pang Tze-ming (*Kuan-ch'a* Ch'ang-ch'un t'ung-hsin), "Sung-hua chiang p'an te yin yang chieh" (The Sungari River Frontier), *ibid.*, II, No. 22 (July 26, 1947), 19–20; Ch'un Sheng, "Shen-yang erh san shih" (Two or Three Things about Mukden), *STPP* (Hong Kong), V, No. 102 (June 15, 1948), 35.

[73] "Our Special Correspondent," "I shih pien ch'ü" (This, Too, Is a Border Area), *Kuan-ch'a* (Shanghai), I, No. 11 (November 9, 1946), 19–20; "Our Special Correspondent" (Chiang nan), "Chiang nan ch'ing" (Conditions in Southern Kiangsu), *ibid.*, I, No. 18 (December 28, 1946), 15–16; Chu Tung-jun, "Wo ts'ung t'ai-hsing lai" (I Have Come from T'ai-hsing), *ibid.*, I, No. 6 (October 5, 1946), 8 (Chu Tung-jun was a professor at National Central University in Nanking); Ho P'eng (*Kuan-ch'a* Pao-ting t'ung-hsin), "Tsai nei-chan tsui ch'ien hsien" (At the Very Forefront of the Civil War), *ibid.*, III, No. 5 (September 27, 1947), 18–19; *Kuan-ch'a* correspondent (Hsi-an), "Lung-tung chih chan chieh-shu i-hou" (After the Battle of Lungtung), *ibid.*, IV, No. 17 (June 19, 1948), 16; *Kuan-ch'a* correspondent (Lan-chou), "Kuan-yü hsi-pei tsui chin chü-shih te pao-kao" (A Report on the Most Recent Situation in the Northwest), *ibid.*, IV, No. 20 (July 17, 1948), 15; and Li Tzu-ching, "Chin nan chieh-fang ch'ü te tou-cheng ch'ing-hsing" (The Matter of Struggle in the South Shansi Liberated District), *ibid.*, IV, No. 2 (March 6, 1948), 15.

[74] *Kuan-ch'a* special correspondent, "K'ung-hsin chan yü ch'uan-hsin chan" (Undefended-Rear Warfare and Strike-at-the-Heart Warfare), *ibid.*, IV, No. 11 (May 8, 1948), 13.

It is not that the government has not seen these things, commented another correspondent. It knows that in dealing with the Communist armies, politics is more important than the military. But the government is not willing to overturn the old society and its tragic fate is thus being sealed.[75]

One of the most positive views of the Communist effort to overturn the old society came from a KMT civil servant who spent three months in Ho-tse, Shantung, in the Shansi-Hopeh-Shantung-Honan Border Area, during the summer of 1946. He went there in an official capacity to participate in relief work associated with the rechanneling of the Yellow River. But having (as he admitted) almost nothing to do, he spent the time talking politics and trying to find out what he could about the Communists. He came away obviously impressed by what he had seen, such as the equalization of wealth, the austere conditions under which Communist officials lived, and most especially what he called their "administrative work style." They are completely different from us, he marveled, in discussing their sincerity, their sense of responsibility in performing any task, and the meetings afterward at which errors were openly admitted and criticized. Unlike some among us, he wrote, they do not say things they know in their hearts to be untrue. Of course, he admitted, "the lower-level cadres cannot avoid shallowness and mechanical answers . . . but better they have that ideology than none at all, and better to be conscientious and self-confident as they are, than negligent and self-deceiving as we are."

He also marveled at the apparent willingness with which the local people cooperated with the Communists in such activities as public works projects, and regretted that he had not made a greater effort to discover the exact methods the CCP was using to activate, organize, and lead the people. He concluded that the Communists were able to develop the strength of the common people by adopting the unusual practice of treating them like human beings, explaining things patiently to them, and allowing them to talk back in return. He was especially surprised and impressed in this regard by the way poor men and women dared to get up on a platform at the struggle meetings and speak out publicly against those who had insulted, cheated, and oppressed them. He had witnesssed many such meetings while he was in

---

[75] *Kuan-ch'a* special correspondent (Lan-chou), "Kuan-yü hsi-pei tsui chin chü shih te pao-kao," p. 15. For a similar comment regarding conditions in western Honan, see Yeh Chün (*Kuan-ch'a* Yü hsi t'ung-hsin), "Chieh-k'ai yü hsi te nei mu" (Behind the Scenes in Western Honan), *ibid.*, III, No. 12 (November 15, 1947), 17.

Ho-tse, including several directed against the German priest and the nuns from the town's Catholic church.[76]

It was specifically land reform, however, that the liberals most often acknowledged as the basis of the CCP's success in changing the social and economic organization in the rural areas, although they did have reservations about the methods being used to implement it.[77] The Communists themselves, of course, made no secret of the fact that they were using land reform as a strategy to strengthen their base of support for the war against the central government. They had admitted on many different occasions that their appeal to the peasants had to be made in concrete and practical terms, rather than in the form of ideological abstractions which they could never comprehend. And since land was the concrete term the peasant understood best, the Communists used it in an effort to strengthen their position in the countryside.

Whether it was generally recognized that the Communists were consciously using the land reform movement in this way is unclear. One schoolteacher who was interviewed in Shanghai shortly after leaving the Communist area in north Kiangsu remarked that although he had never heard them say so, he felt certain that the Communists would not have turned so quickly to land reform from the more moderate policy of rent reduction had the Civil War not created the necessity for such a change. "After the farmer receives his share of land," this observer pointed out, "he will naturally think that the only way to preserve his share of land is to follow the CCP to the very end. As a matter of fact, farmers are fearful of measures of revenge from the landlords, and it is highly probable that they will plunge in with the CCP."[78] One of *Kuan-ch'a*'s correspondents also stated that in his

---

[76] Chiang Sha, "Tsai ho-tse chieh-fang ch'ü suo chien" (What Was Seen in the Ho-tse Liberated Area), *ibid.*, IV, No. 2 (March 6, 1948), 13–16, 18; Part 2 of this article appeared in the next issue, No. 3 (March 13, 1948), 12–13.

[77] P'u Hsi-hsiu (*Kuan-ch'a* Nan-ching t'ung-hsin), "Kuo-min-tang san chung ch'üan hui niao-k'an" (A Bird's-Eye View of the Kuomintang's Third Central Executive Committee Meeting), *ibid.*, II, No. 4 (March 22, 1947), 15; Wu Ch'i-yüan, "Ts'ung ching-chi kuan-tien lun nei-chan wen-t'i," p. 4; Wu Shih-ch'ang, "Ts'ung mei su shuo-tao kuo nei," p. 4.

[78] Cheng Yüeh-chung, "Three Stages of the Land Problem in Northern Kiangsu," *The Economic Weekly* (Shanghai), III, No. 18 (October 31, 1946), as translated in U.S. Consulate-General (Shanghai), *Chinese Press Review*, January 4, 1947.

The general decision to move away from the program of rent and interest reduction, which had been the basis of the Communist land policy during the period of the anti-Japanese united front, was announced in Yenan on May 4, 1946. Land reform was advertised as an effort to realize at once the goal of "land-to-the-tiller" to which everyone, including the KMT, had been giving lip service, at least, since the time of Sun Yat-sen.

view the primary objective of the Communists' land reform program
was the development of their political and military strength in the
countryside. And the results of the effort were obvious. As this correspondent put it: "In the liberated areas, land has been changed both
in terms of its military uses and in terms of social life. This change
has shaken people out of their old ideas about the land. And the deep
military strength of the liberated areas has come as a result of this
great change. Under their new social order, they [the Communists]
have no problems about sources of grain and manpower. . . ." If they
really want to control the rural areas, he concluded, the land reform
movement will make it possible for them to grow roots in the villages
and to grow strong, and the KMT is doing nothing to meet this challenge.[79]

There was nevertheless a large measure of ambivalence inherent in
the liberal intellectual's willingness to acknowledge the nature of the
Communists' strength in the countryside. This ambivalence was indicated by the repeated appeals to the government to find a solution of
its own for the problems in the rural areas. Another indication was
the tone of desperation that began to appear as it became apparent
that no such solutions were even being sought. "There must be a way
out," declared one writer in February, 1948, as he complained that
the government had yet to come forward with a concrete program and
that, even if it did, there was no one in the rural areas capable of
implementing it.[80]

Some criticized the Communist program of land division and redistribution as economically unsound. According to the Communist
method of dividing the land, wrote Professor Wu Shih-ch'ang, each
person would get two or three *mou* of land and he would not be able
to live. Only if there is industrialization, the mechanization of agri-

---

In the Communist areas of north Kiangsu, the land reform program, which involved the
confiscation of the lands of rich peasants and landlords and redistribution to the poor and
landless, reportedly began almost immediately after the general decision was announced
in May, 1946. A major government offensive against the Communist areas there began
that summer. Most of the *hsien* towns were retaken, but the government was never really
able to extend its control much beyond them into the countryside. The Communists were
able gradually to recoup their losses aided in large part apparently by the measures of
retaliation and revenge taken by returning landlords and KMT officials, a fact that was
not lost on the Shanghai press.

[79] *Kuan-ch'a* correspondent, "T'u-ti kai-ko, ti-tao chan" (Land Reform, Underground
Tunnel Warfare), *Kuan-ch'a* (Shanghai), IV, No. 6 (April 3, 1948), 14.

[80] *Kuan-ch'a* correspondent, "Ts'ung chan-chü k'an cheng-chü" (Looking at Political
Conditions from the Military Situation), *ibid.,* IV, No. 1 (February 28, 1948), 16.

culture, and collectivization, can agricultural production be increased and the standard of living be raised.[81] But the real problem was not so much what the Communists were doing in the countryside as how. It was not the class struggle movement and the land reform program themselves, but the manner of their implementation that bothered liberal intellectuals. Although such stories were not uniformly reported from all of the Communist areas, the sensational reports of struggle meetings, liquidations, beatings, and executions were too numerous and too widespread to be dismissed entirely as the work of a few overzealous or misguided local cadres. Violence apparently had to be calculated as part of the cost of the Communists' rural program; and it was a cost which, as Ch'u An-p'ing noted, created serious misgivings about the Communists in many minds.

One of the few who neither overlooked this cost nor seemed to feel too uncomfortable with it was the civil servant quoted above who had visited Ho-tse, Shantung. "As for the method of struggle and the killing incidents," he wrote, "I felt it was not quite right. But after rethinking the matter, I also feel that it cannot be avoided." His reasoning was that social organization in China had been such that the local officials and the gentry had always controlled affairs in the villages, while the peasants always stood in an inferior position to them with no one to protect their interests. He himself had not witnessed any killings while he was in Shantung, but the local newspaper had reported such incidents during his stay, and a Communist official had told him that those among the landlord class who had abused and harmed the people were sometimes killed.

Thus it was possible for the urban intellectual to regard such violence as a form of social justice because it was directed primarily against a specific target which many regarded as legitimate. But the more common response was one of disapproval and apprehension. The reaction of one of *Kuan-ch'a*'s readers to Communist activities in southern Shansi was perhaps more extreme than most. Mentioning briefly the events that had transpired there, she concluded her letter: "Sir, I want to cry. I can scarcely write down such things. Please

---

[81] Wu Shih-ch'ang, "Ts'ung mei su shuo-tao kuo nei," p. 5. Chu Tung-jun was another critic in "Wo ts'ung t'ai-hsing lai," p. 8. Professor Chu also criticized the practice of "division of shops" whereby a store and all of the owner's capital and stocks were divided up and distributed among the employees. He claimed that this was being done in some of the villages which supported the New Fourth Army in the vicinity of T'ai-hsing, Kiangsu.

print this piece of news. I know your publication is neither KMT nor rightist, nor am I a rightist. But I am speaking bitterness for the people of southern Shansi. My head is all confused with what I see and hear. I stand with the people." [82]

A few months later, *Kuan-ch'a* published a story sent from the same area describing in somewhat fuller and more dispassionate detail the events to which Mrs. Chang's letter had referred. The story described how order had been quickly established in the districts of southern Shansi after they were taken by the Communists, how the soldiers had been withdrawn shortly thereafter, and how life had become much more calm and peaceful as compared with conditions under Yen Hsi-shan's rule. Most of the teachers had fled, however, so the children were not in school; but they had been assigned to work in the fields or to other tasks. After the soldiers withdrew, people's governments were set up at the *hsien*, district, and village levels. District and village cadres were sent out to conduct investigations, and a peasant association, whose members were primarily the non-property owners in the villages, was organized. Every family was then designated as rich, middle, or poor peasant, with each grade further divided into upper, middle, and lower levels. The next stage was the class struggle movement in which the peasant association, under the guidance of a peasant cadre, played the leading role.

Rich peasants were the first objects of attack. Their property was confiscated and their buildings sealed for future distribution to the poor. Sometimes, however, mistakes were made and people were wrongly classified as rich peasants. Some of these families were said to have been reduced to destitution. The peasant association also singled out for public censure those among the wealthy who had abused and exploited the villagers. Such persons were brought before general meetings of the entire village to be struggled against and were often physically assaulted by the villagers themselves. Punishment was meted out in a variety of forms which included stoning, clubbing, beating, and stabbing, and the victims sometimes died as a result. What seemed to bother the writer even more than the specific acts of violence, however, was the arbitrariness with which they were carried out. In the Communist areas, he wrote, there seemed to be no rule of law: there were no lawyers, nor courts of law, nor any legal safeguards for the individual. The power of life and death was held not even by

---

[82] Letter signed Chang Ch'iang Li-ch'i, at Sian, October 30, 1947, *Kuan-ch'a* (Shanghai), III, No. 11 (November 8, 1947), 2.

the local government, but lay instead in the hands of the peasant association cadres.[83]

Equally disquieting were reports from north Kiangsu, the proximity of which made information more readily accessible to the Shanghai-Nanking intellectual community. If repeated references are any indication, conditions in north Kiangsu were responsible for a great deal of liberal disillusionment with the Chinese Communists. Although land reform as such was not initiated there until May, 1946, the class struggle movement was begun in the autumn of 1945, shortly after the Japanese surrender. Those who had collaborated with the Japanese were brought before the villagers for punishment. Peasants were encouraged to "settle accounts" with landlords and local bosses who had accumulated large areas of land at the peasants' expense, had charged excessive rentals, or had exploited tenants and farm labor. One observer, who claimed to approve of this liquidation movement "in principle," nevertheless found much to criticize in the manner of its implementation. The problem, he said, was that Chinese society lacked social organization. Once such a movement got started, the peasants, given their "characteristic love of revenge," had a tendency to overdo it. Thus, despite the work teams sent by the CCP to guide the class struggle, many people had still been unfairly treated and many "deplorable" incidents had occurred.[84]

COMMUNISM AS A FORM OF GOVERNMENT

The ambivalence inherent in the response of liberal intellectuals to the Communist program in the countryside was related to their more fundamental misgivings about communism as a form of government. Whatever they may have thought of the achievements of the Chinese Communists, the liberals were almost by definition opposed to the political practices and institutions associated with Communist rule. If they criticized the KMT's dictatorial style of politics, the CCP certainly fared no better. As we have seen, Ch'u An-p'ing criticized both parties for violating the principles of democracy and indulging in one-party rule. This was a theme that was expressed repeatedly. Indeed, it was one reason—probably second only to their desire to see an immediate end to the Civil War—why liberals were so anxious to bring both parties together in a coalition government. Under such an ar-

[83] Li Tzu-ching (*Kuan-ch'a* Hsi-an correspondence), "Chin nan chieh-fang ch'ü te tou-cheng ch'ing-hsing" (The Matter of Struggle in the South Shansi Liberated District), *ibid.*, IV, No. 2 (March 6, 1948), 15.

[84] Cheng Yüeh-chung, "Three Stages of the Land Problem."

rangement, one party could serve as a check upon the other and both might be induced to change from special "revolutionary-type" organizations into ordinary political parties.

Because these intellectuals had little direct experience of political life under Chinese Communist rule, they were much less specific in their criticism of the CCP than of the KMT. But the level of opposition did not seem to be appreciably lowered. They objected to the all-powerful position that the CCP was known to occupy in the liberated areas and to the restrictions placed upon individual freedoms, particularly those which had to do with the expression of political criticism and dissent. Chang Tung-sun, who was willing to relinquish a large measure of freedom and other components of liberal democracy, nevertheless asserted: "As for the CCP, we feel that its organization is too strong to be appropriate in a democratic nation." [85] Professor Chou Chung-ch'i acknowledged that according to Mao's theory of the new democracy, the CCP advocated first the realization of the Three People's Principles, while communism could only be a future goal to be sought after industrialization had been achieved. But when all we want is the Three People's Principles, queried Professor Chou, will it not be overdoing things somewhat to entrust such a function to the CCP? [86]

Another writer tried to explain why liberals had so many doubts about the Communists. "Some people say," he wrote, "that in opposing feudalism the task of the liberals and the CCP is the same and their objective is as one. Truly, with respect to the destruction of the old China, today's students and the CCP are of the same will, and sympathy is related to this. But sympathy is not the same as support. And there is a great distance between them and the CCP on the question of building a new China. This is because the CCP places too much emphasis on the masses and overlooks the individual." Because of this, he concluded, the Communists' style of democracy raises as many doubts as does that of the KMT.[87] An editorial in *Shih-tai p'i-p'ing* was more specific. Denouncing rightist groups for their transgressions against civil liberties, the editor then turned on the leftists: "If they see someone cursing the KMT government in speech or action, then they applaud. But no matter what the CCP says or does, it is evaluated

[85] Chang Tung-sun, "Chui-shu wo-men nu-li chien-li . . . ," p. 7.
[86] Chou Chung-ch'i, "Lun ko-ming" (On Revolution), *Kuan-ch'a* (Shanghai), I, No. 22 (January 25, 1947), 10.
[87] Yü Ts'ai-yu, "T'an chin-t'ien te hsüeh-sheng" (Discussing Today's Students), *ibid.*, IV, No. 9 (April 24, 1948), 18. Yü Ts'ai-yu was editor of the Peiping *Ching-shih jih-pao.*

as being good, and those who disagree are subject to 'liquidation' and attacked as reactionaries, accomplices, running dogs, KMT secret agents, and the like, and all fall into the category of criticizers of the CCP." [88]

Many, however, were not quite so even-handed in their criticism. The more common tendency was to suggest that if the KMT was bad in this respect, the CCP was worse. Professor Yang Jen-keng was one of these. Under Communist control, he wrote, the will of the people has no way of expressing itself because of the Party's discipline and the infantile left-wing disorders of its cadres. The CCP basically denies freedom, he declared, and its intervention is even greater than that of the KMT.[89] Professor Wu Shih-ch'ang's opinion of the Communists was almost identical. If there are those among the liberals who oppose the KMT government, he suggested, it is just because the government has deprived the people of their freedom. But the Communists are even worse, he continued, so that today those liberals who oppose the government absolutely cannot approve of the CCP.[90] What seemed to make them most apprehensive was the CCP's record with respect to freedom of thought and speech. One writer asserted that Communist and liberal concepts of democracy were two different things, pointing out that even though there was no formal news censorship in the liberated areas, the Communists exerted even stricter control over the press than did the government.[91] CCP leaders control the entire Party with iron discipline, commented Chou Shou-chang, editor of the Nanking *Hsin min pao*. But what was even worse in his opinion was that Mao, the political leader, had become the arbiter of art and literature as well. His essay "On Literature and Art" had become the highest creative principle for writers and artists, complained Chou. He recalled a report he had heard about certain writers in Yenan who had developed differences with the political leadership and had been required

---

[88] "Chung-kao Wei-te-mai t'e-shih" (Loyal Counsel for Special Envoy Wedemeyer), *STPP* (Hong Kong), IV, No. 88 (August 1, 1947), 1.

[89] Yang Jen-keng, "Tzu-yu-chu-i che wang ho ch'u ch'ü?" (Where Are the Liberals Headed?), *Kuan-ch'a* (Shanghai,), II, No. 11 (May 10, 1947), 5. Professor Yang also expressed his views on the CCP in "Lun nei chan" (On the Civil War), *ibid.*, IV, No. 4 (March 20, 1948); and "Kuan-yü 'chung-kung wang ho ch'u ch'ü?'" (Concerning "Where Are the Chinese Communists Headed?"), *ibid.*, III, No. 10 (November 1, 1947).

[90] Wu Shih-ch'ang, "Lun ho-p'ing wen-t'i" (On the Problem of Peace), *ibid.*, II, No. 16 (July 14, 1947), 4, 6. Professor Wu also objected to the CCP on the grounds that it was not entirely independent, the implication being that it was too closely tied to the USSR. See "Chung-kuo hsü-yao ch'ung-chien ch'üan-wei" (What China Needs Is the Reconstruction of Authority), *ibid.*, I, No. 8 (October 19, 1946), 7.

[91] Ch'en Yen, "Kuo kung wen-t'i ho-i pu neng ho-p'ing chieh-chüeh te chui-so" (Why KMT-CCP Problems Cannot Be Peacefully Resolved), *ibid.*, II, No. 24 (August 9, 1947), 15.

to continue their work in accordance with principles that were considered politically correct.[92]

On this, as on other matters, Ch'u An-p'ing was perhaps the most outspoken. Since in his view there could be no democracy without freedom of thought, he wondered how the CCP could defend its claim to be a democratic party. For example, he continued, we liberals have been influenced by Anglo-American traditions, yet we still criticize England and the United States. "But have we ever heard the CCP criticize Stalin or the USSR?" he asked. "Have we ever seen leftist newspapers criticize Mao and Yenan? Do you mean to say that Stalin and Mao are saints among the saintly with no points to criticize and that Moscow and Yenan are heavens among the heavenly . . . ?" At least under KMT rule we can still struggle for freedom, he concluded; however circumscribed, this freedom is still a question of "more or less." But if the CCP were in control, this freedom would then change into a question of "having and not having." [93]

THE LIBERAL-COMMUNIST ALLIANCE OF 1949

What then must have been in the minds of people like Ch'u An-p'ing and Wang Yün-sheng when they finally decided to cross over into the Communist areas in late 1948 and 1949; or, like Chang Tung-sun, to remain at their university posts with words of welcome for the victor? Their misgivings about the CCP were deep-rooted and they had made no secret of them. Their first choice had not been a Communist form of government for China; indeed, they had argued consistently and conscientiously against it. They did not go over to the Communists until all hope of a liberal compromise had been extinguished and it was certain that the KMT was finished. They were aware, moreover, that the Communists had equally fundamental reservations about them.

In the 1939 statement so often quoted during the Civil War period, Mao wrote of intellectuals and students: "They do not constitute a separate class or stratum. In present-day China, most of them may be placed in the petit bourgeois category, judging by their family origin, their living conditions, and their political outlook. . . ." Nevertheless, he continued, they are politically alert and can play an impor-

---

92 Chou Shou-chang, "Lun 'shen-hua cheng-chih'" (Of "Myths and Politics"), *ibid.*, I, No. 21 (January 18, 1947), 6.

93 Ch'u An-p'ing, "Chung-kuo te cheng chü," p. 6.

tant role in the revolution. Being dissatisfied with the present system and often living in fear of unemployment or of not being able to continue their studies, they can serve as a revolutionary vanguard among the masses and as an instrument for linking the masses with the forces of revolution. As proof of this assertion, Mao cited the tradition of political activism developed by Chinese students and intellectuals since the turn of the century: their activities abroad before the 1911 Revolution and their roles in the May Fourth Movement in 1919, the May Thirtieth Movement in 1925, and the December Ninth Movement for national salvation from Japan in 1935. Indeed, "the revolutionary forces cannot be successfully organized and revolutionary work cannot be successfully conducted without the participation of revolutionary intellectuals. . . ." Mao warned, however, that intellectuals are not completely reliable, often being "subjective and individualistic, impractical in their thinking and irresolute in action." Because of these inherent weaknesses, some would withdraw, becoming passive and even hostile to the revolution. He suggested that intellectuals could overcome their shortcomings "only in mass struggles over a long period." [94]

Following a discussion of current tendencies within the Party eight years later, Mao found it necessary to warn against "adventurist policies" in the Party's treatment of intellectuals. This was probably an indication that the struggle aspect of his earlier statement was being taken seriously by some comrades. It was also doubtless an indication as to why, during the Civil War years, there were as many reports of teachers and students fleeing the Communist areas as of movement in the opposite direction. According to one *Kuan-ch'a* correspondent writing from southern Kiangsu, among the Communists' biggest failures in that area was their treatment of intellectuals and members of the middle class who were "one after another fleeing the control of the New Fourth Army." [95] Similarly, Professor Wu Shih-ch'ang listed as one of his major points of opposition to the CCP the fact that it had cut itself off from the petite bourgeoisie and that as a consequence the intellectual level of the talent within the Party was "unfortunately limited." [96]

[94] "The Chinese Revolution and the Chinese Communist Party," *Selected Works,* II (Peking: Foreign Languages Press, 1965), 320–22.

[95] "Our Special Correspondent," "I shih pien ch'ü."

[96] Wu Shih-ch'ang, "Chung-kuo hsü-yao ch'ung-chien ch'üan-wei," p. 7. Additional references to teachers and students fleeing the Communist areas appear above. The

What sort of an accommodation, then, did the liberal intellectuals hope to make with the new regime? What kinds of compromises did they anticipate they would have to agree to and how much were they prepared to accept? They did not, of course, address this question directly. But answers can be inferred from two different themes that ran through a number of their writings. One theme emerged from their response to the theory, and doubtless to the practice also, of Mao's new democracy. The other centered around the intellectuals' general recognition of the kinds of compromises that might be necessary if the task of destroying the old society was in fact to be accomplished.

During the Civil War years, the ideas outlined by Mao in his "On New Democracy" (January, 1940) provided the basis of the Party's policies and ideological pronouncements. According to the new democracy theory, communism was a distant goal to be achieved only after the old feudal society had been destroyed and replaced by a new one wherein the Three People's Principles would at last have been realized. The proletariat, the peasantry, the intelligentsia, and other sections of the petite bourgeoisie were to be the "basic forces" of the new society, which would be ruled by a coalition of all anti-imperialist and antifeudal classes under the leadership of the proletariat. A mixed economy and land-to-the-tiller in the rural areas were to constitute the major elements of the new society's economic policy.

Five years after "On New Democracy," when the Seventh National Congress of the CCP met in April, 1945, the Party and the nation

---

student refugees are also discussed in John F. Melby, *The Mandate of Heaven* (Toronto: University of Toronto Press, 1968), pp. 281–82; and Derk Bodde, *Peking Diary* (Greenwich, Conn.: Fawcett Publications, 1967), pp. 31–33, 65–68, 74–77.

The comparative numbers of students and intellectuals fleeing the Communist and the KMT areas respectively is almost impossible to estimate. From available accounts, one gets the impression that the numbers fleeing the Communists were greater, since these tended to be reported in the tens of thousands, whereas those fleeing into the Communist areas were reported only in hundreds and thousands. Even this rough estimate may be deceiving, however, since refugees in the KMT areas tended to be concentrated in a few of the major urban centers, whereas refugees in the liberated areas were much more widely diffused. In addition, the majority of the student refugees in the KMT areas seemed to be middle-school students, and there is some question as to whether their status was entirely voluntary. There were a number of reports of these younger students being told that they must leave and then being given transportation out of an area soon to be taken by the Communists.

In any event, the KMT failed to make any political capital out of the refugees. In fact, its treatment of refugees, intellectual and otherwise, became another issue for which it was widely criticized. This criticism reached a peak after the July 5 (1948) Incident in which government forces in Peiping opened fire on a group of several thousand demonstrating Manchurian student refugees, many of whom had been flown out of the Northeast on government planes. Several of the students were killed.

looked forward to Japan's impending defeat. In his political report to the Congress, Mao outlined the role of the intellectuals in the Party's future tasks based on the principles of the new democracy. The Party's postwar line was to be unity, democracy, peace, and the construction of a new China under a coalition government. Mao called for an immediate end to KMT one-party rule and for its replacement by a coalition government which would include "representatives of all the anti-Japanese parties and people without party affiliation." And to achieve these tasks,

we need large numbers of educators and teachers for the people, and also people's scientists, engineers, technicians, doctors, journalists, writers, men of letters, artists and rank-and-file cultural workers. . . . Provided they serve the people creditably, all intellectuals should be esteemed and regarded as valuable national and social assets. . . . Therefore, the task of a people's government is systematically to develop all kinds of intellectually equipped cadres from among the ranks of the people and at the same time to take care to unite with and re-educate all the useful intellectuals already available.[97]

Thus, despite their weaknesses, intellectuals had an important role to play in the revolution. They would serve as a revolutionary vanguard among the people and as an instrument linking the general population with the forces of the revolution. In addition, intellectuals were essential for the construction of a new society. Hence Mao's warning that the Party must keep its reservations about them within bounds and avoid adventurist policies toward them. The proper course was to "unite with them, educate them, and give them posts according to the merits of each case."[98]

These principles provided the basis of policy statements and directives throughout the liberated areas, statements which increased in number during 1948 and 1949 as the Communist forces took increasing numbers of cities and towns. The directive on policy toward intellectuals issued by the Party's Central China Bureau on September 29, 1948, was widely circulated as a representative statement of official policy for the "attention and reference" of other liberated areas. The intellectuals are important resources for us, the directive began. But because we have been careless and looked lightly on our intellectual and youth work in the districts of central China, and also because of several errors in our policy, together with the KMT's propaganda

---

[97] "On Coalition Government," *Selected Works,* III (Peking: Foreign Languages Press, 1965), 304–5; also 255–56, 288.

[98] "On Some Important Problems of the Party's Present Policy," *Selected Works,* IV (Peking: Foreign Languages Press, 1961), 184.

against us, there are not a few intellectuals who still harbor doubts about us. In order to overcome these doubts as well as the weaknesses of the intellectuals themselves, the Party outlined a specific program of education and thought reform work.

Party and government organs at all levels were directed to use meetings and literary activities as well as newspapers, official statements, notices, pamphlets, and cartoons to explain the Party's policy toward intellectuals and to overcome their reservations. In addition, various kinds of short-course schools and training classes were to be opened in order to mobilize teachers and students in the area for political studies. The instruction of each class was to last for three or four months and concentrate on current events, basic questions of the Chinese revolution, and the basic policies of the CCP. The directive emphasized that in carrying out this work, local leaders were to pay attention to four specific points. First, in setting up the various training classes and cadre schools, undisciplined and anarchical attitudes were to be avoided, as well as liberalism and particularism. Second, intellectuals newly arrived in the Communist areas or in areas recently taken over by the Communists were to be allowed certain privileges in the allotment of food, clothing, study materials, and so forth, but cadres participating in the training work were called upon to make examples of themselves in order to influence the intellectuals. Third, a "free democratic work style" was to be adopted in order to induce the intellectuals to be completely open and candid concerning all their doubts and misgivings. And fourth, these non-Party short-course schools were instructed to rely on discussion meetings, debates, wall newspapers, and various forms of mass activity in order to resolve all problems of thought. Specifically, the methods used for Party rectification and cadre investigations were to be avoided in dealing with intellectuals in newly liberated areas. Once they have gained an elementary knowledge of our policies and their doubts about us have been eliminated, or at least reduced, concluded the directive, all intellectuals should be given jobs in the various organizations where they are needed.[99]

In fact, this effort to win over and re-educate intellectuals had long been the basic policy even though local cadres may have been lax in

[99] Chung kung chung yüan chü (CCP Central China Bureau), "Cheng-ch'ü, t'uan-chieh, kai-tsao, p'ei-yang chih-shih fen-tzu" (Win Over, Unite, Reform, and Train Intellectuals), in Hua-pei hsin hua shu-tien (North China New China Book Store) (ed.), *Kuan-yü ch'eng-shih cheng-ts'e te chi-ko wen-hsien* (Some Documents on City Policy) (n.p.: Hua-pei hsin hua shu-tien, 1949), pp. 37–39.

its implementation. The Party issued repeated warnings during the Civil War years to local leaders to avoid alienating intellectuals in the liberated areas—an indication that they were probably continuing to do just that. But the intellectual issue never seemed to become an object of specific concern involving all the liberated areas until 1948. Nevertheless, at the same time that many intellectuals because of their fears chose to flee from areas of Communist control during the Civil War, other intellectuals became disillusioned with the KMT and, harassed by the government's secret police, fled into the Communist areas. In these cases the students and intellectuals were treated with every consideration. The Communists publicized their attitude toward refugee intellectuals in newspaper editorials, over the airwaves, and doubtless by more covert means as well. These statements of welcome and support probably encouraged many to flee as the central government's harassment increased, and the statements were reinforced in practice once the refugees had arrived. Students from poor families and from the KMT areas were given free board and tuition at liberated area schools, and sometimes free clothing, blankets, and other daily necessities as well. Professors and teachers from the KMT areas were given administrative and technical positions in liberated area schools and were in fact actively encouraged to come and staff them.

Whatever its misgivings about them, then, the Party was quite clearly offering the intelligentsia a place in the life of the new society. Moreover, it was an offer that grew more insistent as the Communist victory approached and the Party realized the immediacy of its need for the technical, administrative, and literary talents of the intelligentsia. Still, most of the intellectuals whose writings have been analyzed here could not be expected to be overly enthusiastic about the sort of "reform and training" which they were all expected to undergo, however elementary and superficial it might initially be. And they entertained no illusions as to the long-term implications of the Communist program for the new democratic society. In fact, many criticized it as a deception since it placed major emphasis on the new democratic phase and was perhaps purposely vague about what was to follow. "The CCP has not abandoned Marxism-Leninism," commented one writer, "nor has it given up anything else; it is only a tactic. Therefore, no matter what democracy the CCP advocates, it can never be a democratic party. . . ."[100]

[100] Tung Ch'iu-shui, "Lun hsin min-chu-chu-i ch'i ts'e-lüeh" (On the New Democracy and Its Policies), *STPP* (Hong Kong), V, No. 97 (January 15, 1948), 20.

Virtually everyone agreed that whatever the CCP's immediate plans for a new democracy, its long-range goal was the transformation of China into a Communist state. For some, however, there were intervening considerations. One of these had to do with timing and the problem of "objective conditions." Thus, when Chang Tung-sun argued in favor of bringing the CCP into a coalition government, he acknowledged that the CCP had never concealed its belief in Marxism or in the necessity of a Communist revolution. But I myself have talked to them, he wrote, and they do not expect to see it in their lifetimes. They say that only their sons or grandsons will live to see it. The problem of a Communist revolution is therefore not one of the present but of the future, he continued, and who can predict that the objective conditions will be ripe for revolution fifty or sixty years from now? Perhaps by then people will have enough to eat and the standard of living will have risen and every household will be self-supporting. The CCP is now at the stage of carrying out the new democracy, he concluded, "and since they do what they say, that is what they will do." There is certainly no need to be afraid of the CCP's brand of "futuristic revolutionary theory." [101]

Shih Fu-liang was another who shared this view. The CCP does not want to carry out communism at the present time, nor does it want to carry out socialism, he wrote, because conditions are not appropriate for it. The most they want to achieve now is the new democracy. Then he continued with reference to the CCP's expressed support for a coalition government: "Some say that this is just a strategy and that when the time is right, the CCP will carry out a Soviet system and a proletarian dictatorship. I do not dare to say they will not and that this is not a possibility. But 'when the time is right' is an objective question. . . . Perhaps China can go its own road and we will be able to move peacefully to socialism from the new capitalism and the new democracy. . . ." At any rate, he concluded, no democratic person nor democratic party need fear the threat of communism.[102]

There is no way of knowing how widespread this particular belief may have been. Chang and Shih could have been speaking only for themselves, but perhaps they were not. There was, moreover, a second consideration that may have helped the intellectuals overcome their doubts about the Communist program at that time. This was the recog-

101 Chang Tung-sun, "Chui-shu wo-men nu-li . . . ," p. 7.
102 Shih Fu-liang, "Lun 'kung-ch'an-chu-i te wei–hsieh'" (On "The Threat of Communism"), STPP (Hong Kong), IV, No. 92 (October 1, 1947), 16.

nition that it might be necessary to compromise certain liberal principles at least temporarily in order to lay the foundations for a new and
more progressive society. As we have seen, this theme had appeared
in some liberal proposals for the achievement of socialism and democracy. Not surprisingly, it appeared also among those who were
genuinely impressed with what the Communists were doing. These
were people like the KMT civil servant who, having visited the Communist areas, was convinced that the violence was perhaps unavoid-
able, and also that the Communists had achieved a certain kind of
democracy because they had done away with local bullies and bureaucrats and KMT secret agents, and had given the peasants the right "to
mount a platform and say the things that someone should say."

Finally, this theme appeared in a student's rebuke to Professor
Yang Jen-keng, who had emphasized the distance existing between the
liberals and the CCP. It is true, the student wrote, that middle-class
liberals have difficulty accepting the violent methods of the CCP and
that they place highest value on the free development of the individual.
But liberals also have a social conscience, and their sense of social
justice has been aroused by the inequities inherent in Chinese society.
This can provide the basis for at least a temporary reconciliation of
the contradictions between the freedom of the liberals and the equality
of the Communists. In fact, he wrote, such a compromise must take
place because, however great an influence the liberals may have
exerted culturally, their tragedy lies in their ineffectiveness. They have
not been able to overturn the old society because they have concentrated too much on the freedom of the individual and have overlooked
the welfare of the majority. They have not put down roots among the
people, nor have they understood that land reform and the awakening
of the peasants are the necessary conditions for the destruction of the
privileged interests that have controlled Chinese society. The liberals,
he asserted, should therefore join with the Communists in order to
destroy their common enemy, and after that task had been completed
there would be time enough to resume the old relationship of mutual
opposition.[103]

This then was the process whereby, to paraphrase Jack Belden, a
decisive minority of the population came finally to embrace the Com-

[103] Li Hsiao-yu, "Tu 'kuan-yü chung-kung wang ho ch'u ch'ü?' chien lun tzu-yu–chu-i
che te tao-lu" (On Reading "Where Are the Chinese Communists Headed?" and on the
Way of the Liberals), *Kuan-ch'a* (Shanghai), III, No. 19 (January 3, 1948), 7–9. Li was
a student at National Central University in Nanking.

munist program.[104] The political arguments which dominated intellectual life during the Civil War years indicated a degree of commitment to liberalism which has perhaps been underestimated because
of the political weakness of its adherents. The strain that the acceptance of the Communist program entailed was clearly apparent in the
anger and frustration which increasingly marked the intellectuals'
political commentaries as they gradually realized that their own ideas
about what ought to be were not going to influence the conduct of the
KMT in any way. Their dilemma was intensified by the simultaneous
realization that the KMT was about to be replaced by a new political
elite likely to be as intransigent as the KMT with respect to certain
fundamental tenets of the liberal creed.

The Communist military victory in fact eased this dilemma for
Chinese liberals. Prior to its occurrence, they had been confronted
by a choice between the KMT, which they had found wanting on
virtually all counts of political principle and performance, and the
CCP, whose political principles were regarded as the negation of some
of the liberal community's most deeply held commitments. All that remained of their loyalty to the KMT was the continuing chance, however limited, that their struggle for a liberal democratic society might
someday succeed. And this chance was the price that would doubtless
have to be paid if they were to go over to the Communists, whose performance otherwise was by and large admired. The force of this dilemma was clearly eased once the KMT military defeat had reduced
it to a choice between immediate and indefinite exile, or acceptance of a
national government led by the CCP in its new democratic phase.

Not everyone, of course, was willing to accept the CCP even in its
new democratic phase. Although the majority of China's liberal intellectuals did remain with the Communists, there were some who chose
otherwise. Hu Shih was one of these. His opposition to the Nationalist
government had never reached the heights of outspoken intensity displayed by so many of his colleagues, but he had nevertheless spoken
out on the liberal side of a number of issues, most notably the student
movement, during the Civil War years. After flying out of the be-
leaguered city of Peiping in January, 1949, Hu was reported to have
told George Yeh, vice minister of foreign affairs of the central government, that there was really very little that could be said for the
KMT. "The only reason why liberal elements like us still prefer to

104 Belden, *China Shakes the World,* p. 398.

string along with you people," he told Yeh, "is that under your regime we at least enjoy the freedom of silence."[105]

Clearly most of the liberal intellectual community did not place so high a price on their own personal freedom of silence.[106] Nor did most of them probably think they would really need it. In his conversations with the anthropologist, Robert Redfield, Fei Hsiao-t'ung, for example, indicated that he felt he could work effectively under a Chinese Communist government, albeit as a member of its "loyal opposition." Although his views on certain matters had been attacked by the Communists—as had the views of many prominent liberals—Fei nevertheless spoke in late 1948 of his hope that he would be able to contribute to China's industrial and agricultural development, meanwhile criticizing the Communists when he felt that criticism was necessary.[107]

But whatever else they may have been, these intellectuals should not be dismissed as political opportunists, half-hearted in their commitment to liberalism, or johnny-come-latelies to the revolutionary cause. This is not to say that there were no opportunists among them. But there were, in addition, those who were committed enough to the path of liberal reform, as they knew it, to pursue that goal until the possibility of achieving it no longer existed, and then to continue to hope that some new path might be found.

Thus, as their position toward the Nationalist government hardened into one of total alienation, and as the KMT's military defeat became more certain, the orientation of the intelligentsia toward the Communists shifted from something like reserved disapproval to qualified support. In whatever way the liberals may have rationalized their decision to accept Communist rule, there is no indication that they extended anything like unequivocal support to the new regime or that the compromises they were willing to make were in any sense fundamental or permanent. Their commitment seemed to extend at most to the Communist program of the new democracy and beyond

[105] Quoted in *Hsin-wen t'ien-ti* (News World) (KMT-affiliated) (Shanghai), No. 68 (April 28, 1949), as translated in U.S. Consulate-General (Shanghai), *Chinese Press Review*, May 3, 1949.

[106] One of Pa Chin's friends used this same argument against the Communists but could not get the novelist to say he agreed with it. Although his anarchist philosophy did not endear him to the Communists, he too remained on the mainland in 1949. See Olga Lang, *Pa Chin and His Writings: Chinese Youth between the Two Revolutions* (Cambridge, Mass.: Harvard University Press, 1967), p. 217.

[107] Robert Redfield, "Introduction," in Fei Hsiao-t'ung, *China's Gentry: Essays in Rural-Urban Relations* (Chicago: University of Chicago Press, Phoenix Books, 1968), pp. 2–3.

that to the realization of a fully socialist economy, but certainly not to the ultimate Communist objective of one-party rule. Communist reservations about the Chinese intelligentsia were as well founded as were the misgivings of the latter about the CCP. And the strain that the alliance with these intellectuals created within the Party was clearly reflected in the repeated admonitions that had to be issued reminding Party members to avoid adventurist policies toward intellectuals and to unite with them and win them over.

The deep-rooted nature of the differences between the liberal intellectual community and the CCP, which was no doubt obscured by their alliance in 1949, may therefore go a long way toward explaining the treatment that the former has received during the twenty-five years of CCP rule in China. Certainly it would seem to explain why the intellectual community has been subjected to repeated re-education campaigns during that time, and perhaps also why such efforts will continue until the Chinese Communist leadership is satisfied that the memory of the old liberal commitments has ceased to exist or at least that these commitments no longer constitute a potential reservoir of serious dissent.

MERLE GOLDMAN

The Chinese Communist Party's *"Cultural Revolution"* of 1962-64

In the early sixties dissent in China was generally expressed through plays, short stories, and literary forums; but by 1962 and 1963 the main medium of dissent had changed to discussions on Chinese history and culture. Like the literati of old, Chinese intellectuals used their interpretations as criticisms of the regime, and the regime used contrary interpretations as rebuttals. While these debates were in actuality a subtle struggle over policy, they touched on some fundamental questions concerning the dynamics of the historical process, the role of traditional values, and the nature of man. They were conducted with a degree of sophistication and balance that had not been exhibited since the Communists had come to power.

Though the debates on history and culture had begun in the early sixties,[1] they gained momentum with Mao Tse-tung's Tenth Plenum speech of September, 1962, when he announced a shift from the relative relaxation of 1961–62 to the imposition of increasing controls. His speech was not published in full, but enough extracts were reprinted to indicate that Mao was obsessed more with the ideological consciousness of the nation than with any other issue. He regarded the intellectual and literary dissidence of the early sixties as the first step to the overthrow of political power and feared that because of this dissidence the revolutionary spirit would not be passed on to the next generation of leaders. Faced with a deceleration of revolutionary momentum, he called for renewed ideological class struggle. Hence,

---

[1] See Merle Goldman, "The Unique 'Blooming and Contending' of 1961–62," in John Wilson Lewis (ed.), *Party Leadership and Revolutionary Power in China* (Cambridge: Cambridge University Press, 1970), pp. 268–303.

the Tenth Plenum marked the beginning of Mao's effort to stem the liberalization set in motion two years earlier.

How is it possible, therefore, to explain the relatively wide-ranging debates that subsequently occurred in intellectual circles? Generally, the response of the Party bureaucracy headed by Liu Shao-ch'i to Mao's demand for increasing controls and revitalization of the revolutionary spirit was lethargic. When compared to the antirightist movement in the wake of the Hundred Flowers campaign, the swing of the pendulum away from relaxation was less sharp and less decisive. It moved ever so slowly and in some places did not move at all. Those responsible for the tightening-up, Lu Ting-i and Chou Yang, director and assistant director of the Propaganda Department, and P'eng Chen, first secretary of the Peking Party Committee, were the very ones who had presided over the relaxation of the early sixties. Verbally they went along with Mao's demand for renewed class struggle, but actually they were reluctant to embark on a new campaign for fear it might lead to disruptions like those produced by the Great Leap Forward (GLF). Disillusionment with Mao's previous policy rendered these Party leaders less responsive to his new demands. Furthermore, as Mao later charged, a process of increasing bureaucratization had taken hold of the cultural apparatus, as is inevitable in any revolutionary organization. The cultural bureaucracy was entrenched, held together by close personal ties developed in the freer atmospheres of Shanghai in the thirties and Yenan in the early forties.

The officials in the cultural sphere may have also been concerned with the erosion of revolutionary spirit; but exhausted and embittered by previous ideological remolding campaigns, they were not ready to launch the intensive, nationwide drives they had engineered in the past. So though their rhetoric was class struggle, their tone was moderate. Though they may not have agreed with some of the intellectuals, whose views were as opposed to theirs and Liu Shao-ch'i's as they were to Mao's, they permitted some genuine ideological debates to take place.

Instead of forcing an end to the indirect attacks made on him in 1961–62 for the policy of the GLF and the purge of P'eng Teh-huai, Mao's call for a renewed struggle activated a new form of dissidence. In academic circles, particularly among historians, Party as well as non-Party intellectuals engaged in debates over the value of class struggle in which the underlying ideological basis of the thought of Mao Tse-tung was questioned. Though the dissidence took different forms, a unifying theme was the desire for less rather than more polarization—for a de-emphasis rather than intensification of class struggle and for a reconciliation rather than accentuation of the differences in Chinese society.

This desire for harmony was not only a response to the severe economic and social disruptions that occurred during the GLF, but was also an expression of Chinese heritage, of the Confucian concept of harmony in social relations and the Taoist concept of harmony with the cosmos. Like the traditional scholar-bureaucrats, some intellectuals feared that unless such harmony were achieved, the regime would not last long. Their debates with more orthodox Maoists emerge as a clash between the traditional Chinese values of harmony and compromise on the one hand and, on the other, the more Western values of struggle and the dialectic, which were filtered through Marx to Mao. As Benjamin Schwartz has pointed out, the Manichaean passion in Western thought and Marxism to see history as a constant struggle between opposites is alien to Chinese culture. Thus, from the Tenth Plenum through 1963, a number of historians as well as some philosophers and aestheticians implicitly subverted Mao's demand for increased ideological struggle by presenting the middle ground in their respective fields.

The Debates on History

While most of China in 1963 was absorbed in the Socialist Education Movement—a drive to halt the spontaneous trend toward individual farming and to inculcate collectivist values—circles of intellectuals were engaged in a series of erudite discussions on historical figures, China's cultural legacy, and peasant rebellions. A major debate over the re-evaluation of Confucianism became one arena for indirect opposition to Mao's Tenth Plenum decree. Several scholars were involved in this debate: among them were Wu Han, Peking University professor and vice-mayor of Peking; the historian Liu Chieh of Sun Yat-sen University in Canton; and the philosopher Feng Yu-lan, also of Peking University. They were acquainted with Western scholarship and had earned their reputations before 1949. Their revived interest in Confucianism was more than a reflection of the nationalist resurgence that resulted from the Sino-Soviet rift. Disregarding Mao's renewed emphasis on class struggle, they sought to unify China by stressing that Chinese culture, and particularly Confucianism, embodied universal and enduring moral values. This effort to universalize Confucianism was not new under the Communist regime. It had begun in the early 1950's, was revived in the Hundred Flowers campaign after the dislocations of collectivization, and was resurrected in the aftermath of the GLF. By mid-1962 it had gained a certain momentum.

An impetus to this re-evaluation was a conference on Confucianism convened in November, 1962, a month after Mao's Tenth Plenum speech. Arranged by Chou Yang and held under the auspices of the Shantung Association of Historians and the Historical Research Institute, it became a platform for historian Liu Chieh's view that China's history had a different pattern than that of the West. Whereas class struggle may have governed Western historical development, it had not governed Chinese development. He specifically stated that the Confucian concept of *jen,* which can be translated variously as humanism or love of mankind, helped make the difference. He and others at the conference contended that it was an abstract, ethical concept which transcended the feudal society from which it came. It ameliorated the relations between different classes in the past and could serve a similar function in the present. Liu Chieh was reported to have said that "it cannot be said that *jen* is not needed in our age and society." [2] There were even some at the conference who suggested that Confucianism helped prepare the way for Marxism-Leninism. For example, the original Confucian view of knowledge as coming from practice, and knowledge in turn informing practice, agreed essentially with the Marxist-Leninist view of acquiring knowledge. There appears to have been a deliberate effort at this conference to entangle Confucianism with Marxism-Leninism, contradicting the Maoist effort to polarize different ideologies.

Following the Confucianism conference, Liu Chieh published several articles in *Hsüeh-shu yen-chiu* (Academic Research) explaining that the Confucian *jen,* as well as other traditional concepts such as Mo Tzu's "love without distinction," had produced an evolutionary rather than revolutionary historical process. According to Liu, since Chinese history was the development of *jen,* various groups and classes worked together and not in opposition to one another. As he stated in an article on Mo Tzu, "It is not in conformity with historical facts to say that the opposing sides were sharply defined and divided . . . and did not mix with each other." [3] This view was also propounded by other promi-

---

[2] Quotes from the conference on Confucianism were reprinted in *KMJP,* August 17–18, 1963, and translated in *SCMP,* No. 3070, p. 2.

[3] Liu Chieh, "Mo Tzu's Love for All without Distinction and His Utilitarianism," *Hsüeh-shu yen-chiu* (Academic Research), No. 1 (1963), translated in *SCMP,* No. 3128, p. 6.

nent historians, among them Chien Po-tsan and Wu Han. It was termed "the policy of concession" (*jang-pu cheng-tze*), which meant that when confronted with peasant rebellion, the ruling class made concessions to the peasants in order to restore the established order. Hence concession, or what Liu Chieh would call the implementation of *jen,* was an effort by the feudal ruling classes to respond to the demands of the peasants in such a way as to benefit both classes.

The scholars engaged in this discussion couched their re-evaluation of Confucianism in Marxist terms and Marxist references, as nineteenth-century Chinese literati had couched their introduction of Western thought in orthodox Confucian doctrine. Like K'ang Yu-wei, who pointed to a commentary on the *Spring and Autumn Annals* as the basis for his arguments, the philosopher Feng Yu-lan, for example, pointed to a small portion of early Marxism, *The German Ideology,* as the authority for his view of the universality of Confucianism.[4] *The German Ideology* maintained that in a transitional period the new class that is replacing the old one must give its ideas the form of universality in order to gain power. At this stage its interests are more closely connected with the common interests of the nonruling classes. Consequently, Feng described Confucius in his time as a representative of the new landlord class which was emerging as China moved from slaveholding to feudalism. He, too, pointed to the Confucian concept of *jen* as an "ideology of universal pattern."[5] In his *New History of Chinese Philosophy,* published in 1961, Feng had presented *jen* as a universal ethic for all times and all classes.[6]

Yet in 1963, in answer to criticisms of his interpretation and in a period of increasing ideological controls, Feng modified his concept by making the universality of *jen* apply specifically to the period in which Confucius and Mencius lived. Still, he circumvented this modification by stating that there are moments in history when common values emerge that have similar meaning to opposing classes. "In certain historical phases, for instance during the revolution or when some nonruling class opposed the old ruling class, there was some uniformity

---

[4] Karl Marx and Friedrich Engels, *The German Ideology,* ed. C. J. Arthur (New York: International Publishers, 1970), pp. 40–41. Douglas Paal has written a comprehensive study of Feng Yu-lan's views in the 1950's and 1960's in an unpublished seminar paper delivered at Harvard University, January, 1971, "Feng Yu-lan: Tradition and Scholarship in Communist China."

[5] Feng Yu-lan, "Criticism and Self-criticism in the Discussion on Confucianism," *Che-hsüeh yen-chiu* (Philosophical Research), No. 6 (1963), reprinted in International Arts and Science Press, *Chinese Studies in History and Philosophy,* I, No. 4 (1968), 77.

[6] Feng Yu-lan, *Chung-kuo che-hsüeh shih hsin-pien* (A New History of Chinese Philosophy) (Peking: People's Publishing Co., 1961).

of interest among them. Under these circumstances, they were still for their own interests, but what was uniform also formed the general interest in the period." [7] There were times, therefore, when there was conciliation of class interests and common goals. To Feng, and formerly to Mao during the Hundred Flowers period, contradictions between classes can be nonantagonistic and are not always irreconcilable.

The historian Wu Han was the boldest and most outspoken advocate of this position. Shortly before the Tenth Plenum, Wu Han had published two articles on the inheritability of values, "On Morality" in May, 1962, and "More on Morality" in August, 1962. These works appeared in the Peking Party Committee ideological journal, *Ch'ien-hsien* (Frontline), under the pen name Wu Nan-hsing. Using as his authority Mao's directive of the early 1950's "to critically assimilate the past," Wu Han insisted that present-day China should incorporate not only *jen* but other values of feudal society, such as loyalty, filial piety, honesty, diligence, and courage, together with certain values of bourgeois society such as democracy and the profit-making motive.

There was no response to these articles until a year later, on August 15, 1963, when Hsü Ch'i-hsien in *Kuang-ming jih-pao* (*KMJP*) charged that Wu Han concerned himself only with the morality of the ruling class and treated it as if it were the morality of all the people when in reality it was opposed to the morality of the masses.[8] Wu Han, four days later and again in *KMJP*, rebutted this criticism. He granted that the ruling class throughout Chinese history had stood in opposition to the people, yet he stated that "under certain conditions and certain limitations, individuals of the ruling class undertook actions compatible with the interests of the people." Likewise, some of the values of the ruled class were adopted by the ruling class as their own. He declared, "It is not right . . . to present without exception any individual of the two classes in any period as opposing each other and not search for the interaction between them. It is because of this interaction of classes that it is possible to inherit the morality of the past." [9] Wu Han not only sabotaged the current Maoist directive for class struggle but subtly hit at the intensifying cult of Mao when he admitted that some of the values handed down by previous generations

[7] Feng, "Criticism and Self-criticism," p. 83.

[8] Hsü Ch'i-hsien, "Kuan-yü tao-te ti chieh-chi-hsing yü chi-ch'eng-hsing ti i-hsieh wen-t'i-yü (Wu Han t'ung-chih shang-chüeh)" (Some Problems on Class Character and the Inheritability of Morality [A Discussion with Comrade Wu Han]), *KMJP*, August 15, 1963, p. 5.

[9] Wu Han, "Shuo tao-te—ching ta Hsü Ch'i-hsien t'ung-chih" (Furthermore on Morality—A Reply to Comrade Hsü Ch'i-hsien), *ibid.*, August 19, 1963, p. 2.

had to change with the times. As an example he pointed to the concept of loyalty, which he said in the present context meant loyalty to the Party, not to a ruler.

Following Wu Han's article, *KMJP*, *Che-hsüeh yen-chiu* (Philosophical Research), *Li-shih yen-chiu* (History Research), *Hsin chien-she* (New Construction), and *Wen-hui pao* published a series of discussions on the issues raised by Wu Han. Although the majority disagreed with Wu, a minority vigorously defended him and elaborated further on his ideas. Several writers mentioned that when China was faced with an alien invasion in the past, some members of the ruling class displayed a spirit of patriotism that was more helpful to the broad masses than to the landlord class. Others paraphrasing *The German Ideology* showed that in the period when a new ruling class was in ascendancy, it joined with the masses against the old ruling class and, therefore, played a progressive role at that time.[10] Several articles asserted that different classes had to make use of certain categories and technical terms common to both classes in order to be understood. One of these common categories, as Shih Liang-jen suggested in *KMJP,* was morality. He defined morality as a form of social consciousness that, "once it has been formed, naturally acquires relative independence." He was even more explicit than Wu Han in his treatment of morality as the blending together of the views of different classes. He asked rhetorically, "Is it not true that conflict is possible between the morality of the ruling class and the morality of the ruled class only under special circumstances in a class society and that under normal circumstances there would be no strife between the moralities of the two classes?"[11]

Those who refuted the views of Wu Han, Liu Chieh, Feng Yu-lan, and their associates engaged in a lively exchange, debating in a nonbelligerent manner and, for the most part, on an academic level. In fact, there appears to have been a concerted effort to circumscribe these discussions within a historical and philosophical context, perhaps to prevent their being used politically against Mao and the GLF as they had in 1961–62. There is a contradictory quality to the Party's rebuttals, most likely reflecting the competing forces within the Party's cultural apparatus. More vigorous than the Propaganda Department hierarchy in debating the philosophical and historical issues was a

[10] Discussion in *KMJP*, October 6 and 7, 1963, p. 5.

[11] Shih Liang-jen, "Ti chi-ke yu-kuan tao-te chieh-chi-hsing ho chi-ch'eng-hsing ti wen-t'i" (Several Questions regarding the Class Nature of Morality and Its Inheritability), *ibid.*, December 1, 1963, p. 4.

group of younger men led by Kuan Feng, Ch'i Pen-yu, Yao Wen-yuan, Lin Yu-shih, and Lin Chieh. For the most part, they had been trained under the Communist regime. Though they were to be Mao's mouthpieces at the start of the Cultural Revolution and would echo his call for renewed class struggle, their arguments in 1963 were not the simplified clichés that they were later to voice. They used a wide range of references and showed a willingness to acknowledge the complexities of a question. At this point they were not in opposition to the Propaganda Department, but instead probably constituted a faction within the cultural apparatus.

Hints of factional rivalry had already appeared in another debate over the re-evaluation of historical figures. A subject of this debate was whether Li Hsiu-ch'eng, the last general of the Taipings, should be treated as a revolutionary hero.[12] As the leader of a peasant uprising, Li suited the Party's desire to point to revolutionary figures in Chinese history. For many years Li had been eulogized by Chinese historians, particularly Lo Erh-kang, who treated Li's surrender at the end of the rebellion not as a capitulation but as an effort to buy time for the Taipings. Suddenly in the August, 1963, issue of *Li-shih yen-chiu*, Ch'i Pen-yu published an article, "Comment on Li Hsiu-ch'eng's Autobiography," in which he stated that Li's surrender was a betrayal of the peasant uprising and a sellout to the landlord class. Li, therefore, should no longer be treated as a hero because when a crisis occurred he had abandoned the struggle. Ch'i used the case of Li to support his argument against any suspension of the revolution or any compromise with other classes. The following month, September, 1963, Chou Yang organized a meeting at the Institute of Modern History attended by prominent historians, including Wu Han, Teng T'o, Chien Po-tsan, and Hou Wai-lu, where Ch'i Pen-yu's view was criticized and the treatment of Li Hsiu-ch'eng as a revolutionary figure was defended.

An intriguing episode in the discussion of Li Hsiu-ch'eng occurred in the theater. Here Yang Han-sheng, vice-chairman and secretary of the Party group of the All-China Federation of Literary and Art Circles and an old associate of Chou Yang, presented a revival of a play on Li Hsiu-ch'eng which had been first performed in 1937. At that time it was part of the National Defense Literature, the cultural policy of the united front. The play advocated class collaboration against

<hr/>

[12] The historical issues in this controversy are analyzed by Stephen Uhalley in "The Controversy over Li Hsiu-ch'eng," *The Journal of Asian Studies*, XXV, No. 2 (February, 1966), 305–17.

the common enemy. But even more threatening, when viewed as an analogy of P'eng Teh-huai's challenge to Mao over the GLF, the play subverted Mao the man. Li is depicted as a courageous figure who dares to risk his own life to challenge the leader of the Taipings, Hung Hsiu-ch'üan, who is unwilling to listen to the advice of his associates and adheres stubbornly to a policy that leads to the defeat of the Taipings. In fact, the intensity of the debate over Li Hsiu-ch'eng at this time may have been because it was in reality a debate over the actions of P'eng Teh-huai and Mao. What is clear is that this historical controversy was part of a factional dispute between the established historians and established playwrights backed by Chou Yang on the one side and their more radical younger colleagues on the other.

Yet even when this controversy reached a climax in the summer of 1964, the prevailing view was neither Ch'i Pen-yu's nor Lo Erh-kang's, but a composite somewhat favoring the establishment, possibly reflecting their respective power. While Li Hsiu-ch'eng was criticized for capitulating to the enemy, he was praised for his contributions to the Taipings. His achievements outweighed his shortcomings. Perhaps this evaluation of Li was also part of an effort to rehabilitate rightists like P'eng Teh-huai whose contributions to the regime were more important than their criticisms of it. Ch'i Pen-yu was upbraided for his polemical assault and charged with crudely selecting facts to fit his conclusions.

Despite these charges against Ch'i, his writings and those of his associates reflected the prevailing tone of toleration and complexity that marked the discussions of 1963. Considering that the views of Wu Han, Feng Yu-lan, Liu Chieh, and their colleagues not only ran counter to the Maoist view of history but also to the current policy of intensifying class struggle, the response was relatively mild and maintained a distinct academic quality. For a brief period there appeared to be a genuine give-and-take in debate. The major criticisms of the historians were that they neglected class struggle and espoused concepts devoid of class content, but these charges were balanced by an acceptance of some of their arguments. Liu Chieh, for example, was chastised for treating Confucianism as an alternative to the thought of Mao, but his views were granted some value because they redressed a defect of the May Fourth Movement which made it impossible to inherit China's cultural legacy.[13] The discussion of Confucianism gave

13 Li K'an, "In Refutation of the New 'Venerate Confucius' Doctrine," *KMJP*, August 17 and 18, 1963, in *SCMP*, No. 3070, p. 3.

the people an understanding of China's spiritual richness. There was a definite policy to tolerate a variety of viewpoints in the academic sphere as expressed by the editorial board of *Hsin chien-she* at the beginning of 1963: "In academic research, scholars of any subject including those of Marxism have no authority to consider their views absolutely correct and suppress views at variance to theirs." [14] There was also a desire to eschew simplifications, as spelled out in a *Nan-fang jih-pao* (Southern Daily) article of November 3, 1963: "Marxists hold that the reflection of social existence by social consciousness, unlike a photograph, is oblique, complex, and indirectly reflective." [15]

Though Kuan Feng, Ch'i Pen-yu, and their associates weighted their arguments in the direction of class struggle, they too displayed a degree of toleration that was to disappear after another one of their colleagues, Yao Wen-yuan, attacked Wu Han's play, *Hai Jui's Dismissal from Office*, in November, 1965. This relatively tolerant approach is seen in the discussion of "historicism and class viewpoint" by another associate, Lin Kan-ch'üan. "Historicism" (*li-shih chu-i*), a method used in the early sixties, interpreted history with more emphasis on the period in which it took place than on current ideological standards. Lin and his allies sought to bring the discussion of history back toward the more class-oriented view of the 1950's. Yet, instead of categorically denouncing "historicism," as might be expected in a time of increasing polarization, he sought to combine it with a class viewpoint. He criticized those who stood historical and class viewpoints in opposition to each other and called instead for a combining of these viewpoints. The historian must "use class analysis as a guiding clue" to the study of the concrete realities of the period of study.[16]

Lin's characterization of class analysis as "a guiding clue" rather than "the method" with which to judge historical events was indicative of the subdued quality of the controversies at this time. The direction of history was obviously toward class struggle, but perhaps in a more subtle, less strictly ideological way. Even the article by Hsü Ch'i-hsien of August 15, 1963, which opened the attack on Wu Han for his essays of late 1962, admitted that "the moral legacies of the ruling class did have a dual character . . . in which some elements of

---

[14] The *Hsin chien-she* editorial was reprinted in *KMJP*, January 23, 1963, in *SCMP*, No. 2924, p. 5.

[15] *NFJP*, November 3, 1963, in *SCMP*, No. 3128, p. 7.

[16] Lin Kan-ch'üan, "Historicism and Class Viewpoint," *Hsin chien-she* (New Construction), May, 1963, in *SCMP*, No. 3162, pp. 15–17.

the people's character and democracy and science were apparent." [17] Though he did not point to the same moral qualities as Wu Han, he too believed that some values of the traditional ruling class could be accepted in the present.

There was little of the personal vindictiveness that marked earlier periods of increasing regimentation. Labels were not applied to individuals involved in the controversies in 1963, and the only persons used as examples of unorthodoxy were dead ones like Li Hsiu-ch'eng. Scarcely any past "evil deeds" were dredged up, as was customary when criticizing an individual for "incorrect" beliefs. For instance, no mention was made of Wu Han's devastating criticisms of Mao during the period 1959–62. His critics debated his ostensibly less political articles on morality written in late 1962 and August, 1963, confining their discussion to narrow philosophical and historical implications.

Whereas the attacks on Wu Han and Feng Yu-lan might be described as flurries, those against Liu Chieh were more severe, perhaps because he did not have the high-powered official protection of P'eng Chen, Chou Yang, and Lu Ting-i that they had. Special meetings were held on Liu Chieh by historical societies in Peking and Canton. Still, their main thrust was against his historical method, not his political views. By the end of 1963 these attacks subsided, though they reverberated into 1964.

Unlike the intellectuals criticized in earlier and later periods, those involved in the historical debates of 1963 for the most part continued to hold their positions. The first of five volumes of a new history of ancient China compiled under Wu Han's direction appeared in October, 1963. A reprinting of the first volume and publication of the second volume of Feng Yu-lan's *New History of Chinese Philosophy* came out in 1964. These works had to be approved by the Propaganda Department before they could be published. Also, pictures in newspapers in January, 1964, showed Liu Shao-ch'i and Chou En-lai holding receptions for philosophers and historians, among whom were Wu Han and Feng Yu-lan. These incidents indicated that the Party apparatus had not categorically rejected these men or their ideas.

THE DEBATES ON AESTHETICS

As the controversies in history waned, new controversies on similar themes waxed in the field of aesthetics. During 1963 and the first half

17 Hsü Ch'i-hsien, "Kuan-yü tao-te ti chieh-chi-hsing yü chi-ch'eng-hsing," p. 5.

of 1964, controversies in the social sciences and humanities dove-
tailed. The natural and physical sciences appeared to have been relatively immune to comparable debates in this period. The controversies
in aesthetics centered on the view of the historian-aesthetician Chou
Ku-ch'eng that art transcended class division and reflected the spirit
of all groups in society. As his colleagues Wu Han and Feng Yu-lan
saw history in universal rather than class terms, Chou regarded art
as the reflection of an amalgam of all social classes of a particular era.

Chou Ku-ch'eng, a professor at Futan University in Shanghai, was
an established theoretician in aesthetics and history. Many of his ideas
on aesthetics were formulated in a debate he had with the highly respected aesthetician, Chu Kuang-chien. In refuting Chu's theory that
artistic beauty lies in the subjective impression of the appreciator,
Chou presented a view of art which closely resembled that of Hu Feng,
a literary theorist he had helped to purge in 1955. Like Hu Feng,
Chou saw the creative process as an acute struggle between the artist's
subjective nature and objective reality. As the process is completed,
the subjective merges with the objective, thereby solving the contradiction and producing a work of art. The writer's own subjective feelings, which may or may not include class feelings, are the crucial
factor in the creative process. Chou expounded on this concept repeatedly even after Mao's Tenth Plenum speech.

It was not Chou's theory of art, however unorthodox, but his view
of consciousness that more directly opposed the thought of Mao and
provoked the most controversy. In "A Critique of Some Problems of
Artistic Creativity," published in the June, 1963, issue of *Hsin chien-
she,* Chou wrote: "The age of feudalism had various ideologies and
ideological consciousnesses which merged to become the spirit of the
age; the age of capitalism also had a variety of beliefs which merged
to become the spirit of the age. The spirit of the age of each era,
while it is a unified integral whole, is nevertheless reflected through
different classes and individuals all of which are distinct." [18] This view,
which saw consciousness as the unified expression of various ideologies
representing different groups coexisting in society, conflicted with the
Maoist vision of consciousness as the expression of one class in conflict with another or one class transforming another.

The principal critic of Chou's theory was Yao Wen-yuan. The son

[18] A section of this article was reprinted in Yao Wen-yuan, "Lüeh-lun shih-tai ching-
shen wen-t'i yü Chou Ku-ch'eng hsien-sheng shang-chüeh" (A Brief Discussion of the
Problems of the Spirit of the Age), *KMJP,* September 24, 1963, p. 3.

of Yao P'eng-tzu, a Shanghai writer of the 1930's, Yao already in the early fifties was an occasional contributor to *Wen-i pao* (Literary Gazette). Like other aspiring writers, he rose to prominence in the Hu Feng and Antirightist campaigns because of his vigorous role in attacking its victims. He was even more conspicuous in the brief antirevisionist drive of early 1960 when he was the first to label the writer Pa Jen a revisionist. Pa Jen had also become famous in Shanghai in the 1930's, a cosmopolitan place and period whose lingering influence, Yao and his associates later charged, had eroded the revolutionary spirit. Most likely because of his ideological crusades, Yao very quickly made a name for himself in Shanghai cultural circles. He became an editor of *Wen-i yüeh-pao* (Literary Monthly), under its chief editor Pa Chin, and a member of the editorial board of *Chiehfang jih-pao* (Liberation Daily). These activities brought him into contact with K'o Ch'ing-shih, then the first secretary of the Shanghai Party Committee and a close associate of Mao's, and with Chang Ch'un-ch'iao, then director of literary work in Shanghai, who became an activist in the Cultural Revolution.

Though Yao was to be Mao's chief ideologue in the Cultural Revolution, his arguments in 1963, like those of his associates involved in the historical and philosophical debates, showed some scholarship and made use of non-Communist references. He was then willing to accept certain aspects of Chou Ku-ch'eng's arguments while rejecting others. His discussion with Chou in the pages of *KMJP* emerges as a genuine debate. In his refutation of a "A Brief Discussion of the Problems of the Spirit of the Age," Yao compared Chou's view to Taine's, who believed that the consciousness of a historical period evolved into an abstract spirit. While Yao agreed with Chou that society was composed of a variety of complex, contradictory class views, he disagreed with the corollary that the combination of these various views assumed the spirit of the age. Yao contended that mutually antagonistic class consciousnesses can never form an integrated spirit. In the present age, Yao insisted, it is the revolutionary consciousness of the proletariat that represents the common spirit, not a combination of various class consciousnesses. He warned that "if one completely separates oneself from all moorings with present realities, he will inevitably move into absurdity." [19]

This charge of "unreality" was exactly what Chou and his colleagues thought of Yao's—that is, Mao's—contention that the spirit

[19] *Ibid.*

of the present age was one of proletarian revolutionary consciousness. They maintained that the current spirit was not one of revolutionary consciousness but of various contradictory strains that produced a nonrevolutionary whole. Chou wrote in his article, "Unified Whole and Separate Reflections," "Yao holds that the spirit of the contemporary age is revolutionary. . . . If the facts were analyzed, we would find that this is not so. Besides a revolutionary spirit, there is also some nonrevolutionary and even antirevolutionary spirit." He charged that Yao was "fond of making abstract generalizations, but does not like to analyze facts." This article differed from Chou's earlier one in that he stated his views explicitly within the context of present-day China. He saw the prevalent conflicting forces ultimately converging to form a unified whole. Foreshadowing the debate that was to burst forth the following year over Yang Hsien-chen's concept of two combining into one, he asked, "Though it incorporates different classes, different nationalities, different languages, or different religious beliefs, is not the People's Republic of China a unified whole? If it is held that different parts cannot form the whole, then a unified China, Chinese history, and the Chinese cultural legacy could not exist." [20]

Yao's reply, in an article entitled "On Mr. Chou Ku-ch'eng's View on Contradictions," was surprisingly bland and belated considering Chou's direct challenge of his and Mao's assumption that China was a revolutionary society.[21] In fact, Yao did not even confront the issue but asserted instead that it was Chou who was not revolutionary because he denied that different kinds of consciousness were being transformed into proletarian consciousness. The major part of Yao's reply, however, was not concerned with the subject of consciousness, but was a critique of Chou's aesthetic theory, as if he sought to divert the debate to a less controversial issue. Yao charged that Chou's theory was based on what he called the bourgeois idealistic thinking of Western philosophy. It was in the same tradition as Schopenhauer, who considered aesthetics to be the identity of the subjective and the objective, and Bergson, who held that nonrational intuition enters the object and thus deprives a work of art of correct ideological content.

[20] Chou Ku-ch'eng, "T'ung-i cheng-t'u yü fen-pieh fan-ying," *KMJP*, November 7, 1963, p. 2.
[21] Yao Wen-yuan, "P'ing Chou Ku-ch'eng hsien-sheng ti mao-tun kuan," *ibid.*, May 10, 1964, p. 2.

CHOU YANG'S ROLE IN THE DEBATES OF 1963

The heat of the 1963 controversies appeared to be burning out in the early months of 1964. Despite the fact that Mao's views and policies were challenged, the Party's attitude toward ideological orthodoxy in the intellectual community continued to be sluggish. There had been discussion, debate, and even argument, but there was not the customary campaign that accompanied a shift toward ideological regimentation and there was no imposition of one specific line. This hesitancy to move in the ideological realm was reflected in the thinking and actions of the assistant director of the Propaganda Department, Chou Yang, whose realm was the literary and intellectual community. Little that he said or did directly following the Tenth Plenum showed a responsiveness to Mao's criticism or demand for renewed class struggle. True, he did make a self-criticism in which he admitted he had not been alert to subversive tendencies in literary works, but he also insisted that the cultural sphere was basically ideologically correct.

It was not until over a year later, on October 26, 1963, that Chou gave strong backing to Mao's policy. As if in anticipation of further pressure from Mao, Chou Yang's speech before the philosophy and social sciences faculties of the Chinese Academy of Sciences, which he entitled "The Fighting Tasks Confronting Workers in Philosophy and Social Sciences," was widely hailed in all the media, the domain of the Propaganda Department, as the definitive line on academic work. One whole issue of *Hung-ch'i* (Red Flag) was devoted to it, marking the first time that the journal had published a single author. Not even Mao had received such treatment. Forums were held to discuss Chou's speech in academic communities throughout the country.

He decried the current reluctance in intellectual circles to apply class struggle to research and cultural activity. In ringing words he declared, "We should systematically refute modern revisionism on the academic front and carry on revolution on the ideological front." [22] He then used the phrase that was to gain wide currency even when he himself was condemned: "Everything tends to divide itself into two." [23] This opposed the views of Chou Ku-ch'eng and Wu Han by saying that contradictions in society were irreconcilable and must be resolved through struggle. Contradiction and struggle, not unity and

[22] Chou Yang, "The Fighting Tasks Confronting Workers in Philosophy and Social Sciences," *CB*, No. 726, p. 2.
[23] *Ibid.*, p. 4.

reconciliation, were the forces that pushed society forward. He labeled theories on merging of contradictions as "revisionism" and claimed that they provided a philosophical basis for the concept of "a state of the whole people."

Though certainly in line with the Maoist vision of the Tenth Plenum, there were other elements in Chou's speech that may have beclouded the vision. Chou spoke primarily in terms of Soviet revisionism rather than Chinese revisionism. His accusations were general rather than specific. He also touched upon a topic seldom discussed under the Chinese Communist regime—the Marxist theory of alienation. Though he ultimately rejected the validity of this concept for present-day China, he presented it with a degree of understanding. The fact that he gave so much attention to alienation indicated that the feeling did exist among some groups in Chinese society. He observed that there were some people who believed that a socialist society under the dictatorship of the proletariat was not free politically, economically, and ideologically, and that "these restraints imposed by society on the individual had produced the alienation of man." [24] The only way for man to return to himself is to eliminate all kinds of social constraints. Yet despite his straightforward discussion of alienation, Chou condemned it as a typically bourgeois, revisionist concept.

The second half of his speech qualified and somewhat contradicted his call in the first half for the application of class struggle to cultural matters. He urged intellectuals "to learn from all peoples in science and culture," including those in their own heritage.[25] Although he had called for an ideological approach, he also demanded a disciplined, academic approach: "In studying a problem, it is necessary to investigate and derive its inherent laws, not imaginary ones. . . . To use the simplified method of sticking the orthodox label on something may seem to conform with historical materialism and class viewpoint, but it is subjective." [26] These words may have been directed at the young Turks, Ch'i Pen-yu and Yao Wen-yuan, who disputed the older scholars.

Finally, he made a plea for academic procedures akin to those used in Western academic communities: "If free exploration, debate, and independent thinking are discouraged and if the method of issuing administrative decrees to solve complicated questions in intellectual

24 *Ibid.*, p. 15.
25 *Ibid.*, p. 21.
26 *Ibid.*, p. 23.

fields is employed, then the result will be the ossification of thought in the academic world." [27] Perhaps this thinking was behind his relative restraint in academic matters in 1963. As opposed to Mao, he looked forward to a society that would not only produce a host of self-sacrificing "ordinary" heroes like Lei Feng, but "also a galaxy of brilliant scholars." [28] Herein lay one of the major differences between Mao and the Party's cultural officials.

MAO'S RESPONSE

The pressure Chou had anticipated came in the form of a directive from Mao on December 12, 1963. Though Mao specifically referred to the arts, his directive was applicable to all areas of cultural endeavor. He voiced obvious displeasure with the inertia of his cultural apparatus: "Problems abound in all forms of art. . . . In many departments very little has been achieved so far in socialist transformation. . . . The social and economic base has changed, but the arts, as part of the superstructure which serves this base, still remain a serious problem. Hence, we should proceed with investigation and study and attend to this matter in earnest." [29] The following day Mao expressed even harsher criticism in his December 13 instruction to the Central Committee, in which he charged some members with "conservatism, arrogance, and complacency." [30] He accused them of talking only of their achievements and not admitting their shortcomings or else dealing with them only superficially. Though he did not mention any names, Chou Yang's self-criticism after the Tenth Plenum was an obvious example. Mao, too, used the phrase, "one divides into two," but in a different context, applying it specifically to the need to distinguish between one's achievements and shortcomings. What disturbed him was that his followers had not acknowledged or remedied the shortcomings he had pointed out.

Most revealing of Mao's feelings at this time were his poems. Allusive, figurative phrases in his poetry often expressed political sentiments. Ten poems written over a period of fourteen years were published with great fanfare on January 4, 1964, in all major newspapers

[27] *Ibid.*, p. 24.

[28] *Ibid.*

[29] Mao Tse-tung, "Comment on Comrade K'o Ch'ing-shih's Report," *Long Live Mao Tse-tung Thought (CB,* No. 891), p. 41.

[30] Mao Tse-tung, "Instruction of the Central Committee on Strengthening of Learning from Each Other and Overcoming Conservatism, Arrogance, and Complacency," *Long Live Mao Tse-tung Thought (CB,* No. 892), p. 15.

and journals. It was as if the poems were brought out at this time to draw attention away from Chou's much-heralded speech before the philosophy and social science faculties. At the time of their publication, most of the poems were interpreted not only by Western scholars but also by Party officials as implicit attacks on Soviet revisionism. Yet with the hindsight of the Cultural Revolution, it appears that these poems were also implicit attacks on Mao's cultural apparatus and its Party backers. In the same manner as his critics, Mao at this point chose an indirect means of response. The principal interpreters of these poems came from Chou Yang's department, and it is natural that they might try to deflect criticism from themselves and aim it at Soviet officials. Given the subtlety and abstruse references in Mao's poetry, they are open to a wide range of interpretations, so that within certain limits the commentator can mold his interpretation to his own needs.

The poem that appears directed more against his internal than his external "enemies" is "Reply to Comrade Kuo Mo-jo," written in January, 1963.[31]

> In this small globe there are several flies crashing against
>   the wall
> They hum in a bitter tune and sob once and again
> The ants taking their abode inside the ash tree claim their
>   place is a large kingdom
> It is not easy for the ants to take a tree
> The direct Westerly wind tears down the leaves and passes
>   Ch'ang-an
>   Howling like whizzing arrows
>   So many things happened; they happen always fast
>   The earth is revolving; the time is too short
> Ten thousand years is too long; we only seize the morning
>   and the evening
> The four seasons are in a fury and the clouds and water in
>   a rage
> The five continents are in eruption under strong gales and
>   loud thunder
> It is necessary to wipe out all harmful insects to become
>   invincible.

The "flies" could just as well be those who disagree with Mao within his own Party as revisionists in the international Communist

---

[31] URS, XXXIV, No. 13 (February 14, 1964), 224. For an interpretation of this poem as an attack on China's external enemies, see Stuart Schram, "Mao as a Poet," *Problems of Communism*, VIII, No. 5 (September–October, 1964), 42–43.

movement. Flies, ants, and insects were terms used in traditional China to give a negative connotation to scholar-bureaucrats.[32] In the 1930's, Lu Hsün had used "flies" to refer specifically to Chou Yang, Yang Han-sheng, and their associates when they were in conflict with him because of his refusal to go along wholeheartedly with the united front. Considering that Lu Hsün later became a hero in the Cultural Revolution, it is possible that Mao may have identified with Lu Hsün in his struggle with the same cultural apparatus in the 1960's. The "flies crashing against the wall" could refer to those who hit at the thought of Mao Tse-tung. "They hum in a bitter tune and sob once and again" may allude to the intellectuals' distress over the GLF and their complaints against Maoist policies. "The ants" claiming "a large kingdom" probably connotes "the independent kingdoms" Mao later charged were set up in his domain, "the ash tree." These lines and variations of them were used repeatedly during the Cultural Revolution to describe the attempts by Lu Ting-i, P'eng Chen, Chou Yang, and others to subvert Maoist policies.

"The direct Westerly wind tears down the leaves" may mean that Western influence, Soviet revisionism, or anti-Maoist ideas will destroy the fruits of revolution, and "passes Ch'ang-an" could refer to the decline of the capital city of the T'ang dynasty, a fate that awaits the capital of the revolution. In the next five lines Mao expresses his feelings of urgency that the revolution be continued, and that its internal as well as external subversion be stopped. He concludes, therefore, that "all harmful insects" must be squashed if the revolution, which he equates with himself, is to succeed.

The Party's cultural officials either did not understand, misinterpreted, or chose to ignore Mao's directives and poems. They may have felt sure enough of their positions and support in the Party to pay lip service to the thought of Mao Tse-tung, while disregarding his instructions of December, 1963, to carry out an "ideological transformation" and investigate "in earnest." The Propaganda Department sent groups of intellectuals and cultural cadres to the countryside and factories. Still, in the early months of 1964, there was neither an ideological remolding campaign nor purge. Even the intellectual controversies had petered out.

Then, on May 29, 1964, two students at the Higher Party School

---

[32] Jeremy Ingalls, in an unpublished manuscript, has analyzed the relationship between Mao's poems and the Chinese classics, the Chinese language, and political developments.

in Peking, studying with the Russian-trained Central Committee member Yang Hsien-chen, published an article on the philosophical page of *KMJP* in which they agreed with the dictum that one divides into two, but they insisted that the corollary, two combines into one, was also valid. They held that everything from the physical world to human society was composed of opposites, so that one divides into two; but that these opposites were united by dependence as well as conflict, hence two combines into one. Their corollary to one dividing into two completely changed its meaning and was in direct opposition not only to Mao's overall approach but even to his most recent instructions. Mao's December 13, 1963, statement against the "complacency" of some Party members also asserted that "the contradictions and opposite aspects of a thing in a given condition transform themselves into the opposite." [33] The students' corollary of the unity of opposites not only denied the concept of transformation, but also implied a rejection of the struggle needed to produce the transformation. They sought reconciliation rather than struggle between opposites. To a certain extent, the unity of opposites was a theoretical restatement of Chou Ku-ch'eng's "spirit of the age" and Wu Han's "universal ethics." When the two students used their theory in a political context, their rejection of revolutionary struggle for present-day China was even clearer. They held that the method of one into two should be used in achieving power, but that once one moves from attaining power to socialist construction, then the two into one approach comes into play. Moreover, they criticized those who "see only absolute good and bad" because it renders them unable "to make a unity of opposites." [34] Hence, their concept would result in a period of consolidation and moderation rather than the struggle and polarization that Mao advocated.

Despite the fact that they recommended an opposite approach to Mao's, their article initially did not cause much of a stir outside the Higher Party School and the philosophical page of *KMJP*. Their article resulted from a discussion that had been developing for some time at the school and among Party ideologists. A rejoinder to the May 29 article was published on June 5 in *KMJP* in which Hsiung Ch'ing charged that the two students had repudiated class struggle. However, this accusation drew little support, and Hsiung Ch'ing was

---

[33] Mao, "Instruction of the Central Committee," p. 15.

[34] Ai Heng-wu and Lin Ch'ing-shan, " 'I fen-wei erh' yu 'ho erh erh i' " (One Divides into Two and Two Combines into One), *KMJP*, May 29, 1964, p. 5.

even chastised in another *KMJP* article seven days later for finding any difference between one into two and two into one. The article mistakenly claimed that the corollary meant the same as the proposition, and this view was repeated several times throughout June in *KMJP*. Most of the discussion was a quiet philosophical debate comparable to those of 1963.

At this time there was also a resurgence of interest in peasant rebellions, a subject that had sparked much controversy in the early sixties, when several scholars challenged the accepted Maoist interpretation of peasant uprisings as revolutionary movements. Some had argued on strictly Marxist terms that the peasantry was a conservative force that desired not a new order, but wealth and power like the upper classes. Though they argued with historical examples, it was obvious that they were disputing Mao's glorification in the GLF of the peasants as revolutionaries.

The debate on the peasantry simmered throughout 1963, but again broke out into the open in June, 1964, as the Socialist Education Movement was reaching a climax. Using arguments similar to those in 1961–62, Chou Liang-hsiao in *Jen-min jih-pao* (People's Daily; hereafter *JMJP*) contended that the peasant's chief goal was not the establishment of a new kind of egalitarian society, but improvement in his own livelihood. In Chinese history, he pointed out, "it is wrong to regard peasant wars as . . . giving rise to a new social system." He explained that "in feudal times peasants did not oppose all forms of exploitation. The equality they desired was to throw off the landlords in order to make a profit or become small property owners." The peasants, therefore, "are not revolutionary, but conservative." Yet, he complained, "some comrades attributed greater awareness to peasants than is warranted." They "believe that peasant wars have egalitarian goals and the desire for a new kind of society." Indirectly criticizing Mao, he called these beliefs illusions which he charged were "the result of deficiencies in the knowledge of the realities of social development." [35] While he added that the description of peasants as conservative depicted their historical and not their current role, his and his colleagues' concern with this issue in mid-1964 seemingly expressed their fear that Mao once again was overestimating China's ideological readiness for revolutionary change.

Though the propaganda and cultural apparatuses did not respond to

[35] Chou Liang-hsiao, "Tui nung-min chung-cheng fan feng-chien hsing-chi ti li-chieh" (The Antifeudal Nature of Peasant Wars), *JMJP*, June 2, 1964, p. 6.

these developments, Mao finally did on June 27, 1964, with a more emphatic and accusatory directive than those of December, 1963. Again his anger was not directed at those engaged in the debates, but at the cultural bureaucracy that permitted them to take place. "In the past fifteen years, most of their publications (it is said a few are good), and by and large the people in them (that is, not everybody has not carried out the policies of the Party) have acted as high and mighty bureaucrats, have not gone to the workers, peasants, and soldiers, and have not reflected socialist reality and socialist construction. In recent years, they have slid right down to the brink of revisionism. Unless they remold themselves in real earnest in the future, they are bound to become a group like the Hungarian Petofi Club." [36] In no way could this directive be misinterpreted or ignored.

THE RECTIFICATION OF 1964

Immediately following Mao's June 27 statement, a rectification was launched in the academic and cultural spheres. Though it was undertaken in response to Mao's directives, its implementation was under the control of Liu Shao-ch'i, P'eng Chen, and the Propaganda Department rather than the ideologues closer to Mao. Liu is referred to as an authority as much as Mao and is profusely quoted, sometimes without an accompanying quote from Mao. Since the early sixties, Mao had used the People's Liberation Army (PLA) increasingly in the ideological and cultural realm. In late 1963 he initiated a campaign for the whole nation "to learn from the PLA," and in the theater and opera the PLA was setting up organizations parallel to those of the Party. Yet, at this time Mao was utilizing the army to reinfuse the nation with revolutionary élan, not to replace the Party. The Party was still very much in charge of the rectification and was determined to keep it within bounds.

Most likely, the Party hierarchy was not only responding to Mao's pressure but was itself concerned about the deterioration of ideological discipline. It was probably as determined as Mao to halt the slide toward revisionism, but its methods differed from the ones Mao had in mind. It did not purge the "high and mighty bureaucrats" Mao had criticized, nor did it carry out the full-scale remolding movement Mao demanded. The intellectuals who had been the center of the controversies of 1963 were virtually ignored, though their arguments were

[36] "Instructions concerning Literature and Art," *Long Live Mao Tse-tung Thought* (*CB*, No. 891), p. 41.

condemned. Chou Ku-ch'eng was given attention, but he was not a prime target. Not being Party members, they were not in the position to influence large groups. Those who were attacked had long careers in Party propaganda and ideology, but they were not the ones who had most sharply criticized Mao and the GLF. For instance, Teng T'o, head of the secretariat of the Peking Party Committee, whose satires of the early sixties had amounted to a barrage against Mao, was not even mentioned.

The first and foremost target was the Party ideologist, Yang Hsien-chen. Though Yang's Soviet training must have played a role in selecting him for criticism, the campaign was more concerned with countering the desire for compromise expressed in the two into one slogan than in his Soviet connections.[37] The attack on him was based on the article by his two students and on his lecture notes of the early sixties. In these notes, Yang, in another example of the historical-mindedness of Chinese intellectuals, traced the concept of one into two, two into one, to Chinese tradition. Claiming that the dialectic was part of the Chinese heritage, he pointed to the thinking of the Ming scholar Fang Ming-chih, who described the underlying principle of the cosmos as one of opposites, such as yin and yang, day and night, sadness and happiness. But Yang insisted it was a dialectic in which the elements did not work in opposition to each other, but in harmony. For example, in the Chinese language, the word, "thing" is made up of the words east and west (*tung-hsi*), and the verb "to breathe" is made up of exhale-inhale (*hu-hsi*). He also found the harmony of opposites in some Chinese philosophical concepts like Lao Tzu's definition of origin, which is composed of the words for existence and nonexistence. Hence, two into one was very much a part of China's cultural heritage.

However, it was not so much Yang's concept of the unity of opposites that disturbed the authorities. After all, Mao had talked of non-antagonistic contradictions in "On the Correct Handling of Contradictions among the People" and of the interrelation of opposites in "On Contradiction"; Mao as well as Lenin allowed for a temporary union of opposites. But whereas they emphasized that the transformation of one force by the other in an endless struggle was more fundamental than union, Yang emphasized that the union did not dissolve the opposites, that each remained separate, held together by mutual need. Consequently, he advocated seeking common ground with op-

[37] This aspect of the campaign is also discussed by Donald Munro, "The Yang Hsien-chen Affair," *CQ,* No. 22 (April–June, 1965), pp. 75–82.

posing ideologies, but allowing differences to remain. Again he found
the basis for his view in Chinese tradition. The contrasting philosophies of Confucianism and Taoism existed together, but they did not
transform each other; they lived together in a spirit of syncretism.[38]
Similarly, through his concept, Yang had "sinicized" the Marxian
dialectic. Instead of thesis and antithesis producing a synthesis, it was
thesis and antithesis producing a syncretism. The ultimate implication
of this view for present-day China would be toleration of a diversity
of viewpoints and of classes.

Though Yang had expressed his ideas in a philosophical context, the
regime rebutted them in a political context. The main critics of Yang
were not the young ideologues who figured so prominently in the controversies of 1963, but the established Party ideologues, of whom Ai
Ssu-ch'i was the major spokesman. They insisted that if Yang's theories were carried out in practice, they would lead away from uninterrupted class struggle toward class conciliation. If contradictory elements united without a struggle, without one vanquishing the other,
then the capitalist system would remain and socialism would not be
victorious. His critics asked, "Does not the unity of opposites between
the proletariat and the bourgeoisie signify that the interdependence of
these two classes is unconditional and absolute and the bourgeoisie
must be preserved forever?" [39]

Because the regime was not yet ready to denounce the Chinese
heritage, Yang's views were attributed to Soviet revisionist influence.
Yang could easily be identified with the Soviet Union. He had studied
at the University for the Toilers of the East in Moscow in the 1920's
and was head of the Chinese Department of the Soviet Foreign Languages Institute in the 1930's. Still, in the excerpts that were printed
of Yang's unpublished works there is little mention of the Soviet
Union. Even though he attributed his views to Chinese cultural tradition, his critics made him a disciple of Bernstein, Plekhanov, and
Bukharin. His theory of two into one was traced directly to the Deborin
school of philosophy which developed in the USSR in the late 1920's.
Its founder, Abram Deborin, was a Menshevik before the Russian
Revolution, a Party member after. His words that "thesis and antith-

[38] Joseph Levenson analyzed the syncretism of traditional China in Joseph R. Levenson and Franz Schurmann, *China: An Interpretive History from the Beginnings to the
Fall of Han* (Berkeley and Los Angeles: University of California Press, 1971).

[39] Wang Chung and Kuo P'ei-heng, "Chiu 'ho erh erh i' wen-t'i ho Yang Hsien-chen
t'ung-chih shang-chüeh" (Discussing with Comrade Yang Hsien-chen "Two into One"),
JMJP, July 17, 1964, p. 5.

esis are not mutually exclusive opposites but mutually conciliatory opposites" were similar to Yang's.[40] Stalin regarded Deborin's theory as an effort to conciliate the rich peasants and bourgeoisie who opposed his drive toward collectivization in the late twenties and early thirties. Whether or not Yang was directly influenced by Deborin, it is most likely the Chinese regime shared Stalin's fear.

The Yang Hsien-chen campaign was also used to attack the classical Marxist view of history that had been implicit in Chou Liang-hsiao's discussion of peasant rebellions and explicit in Yang Hsien-chen's thinking. In the midst of the GLF, a discussion was initiated in academic circles on "the question of thinking and being" in which Yang argued that no one, no matter how omniscient, can afford to disregard the inexorable laws of history or oppose his will against the limitations of objective reality. These views emerged as a major issue in 1964. Whereas 1963 was characterized by debates on Chinese history, 1964 was characterized by debates on historical materialism.

As in the attack on the concept of two into one, these ideas were attributed to Yang largely on the basis of unpublished articles. In 1958, after a visit to the countryside, Yang wrote "A Brief Discussion of Two Categories of Identity" in which he attacked the belief that China was ready for revolution and denied the dynamic role of the masses in the GLF. Though he was stopped from publishing the article, it finally came out in a revised form under what was later called "the guise of an academic exploration." In the original article, Yang supposedly wrote that "the abandonment of objective laws and one-sided discussion of subjective ability means metaphysics and the sole obedience to the will." [41] In another work, "What Is Materialism?" Yang wrote, "For a certain concrete problem, if thought cannot correctly reflect objective realities and the subjective is not in conformity with the objective, this thought is idealism." [42] Yang attributed the failure of the GLF to the discrepancy between the subjective and the objective.

The "objective reality" that Yang saw was quite different from the one Mao saw in the GLF. In this respect, there may be some validity to the Party's charge that Yang's arguments resembled Bukharin's objection to Stalin's five-year plan. Both Yang and Bukharin favored

[40] Deborin is quoted in Hsiao Shu, "Anti-dialectical Substance of the 'Uniting Two into One,'" *JMJP*, August 14, 1964, in *SCMP*, No. 3296, p. 5.

[41] Ts'ung Wei, "Yang Hsien-chen and the 'Identity of Thinking and Existence,'" *KMJP*, December 11, 1964, in *SCMP*, No. 3380, p. 5.

[42] "A Critique of Yang Hsien-chen's Theory of Reflection," *KMJP*, December 18, 1964, in *SCMP*, No. 3386, p. 2.

an economy in which socialism and capitalism would develop side by side for a period of time. In another unpublished article, written in the midst of the collectivization drive of 1955, Yang wrote that what existed in China was "a semisocialist system of ownership which allows some ownership by individual peasants." To deny this, Yang declared, "was the same as saying that socialism can be built without agriculture because it is clear even now that individual agriculture still occupies a dominant position." [43] Yang asserted that even those who advocate an economy without individual holdings "have to eat every day," and yet they refuse to acknowledge the role the individual peasant plays in providing certain needs in a socialist society.[44] Moreover, the superstructure or ideology that derives from this economic base should not serve one single economic underpinning but all economic groups, otherwise its programs will not be in accord with the people for whom they were created. Like Bukharin, Yang saw a single economic form evolving gradually as the socialist economy expanded and the capitalist economy contracted. But up to the present time this had not happened because the population was not ready. Consequently Yang felt ideology and its accompanying programs should respond to the existing situation, not the future one. When ideology was not in tune with reality, its programs would be counterproductive.

The regime did not respond publicly to Yang's views until the rectification of 1964, when, in line with the Socialist Education Movement, it sought to reject Yang's belief that two economic systems could coexist for a period of time. A quote from Liu Shao-ch'i was used repeatedly: "If China does not become a socialist nation, then it will become a capitalist country. Instead of capitalism giving in to socialism, it will hinder it." [45] More important than rejecting the specific content of Yang's view was the rejection of his approach, which the regime believed would not necessarily lead to socialism. As a *KMJP* article of December 18, 1964, pointed out, in Yang's opinion a man's understanding of any problem must be a complete reflection of objective existence and only after achieving such complete reflection will he take action. But "if we wait to achieve perfect reflection before we act,

43 "Yang Hsien-chen's Composite Economic Base Theory," *JMJP*, November 1, 1964, in *SCMP*, No. 3337, p. 13.

44 *Ibid.*, p. 14.

45 "Comrade Yang Hsien-chen's 'Theory of Balanced Development' Is a Reprint of Bukharin's 'Theory of Equal Development,'" *KMJP*, February 19, 1965, in *SCMP*, No. 3428, p. 4. This quote is from Liu Shao-ch'i's "Report on Drafting the Constitution of the Chinese People's Republic."

we will certainly eliminate action and revolution." [46] This was an admission that revolutionary policies did not necessarily reflect present-day realities. The fear as expressed in another *KMJP* article a week earlier was that "if . . . we assume a passive stand and lose initiative, we cannot fulfill our tasks." [47] The conclusion was that Yang had failed to understand the dynamic revolutionary theory of reflection.

The questions that preoccupied the intellectual community in China in the summer of 1964 resembled a number of Western philosophical and ideological debates in the nineteenth and early twentieth centuries between those who believed in the existence of immutable laws of history and those who believed in man's ability to shape his own history. At the beginning of the twentieth century, the Russian theorist Plekhanov and other orthodox Russian Marxists argued the doctrine of technical-economic causation in opposition to Lenin, who did not have their faith that impersonal historical forces would produce communism. Plekhanov asserted that the Promethean will could not change the course of history or the limits imposed by material existence, to which Lenin replied that man's function was not only to understand the objective world but, more importantly, actively to change it. In 1964 Yang was associated with Plekhanov's position and of course Mao with Lenin's. Mao had stated Lenin's view many times, most recently in May, 1963, in "Where Do Correct Ideas Come From?" He wrote, "Once correct ideas . . . are grasped by the masses, these ideas turn into a material force which can change society and change the world." [48] The question whether one knows if he correctly reflects the laws of the objective world is not proved until "the stage leading from consciousness back to matter in which they are applied in practice." [49] Thus, Mao insisted that one must act in order to know if he accurately reflects the objective world.

Whereas Mao believed one's ideas depend on action, Yang was charged with believing that ideas are only a passive reflection of material progress. He was chastised for his rejection of subjective initiative and revolutionary spirit. These charges were an unfair polarization of Yang's views. As late as January, 1964, in a lecture at the Higher Party School, he is reported to have said that "the revolu-

[46] "A Critique of Yang Hsien-chen's 'Theory of Reflection,' " p. 3.

[47] Ts'ung Wei, "Yang Hsien-chen and the 'Identity of Thinking and Existence,' " p. 6.

[48] Mao Tse-tung, "Where Do Correct Ideas Come From?" *Four Essays on Philosophy* (Peking: Foreign Languages Press, 1966), p. 134.

[49] *Ibid.,* p. 135.

tionary spirit alone cannot help us to be free." [50] A reverse of this statement had been expressed by his supposed mentor Plekhanov, who pointed out that no freedoms existed unless they were consistent with economic realities.[51] Yang did not reject the revolutionary spirit, but he maintained that it had to be combined with a sober respect for objective limitations. Undoubtedly, as evidenced by the dissent in 1961–62, he and several members of the Party hierarchy who shared his views felt they were acting in good Marxist-Leninist tradition. After all, Lenin's emphasis on the subjective factor and revolutionary will was also accompanied by a genuine effort to comprehend "objective reality" accurately.

While Mao and Yang had the same goals—the establishment of communism—their methods differed. Whereas Yang believed communism would come with economic and technical transformation, Mao increasingly believed it would come with moral transformation, the making of a new revolutionary soul. But this clash was more than one between Rousseauan-Jacobin voluntarism diffused through Marxism-Leninism to Mao and the orthodox Marxist view of stages of development. Certainly Yang protested against the GLF because he was committed to the orthodoxy that an economically backward country could not leap into communism. Yet also implicit in his writings, as in Chou Ku-ch'eng's, was the belief that radical policies were self-defeating because they were not in tune with the Chinese reality: the revolutionary spirit that must accompany radical programs did not yet predominate among the Chinese masses.

An offshoot of the Yang Hsien-chen campaign was a drive against the literary official, Shao Ch'üan-lin, in the fall of 1964. At a writers' conference in Dairen in August, 1962, Shao, like Chou Liang-hsiao and Yang Hsien-chen, portrayed the peasants as less revolutionary than Party propaganda had painted them. Shao coined the phrase "the middle men" (*chung-chien jen-wu*)—meaning people who were caught between the old ways of life and the new—as a more realistic description of the Chinese masses than "revolutionary." Though speaking in a literary context, his views were similar to those that Yang had voiced in "the question of thinking and being" and that Chou Ku-ch'eng had

50 Ch'eng Hsin, "Expose Comrade Yang Hsien-chen's Substitute of Metaphysical Mechanical Theory for Dialectic Materialism," *KMJP*, December 25, 1964, in *SCMP*, No. 3392, p. 1.

51 This debate between Plekhanov and Lenin is discussed in Leopold Haimson, *The Russian Marxists and the Origins of Bolshevism* (Cambridge, Mass.: Harvard University Press, 1955).

presented in his theory on "the spirit of the age." As Yang and Chou had urged that ideology express current realities, not future utopias, so Shao urged writers to depict the peasants as they respond to rapidly changing realities rather than as heroic, revolutionary models. He wrote that "the complexity of the struggle is not adequately reflected. . . . Our creativity should take a step toward real life and solidly reflect reality." [52] His advice to writers was not meant to deny the revolutionary will, but like Yang he feared that unless China's problems were approached with more realism and less utopianism, there would be an overestimation of the ideological readiness of the Chinese people to participate in a revolutionary movement, which would again produce setbacks like the GLF.

The purpose of the campaign against Shao was to reject the portrayal of the peasant as nonrevolutionary. Whereas in 1963 the regime merely charged that the backwardness of the peasants had been exaggerated, in the fall of 1964 it denied categorically any view that considered the poor and lower-middle class peasants nonrevolutionary. Shao's picture of the majority of Chinese peasants as ambivalent toward the revolution clashed directly with the Socialist Education Movement then underway. More crucial than the clash of views was the implication that the regime had not understood the real demands of the peasantry. Instead of confronting this issue, the regime threw Shao's criticism back at him by charging that it was Shao and his allies who were out of touch with the peasantry. Among his allies were allegedly two authors, Chao Shu-li and Chou Li-po, who in the previous decade had been praised for their authentic portrayal of ordinary peasants, which included the ambivalence that Shao had described. Now in 1964 it was they who were called "unrealistic." At a forum to censure Shao, his critics said of his remarks at the Dairen conference: "How remote from the times and the desires of the people." [53]

The drive against Shao moved quickly from a negative to a positive stage in which it sought to define new behavior patterns, new values, and new beliefs for a new socialist man. In contrast to Shao's image of the peasant as suspicious of the revolution, riddled with conflict, and desirous of some material benefits, the regime depicted the peasant as a hero of unqualified optimism, unstinting self-sacrifice, and abiding faith in the revolution. This aspect of the rectification became a more

---

[52] Shao's speech was not published at the time, but excerpts of his remarks were published in *Wen-i pao*, No. 8–9 (September 30, 1964), pp. 15–20.

[53] *JMJP*, February 18, 1965, in *SCMP*, No. 3411, p. 4.

sophisticated edition of the Lei Feng movement directed toward the intellectuals. It was carried out not only by the established propaganda officials, but also by the younger ideologues, most prominently Yao Wen-yuan. Yao faced the fundamental question posed by the dissident officials and intellectuals: if the vast masses do not wholeheartedly support the revolution, then how can it be carried out? But instead of answering it, he reformulated the issue by saying that those who "loyally devote all their strength to advancing the revolution are not just a minority," as Shao claimed, but the overwhelming majority of the peasantry. This majority was not a suffering mass but heroic, conscious peasants who "love socialism and are the firmest [of all classes] in the revolution." [54]

This shift from the negative to positive phase of the rectification was carried further by a drive against another Soviet-trained Party ideologue, Feng Ting. Like Shao Chüan-lin's middle men, the image of man presented in Feng Ting's writings was contrasted with the new socialist man the regime sought to imprint. Feng's affirmation in his writings of the simple pleasures of normal life was exaggerated to mean that personal happiness takes precedence over revolutionary activity. This approach was condemned by comparing it with that of Lei Feng and other figures for emulation who supposedly sacrificed their lives for the revolution.

Feng was also condemned as part of the effort to combat what the regime called "Social Darwinism," a concept that played an important role in the May Fourth Movement. In 1964 this concept was defined as a view of man based on his biological development rather than on his class relationships. Though criticized earlier, it was given renewed attention in 1964 because there was a growing concern that intellectuals considered the main contradiction in society to be not between classes but between man and his environment. Quotations from Feng's writings about the ordinary person's concern for adequate food and housing were presented as examples of Social Darwinism because they stressed a common instinct for self-preservation and material improvement. Instead of treating selfishness and individualism as traits of the bourgeoisie, as doctrine decreed, Feng is accused of regarding them as innate emotions of all classes. In opposition, the regime insisted that these traits were not universal: workers, peasants, and soldiers were not motivated by selfish drives, but by a selfless, communist spirit. In juxta-

[54] Yao Wen-yuan, "A Theory Which Causes Socialist Literature and Art to Degenerate," *KMJP*, December 20, 1964, in *SCMP*, No. 3374, pp. 3, 6.

position to Feng's views, Lei Feng is quoted as saying, "Man is happiest when he contributes everything of himself to the cause of liberating mankind." [55]

THE UNIQUENESS OF THE 1964 RECTIFICATION

These were the major themes of the 1964 rectification in the intellectual community.[56] Though the pattern was similar to other campaigns in Chinese Communist history in its use of all forms of media, criticism and self-criticism sessions, and examples of personalized targets, the method and the substance were different. For the most part the same Chou Yang group that conducted the Hu Feng campaign of 1955 and the Antirightist Campaign of 1957–58 was in charge. Yet, its approach was less direct, less thorough, and more tolerant of its victims.

Though the group most likely deliberately misinterpreted Mao's wishes, there was room for genuine misinterpretation. For example, Mao's speech before the Propaganda Department on March 12, 1957, in the midst of the Hundred Flowers campaign, which had not previously been published, appeared in June, 1964, just as the rectification was to be launched. Whether Mao or the Party had ordered it printed is not clear. This speech, given at a time when Mao was less disillusioned with the Party, called for criticism of intellectual cadres, but with restraint and understanding. He cautioned that criticism of intellectuals must be "fully reasoned, analytical, and convincing, and should not be brutal, bureaucratic, or dogmatic." Furthermore, he advocated a gradual approach: "Changing the world view of intellectuals will take a long time." [57] This speech, plus Mao's short directives, were ambiguous on how the rectification was to be implemented and, if anything, advocated persuasion rather than coercion.

Whether purposely or not, the propaganda apparatus chose to interpret Mao's words as an order for a mild rectification. As in the past, personalized targets served as vehicles for transmitting ideological themes. But this time, instead of one specific target like Hu Feng or one specific group like the Ting Ling clique or the Chinese Democratic

[55] Quoted in *Yang-ch'eng wan-pao* (Yang-ch'eng Evening News), January 20, 1965, in *SCMP*, No. 3407, p. 4.

[56] The impact of the rectification on the performing arts, particularly the opera, theater, and film, is an aspect of the rectification which I plan to discuss in another paper. The rectification in the performing arts differed from that in the social sciences and humanities in that the PLA and Chiang Ch'ing played a greater role. It was carried out more in accordance with Mao's directives.

[57] Mao Tse-tung, "Talk at the National Conference on Propaganda Work of the CCP," in *CB*, No. 740, p. 16.

League, there were several different campaigns going on simultaneously against several related but different targets. The overall impact was to diffuse the movement. It was a broad campaign encompassing philosophy, history, literary theory, and the arts, but it was not very deep.

Those affected were a limited group of Party intellectuals and students in the large cities. As opposed to the Hu Feng campaign, which was conducted on a nationwide scale so that even a humble peasant in a remote area of Inner Mongolia was ferreting out latent "Hu Fengism," there was slight effort to incorporate large numbers of workers and peasants, either as the targets of indoctrination or as critics. There were no big struggle meetings or big-character posters, features that characterized past campaigns. As opposed to the publication of Hu Feng's letters or the republication of some of Ting Ling's stories, there was what appears to be a deliberate paucity of materials so that it was difficult to generate large-scale criticism. Except for the slogan "one into two, two into one," little effort was made to simplify the ideological themes in terms that could be understood by the uneducated. Most of the discussion had the character of abstruse intellectual exercises filled with Marxist abstractions as if to distract from the political implications of the issues. There was even debate, for instance, as to whether the "two into one" matter should be treated as a philosophical or political question. As opposed to P'eng Chen's unsuccessful effort in the early stage of the Cultural Revolution to treat these questions as scholarly ones, though the campaign in 1964 was definitely political, the discussion had a distinct academic quality.

The personalized targets were treated leniently. They were referred to throughout as "comrade," an appellation that Hu Feng and Ting Ling lost with the first volleys fired against them. Nor did the 1964 campaigns end with abject self-criticisms published throughout the land as a source of further indoctrination; no public confession came forth from Yang Hsien-chen, Shao Ch'üan-lin, or Feng Ting. Nor did the individuals or journals that had not recognized their "mistakes" suffer to any extent. In contrast to the purge of Feng Hsüeh-feng and his associates from *Wen-i pao* in 1954 for rejecting the students' criticism of Yu P'ing-po, *Chung-kuo ch'ing-nien pao* (Chinese Youth News) issued a mild self-criticism for its turning down the initial attack on Feng Ting and that was all. Certainly those under attack did lose their power, but Yang Hsien-chen and Feng Ting continued to teach at their respective institutions.

Shao Chüan-lin, together with a few other intimates of Chou Yang in the cultural hierarchy, were purged, marking the beginning of the end of the formidable cultural bureaucracy that Chou had established almost thirty years before.[58] Yet, as opposed to the earlier campaigns when all disciples, as in the case of Hu Feng, and all associates, as in the case of Ting Ling, suffered a fate similar to the chief target, the purge stopped with Shao and a few others. Shao was treated as the sacrificial lamb. His and Chou's other close colleagues, Lin Mo-han, Yuan Shui-po, and Ho Ch'i-fang, were not even criticized at this time. Another associate, Liu Pai-yü, who was in charge of the rectification in the Chinese Writers' Union, assumed Shao's place as head of its Party group. Chou was able to shelter most of his apparatus from attack. Furthermore, he appeared to have protected it against the infiltration of the PLA. Whereas by the end of 1964 the establishment of political departments on the PLA commissar system made some headway in the economic ministries, there is little evidence of this system in the Ministry of Culture, which was actually under the command of the Propaganda Department. The personal vehemence against the victims of previous and later purges was also missing. Hu Feng had been derided as "an imperialist dog of the United States and Chiang Kai-shek," but the worst epithets employed against the objects of the 1964 rectification were "revisionist" and "bourgeois humanitarian."

Even in substance the pattern was different than in previous rectifications. Whereas in earlier campaigns there was a unanimity of view in the negative appraisal of the victim and the imposition of a definitive line, this time there was a diversity of views with some defense of the victims and with some qualifications to the line being imposed. The attackers dominated, but the defenders and modifiers did not vanish from the scene as they had in other campaigns. The themes that were to dominate the Cultural Revolution were all present in the 1964 rectification—class struggle, transformation of consciousness, and concern over the deterioration of revolutionary spirit particularly among the youth—but the discussion, as in 1963, was contradictory, reflecting again the competition between the established authorities and the younger ideologues.

Some articles that purportedly criticized Yang Hsien-chen actually defended his ideas. Though Yang was criticized in a December 11,

---

[58] The purgees included the writer Hsia Yin, Yang Han-sheng (vice-minister of culture), Kang Cho (vice-chairman of the Hunan branch of the Chinese Writers' Union), and Mao Tun (minister of culture), who though not an intimate of Chou Yang, had been associated with him for many years largely in ceremonial positions in the cultural hierarchy.

1964, article in *KMJP* for his obedience to the objective laws of history, the author, Ts'ung Wei, nevertheless insisted that "we must also oppose the theory of sole obedience to the will and subjective idealism . . . because that would be a rejection of the primary quality of matter and the secondary quality of will." A line of criticism of the GLF expressed in the early sixties was now found in the discussions on Yang Hsien-chen. Ts'ung Wei went on to condemn the belief that "the will can determine everything and that man can do what he likes according to the dictates of his own will." [59] Similarly, though the major argument against Feng Ting was that individual enjoyment must be sacrificed to the revolution, a vocal minority modified this to read that personal and material pleasures were secondary to the revolution, rather than obliterated by it. Thus, the new kind of man was one to whom the revolution was not his whole life but the major part of it, leaving room for personal fulfillment. This was certainly a modification of the totally revolutionary image of Lei Feng.

Another distinctive feature of this rectification was that as it was unfolding, there was open criticism of some of the critics, particularly the younger ideologues. Like Ch'i Pen-yu in 1963, Yao Wen-yuan was censured in 1964 for his earlier comments on Chou Ku-ch'eng in an article which termed Yao's criticism "contradictory" and "not in correspondence with history." [60] Even more significant, the writers defended Shao Ch'üan-lin's concept of "the middle men" just as the campaign against this concept was getting underway. They charged that "if at all times, only the positive, advanced typical images can give direct expression to the spirit of the times . . . it means that representatives of the times may have no representation and things which do not represent the spirit of the times may become representative." [61] It is as if, they pointed out, in nineteenth-century Russia Chernyshevski's image of the peasant as ready for revolution was the only accepted form of literature and the landlords and bureaucrats of Gogol and Oblomov-type characters were rejected. They repeated the arguments that Chou Ku-ch'eng had made a year earlier, though in a parenthetical phrase, perhaps signifying that the period of debate was ending: "(In this period, there are not only revolutionary and advanced spirits, but also the normal feelings of ordinary people which we usually come across. Such feelings are not revolutionary or advanced, but also are

[59] Ts'ung Wei, "Yang Hsien-chen and the 'Identity of Thinking and Existence,' " p. 5.
[60] Chin Wei-min and Li Yun-ch'u, "Some Queries on the Spirit of the Times," *JMJP*, August 2, 1964, in *CB*, No. 747, p. 25.
[61] *Ibid.*, p. 27.

not nonrevolutionary or counterrevolutionary spiritual factors.)" [62] In an indirect criticism of Mao, they concluded that Yao's "arguments lack historical concreteness. They are only abstractions and rigid formulas," and they provide an inaccurate picture of the times.

By the beginning of 1965 the rectification appeared to have run its course. When it spread into the Ministry of Culture in the closing months of 1964, Chou Yang quickly sought to bring the campaign to a close. He suspended the rectification in various unions of the All-China Federation of Literary and Art Circles in November, 1964, on the grounds that the cadres had to be used in the Four Cleanups Campaign. But a sign of his waning power was that the rectification continued in the Peking Film Studios, Peking Opera, and Institute of Fine Arts in which Mao's wife, Chiang Ch'ing, had personally intervened. At the end of February, 1965, Chou called a meeting of press commentators and denounced recent articles on the rectification as dogmatic and exaggerated. The criticisms subsequently faded away. As was his custom in previous campaigns, Chou on April 15 and 16, 1965, summed up the results of the rectification and announced its conclusion. Though he acknowledged once again in his final report that he had been slow in recognizing revisionism and in implementing rectification, he did not admit any serious shortcomings as Mao had demanded in his December 13, 1963, instruction. In reference to some of his dismissed colleagues, he agreed that they did things for which they should be criticized, but he claimed that they were true Marxist-Leninists and opposed revisionism. Therefore, they could not be labeled revisionists or ousted from the Party.

There was reason, therefore, for Mao to be dissatisfied with the rectification of 1964. Instead of swelling into a major mass movement, it had fizzled into a superficial, perfunctory affair. There was an inconclusive quality to the whole campaign. Mao's summons to return to a revolutionary course was blocked by the entrenched cultural bureaucracies within his own political system. Their efforts to purge their organizations, stamp out dissent, and transform themselves and the nation ideologically were neither thorough nor far-reaching. It was evident to Mao by 1965 that he could not achieve the results he desired because of lack of commitment in the very departments that were to implement the ideological and organizational transformation. He abandoned his policy of persuasion from within to one of coercion from without with the assistance of Chiang Ch'ing, the PLA, and the young

62 *Ibid.*, p. 28.

radical faction in the cultural apparatus. In contrast to the Party's weak rectification, Mao's Cultural Revolution compelled unanimity in ideology, activation of the masses, and a thorough purge of those who did not follow his orders.

Although the genuine concerns expressed by the intellectuals in 1963 and 1964 for common values on which to reconcile the country, for concurrence between ideology and reality, and for an awareness of the real demands of the masses were pushed underground and their advocates purged, these concerns still remained. Since the conclusion of the Cultural Revolution, there has been a renewed concern with the idea of two into one and "the identity of thinking and being," an indication that in the aftermath of the upheaval of the Cultural Revolution, as in the aftermath of the Great Leap Forward, there is an underlying desire within the population for a period of consolidation and harmony as was reflected in the debates of 1963–64.

PART III

Maoism in Action

BYUNG-JOON AHN

Adjustments in the Great Leap Forward and Their Ideological Legacy, 1959-62

The period 1959–62 was one of the most critical in the history of the Chinese Communist Party (CCP) since its rise to power, for it was in these years that the Party weathered a major crisis by making a series of adjustments in the aftermath of the Great Leap Forward (GLF). Since the GLF emerged in 1958 as a prototype for Maoist revolution and development, as Mao Tse-tung defined it, the course of such adjustments revealed many problems of Maoist ideology and practice. Moreover, the adjustments of 1959–62 left the Party with an enduring legacy of unresolved ideological problems.

To understand the adjustments period it is necessary to take brief account of some basic assumptions underlying the GLF. Three broad themes can be delineated in this perspective.[1] First, the doctrine of

[1] These themes abound in the following documents: Mao Tse-tung, "On the Question of Agricultural Co-operation," *Selected Readings from the Works of Mao Tse-tung* (Peking: Foreign Languages Press, 1967), pp. 316–39; Mao, *Socialist Upsurge in China's Countryside* (Peking: Foreign Languages Press, 1957); Liao Lu-yen, "Explanation on the Draft 1956–1967 National Program for Agricultural Development," NCNA, January 25, 1956; Mao, "On the Ten Major Relationships," *CB*, No. 892 (October 21, 1969). pp. 21–34; Mao, "On the Correct Handling of Contradictions among the People," *Selected Readings*, pp. 350–87; Mao, "Sixty Points on Work Methods," February 10, 1958, *CB*, No. 892 (October 21, 1969), pp. 1–14; "Chairman Mao's Speech at the Ch'engtu Conference," *JPRS*, No. 49826 (February 12, 1970), pp. 45–52; Liu Shao-ch'i, "Report on the Work of the Central Committee of the Communist Party of China to the Second Session of the Eighth National Congress," May 5, 1958, *Second Session of the Eighth National Congress of the Communist Party of China* (Peking: Foreign Languages Press, 1958), pp. 16–66; "Resolution of the Central Committee of the CCP on the Establishment of People's Communes in the Rural Areas," August 29, 1958, in *Communist China, 1955–*

uninterrupted revolution provided the GLF with an ideological rationale. The Three Red Banners—that is, the general line, the GLF, and the people's commune—all derived from Mao's belief in uninterrupted revolution; they represented an admixture of dialectical materialism, Marxist-Leninist doctrine, and some concrete policies. These slogans amounted to a projection of what Mao conceived to be a good Communist society in China, but as such they lacked an operational ideology based on a compromise between the Party's professed goals and its available means. There was little differentiation between ideology and practice, for the Chinese were to build communism directly according to the dictates of uninterrupted revolution. With this doctrine, Mao asserted most of his ideological themes, such as voluntarism, populism, thought reform, and egalitarianism, stressing such positive functions of ideology as orientation, mobilization, motivation, and socialization.

Second, the strategy of simultaneous development underlay the policy of the GLF. The lack of an operational ideology led to the lack of a system of priorities, or of sequences, in the GLF's policy prescriptions. Under the slogan of "walking on two legs," the Party set out to promote simultaneously both revolution and production, agriculture and industry, local industry and central industry, aiming at a simultaneous servicing of all desired goals through a comprehensive mobilization of resources. Symbolizing this was the general line of "aiming at higher, faster, better, and more economical results." As shown by the multifunctional structure of the commune, the aim of the policy was to enhance equality, and the basic work methods were self-reliance and mass movements.

Third, at the height of the GLF, there emerged a form of mass polity in which the elite and the masses were to meet directly in a mass movement. The masses were "accessible" to the elite and the elite was "available" to the masses.[2] Crucial to this relationship was Mao's personal leadership. However, Mao made policy in such an informal way as to render the Party's formal decision-making machinery inoperative. At the apex of power, he perceived the Party's pressing problems, ar-

---

1959: Policy Documents with Analysis (Cambridge, Mass.: Harvard University Press for the Center for International Affairs and East Asian Research Center, 1962), pp. 454–63.

[2] See William Kornhauser, *The Politics of Mass Society* (New York: Free Press, 1959); also see Robert Tucker, "Toward a Comparative Politics of Movement-Regimes," *American Political Science Review*, LV (June, 1961), 281–89.

ticulated them into "correct ideas," and then imposed them on the Party. In fact, whatever he said served as policy, and the press reported and popularized it as such. The masses' response was almost instantaneous and in turn produced movements like extremely rapid communalization. If this authority structure failed to measure up to expectations, it was to renew itself through criticism and self-criticism.

These three themes represented Mao's self-fulfilling prophecy of a "great leap forward" toward communism. As soon as the Party tried to translate them into action, however, they had to undergo a process of reality-testing. Just what took place in these years and what legacy did it leave?

RETREAT FROM THE GREAT LEAP FORWARD

In the two years between the Pei-tai-ho Conference in August, 1958, and the Pei-tai-ho Conference in August, 1960, the Party had to readjust the relationship between its professed ideology and its actual practice in the light of emerging problems. In coping with these problems, the Party tried to make a series of compromises between the center's demands and the localities' responses.

ADJUSTMENT AND CONSOLIDATION

When the Pei-tai-ho Politburo meeting declared that the commune would be developed into the "basic social unit of Communist society" with its "big size and two ownerships" (collective ownership and ownership by the whole people),[3] there followed an atmosphere of euphoria exemplified by such statements as uninterrupted revolution leads to a new society, people need no money for food, communism is heaven and the commune the step to it, and people become omnipotent in the commune.[4] It was under the pressure of these slogans that the local cadres to whom communization was entrusted erred on the side of excessive zealousness, even if it resulted in "Communist style" (by transferring or confiscating resources and manpower) and "commandist style" (by coercing the peasants into the steel-smelting and irrigation projects); to do otherwise would have left them vulnerable to the charge of "lagging behind the masses." Because of such excesses,

---

[3] *Communist China 1955–1959*, p. 454.

[4] Wang Kuo-fan, "Uninterrupted Revolution for the Communes," *KMJP*, October 30, 1958; *Shansi jih-pao* (Shansi Daily), September 5, 1958; Ch'en Po-ta, "Under the Flag of Comrade Mao Tse-tung," *Hung-ch'i* (Red Flag), No. 4 (July 16, 1958), p. 5; *KJJP*, October 10–19, 1958.

criticisms were soon voiced that the communes had been established "too early, too quickly, and too crudely." As for the slogan, "All people smelt steel," it came to be called "the greatest mess in the world." [5]

As these results of the commune movement surfaced, the Party held consecutive central and provincial conferences to cope with the rising problems. In November, 1958, Mao convened the first Chengchow Conference, where it was decided to rectify "communist style." Soon after this, he summoned another conference of provincial leaders in Wuhan; and in December, the Sixth Party Central Committee Plenum produced the "Wuhan Resolution." [6] This resolution was notable for its ideological retreat from uninterrupted revolution by warning against the "utopian dream of skipping the socialist stage" and calling instead for "revolution by stages." Describing the attempt to "enter communism immediately" as a "petit bourgeois trend toward egalitarianism" because it "distorts and vulgarizes" the ideal of communism, the resolution called upon the Party to carry out "adjustment and consolidation" in the communes.[7]

In January, 1959, Mao called another conference of central leaders in Peking. From February through March he convened the second Chengchow Conference, where he acknowledged some defects in the communes but argued that the relationship between the achievements and the defects was like that between nine fingers and one. After labeling those "skeptics" who still denied the superiority of the communes as "tide watchers" or "right opportunists," he asked the local cadres to rectify "communist and commandist styles." But he also asserted that under no circumstances should mass enthusiasm be allowed to decline just because such "leftist" tendencies had appeared.[8]

While these conferences were being held, the communes experimented at the local level with various methods of work assignment to cope with the communes' unwieldy organizational structure, which was too big and too centralized. From these experiments came the system of responsibility for fixed output quotas (*pao-ch'an-chih*) at the production brigade level by which a sort of contract (called *pao* or *ting*) was concluded between the commune and the brigades, thus making

[5] "Long Live People's Commune," *JMJP*, August 29, 1959, editorial.

[6] *The Case of Peng Teh-huai, 1959–1968* (Hong Kong: URI, 1968), p. 120; NCNA, December 17, 1958; *JMJP*, December 18, 1958.

[7] "Resolution on Some Questions concerning the People's Communes," December 10, 1958, *Communist China, 1955–1959*, pp. 494–95.

[8] Mao, "Speech at the Central Politburo's Chengchow Conference," February, 1959, and "Speech at the Second Chengchow Conference," March, 1959, in *Chinese Law and Government* (hereafter *CLG*), I, No. 4 (Winter 1968/69), 22–24.

the brigade the basic unit of labor.[9] With this system in operation, the unified leadership of the commune gave way to the two-level management structure, and gradually the brigade restored the work-point system of distribution based on piece-rates instead of time-rates.[10]

In April, 1959, the Seventh Plenum in Shanghai reaffirmed its faith in the commune while making some adjustments.[11] It was at this plenum that P'eng Teh-huai first criticized Mao for discarding the Politburo in making decisions.[12] After this Shanghai plenum, the Party called upon the communes to put at least 85 per cent of the labor force into grain production, thereby shifting away from the earlier emphasis placed on basic construction and steel-smelting. And in response to excesses at the basic level, the Party tried to rectify them by sending down (*hsia-fang*) higher-level cadres.[13]

THE LUSHAN CONFERENCE AND ITS AFTERMATH

The Politburo meeting at Lushan held in July, 1959, was again engaged in discussions about the maladies afflicting the communes. According to Mao, this was a "work conference"; but it soon turned into a forum for debate after P'eng Teh-huai "jeopardized the work." [14] Through his inspection of the northwest regions, P'eng had observed that production actually decreased as a result of the GLF. He therefore made up his mind to challenge Mao. Indeed, at the Lushan Conference he both spoke out at the northwest subgroup meeting and also sent an open letter to Mao.[15]

Alluding to the doctrine of uninterrupted revolution, P'eng pointed out: "We always wanted to enter into communism at one step," and "we held the illusion that communism was around the corner." He called this a "left" tendency caused by "petit bourgeois fanaticism." Also questioning the strategy of the GLF, he asserted: "Politics and economics have their respective laws. Therefore, ideological education cannot replace economic work." He pointed out that there were only tasks and targets in the GLF, but neither concrete measures nor spe-

---

[9] *Fukien jih-pao* (Fukien Daily), January 27, 1959; *Szechwan jih-pao* (Szechwan Daily), January 24, 1959; "People's Communes Must Establish a Sound and Responsible Production System," *JMJP*, February 17, 1959, editorial.

[10] *Szechwan jih-pao*, January 10 and February 17, 1959; *Nan-fang jih-pao* (Southern Daily), January 22, 1959; *Yun-nan jih-pao* (Yunnan Daily), January 22 and 23, 1959.

[11] *JMJP*, April 8, 1959.

[12] *CLG*, I, No. 4 (Winter, 1968/69), 81.

[13] *Szechwan jih-pao*, April 12, 1959; *Nan-fang jih-pao*, April 4, 1959. *Szechwan jih-pao*, January 15, 1959; *Liaoning jih-pao* (Liaoning Daily), January 24, 1959.

[14] *CLG*, I, No. 4 (Winter, 1968/69), 92.

[15] "Peng Teh-huai's Testimony," *The Case of Peng Teh-huai*, p. 120.

cific plans for achieving them, and that steel-smelting in particular resulted in "a relatively big loss." Lastly, he touched upon the way Mao
had led the GLF. It occurred to him that the CCP had had "a fever in
the brain" since the Antirightist Campaign in 1957 and that with the
GLF the Party had actually damaged its own prestige. The collective
leadership of the Politburo had been ignored as the first secretary decided everything, and the State Planning Commission no longer
planned. Echoing this point, Chang Wen-t'ien also revealed that Politburo meetings at that time were only "large-scale briefings without
any collective discussion." [16]

Confronted with these challenges, Mao asked the Party to choose
between him and P'eng, under an ominous threat: "If the Chinese PLA
should follow P'eng Teh-huai, I will go to fight a guerrilla war." [17]
As Mao saw the situation, the "left" tendencies had been rectified since
the first Chengchow Conference; therefore, the major danger at present was "right opportunism." [18] With this counterattack, he managed
to overcome the immediate crisis; but he had in effect left the Party
actually torn apart, for he was also aware that the majority of the
Party leadership was against his policy. He lamented: "The fact is that
you have all refuted me, though not by name perhaps." [19] He acknowledged that he had, together with K'o Ch'ing-shih and T'an Chen-lin,
shot "three big cannons": the communes, backyard steel-smelting, and
the general line. Hence, he held himself responsible for everything that
had occurred since August, 1958. He sounded an apology by saying,
"Being basically unversed in construction, I knew nothing about industrial planning." [20] Nevertheless, he rejected the charge that the Party
had lost the support of the masses, and he envisioned the current difficulties lasting only for two or three months.

Despite Mao's attack on P'eng Teh-huai, the Eighth, or Lushan,
Plenum did make substantial adjustments in the communes. Not only
did it revise the grain production target for 1959 but the Lushan Resolution also formally declared the brigade to be the basic unit of ownership within the "three-level ownership" structure, and it allowed the
peasants to use the mess halls "voluntarily." [21] In a letter sent to pro-

[16] *Ibid.*, pp. 2–5, 8–10, 21. Chang's comments are on pp. 36–37.
[17] *CLG*, I, No. 4 (Winter, 1968/69), 26.
[18] "Speech at the Lushan Conference," *ibid.*, p. 35.
[19] *Ibid.*, p. 40.
[20] *Ibid.*, pp. 36–41.
[21] *The Case of Peng Teh-huai*, pp. 41, 297–305.

duction teams soon after the Lushan Plenum, Mao himself endorsed the system of fixing output quotas through the production teams, admitting that many exaggerations at the lower levels were results of the pressures coming from the higher levels.[22] Yet the communiqué of the Lushan Plenum still claimed that the Three Red Banners had been successful.[23] And the subsequent Antirightist Campaign made it difficult for the Party to halt some of the disruptive aspects of the Leap, hastening the demise of the GLF. During the post-Lushan Antirightist Campaign, some mess halls were restored and demands were even heard that the communes be transformed back into larger units.[24]

In the wake of the Antirightist Campaign, the spring of 1960 saw a resurgence of GLF policies. In March, Mao personally enacted the Constitution of the Anshan Iron and Steel Company, which laid down the mass line and multifunctional principles as the basic tenets of industrial management corresponding to the features of the commune.[25] In April, when the second National People's Congress (NPC) was held, Li Fu-ch'un upheld the Three Red Banners as the Party's "three beacons" for socialist construction; the congress passed the Twelve-year Agricultural Program into law; and T'an Chen-lin stated that the commune was the fundamental guarantee for fulfilling the program ahead of schedule.[26] Externally, the CCP made it clear that it did not share Khrushchev's ideas on general disarmament. Internally, the urban communes were being set up in the cities, and the Party intensified the *hsia-fang* campaign in the countryside, urging the cadres to go down to the masses and practice "Four Togethers"—eating, living, working, and discussing together.[27]

THE PARTY'S RESPONSE TO THE AGRICULTURAL CRISIS

The Party's initial response to the deteriorating situation in the communes was the *hsia-fang* campaign. Ever since Mao had blamed the local cadres at the Lushan Conference for not heeding Party di-

[22] "A Letter to Production Team Leaders," November 29, 1959, in *CB,* No. 891 (1969), pp. 34–35.

[23] *The Case of Peng Teh-huai,* pp. 41–42.

[24] "Unlimited Future of the Mess Hall," *JMJP,* September 22, 1959, editorial; *Szechwan jih-pao,* September 19, 1959, editorial.

[25] "Constitution of Anshan Iron and Steel Company Spurts Revolution and Production," *Peking Review,* No. 16 (April 17, 1970), pp. 3–5.

[26] *Jen-min shou-ts'e* (People's Handbook), 1960, pp. 175–76, 190.

[27] "Long Live Leninism!" *JMJP,* April 22, 1960; *ibid.,* July 4, 1960; *CFJP,* July 8, 1960.

rectives,[28] the Party has maintained that its policies had been correct but that the cadres' errors in implementing them had damaged the commune program.

Among such cadre errors, the leadership singled out the five most prevalent ones and called them the "five styles": communism, commandism, privileged behavior, blind direction, and exaggeration.[29] Of these, the most common were communism and commandism, which resulted from the local cadres' excessive responses to the CCP's calls "to dare to think and act." As the local cadres were caught up in a cross fire between the center's demands and the peasants' grievances, commandism in particular lay at the heart of the cadre problem. The more the center demanded that cadres be "activist," the more likely it was for them to commit commandism; but the less demand for activism, the more they manifested "goodmanism" (*hao-jen chu-i*). By and large, then, the local cadres' behavior was a function of the center's demands, for they generally did what they were told to do. Unless the Party changed the political climate in which the cadres implemented Party policy, the *hsia-fang* campaign could do little to curb the excesses. The general mood at a particular time had as much influence as the policy line.

During the late summer of 1960, the full impact of the crisis began to be felt. An important external event that compelled the Party to change policy was the sudden pull-out of Soviet technicians in June. In the long run, this move forced the Chinese to pursue a strategy of self-reliance more vigorously and left the CCP with a legacy of bitterness toward the Soviet Union. In the short run, however, it gave the Chinese leaders an immediate shock and forced them to re-examine their policies.

According to Liao Lu-yen, Mao in 1959 had already put forward the policy of "taking agriculture as the foundation and industry as the leading factor." In his report on the 1960 economic plan at the NPC in April, 1960, Li Fu-ch'un confirmed that this was Party policy.[30] Now that the Soviets had pulled out their technicians and another year of adverse climate continued to produce natural calamities, the top Party leaders discussed the impact of these events at a central work conference at Pei-tai-ho from July through August which was attended by the first secretaries of provincial committees. There the Party decided

---

[28] *The Case of Peng Teh-huai*, pp. 36–41.

[29] *KTTH*, No. 6 (January 27, 1961), pp. 12–14; *ibid.*, No. 13 (March 20, 1961), pp. 1–15.

[30] *Hung-ch'i*, No. 17 (September 1, 1960), p. 1; *Jen-min shou-ts'e*, 1960, pp. 175–76.

actually to implement China's new economic policy of "agriculture as the foundation and industry as the leading factor." The Party also decided to resume its central direction of policy implementation by reestablishing the six regional Party bureaus.[31]

During the harvest of the autumn crops, it became painfully clear that a mere rectification of cadres could hardly alleviate the agricultural crisis. Nor could the summer's reordering of priorities, for it came too late to have any immediate results. Another year of natural calamities had also dealt a severe blow to the commune program. The Party had already attributed the failure to these calamities, as well as to the Soviet pull-out. More than any other group of citizens, the peasants suffered most and knew that the stopgap measures taken by the Party thus far were inadequate. The CCP was hard pressed to do something drastic. Responding to this need, the Central Committee in November issued in letter form its "Urgent Directive on Rural Work," commonly known as the "Twelve Articles."[32]

In all probability this directive spelled the end of the GLF. First of all, it laid down concrete guidelines free of ideological pronouncements for curbing excesses, and it banned "one equal and two transfers," or equalitarianism in distribution and the transfer of manpower and goods, the two most salient manifestations of communism and commandism. It specified the ratio of supply to wages as three to seven, made the team a unit of "partial ownership," and legitimized the contract system between the brigade and the team by approving the "four-fixes" and the "three guarantees and one reward" systems. Most important, this directive restored the private plots, the family sideline occupations, and the free markets. Finally, it promised further "adjustments" in the commune, but with the proviso that the current policy would not be changed for at least seven years.

READJUSTMENT AND CONSOLIDATION: THE PEOPLE'S LIBERATION ARMY VS. THE PARTY

The Twelve Articles were the Party's urgent response to the deteriorating rural situation. As to just how serious it was, the *Kung-tso t'ung-hsün* (Work Bulletin) of the People's Liberation Army (PLA) gave a vivid account. But implementing a reversed policy after

[31] *CB,* No. 884 (1969), p. 18.

[32] *KTTH,* No. 6 (January 27, 1961), pp. 6–7. For a full text, see *Jinmin kōsha sōron* (Survey of People's Communes) (Tokyo: Ajia Keizai Kenkyūjo [Asian Economic Research Institute], 1965), p. 573. For a fragmentary collection, see URS, Vol. XXVIII, No. 12, pp. 200–1.

so much change was not simple, and the Party faced various difficulties in convincing local cadres that they had to comply with the new directive. Since these cadres had been told that the Three Red Banners were correct, and were now suddenly asked to do away with them, it was natural that they were confused. The local cadres raised some fundamental questions hitting at the heart of the problem.

"How do you interpret the fact that now you speak of only one bigness while in the past you spoke of one bigness and two publics? . . . Do we still have ten superiorities of the commune or don't we? As the communes and brigades enter into contracts and the brigades resume distribution by work-points, not to mention the private plots, what differences are there between the brigade and the advanced APC's [Agricultural Procedures Cooperatives]?"[33] These were some of the local cadres' complaints about the new directive. As for the current situation, they said that conditions had really been worse before the Twelve-Articles directive, but that even now prices were still too high and were chaotic.[34]

These complaints begged the question of why such a crisis had come about in the first place. However, they rebuked the official explanation by saying, "Where do those 'five styles' come from? Isn't it true that without the commune there would be no 'five styles?'" And they hit close to home with: "Party policies are good but are unimplementable; it was inevitable for the cadres to commit mistakes."[35] In recommending a new course of action, they made it clear that more material incentives were the best remedy: "It is still material incentives that count in management, for without them politics in command loses its soul. Material incentives and politics in command are both important, but the former is the basis and superior to the latter."[36]

In the CCP's efforts to deal with this unrest among the peasants, one can discern two broad trends, which in turn established the two main orientations of Chinese political development in the 1960's. The first was a trend toward continuing more of the same of what the Party had done during the GLF, that is, mass persuasion and mobilization. The second was a trend to reverse this by restoring the pre-Leap practices of material incentives and regularized administration. By and large, the PLA under Lin Piao's leadership followed the former course,

[33] "Comrade Yang Chiu-ju and Others' Report," *KTTH*, No. 17 (April 15, 1961), p. 3.
[34] *Ibid.*, p. 4.
[35] *Ibid.*, p. 6.
[36] *Ibid.*, p. 4.

and the CCP under Liu Shao-ch'i's direction, the latter. Addressing himself to this problem in December, 1960, Lin Piao stated:

Because of the great calamities of this year, there are some difficulties in grain food supply and some tensions in the supply of subsidiary food. The soldiers are peasants and workers wearing military uniforms; hence, whatever problems there are in the localities, they are reflected in the army. In some army units political incidents have increased on account of the comparatively difficult situation of the current economic life.[37]

To stabilize the sentiment of the troops and to insure that there would be no more incidents, Lin stressed the need for ideological indoctrination within the army.

On the other hand, it was under the same circumstances that Liu Shao-ch'i remarked that the free market must continue even if it produces some capitalist elements, for without the interests of the individual there are no interests of the whole. What should be advocated, he claimed, were not public interests without private interests, but public interests with private interests, although public interests take precedence. In 1967 Mao's supporters labeled this posture a bourgeois outlook, a "theory of convergence of public interests and private interests." [38]

THE PLA: "READ CHAIRMAN MAO'S WORKS, LISTEN TO HIS WORDS,
DO AS HE INSTRUCTS, AND BECOME A GOOD SOLDIER
OF CHAIRMAN MAO"

Beginning in 1960, the General Political Department (GPD) of the PLA embarked upon an intensive campaign of ideological revitalization among the soldiers to prevent unrest among their dependents and relatives. Lin Piao personally initiated this movement.[39] Lin presided over an enlarged meeting of the Military Affairs Committee (MAC) from September through October, 1960, and proposed the "four firsts" principle as the key to political work—namely, man first over weapons, political work first over other work, ideological work first over administrative work, and living ideology first over book ideology. The resolution of the MAC declared:

In an era in which imperialism is heading for collapse and socialism is advancing to victory, the Thought of Mao Tse-tung has applied the universal truth of Marxism-Leninism and creatively developed it in the concrete practice of the Chinese

---

37 *KTTH*, No. 1 (January 1, 1961), pp. 7–8.
38 *SCMM*, No. 652 (1969), p. 4; *JMJP*, October 26, 1967.
39 *KTTH*, No. 1 (January 1, 1961), pp. 1 6; *CB*, No. 894 (1969), p. 24.

revolution and in the collective struggle of the Party and the people. It is the
guide to the Chinese people's revolution and socialist construction, and the powerful weapon for opposing imperialism, revisionism, and dogmatism.[40]

Lin elaborated upon this resolution in an October, 1960, article en-
titled, "Hold High the Great Red Banner of the General Line and of
Mao Tse-tung's Military Thought," which criticized indirectly P'eng
Teh-huai's military line and proposed a campaign for the study of
Mao's thought.[41]

The October MAC resolution also quoted Lin's famous dictum,
"Read Chairman Mao's works, listen to his words, do as he instructs,
and become a good soldier of Chairman Mao." The resolution reaffirmed several themes of the GLF, such as the mass line; democracy
in the areas of politics, the military, and economics; and the "three-
eight work style." [42] Pointing out that one-third of all army companies
did not have a Party branch, it also demanded the building of Party
branches in every company. It further called for intensifying youth
work, training Red-and-expert cadres, army participation in construction, and militia work.

This resolution was directed not only at the PLA but at the whole
Party. The Central Committee endorsed the MAC resolution and
transmitted it to all regional bureaus and to provincial and district
committees. During 1961 political work stressed particularly the need
for "education concerning the situation" (*hsing-shih chiao-yü*). Lo
Jung-huan, director of the GPD, revived Mao's theme that classes do
exist in a socialist society. Liu Chih-chien, a deputy director, specified
the method of education as "two recollections and three investigations," that is, every cadre had to recollect his class and the nation's
sufferings in the past while investigating his own standpoint, his will to
struggle, and his work.[43] Through this education, the cadres were told
that the Three Red Banners had been correct and that the Party would
overcome the temporary difficulties.

This education was accompanied by an intensive effort to simplify
administration. According to Lo Jui-ch'ing, Lin Piao ordered one-third
of the cadres above the regimental level to go down to the companies
while criticizing the "five many" (too many tables, documents, local
investigations, general calls, and reports). Lo pointed out: "Some say

[40] *KTTH*, No. 3 (January 7, 1961), p. 1.
[41] *Ibid.*, No. 1 (January 1, 1961), pp. 1–6.
[42] *Ibid.*, pp. 7–8.
[43] *Ibid.*, No. 8 (February 6, 1961), pp. 11–19; *ibid.*, No. 15 (April 5, 1961), pp. 1–8;
ibid., No. 4 (January 11, 1961), pp. 1–10.

that of so many figures only 30 per cent is statistics and 70 per cent guesswork; I say that all of them are guesses." [44] In December, 1960, the MAC decided to nurture "five-good soldiers" (who must be good in politics and ideology, military techniques, three-eight style, fulfilling their duties, and steeling the body). In 1961 the army followed this up with the "four-good company" movement (good in politics and ideology, three-eight style, military training, and management of living).[45] The high intensity of these campaigns is suggested by the fact that between July, 1960, and February, 1961, 85 per cent of all Party branches in the army had been rebuilt. In one unit the effort induced three soldiers to commit suicide, prompting Lin Piao to issue a directive banning the use of crude methods.[46]

An important aspect of the PLA's political work was its special emphasis on youth. A noteworthy method for propaganda among youth was the use of quotations from Mao's works. The GPD compiled Mao's quotations and arranged them according to several themes, such as overcoming difficulties in hard times, the mass line, self-reliance and frugality, bravery, and dedication to the people. These quotations were not intended to idolize Mao alone, for a few quotations from Lin Piao and even from Liu Shao-ch'i were included. At the end of 1961, the GPD selected eighteen of the 158 articles in Mao's four-volume *Selected Works,* added three passages from his "On the Correct Handling of Contradictions among the People," and edited them into *Selected Readings from the Works of Mao Tse-tung.* The department then issued the book to all military units for study. Lin Piao also instructed the army-run schools to shorten their school year.[47]

The GPD apparently took charge of the planning and operation of these programs. Lo Jung-huan and his deputies worked out the details, and as the first vice-chairman of the MAC, Lin Piao personally supervised their work. Out of this endeavor, the army produced two documents in 1960 and 1961 respectively entitled, "Regulations Governing Political Work" and "Regulations Governing Company and Educational Work." In sum, after P'eng Teh-huai's fall, Lin Piao became the *de facto* head of the MAC and made the PLA a national model for political work. Yet it would be a mistake to suggest that Lin promoted

---

[44] *Ibid.,* No. 23 (June 13, 1961), p. 8.

[45] *JMJP,* January 23, 1964, p. 2.

[46] *KTTH,* No. 23 (June 13, 1961), p. 1; *ibid.,* No. 13 (March 20, 1961), p. 21; *ibid.,* No. 14 (March 29, 1961), p. 1.

[47] *Ibid.,* No. 12 (March 10, 1961), pp. 9–15; *ibid.,* No. 6 (January 27, 1961), pp. 1–11; *JPRS,* No. 50,477 (May 7, 1970), p. 70.

political work at the expense of professional training; indeed, he advocated a professional-political ratio of seven to three for specialized units and six to four for other units.[48] The important point, however, is that Lin was more steadfast than any other leader in marshaling Mao's thought during the hard times. The other leaders displayed doubts about the utility of Mao's thought.

THE CCP'S POLICY REVIEWS: "READJUSTING, CONSOLIDATING,
FILLING OUT, AND RAISING STANDARDS"

The Party's policy review was in marked contrast to the one made by the PLA. In January, 1961, the Party convened an enlarged Politburo meeting and immediately followed it with the Ninth Plenum.[49] This plenum adopted an operational ideology in tune with the actual reality, that is, the line of "readjusting, consolidating, filling out, and raising standards." Under this slogan, the Party scaled down the scope of capital construction and the rate of development, thereby putting an end to the general line, because rapid speed had been regarded as the soul of the general line.[50] The Party also readjusted the relationship between industry and agriculture by demanding that the whole nation implement the policy of "taking agriculture as the foundation of the national economy" and that "the whole Party and the entire people go in for agriculture and grain production." In line with these changes, the CCP advanced a new slogan: "Listen to the Party and act according to Party policies."[51]

From the Ninth Plenum to the Tenth Plenum of September, 1962, the Party's central machinery—mainly the Politburo's Standing Committee and Secretariat—carried out some sweeping reviews in the name of "readjusting and consolidating" and regularized their findings into a series of comprehensive directives. This endeavor covered all five major systems of policy, excluding only foreign and military policy: (1) agriculture and forestry; (2) industry and transportation; (3) finance and trade; (4) culture and education; and (5) political-legal. Since agriculture, political-legal matters, and finance concerned most of the population, policy adjustments in these areas stemmed from the interactions between the center and the localities. Decision-making in-

[48] *KTTH,* No. 1 (January 1, 1961), pp. 5-6.
[49] *SCMM,* No. 635 (1968), p. 21; *Peking Review,* No. 4 (January 27, 1961), p. 6.
[50] *Peking Review,* No. 4 (January 27, 1961), p. 6; *Hsüeh-hsi* (Study), No. 139 (July 3, 1958).
[51] *Peking Review,* No. 4 (January 27, 1961), pp. 5-6. *JMJP,* November 26, 1960; *Nan-fang jih-pao,* December 22, 1960.

volved frequent Party use of the central work conference (*chung-yang kung-tso hui-i*), which regional and provincial leaders attended. For such specialized areas as industry and culture and education, adjustments resulted from the interaction between the specialized Party-state organizations and the practitioners in the field; as for decision-making in these areas, the Party relied on more specialized forms of the central work conference at which the specialized officials as well as practitioners were present.

The first "readjustment" document emerging from these reviews was entitled "Draft Regulations concerning the Rural People's Communes," commonly called the "Sixty Articles on Agriculture." In March, 1961, the Secretariat convened a central work conference at Canton and discussed the Sixty Articles. It appears that the Secretariat under the aegis of Teng Hsiao-p'ing and P'eng Chen drafted this document without consulting Mao. When criticizing Teng and P'eng at the Canton conference, Mao reportedly asked, "Which emperor decided this?"[52] As Liu Chih-chien explained, the Sixty Articles were written in the light of Mao's speech at the second Chengchow Conference in 1959, in the spirit of a *Tang-nei t'ung-hsün* (Intra-Party Bulletin), and with consideration for the Twelve Articles, thus summing up three years of experiences.[53] In fact, the accumulation of the Party's incremental decisions made in retreating from the GLF, beginning with the first Chengchow Conference in November, 1958, culminated in this document.

The Sixty Articles were the first comprehensive manual for commune management drawn up on a nationwide basis. Though quite similar in spirit to the Twelve Articles, their provisions were more detailed and workable, for they stipulated with clarity what was permissible and what was banned in such a way that the communes could easily consult and apply them. They specifically banned any coercive measures, discouraged industrial enterprises except in slack seasons, allowed suspension of the mess halls if the commune desired, specified that the private plots should not exceed 5 per cent of the arable land, and prohibited commune authorities from interfering in family sideline occupations or daily necessities.[54]

---

[52] Ting Wang (ed.), *Chung-kung wen-hua ta-ke-ming tzu-liao hui-pien* (Compendium of Materials on the Great Cultural Revolution in Communist China), I (Hong Kong: Ming-pao yueh-k'an, 1967), 486, 491.

[53] *KTTH*, No. 15 (April 5, 1961), p. 3.

[54] See Articles 34, 37, and 40 of *Nung-ts'un jen-min kung-she t'iao-li ch'ao-an* (Draft Regulations concerning Rural People's Communes) (Taipei: Nationalist Chinese Government, 1965).

To implement this directive, the Party center transmitted it with an explanatory letter to the Party branches, asking them to study these documents in April and May, and to make suggestions.[55] The actual implementation fell into two categories: the general "plane" (*mien*) and some "spots" (*tien*) specially selected for further experimentation. On the plane the Party branches punctually took charge of its implementation, whereas in the spots central and provincial leaders or special task forces in the form of "work teams" (*kung-tso tui*) carried out investigation and experimentation, quite often "squatting" (*tun-tien*) there. As part of the attack upon rural problems, Mao especially called upon central Party leaders to investigate rural conditions in person. Most central leaders (including Liu Shao-ch'i, Teng Hsiao-p'ing, Ch'en Yün, and P'eng Chen) went on inspection tours. Teng, for example, went to Sunyi *hsien*, together with P'eng Chen and Liu Jen; and during the Cultural Revolution the Maoists accused them of having collected "black" materials to attack Mao's policies.[56] To encourage investigation, the center also dispatched Mao's 1930 essay, "On Investigation Work," together with an explanatory letter to Party committees above the *hsien* level. The Party required its cadres to study these materials in hope of changing their work style.[57] Indeed, cadres began investigations, and they sent back many reports to higher levels. Based on these findings, the center issued more instructions and regulations through central conferences.

As before, policy formulation involved a series of compromises between the center's demands and local responses. But at this time the process occurred under the direction and the approval of the Party center, the regional bureaus, and the provincial committees. For instance, at the May–June, 1961, central work conference, Liu Shao-ch'i took the lead in pointing out that the peasants still had "no ease of mind." [58] At this conference, Mao apparently offered his own self-criticism for his responsibility in the GLF. In August–September, the Party convened the second Lushan Conference to discuss further adjustments in the communes.[59] As one report from PLA sources recorded, the local cadres maintained that even the Sixty Articles were

55 *KTTH,* No. 15 (April 5, 1961), p. 1.
56 Ting Wang (ed.), *Chung-kung,* I, 491.
57 *KTTH,* No. 15 (April 5, 1961), p. 1.
58 "Along the Socialist or the Capitalist Road?" *JMJP,* August 15, 1967.
59 *JPRS,* No. 50,792 (June 23, 1970), p. 45; Ting Wang (ed.), *Chung-kung wen-hua ta-ke-ming tzu-liao hui-pien,* II (Hong Kong: Ming-pao yueh-k'an, 1969), p. 550; *SCMM,* No. 640 (1969), p. 19.

"not good enough." To cater to these grievances, the Party could not avoid allowing some experimentation that exceeded the limits imposed by the Sixty Articles. A poignant instance in this regard was the emergence of *san-tzu i-pao,* the extension of private plots, free markets, and small enterprises that maintained independent accounts with the sole responsibility for their own profits and losses, and the fixing of output quotas at individual households.[60]

Ironically, Anhwei and Honan, the very provinces that had set the pace for the early communization, were at the forefront of the retreat.[61] An obvious reason for Anhwei's action was its widespread devastation by floods from the Yangtze River. To restore production in the fall of 1961, Anhwei assigned output quotas to individual households. This action, called "fixing output quotas with the households" (*pao-ch'an tao-hu*), was a drastic measure which virtually abandoned collective farming; but elsewhere, too, Party organizations discussed fixing quotas at the households or even dividing lands among the households (*fen-t'ien tao-hu*). After Liu Shao-ch'i called a meeting in October to discuss the prevention of commodities from flowing onto the black market, provincial authorities began to extend free markets and private plots.[62] Thus, illegal activities, in effect, were halted by granting them legitimacy.

Take Honan as an example. In June, 1961, Liu Chien-hsün replaced Wu Chih-p'u as first secretary, saying that his purpose in coming to Honan was to solve the food problem. He encouraged diversity and experimentation, with the comment that "he who produces grain is Marxist-Leninist, and sweet potatoes are as good as politics." In cooperation with Hua Yu-ch'un, secretary of the district committee, Liu promoted the cultivation of sweet potatoes in Anyang Special District. Elsewhere, he permitted Keng Ch'i-ch'ang, first secretary of Hsin-hsiang Special District, to experiment with renting out land while Juang Lien-hsi of Wuchiu *hsien* was allowed to go ahead with fixing output quotas with households. In doing so, he swiftly put a halt to the zealous policies of Wu Chih-p'u, saying, "In recent years, many things have been done on impulse. They did not come from the masses. Instead of the movement being directed by the masses, the movement directed the masses." When in 1963 he was accused of being rightist

[60] *KTTH,* No. 17 (April 25, 1961), p. 4; "The Struggle between the Two Roads in China's Countryside," *JMJP,* November 23, 1967.

[61] Interview Protocols No. 2 (November, 1969) and No. 53 (March, 1970). Interviewees were middle-level cadres in Canton.

[62] *SCMM,* No. 652 (1969), p. 4; *JMJP,* November 23, 1967.

for this kind of talk, his answer was equally forceful: "You said that I was right-inclined. I think the right is good because I have work and grain to eat. Some people said that I was an opportunist. If a favorable situation could come out of opportunism, why should I oppose it? If you search for my mistakes, get the big ones, not the small ones." [63]

The experimentation in rural policies spread into other areas as well, ranging from Shanghai to Szechwan. Following the Sixty Articles, Li Ching-ch'üan and Chia Ch'i-yun of Szechwan formulated an eighteen-article directive on the communes which made allowance for *san-tzu i-pao*.[64] The Lien-chiang documents also indicate that in Fukien the trend for dividing land and fixing output at the household level (also called *tan-kan feng*, or "going it alone") continued in 1962. Indeed, in one brigade over 98 per cent of the teams engaged in it, and the local cadres themselves pleaded for it in order to overcome difficulties. Peasant aphorisms caustically described Party opposition and their own attitude toward *san-tzu i-pao*: "The government is afraid that the masses will eat too well, so they promote the collectives." But "there is not one Chinese with an unselfish public spirit"; hence, "only under individual enterprise will he redouble his efforts." [65]

As the contract system of fixing output or labor to a small group of five or ten members or even to individual households prevailed, the brigade was found to be too big to handle their assignments. Wide economic disparities also existed among teams in the same brigade simply because of ecological differences. Eventually the Party center concluded that it was unfair for the brigade to enforce a uniform distribution over the teams. The obvious solution was to make the team the basic accounting unit—the unit which determined the income of its members—and the Party officially took that step on January 1, 1962. In effect, this decision was a retreat to the level of collective organization under the lower APC's, since both the 1955 unit and the team had about twenty households.[66]

Returning to the Honan case, T'ao Chu, first secretary of the Party's Central-South Bureau, who had been in the vanguard of the commune movement of 1958 with Wu Chih-p'u, personally presided over a

[63] *Facts about Liu Chien-hsün*, a pamphlet published by the General Committee Headquarters of Revolutionary Rebels of Organs of the CCP Honan Provincial Committee, March 12, 1967.

[64] *JMJP*, August 28, 1967; *Kweichow jih-pao* (Kweichow Daily), June 4, 1967; *Wen-hui pao* (Cultural Exchange Daily) (Shanghai), April 18, 1967.

[65] C. S. Chen (ed.), *Rural People's Communes in Lien-chiang*, translated by Charles Price Ridley (Stanford, Calif.: Hoover Institution, 1969), pp. 105–6.

[66] *JMJP*, January 1, 1962, editorial.

meeting of Honan provincial secretaries at Chengchow in April, 1962, and worked out a document called the "Six-Year Plan for Recovering and Developing Agriculture in Honan (1962–67)." This plan allowed the brigades or teams to devote a maximum of 7 per cent, or in some exceptional cases 20 per cent, of the arable land to private plots, to fix output quotas and divide land at the household level, and even to rent commune land to households. In Wutao *hsien,* over 63 per cent of the teams assigned output quotas to individual households. About 12 per cent of the land in the province was rented out. In July, 1962, the Honan Provincial Committee instructed the production teams to extend the family sideline occupations. Chin Ming, secretary of the CCP Central-South Bureau, supervised the implementation of these measures. Liu Shao-ch'i allegedly commended Keng Ch'i-ch'ang for his involvement in these activities.[67]

As these experiments at the local level increasingly turned away from the stipulated rules, they were bound to be raised at the center and to cause policy debates. By the time of the Pei-tai-ho Conference of August, 1962, Mao had come to realize that some leaders' support for *san-tzu i-pao,* if fully adopted, would deny the very principle of collectivism altogether. Therefore, at the Pei-tai-ho Conference he put a halt to the debate by invoking the ideological specter of class struggle, and he vetoed the current quest for *san-tzu i-pao.* In light of the interaction between the Party's policy initiatives and the local responses, and between the Party center's implementation and Mao's veto, the Party summed up the experience acquired on the "plane" as well as on the "spots" and amended the draft of the Sixty Articles into a "revised draft." Finally, the Tenth Plenum in September, 1962, ratified this revised draft of the Sixty Articles and adopted a "Resolution on Collective Economy."[68]

As for the situation in industry, in June, 1961, Po I-po went to Shenyang to study the "Twelve Articles on Coal Mine Work in An-p'ing, Fuhsin," which Sung Jen-ch'iung had drafted in April. Po and Sung worked together in formulating the "Seventy Articles concerning Industrial Enterprises and Mines," commonly called the "Seventy

[67] "Liu Shao-ch'i's and Teng Hsiao-p'ing's Black Winds of Individual Farming in Honan," *Wei-tung* (Defend the East) (Peking), No. 21 (May 12, 1967).

[68] *Nung-ts'un jen-min kung-she t'iao-li (hsiu-cheng ch'ao-an)* (Regulations concerning Rural People's Communes [Revised Draft]) (Taipei: Nationalist Chinese Government, 1965). Also see "Resolution on the Further Strengthening of the Collective Economy of the People's Communes and Expanding Agricultural Production," in Chen (ed.), *Rural People's Communes in Lien-chiang,* pp. 81–89.

Articles on Industry." This document contradicted many aspects of Mao's 1960 Constitution of the Anshan Iron and Steel Company. In July Po completed his first draft, and in August a central work conference presided over by Teng Hsiao-p'ing at Pei-tai-ho revised it. In September the Secretariat transmitted the Seventy Articles on Industry throughout the country.[69] This directive aimed at doing away with the mass line method in industrial management. It restored the director-responsibility system coupled with Party leadership, increased material incentives by adopting the piece-rate system of the "three fixes and four guarantees" from the readjusted communes, and restored bonuses for innovation and overfulfillment. It also provided for technicians' and engineers' prerogatives in quality control and supervision, specifically banned any transfer of workers by the local authorities, and discouraged large-scale capital construction. Also new was the stratified "five-personnel" rank structure by which the duties and responsibilities of inspectors, custodians, procurement officers, supervisors, and safety experts were specified. Yu Ch'iu-li led in implementing these measures in the Ministry of Petroleum, and in 1963 he himself formulated a similar directive for the petroleum industry.[70]

Regarding finance and trade, in March, 1961, Li Hsien-nien, acting on Liu Shao-ch'i's instructions, formulated the "Six Articles on Finance and Banking" which laid down the principles of vertical leadership, uniform planning, profit-making, and supervision by upper echelons. Through another directive on accounting, Li instituted a "Western" system of double-entry bookkeeping.[71] In regard to commodity exchange, Li advocated the procurement of commodities through administrative agencies (*p'ai-kou*) so that the State Planning Commission could operate on a nationwide network of supply and demand. This unified transaction of commodities contrasted with Mao's policy of "guaranteeing supply" to the peasants; for this reason, a comprehensive directive on finance and trade was delayed until the Tenth Plenum.

[69] For the process of drafting this document, see *Tsu-kuo* (China Monthly), April, 1970, p. 43; *Kirin jih-pao* (Kirin Daily), July 29, 1967; *CFJP*, June 4, 1967; *Yu-t'ien chan-pao* (Post Office Combat News) (Peking), June 28, 1967; *Nihon keizai shimbun* (Tokyo), April 19, 1967, morning edition; *CB*, No. 878 (1969), p. 10.

[70] *Kung-fei kung-yeh cheng-ts'e ch'i-shih-t'iao chu-yao nei-jung* (Main Contents of Chinese Communists' Seventy Articles concerning Industrial Policy) (Taipei: Nationalist Chinese Government, 1965); for Yu Ch'iu-li, see *Hsien-feng* (Dangerous Peak), April 10, 1967, p. 5.

[71] "Antirevolutionary and Revisionist Black Line in Finance and Trade as Seen from the Hsi-lou Conference," *Pei-ching kung-she* (Peking Commune), May 26, 1967.

A similar pattern existed in the cultural and educational systems. The Party leaders in operational control of this field were most critical of Lin Piao's promotion of Mao-study within the PLA. Alluding to Lin's claim that Mao's thought is the peak, Chou Yang, deputy director of the Propaganda Department, stated in October, 1960: "If everything is the peak, there will be no peak." [72] As for the quotations from Mao popularized in the army, Chou Yang similarly maintained that they were too simple and that while they might be suitable for soldiers, they were definitely not for the cadres in the cultural field. At a work conference on science and technology held in 1961, Chou stated: "The Thought of Mao Tse-tung should be studied properly, but it must not be simplified or vulgarized." And he asked: "How can we ask one to put what he has learned to use on the same day? How can one learn something and then use it immediately?" [73] Six years later, in his acceptance speech as the sole vice-chairman of the Party at the Eleventh Plenum in 1966, Lin Piao confirmed that leaders such as Lu Ting-yi and Chou Yang "smeared" the study of Mao's thought as "eating Hsuan-wei ham, saying that one would get sick of it if they ate it every day!" [74]

In the eased atmosphere of 1961, however, the Propaganda Department was able to enact several "revisionist" regulations. In February, Chou Yang and Lin Mo-han (deputy director of the department in charge of drama and films) convened "investigation meetings" to examine all the art forms, including movies, plays, music, graphic art, and the press and literature. Representatives from each of the professional associations took part in the meetings. In April, Chang Kuang-nien, secretary of the Chinese Writers' Association and editor of *Wen-i pao* (Literary Gazette), summarized the discussions in an article entitled "The Questions of Themes." In May, Yuan Sui-p'o, another editor of *Wen-i pao*, and two leaders of the Propaganda Department drafted the "Ten Articles on Literature and Art," which Lin Mo-han later revised several times. At a nationwide forum on literary work held from June through July, Chou Yang and Lin Mo-han explained the draft. After these discussions they revised it again, and circulated the original and the revised draft to the propaganda departments of the provincial committees to solicit further suggestions.

In October, Lu Ting-yi took direct charge of the drafting. He in-

[72] *SCMM*, No. 646 (1969), p. 2.
[73] *Ibid.*, pp. 4–5, 10.
[74] *JPRS*, No. 49,826 (February 16, 1970), p. 16.

structed his deputies that the document should seek to eliminate
"political vulgarization" in the arts and should embody the "united
front" policy of listening to all the intellectuals, including the bourgeoisie. Under Lu's direction, the Ten Articles were revised in December into Eight Articles. Lin Mo-han and Chang Kuang-nien added
still more revisions. Finally, the department dispatched its draft to all
relevant Party units, including the various literary associations, not as
a regular internal document but as a draft directive, pending further
consideration. At the NPC held in April, 1962, Chou Yang circulated
the draft to some concerned delegates and submitted it afterward to
the Secretariat and the Politburo's Standing Committee for approval.
When it was approved, the Secretariat transmitted it as a Party directive to the Party units.[75]

This episode vividly reveals the inner working of the Party's decision-making process. Of importance here was the fact that the CCP's
central department not only sought opinions of the professional associations but also took them into consideration. The revised draft of
the Ten Articles was a product of interaction between the center's
goals and those of the practitioners, reflecting both the center's desires
and the intellectuals' wishes. Pertinent to the later Cultural Revolution, the document encouraged artists to seek inspiration from the
literary and artistic legacy of Chinese history and folk culture, and to
absorb the cultural achievements of foreign countries. It called for
guarantees of time for artistic work, correct standards of criticism,
training of talent, spiritual and material incentives, unity of all active
elements, and reform of leadership style.[76]

A drastic reform was introduced in education, too. In January, 1961,
Liu Shao-ch'i instructed Lin Feng, vice-chairman of the NPC Standing
Committee, to lead an investigation group composed of Yang Shu, Wu
Tzu-ma, and P'eng Pei-yün at Peking University. This group discovered many excesses of the GLF, particularly too much emphasis
on politics and production (which caused the downgrading of teaching
and learning) and too tight control of schools by the Party branch
(which disrupted academic activities). The first task they identified
was the restoration of regularized teaching. In February, P'eng Chen
presided over a Secretariat meeting at which he demanded that all

---

[75] *Wen-hsüeh chan-pao* (Literature Combat News) (Peking), June 30, 1967; Yao
Wen-yüan, "Criticizing Antirevolutionary Double-Dealer Chou Yang," *Hung-ch'i*, No. 1
(Jaunary 1, 1967), p. 29.

[76] "Ten Articles on Literature and Art," *Wen-hsüeh chan-pao*, June 30, 1967, pp. 5–6, 8.

teachers prepare "a clearly printed copy of teaching materials" before going to classes.[77]

P'eng placed Chiang Nan-hsiang, vice-minister of education, in charge of compiling new teaching materials in science, engineering, agriculture, and medicine; and he entrusted Chou Yang with the same task in the social sciences and literature and art. In March, Chiang convened a meeting at the Ministry of Education, and in April, Chou convened a similar meeting at the Propaganda Department. They found that during the previous period of "collective scientific research," some people "only ran around to fetch materials, tea, and water" and that, as a result, specialized training had been put aside. To rectify this, they proposed that "experts" be allowed to compile teaching materials. Teng Hsiao-p'ing approved this proposal. Lu Ting-yi also instructed Chou Yang and Chiang Nan-hsiang to exclude the Mao quotations from teaching materials, saying that Mao's thought was a new "label" which actually led the young to an "ideological stalemate." Yang Hsiu-feng, minister of education, maintained that there had been anarchy in education.[78]

The ministry convened a number of national conferences to readjust educational policies. In March, 1961, Lu Ting-yi, Lin Feng, and Chang Chi-ch'un organized a task force for drafting a directive on higher education. In August, Teng Hsiao-p'ing convened a central work conference at Pei-tai-ho, at which P'eng Chen, Lo Jui-ch'ing, Po I-po, Wang Chia-hsiang, and Yang Shang-k'un were present. The conference discussed the "Draft Sixty Regulations Governing Work in Institutes of Higher Education," commonly called the "Sixty Articles on Universities." Teng in particular praised the draft as a "good document" and proposed including in it a provision that rightist teachers might also play a leading role in education. In September the ministry put it into practice on a trial basis, and in November, with the approval of the Standing Committee, the Secretariat transmitted it as a Party directive.[79] The thrust of this document was to restore three aspects of higher education: (1) teaching and research as the main task of the universities, (2) specialized training and research, and (3) relative autonomy of the teaching staff from Party control.[80]

[77] *Chiao-hsüeh p'i-p'an* (Criticism and Repudiation of Pedagogics), a pamphlet by the Cultural Revolution Committee of Peking University, No. 2 (1967).

[78] *Ibid.*

[79] *Ibid.; Chinese Education*, No. 1 (Spring, 1968), pp. 3–58.

[80] *Chiao-hsüeh p'i-p'an*, No. 2 (1967); *JPRS*, No. 42,887 (October 9, 1967), p. 27; *JMJP*, November 9, 1967, p. 4; *KMJP*, August 11, 1967, p. 4.

In January, 1962, Chiang Nan-hsiang headed a group of one thousand experts to compile teaching materials, revise the curriculum, and reform examination systems. In February, the Scientific and Technological Commission convened the National Conference on Scientific and Technological Work at Canton. On the basis of the discussions at the conference, the Ministry of Education drafted the "Regulations Governing Work in Natural Sciences," also known as the "Fourteen Articles on Science." [81] At this conference Chou Yang repeated his famous characterization of Mao study: "oversimplification, vulgarization, and dogmatism." [82] In June Chiang Nan-hsiang's group formulated the "Regulations Governing Examinations," which made examination the yardstick for evaluating students' academic and political performances. In the latter part of the year, through similar processes, the ministry drafted two additional directives: "Fifty Articles on High Schools" and "Forty Articles on Primary Schools." These documents reversed the half-study and half-work system of the GLF into the full-time school system.[83]

In journalism, too, upon an instruction from Liu Shao-ch'i and P'eng Chen, Lu Ting-yi in the spring of 1961 sent a work team headed by Teng T'o to the Journalism Department of People's University, Peking. This team adopted the principle of "truthfulness, objectivity, and fairness" in journalistic reporting. It should be noted in this regard that already at the Lushan Conference of 1959 Liu had criticized New China News Agency and *Jen-min jih-pao* (People's Daily) for creating "communist and commandist styles" in reporting statements made by central leaders without requesting their approval. In 1961 Liu again called upon the reporters to "maintain links with current reality while keeping a certain distance from it." This, as he saw it, was necessary to ward off sensationalism and to enhance "service for the people." [84]

The key to these adjustments was the way in which the Party carried them out. To restore the Party's tarnished prestige in the aftermath of the GLF, the Ninth Plenum sternly declared: "It is of the utmost importance to strengthen the ties of the Party and government organiza-

[81] *Chiao-hsüeh p'i-p'an*, No. 2 (1967); *Ajia keizai jumpō* (Asian Economic Trimonthly), No. 7114 (1968), p. 4.

[82] *CFJP*, August 4, 1966.

[83] *Chiao-hsüeh p'i-p'an*, No. 2 (1967).

[84] *Carry the Great Revolution on the Journalistic Front through to the End* (Peking: Foreign Languages Press, 1969), p. 34; "Antirevolutionary and Revisionist Wu Leng-hsi's Remarks," *Kung-jen p'ing-lun* (Workers' Forum) (Canton), June, 1968; *JMJP*, August 24, 1967, p. 4.

tions at various levels and all their functionaries with the masses of the people." [85] This plenum formally authorized the establishment of six regional bureaus which would act for the Central Committee in strengthening its leadership over the Party committees. And Mao's withdrawal from the first line of the Politburo probably helped the collective leadership under Liu Shao-ch'i to take firm control of the Party's central machinery. In 1961 Liu assigned Ch'en Yün to lead a five-man group for reviewing the economic policies; as for the cultural and educational systems, apparently P'eng Chen assumed a similar role, as did Teng Hsiao-p'ing for the political and legal systems.

From the Ninth Plenum on, the Secretariat had made special efforts aimed at regularizing cadres' duties and responsibilities by issuing central directives.[86] Yet because of continued uncertainty and decentralization, the Party still faced numerous difficulties in achieving unified control over the cadres, which was necessary for coherent policy implementation. To cope with this problem of "dispersion" in implementation, the Party convened an "enlarged central work conference" in January, 1962, to which some seven thousand cadres from five levels—central, provincial, district, *hsien,* and commune—were invited. Contending that the violation of democratic centralism was the basic cause of such dispersion, Liu Shao-ch'i went out of his way to stress the need for normalizing Party life.[87]

In response, Mao explicitly endorsed the need for eliminating "separatism" and for strengthening centralized and collective leadership. He also gave approval to both the policy reviews in the seven areas—industry, agriculture, trade, education, the military, the government, and the Party—and the formulation of "specific policies" such as the "Sixty Articles on Agriculture" and the "Seventy Articles on Industry." He actually conceded that the lack of such "comprehensive guiding principles" had been an important cause in the failure of the GLF.[88] He also acknowledged that the Party had handled certain cadres improperly in the past.

Once the political mood at the center shifted, Teng Hsiao-p'ing proposed in February, 1962, to correct some wrong verdicts imposed on cadres in the previous Antirightist Campaign, indicating that over 80

---

[85] *Peking Review,* No. 4 (January 27, 1961), pp. 6–7.

[86] *Ching-kang-shan* (The Chingkangshan Mountains) (Peking), April 18, 1967; "Teng Hsiao-p'ing's Hundred Cases against the Thought of Mao Tse-tung," *ibid.,* March 8, 1967; *Pa-i-san hung-wei-ping* (August 13th Red Guard) (Tientsin), April 17, 1967.

[87] *SCMM,* No. 652 (1969), pp. 24–25.

[88] "Democratic Centralism," January, 1962, in *JPRS,* No. 50,792 (June 23, 1970), p. 52.

per cent of them had been subject to false charges.[89] In 1967 Mao's supporters labeled this move a "reverse wind" designed to usurp Party leadership. But the evidence from 1962 reveals only a few instances of rehabilitation. Chang Wen-t'ien became a special researcher at the Economic Research Institute, where he coauthored a book on socialist economy with Sun Yeh-fang. Huang K'o-ch'eng, vice-governor of Shansi, and Teng Hua, vice-governor of Szechwan, were also rehabilitated. In June, P'eng Teh-huai was also allowed to go to the countryside for investigation; he brought back an eighty-thousand-word report vindicating his previous views and allegedly saying: "I will not keep quiet any more. I want to be a Hai Jui." [90]

CRITICISM AND SELF-CRITICISM

Once the shift of political mood described above had taken place at the center, there followed a wave of self-examination about what had gone wrong with the GLF and why. All sectors of the population, ranging from local cadres to Mao, were engaged in this, scrutinizing every aspect of the Leap. The net effect of these campaigns was that Maoist ideology suffered a gradual erosion.

Mao actually initiated the movement for such self-examination by offering his own in June, 1961. This was revealed in his speech to the seven thousand cadres conference, although the exact content of his self-criticism was not made public. He stated in the speech:

On June 12 last year, the last day of the Central Conference in Peking, I spoke on my shortcomings and mistakes. I asked the comrades to report what I said to all provinces and areas. Subsequently, I learned that this was not disseminated in many areas. It seemed that my mistakes could and should be concealed. Comrades, they cannot be concealed. For whatever mistakes are committed by the Central Committee, I bear direct responsibility and share the indirect responsibility, for I am chairman of the Central Committee. While I do not intend to encourage others to shirk responsibilities, nevertheless I should be the first to bear responsibility.[91]

Following this statement, some provincial leaders also underwent self-criticism; those who were reluctant were forced to do so, as was the case in Honan, Kansu, and Tsinghai.[92]

While policy review and self-criticism were being undertaken at the

---

[89] *Pa-i-san hung-wei-ping*, April 17, 1967.

[90] *Ibid.; Ching-kang-shan*, February 1, 1967; *The Case of Peng Teh-huai*, pp. 138, 217; *Hung-an chan-pao* (Red Rock Combat News), April 15, 1967; *JMJP*, August 16, 1967.

[91] *JPRS*, No. 50,792 (June 23, 1970), p. 45.

[92] *Ibid.*, p. 42.

central level, similar processes also got underway at the provincial and local levels. A most conspicuous example at the local level, one that had a great bearing on the Cultural Revolution, was the case of the Peking Municipal Party Committee. Responding to Mao's demand for investigation, P'eng Chen in May, 1961, directed the Standing Committee of the Peking committee to investigate conditions in agriculture, industry, finance, culture, and education. Their most important conclusion was that many shortcomings at the local level had resulted from the center's "blind direction." [93]

In November, 1961, P'eng Chen instructed his closest deputies to review thoroughly the central directives issued between 1958 and 1961. He said to Hsiang Tzu-ming, secretary-general of the Secretariat of the Peking committee:

The Pei-tai-ho Conference [of 1958] talked about setting up an initial framework for the people's communes. I do not know exactly what happened, but every place rose with a roar. In some provinces the "five styles" are very serious. The Central Committee has a responsibility in this. . . . Some documents were issued on the basis of the comments of an individual, and it could not be guaranteed that they were free of problems. You had better organize some people to go through the documents issued by the Central Committee to see what problems there have been. See what those hotheaded people have done, and what are the documents of the Central Committee which have advocated the "five styles." We must gain experience and learn lessons from them. For example, some slogans contain subjective idealism.

And he continued:

The proposition of "destruction before construction" is debatable. For example, the operational procedure left behind by the Soviet experts at the Anshan Steel Company was set aflame even before our own plan had been drafted. As a result, production declined; there was no order to speak of. Why should we act in such a hurry? [94]

P'eng Chen entrusted the supervision of this review to Teng T'o, secretary of the Peking committee. Teng then divided the work into several groups. In December, 1961, Teng's teams gathered at a house called Ch'ang-kuan-lou in the Western Suburbs Park of Peking and went through the central documents. What they found largely confirmed the views expressed by P'eng Teh-huai in 1959.

[93] "Before and After the Ch'ang-kuan-lou Affair," *Tung-fang-hung* (The East Is Red) (Peking), April 20, 1967; *Pei-ching jih-pao* (Peking Daily), August 7, 1967; *T'i-yü chan-pao* (Athlete Combat News) (Peking), May 18, 1967; *Hung-she tsao fan tse* (Red Rebels) (Canton), May 13, 1967.

[94] *Tung-fang-hung* (Peking), April 20, 1967.

First, most mistakes were the result of "left" deviation rather than "right" opportunism. Mao's decision to launch the GLF had been hastily made and had led to waste. It was acknowledged that man's subjective initiative could play an important role, but to overemphasize it amounted to subjective idealism. It was one thing to dare to think and speak, but it was something else to dare to act. As men had been drawn off to irrigation and steel-smelting projects, the people's communes had become "women's communes." In order to rectify this, some cold water had to be poured on the mass movement. Second, many GLF policies, such as high speed, simultaneous development, and the reliance on political incentives, were all divorced from economic science. To do something by the whole, people rejected by definition any division of labor. Third, the Central Committee had changed policies so frequently that some of them contradicted each other. The center received false information from the localities, while the localities were not clear about the center's intentions. As a result, "nobody dared to tell the truth." Specifically, the high tide generated by the 1958 Pei-tai-ho Conference and the 1959 Lushan Conference widened this chasm of confusion.

The Ch'ang-kuan-lou review was a secret affair contained within the Peking Party apparatus. Hsiang Tzu-ming specifically directed the participants not to divulge anything about it to outsiders. This review culminated in a two-thousand word report to P'eng Chen. During the Cultural Revolution, it was challenged that Teng T'o had used the report in his jointly authored satirical newspaper articles, "Notes from Three Family Village"; and the fact that the Peking Committee had autonomously conducted such a highly classified review was cited as evidence that it had become an "independent kingdom" similar to the Petofi Club.

In the new political mood of 1961–62, intellectuals in addition to Party officials were allowed to air their views, but they could do so only in an esoteric language. Despite the changed atmosphere, the Party laid down the ground rules for literature and art, since the revised version of Mao's February, 1957, speech precluded open discussion of any political subject: there had to be a clear separation between purely academic-artistic discussion and political-ideological contention, and freedom was granted only in the first area.[95]

95 Dennis Doolin, "The Revival of the Hundred Flowers Campaign and Chinese Intellectuals: 1961," *CQ,* No. 8 (October–December, 1961), pp. 34–41. Also see Merle Goldman, "The Unique 'Blooming and Contending' of 1961–62," *ibid.,* No. 37 (January-March, 1969), pp. 54–83.

Under these restrictions, however, the writers groped for some better forms of expression. Some chose historical allegories, as did Wu Han, or ghost stories, as did Meng Ch'ao in his *Li Hui-niang*. Others, such as Teng T'o, used newspaper comments. However, no matter what form the authors used, they all chose ancient themes taken from the Ming or Sung dynasties and made the emperors and ministers in their works speak for them. In this way they could couch political debates in terms of academic issues, such as whether a particular Ming emperor (possibly meaning Mao) improved the lot of the peasants.

The first work in this genre was *Hai Jui's Dismissal from Office*, written by Wu Han, a historian and vice-mayor of Peking, and published in January, 1961. The play portrayed an upright Ming official, Hai Jui, in the reign of Emperor Chia Ch'ing. Hai Jui had apprehended a corrupt local tyrant, Hsu Chieh, a retired prime minister, and forced him to return the land he had confiscated from an innocent peasant. Hai Jui scrupulously punished Hsu for his crime, but the emperor dismissed Hai Jui on the advice of a eunuch at the court whom Hsu had bribed.[96] Wu Han contended that this ancient "virtue" of Hai Jui was worthy of being emulated by contemporary rulers. Though not a professional playwright, Wu Han claimed that the play was a "product of daring to think and speak." [97]

After Wu Han's play was staged in February, Teng T'o in March launched the column, "Evening Chats at Yenshan" ("Yen-shan yeh-hua"), in *Pei-ching wan-pao* (Peking Evening News). In October, Wu Han, Liao Mo-sha (director of the United Front Department), and Teng T'o jointly started the column, "Notes from the Three Family Village" ("San-chia-ts'un ch'a-chi") in *Ch'ien-hsien* (Frontline) under the pen name of Wu Nan-hsing.[98] These columns were mostly social criticism couched in ancient anecdotes or foreign fables. Of the three writers, Teng T'o stood out as the most biting critic of the GLF in general and of Mao's leadership in particular.

[96] "Hai Jui's Dismissal from Office," *Wen-hui pao* (Shanghai), December 7, 1965, pp. 4–6.

[97] Wu Han, "Preface to *Hai Jui's Dismissal from Office*," *Wen-hui pao* (Shanghai), December 7, 1965. Also see his "On Hai Jui," in "Wu han yü 'Hai Jui pa-kuan' shih-chien" (Wu Han and the Incident of *Hai Jui's Dismissal from Office*), in Ting Wang (ed.), *Chung-kung wen-hua ta-ke-ming tzu-liao hui-pien*, IV (Hong Kong: Ming-pao yueh-k'an, 1969), 155–73.

[98] Yao Wen-yüan, "On the 'Three Family Village,'" in *The Great Socialist Cultural Revolution in China* (Peking: Foreign Languages Press, 1966), I, 34; Lin Chieh *et al.*, "Teng T'o's *Evening Chats at Yenshan* Is an Anti-Socialist Black Talk," *Chieh-fang-chün pao* (Liberation Army Daily), May 8, 1966; *Wen-hui pao* (Shanghai), May 14, 1966.

First and foremost, these writers questioned the ideological under-pinnings of the Three Red Banners. Hitting at the basic premise of the GLF, Teng T'o castigated the idea of realizing communism through the communes as "substituting illusion for reality." [99] He told of Ernst Mach's positivism which, incidentally, was also used by Lenin in his *Materialism and Empirico-criticism* to satirize what he thought was antiscientific thought:

Followers of Ernst Mach exaggerated the role of what they called the "psycho-logical factor" and talked boastfully to their heart's content. Is this not the same as the titlark's nonsense about boiling the sea dry? Nevertheless, the *Machians imagined that through reliance on the role of the psychological factor they could do whatever they pleased, but the result was that they ran their heads against the brick wall of reality* and went bankrupt in the end.[100]

Perhaps the most humorous comments Teng made were on the slogans of the GLF. He bluntly called them "trumpet-blowing" and caricatured them in old stories. One of these was "A Fortune Built on One Egg," a story from the Ming dynasty,[101] which related to Mao's call for China to overtake Britain in fifteen years (during which time the fifteen years depended on achievements of the first five years and the first five years on the first three years, and so on). A poor peasant picked up an egg and made up his mind to make a fortune by raising chickens. The chickens would multiply over the years and he would buy cows; finally, in ten years he would become rich. When he di-vulged this idea to his wife, he could not help telling her that he would then be able to have a concubine. She was so angry at this that she crushed the egg. The whole story was based on the premise that every step to be taken would be fulfilled within ten years. When this angered his wife, the whole dream collapsed, suggesting that the GLF also collapsed because of the anger of the Chinese peasants.

It should be clear that the thrust of the Hai Jui drama and Three Family Village column was not so much their quest for artistic quality as their critique of GLF policies. Behind these writings was a profound disillusionment with the way Mao had led the GLF. For this reason the Maoists later labeled the authors of such works as "academic au-thorities" or "ghosts and monsters," charging that they attempted to

[99] Teng T'o hsüan-chih" (Selected Works of Teng T'o), in Ting Wing (ed.), *Chung-kung*, II, 57; *KMJP*, May 17, 1966.

[100] *Ibid.*, p. 166, translated in *The Great Socialist Cultural Revolution in China*, II, 21 (emphasis in original).

[101] "Teng T'o hsüan-chih," pp. 56–58.

form "public opinion" before undertaking a "comeback" through "peaceful evolution." It seems no exaggeration to say that the substance of their writings amounted to a de-Maoization of sorts. That their veiled criticisms did not encounter a successful Maoist counterattack *at that time* is explained by the circumstances under which they wrote. There is little doubt, however, that Mao and his supporters were aware of them. Not only did Chiang Ch'ing try to stop them, but in March, 1962, Yao Wen-yüan also attempted a counterattack. Lin Mohan dismissed Yao's critique as being "oversimplified and rude." [102]

Although all aspects of the GLF except military and foreign policy had been reversed by the end of 1961, the specific direction and permissible extent of the new policies had yet to be clarified. In 1962 this uncertainty led the top Party leaders to engage in policy debates. Some of these debates occurred at the conference of seven thousand cadres in January, 1962. In a written report to the conference, Liu Shao-ch'i set the basic tone of the debate. His point of departure was the appraisal of the "current situation," wherein he considered the GLF basically a failure: "In the last several years many shortcomings and mistakes have occurred in our work. The cadres and members of the whole Party and even the great majority of the people all have had personal painful experience of this. They have starved for two years." [103] Two months later, Liu concluded that the economy was still on the brink of collapse and could not be rehabilitated in less than seven or eight years, even with a decisive administration.[104] In May, 1962, he again argued that the center had not yet accurately assessed the gravity of the situation. On this point, Wang Kuang-mei admitted in 1967 that her husband had "overestimated" the difficulties in 1962.[105]

By contrast, Mao asserted at the conference of seven thousand cadres that the difficult years were over. Liu interpreted Mao to mean that the political situation was improving, for Liu saw no sign that the economic situation was better. In addition, Liu disagreed with Mao over how the Party should account for the depression. For him, the CCP had given the masses only a partial explanation by attributing the crisis to the climate in order to prevent the cadres from losing the

---

102 *Wen-hua ke-ming t'ung-hsün* (Bulletin of the Cultural Revolution) (Peking), No. 11 (May, 1967); *CB,* No. 842 (1967), p. 51.
103 *SCMM,* No. 652 (1969), p. 24; *Ching-kang-shan,* April 18, 1967.
104 *KMJP,* August 8, 1967; URS, Vol. XLVIII, p. 83.
105 *Ching-kang-shan,* February 1 and 8, 1967; *CB,* No. 848 (1968), p. 22.

confidence of the people. He saw in this neither genuine courage nor a Leninist attitude.[106]

Hence, the debate led to the reasons why such a grave situation had come about. Again Liu was quick to point out that the center had to take the primary responsibility. To put the matter in perspective, he cited the views of the peasants he had heard in Hunan: they had said to him that 30 per cent of the difficulties were brought about by natural calamities and 70 per cent were man-made, an inversion of the official explanation.[107] He told the seven thousand cadres that the Party had set up too many communes at one stroke, for attention was given only to faster and greater results and not to better and more economical results, and that things would certainly have been better without the communes.[108]

With regard to these points, Mao conceded that the prime responsibility lay with his leadership. He confessed that he had not "really" known much about economic matters, as he had told Edgar Snow in 1960. He argued, though, that the whole Party had lacked experience in construction and was still groping for a long-range view. He stressed that just as the Party had learned how to make revolution in twenty-eight years, so it had to learn construction from practice. In stark contrast to 1958, when he had urged the Chinese to surpass Great Britain in fifteen years, he reminded the cadres of his talk with Marshal Montgomery in 1961, when he had said that China would need at least one hundred years or more for industrialization.[109]

These debates inevitably raised the question of what to do about the situation. Liu's prescription was to do everything possible to restore a sound material base. He revived his thesis of 1956: "During the transitional period we may employ every possible means that contributes to the mobilization of the productive enthusiasm of the peasants. We should not say that such and such a means is the best and the only one."[110] Concurring with Liu's position, Teng Hsiaop'ing put it most succinctly at the Seventh Plenum of the Third Communist Youth League Central Committee in July: "So long as it raises output, 'going alone' is permissible. Whether cats are white or black, so long as they can catch mice, they are all good cats."[111]

---

[106] *Ching-kang-shan,* April 18, 1967; *SCMM,* No. 652 (1969), p. 26.

[107] *JMJP,* August 15, 1967; *SCMM,* No. 652 (1969), p. 27.

[108] *SCMM,* No. 652 (1969), p. 22; *JMJP,* November 23, 1967.

[109] *JPRS,* No. 50,792 (June 23, 1970), p. 50.

[110] *URS,* Vol. XLVIII, p. 83.

[111] *JMJP,* November 23, 1967; *Hsin pei-ta* (New Peking University) (Peking), January 20, 1967. According to the latter source, Teng asked Hu Yao-pang, chairman of the

The question of leadership was also a main topic of the cadre conference. Liu told the cadres:

We stirred up the "communist style," thereby violating the principle of pay according to labor and the principle of exchange of equal values. . . . We arrived at decisions rashly and implemented them in wide areas. Moreover, things were done in short order. This was a violation of the principle of democratic centralism in Party life, the life of the state, and the life of mass organizations. This is the basic cause of the serious mistakes which we committed in certain fields of work over the past several years.[112]

This statement cut to the core of the problem by suggesting that Mao's personalized decision-making disrupted democratic centralism and resulted in commandism among the local cadres. Liu allegedly went so far as to say that to oppose Mao was only to oppose an individual.[113]

Toward these criticisms, Lin Piao and Chou En-lai were said to have defended the GLF at the cadre conference of January, 1962. Lin argued that since the Three Red Banners were unprecedented, the Party lacked experience in carrying them out and problems were inevitable. Insisting that the GLF policies were nevertheless "correct," he championed again the Thought of Mao Tse-tung as "the soul and root of life"; hence, the Party had to act according to Mao's instructions. Chou delivered a speech to "sum up the great achievements" of the GLF, but what he said has not been made public.[114] In his speech on democratic centralism, Mao largely conceded the points Liu had raised. He upheld the principle of collective leadership, saying that he had yielded quite often to the majority view of the Politburo whether it was correct or not! But he placed more emphasis on democracy than Liu did. In the name of democracy, he had Liu's written report circulated among the cadres to seek their views. On the basis of their suggestions, the twenty-one-member committee under Liu prepared a second draft of the report. Mao also warned that the word "separatism" should not be used indiscriminately. Perhaps this was a veiled criticism of Liu, for he said that he was actually criticizing "some comrades without naming anyone." [115]

Lastly, Liu and Teng put the brakes on "brutal inner-Party struggle." Liu maintained that the antirightist struggle after the Lushan

Communist Youth League, to delete his remark from the record soon after returning to his office.

112 *SCMM*, No. 652 (1969), pp. 24–25.
113 *Ibid.*, No. 651 (1969), p. 19.
114 *CB*, No. 884 (1969), p. 19; Ting Wang (ed.), *Chung-kung*, I, 287.
115 *JPRS*, No. 50,792 (June 23, 1970), pp. 43, 51–52, 57.

Plenum had gone "too far." As a result, there had been no exchange of opinions between the top and bottom levels, and many mistakes had gone unresolved. He decreed that anyone who had views similar to P'eng teh-huai's but who had no illegal relations with foreign countries might have his verdict reversed, and that those who spoke at Party meetings would not be punished. In reference to this, Mao also admitted that "certain cadres" had been handled wrongly, but he contended that demotion could sometimes be beneficial in tempering the revolutionary will.

In February, 1962, the Party center convened an enlarged meeting of the Politburo at the Hsi-lou building within Chungnanhai (part of the Forbidden City reserved for use by the top leaders of the regime) to deal with the direction of the new economic policy. Reporting on the findings of the five-man finance group, Ch'en Yün pictured a bleak state of the economy. Due to the decline of agricultural production, food and goods were in short supply. Millions of *mou* of fertile soil had been wasted; pigs could not be raised because of inadequate feed; farm implements had become unusable; and even seed grains were in short supply. At the same time, the efforts in industrial construction were still excessive, and the inventories of materials and the supply of labor had declined. These conditions were leading to inflation as money flowed from the cities to the countryside, causing speculation there. Worst of all, the government's financial deficit had soared to two billion *yuan* in the previous four years. Liu Shao-ch'i, Teng Hsiao-p'ing, and Li Hsien-nien concurred in this appraisal. The Party center approved of the report and disseminated it to the provinces.[116]

As for the remedy, Ch'en Yün went further than any of the other leaders by saying that Teng Tzu-hui's idea of fixing output quotas to the households was not enough. He asked that land be redistributed to the households. When someone asked him how he would justify this in terms of Mao's Thought, he replied: "After all, the People's Republic will last ten thousand years! We can try once more later." Teng Hsiao-p'ing agreed with Ch'en Yün, arguing that there was really no difference between fixing output quotas with the households in Anhwei and private farming.[117] Teng regarded the practice of "going

116 *Pei-ching kung-she,* May 26, 1967; "Down with Counterrevolutionary and Revisionist Ch'en Yün," *Tung-fang-hung* (Peking), January 27, 1967. For Liu's role, see his "Self-Criticism," in *Collected Works of Liu Shao-ch'i, 1957–1967* (Hong Kong: URI, 1969), p. 361.
117 "Ch'en Yün Is the Vanguard in Restoring Capitalism," *Ts'ai-mao hung-ch'i* (Finance and Trade Red Flag) (Peking), February 8 and 23, 1967.

it alone" as a necessary step toward "going a step forward later." [118]

Against this background the revised version of Liu's *How to Be a Good Communist* appeared on August 1, 1962. The new edition was distinguished for its severe criticism of "dogmatism" and for its emphasis on the need for different opinions within the Party.[119] Liu deplored such dogmatism as follows:

Some comrades [have a] mechanical conception of inner-Party struggle and self-criticism. People with this attitude believe that inner-Party struggle must be launched under any and all circumstances—the more frequently and bitterly, the better. They magnify every trifle into a matter of "principle" and brand every tiny fault with such labels as political opportunism. They do not carry on inner-Party struggle properly and specifically in accordance with objective needs and objective laws of development, but instead "struggle" mechanically, subjectively, and violently, regardless of the consequences.[120]

Liu also called upon the cadres to be good pupils of Marxism-Leninism, stating that a good Communist must be able to "make timely changes in strategy and tactics to meet changing circumstances." [121] In 1967, Liu rejected the Maoist charge that he revised the book in order to usurp power by pointing out that the revision was actually made by someone else.[122]

Mao was well aware of these trends of ideological erosion and "reverse wind," but not until the Politburo meeting at Pei-tai-ho in August did he interfere with the way in which these issues had been handled. A passage in Liu's self-criticism made in 1966 threw some light on the relationship between Mao and Liu:

In the summer of 1962, at the Pei-tai-ho Conference I committed the error of leaning toward the rightist line. After having returned to Peking, the Chairman undertook drafting the decision on further developing and consolidating the collective economy and the decision on commerce. Also at this conference, he brought up class struggle and contradictions. In September, the Tenth Plenum was held and it passed the decisions and a communiqué. Only then were my errors corrected and the situation changed fundamentally.[123]

---

118 *JMJP*, December 3, 1967.

119 For the background of this revision, see Howard L. Boorman, "How to Be a Good Communist: The Political Ethics of Liu Shao-ch'i," *Asian Survey*, No. 8 (August, 1963), pp. 372–83.

120 Liu Shao-ch'i, *How to Be a Good Communist* (Peking: Foreign Languages Press, 1964), p. 80.

121 *Ibid.*, p. 27.

122 *JMJP*, June 5, 1967; for Liu's reply, see "Confession," in *Collected Works of Liu Shao-ch'i*, p. 366.

123 "Self-Criticism," *Collected Works of Liu Shao-ch'i*, p. 361. The translation has been slightly changed in light of a Chinese text available at Columbia University.

The Pei-tai-ho Conference was a work conference lasting a month, which discussed problems of agriculture, commerce, industry, and Party unity. Ch'en Po-ta reported on agriculture, Li Hsien-nien on commerce, and Li Fu-ch'un (possibly also Po I-po) on planning. The conference also discussed the expansion of the Control Commission and the transfer of cadres.[124] When Li Hsien-nien advocated the unified supply of commodities under state control, Ch'en Po-ta opposed him because it was against the mass line. Mao then criticized the spread of *san-tzu i-pao* and its supporters, including Ch'en Yün and Li Hsien-nien. He derided the Ministry of Commerce as the "Ministry of Destruction" and referred to both the State Planning Commission and the State Economic Commission as "independent kingdoms," asking them to go down to the countryside to "make revolution." [125]

Clearly Mao was questioning the current course of policy, but he presented no alternative. In a speech on the "current situation, contradictions, and class struggle," he instead raised the ideological specter that what was going on had the earmarks of *class struggle* —that this was not an internal dispute among Communists, but one between antagonistic classes. He sternly warned the Party, "Never forget class struggle," and reiterated his belief that "socialist society is a fairly long historical stage. During this historical stage, classes, class contradictions, and class struggle continue to exist, the struggle between the road of socialism and the road of capitalism goes on and the danger of capitalist restoration remains. It is necessary to recognize the protracted and complex nature of this struggle." [126] Instead of further retrenchment, Mao called for socialist education. By suggesting that the current intra-Party debates were a "struggle between the two roads," he halted the debates overtly, but in reality drove them underground.

In September, 1962, the Central Committee called its Tenth Plenum in Peking to transform the minutes of the Pei-tai-ho Conference into the Party line. In his speech to this plenum, Mao repeated a number of themes from his Pei-tai-ho remarks. The communiqué of the plenum stated the thesis that class struggles inevitably find their expression within the Party because of the pressures from imperialism abroad and bourgeois influence at home. The prevention of a capitalist

[124] "Speech at the Tenth Plenary Session," *CLG*, I, No. 4 (Winter, 1968/69), 86.
[125] "Summary of Revisionist Li Hsien-nien's Anti-Mao Remarks in Finance and Trade," *Pei-ching kung-she*, May 26, 1967.
[126] "Theoretical Weapon for Carrying Out Revolution under the Proletarian Dictatorship," *Peking Review*, No. 26 (June 24, 1967), p. 28.

restoration required the Party to be continuously vigilant against "various opportunist ideological tendencies in the Party." Mao also perceived the Sino-Soviet dispute to be part of the class struggle, that is, the "problem of struggle between Marxism-Leninism and revisionism." [127]

Mao then put an end to the "reverse wind." First, he made some conciliatory remarks to the "rightists": "I welcome several of the comrades here. . . . I wish to advise our comrades that even if you have conspired with foreign countries, if you will expose everything and speak out truthfully, we would welcome you, also give you work to do and never take the attitude of apathy. Nor would we adopt the method of execution." He hedged this with a warning, however: "The recent vogue of rehabilitation is not correct." Only rehabilitation by individual cases, not blanket rehabilitation, could be allowed. The communiqué reaffirmed that the Lushan Plenum had correctly smashed attacks by "right opportunism, i.e., revisionism." [128]

As for the intellectuals' criticism of his policies, Mao commented: "Isn't the writing of novels very popular now? To utilize novels to engage in antiparty activities is a great invention. In order to overthrow any political power, one must first create public opinion and engage in ideological and philosophical work. This applies to the revolutionary class as well as to the counterrevolutionary class." [129] Lastly, the communiqué insisted that "the broad masses and cadres of our country have always firmly believed in the correctness of the general line for socialist construction, the big leap forward, and the people's commune—the three red banners." [130]

While the Tenth Plenum reaffirmed the bulk of Mao's ideological positions, it also legitimized most of the adjustment policies. It adopted three documents: (1) the resolution on strengthening the collective economy, (2) the revised draft of the Sixty Articles on Agriculture, and (3) the decision on commerce.[131] Unlike Mao's twelve-year agricultural program, the resolution anticipated that the basic completion of technical reform in agriculture would require four or five five-year plans. It promised to stabilize the ratio of agricultural

---

127 *Ibid.*; "Speech at the Tenth Plenary Session," p. 89. Also see the communiqué of the Tenth Plenum in *Peking Review*, No. 39 (September 28, 1962), p. 6.

128 "Speech at the Tenth Plenary Session," p. 91; *Peking Review*, No. 39 (September 28, 1962), p. 7.

129 "Speech at the Tenth Plenary Session," pp. 92–93.

130 *Peking Review*, No. 39 (September 28, 1962), p. 6.

131 "Speech at the Tenth Plenary Session," p. 85; Chen (ed.), *Rural People's Communes in Lien-chiang*, pp. 80–90.

taxes and procurement at "an appropriate level." Although the decision on commerce has not been made public, according to the resolution on collective economy, the Party apparently adopted Ch'en Yün's and Li Hsien-nien's idea of the unified supply of commodities.[132]

The revised Sixty Articles clearly designated the production team as the basic accounting unit, made allowances for smaller communes, discouraged commune enterprises, increased the scope of private plots from 5 to 7 per cent of the arable land, and sanctioned the fixing of output quotas to small groups. These measures made it clear that Mao had succeeded only in arresting the drift toward *san-tzu i-pao,* thus preventing it from slipping further into private farming, but that he had accepted all the other practices of the communes that went beyond the 1961 commune charter. The 1962 charter stipulated that the refurbished team would not be changed for at least thirty years! [133]

Finally, the Tenth Plenum endorsed the Party-state authority structure that had emerged in the course of adjustment. Its resolution stated that agricultural development must be carried out under "uniform Central Committee policies and uniform national planning." Indeed, in the two years after 1960, the State Planning Commission almost doubled its size by adding seven more members. The plenum also strengthened the Party control commissions, particularly the Central Control Commission, by establishing a new standing committee and tripling the membership of the commission. It elected Lu Ting-yi, K'ang Sheng, and Lo Jui-ch'eng as new members of the Secretariat, while dismissing Huang K'o-ch'eng and T'an Cheng.[134]

Adjustments and Their Legacy: An Assessment

As the ideology of the GLF confronted reality, it underwent major adjustments. The Wuhan Resolution of December, 1958, already marked an ideological retreat from "uninterrupted revolution" to "revolution by stages," via its warning against the "utopian dream of skipping the socialist stage." At the Lushan Conference of July, 1959, P'eng Teh-huai castigated the uninterrupted revolution as "petit bourgeois fanaticism." The Antirightist Campaign in 1959–60 saw a brief

---

[132] Chen (ed.), *Rural People's Communes in Lien-chiang,* pp. 81–83.

[133] *Nung-ts'un jen-min kung-she t'iao-li (hsiu-cheng ch'ao-an),* Article 20.

[134] "Resolution on the Further Strengthening of the Collective Economy," item 12, in Chen (ed.), *Rural People's Communes in Lien-chiang,* p. 88; *Peking Review,* No. 39 (September 28, 1962), p. 5; The Research Office of the Japanese Cabinet Secretariat, *Chūka jinmin kyōwakoku soshikibetsu jinmeihyō* (Who's Who in the People's Republic of China Arranged according to Organizations) (Tokyo: Naikaku kanbō, 1967), p. 205.

revival of the commune movement, but with the enactment of the Twelve Articles in November, 1960, the original form of the commune ceased to exist. From that time on, the practice in commune management so diverged from the Party's official ideology that few cadres and peasants took the ideology seriously. In 1961, not only did the local cadres voice open complaints but some outspoken intellectuals went so far as to vilify Mao's ideological exhortations as "empty talk" or "vulgar." As many Party leaders also questioned the basic premises of the GLF, ideological erosion became apparent among the peasants, the cadres, the intellectuals, and the top Party leaders.

It was against this background that the Ninth Plenum adopted the slogan of "readjusting, consolidating, filling out, and raising standards." This slogan served as an operational ideology enabling the Party center to pursue its goal of restoring economic order with the means at its disposal. Faced with the food crisis, the CCP had to shelve its goal-oriented program of the GLF and concentrate on the solution of pressing problems of survival. Its operational code ceased to have utility for defining long-term communist ends, since it sought rather to ascertain the most effective means for solving current problems and only those ends were chosen that were appropriate to the available means. The operational leaders at the center under Liu Shao-ch'i stressed the integrative, legitimating, and social control function of ideology rather than such functions as orientation, motivation, mobilization, and socialization. They basically approached problems "pragmatically"; if changes in the external world forced practice to depart from ideological imperatives, they adapted the ideology to the practice.

As the Party became preoccupied with increasing production, it also reverted to a strategy of sequential development. The GLF strategy of "simultaneous development" gave way to that of "agriculture as the foundation and industry as the leading factor." The basic goal of adjustment policy was to maximize efficiency and productivity. Management practices of the communes and enterprises under the new directives, such as work points, material incentives, and differential work assignments, stemmed from the quest for efficiency. As the promotion of "productive forces" was given the foremost priority, revolution—changing attitudes and "productive relations"—had to be put aside at least for the time being, and economics took command. In 1966, Wang Jen-chung, first secretary of Hupeh province, recalled this period: "It was principally in 1961 and 1962 that we did not do a good job in put-

ting politics in command or did nothing to put politics in command."
And at the Eleventh Plenum in 1966, Mao himself asserted that a
"right deviation" had existed in this period.[135]

In the course of making its adjustments, the Party center gradually
turned away from the erratic mass polity of the GLF and consolidated
the institutional arrangements of the policy process that had been developed in the post-Leap period. In many ways the new policy organs
had the qualities that Samuel Huntington attributes to an institutionalized polity: coherence, autonomy, complexity, and adaptabil-
ity.[136]

There were several key elements in this emergent authority structure. First was the recentralization of authority, which occurred
gradually during the two hectic years between the Pei-tai-ho conferences of 1958 and 1960 while the Party was retreating step by step
from the GLF. In order to give coherence to this change, especially
from the Pei-tai-ho Conference of 1960 on, the Party center reestablished a firm grip over the process of policy readjustment. The
Ninth Plenum legitimized the principle that the adjustments must
take place under central direction. After that, the Party center carried
out policy reviews and codified their findings into central directives.
The locus of decision-making was the Politburo's Standing Committee
and the Secretariat, which functioned under a collective leadership
headed by Liu Shao-ch'i and Teng Hsiao-p'ing. Mao seemed to have
withdrawn from operational decisions after the Pei-tai-ho Conference
of 1960, making it easy for the Party center to adjust policy in a more
regularized manner.

A second characteristic of the national policy-making mechanism
was a growing specialization. A division of labor at the center had become apparent by 1962. In economic affairs, the reactivated Ch'en Yün
headed the five-man finance group; Li Fu-ch'un and Po I-po resumed
their leadership in planning; T'an Chen-lin, Liao Lu-yen, and Ch'en
Cheng-jen took charge of agriculture; Po I-po and Yu Ch'iu-li, industry; and Li Hsien-nien and Yao Yi-lin, finance and trade. As for
culture and education, P'eng Chen led the team made up of Lu Ting-
yi, Chou Yang, Hu Ch'iao-mu, Yang Hsiu-feng, and Chiang Nan-

---

135 Wang Jen-chung, "Bring Politics to the Fore, Put the Thought of Mao Tse-tung in
Command of Everything," *Hung-ch'i*, No. 5 (April 5, 1966), translated in *SCMM*, No.
523 (1966), p. 5; for Mao's remark, see "Bombard the Headquarters—My First Big-
Character Poster," August 5, 1966, *CB*, No. 891 (1969), p. 63.

136 Samuel P. Huntington, *Political Order in Changing Societies* (New Haven, Conn.:
Yale University Press, 1968), pp. 12–13.

hsiang. As for the Party and security operations, Teng Hsiao-p'ing led the team of Liu Lan-t'ao, An Tzu-wen, Hsieh Fu-chih, and Yang Shang-k'un.[137] The ten secretaries of the Secretariat also each assumed a special task. It would seem—and Mao's supporters certainly later argued—that this specialization introduced a note of autonomy to the policy process, with each system of specialists having a measure of independence in its realm.

A third aspect of this policy process was that decisions were reached through a complex process of consensus building. In fact, two slightly different types of policy processes evolved, one for general problems embracing all localities (such as general economic policy, agriculture, cadre problems, and ideology), and the other for some specialized policy areas (such as industry, culture, and education). Both processes involved Party utilization of a forum called the "central work conference," which came into prominence during this period. Formulating policies for general and nationwide problems necessarily involved compromises between the center's demands and the localities' capabilities and responses. For example, the policy of "agriculture as the foundation" was adopted at the central work conference at Pei-tai-ho in August, 1960, which the Peking conference in January, 1961, further discussed and the Ninth Plenum formally ratified. Participants in these general conferences seem to have varied but probably included members of the Politburo and the Secretariat, responsible heads of the central departments and the State Council, first secretaries of the regional bureaus and the provincial committees, and representatives of the PLA commands.[138]

The Party also used such conferences to legitimate spontaneously initiated practices through the issuance of directives approving them. Directives on communes were a case in point. In November, 1960, the Party center issued the Twelve Articles ratifying the measures that had sprung up in the countryside. Then, the Canton conference of March, 1961, expanded the Twelve Articles into "The 'Draft' [*ch'ao-an*] Sixty Articles on Agriculture." The Politburo's Standing Committee apparently accepted the ideas coming from lower levels, and the Secretariat then convened a conference to prepare the draft. At these conferences, substantive discussions were held, regional and local activities coordinated, and conflicts resolved. The results of the con-

[137] "Thoroughly Overthrow Liu Shao-ch'i's Traitor Group," *Ching-kang-shan*, February 9, 1967.

[138] Parris H. Chang, "Research Notes on the Changing Loci of Decision in the Chinese Communist Party," *CQ*, No. 44 (October–December, 1970), pp. 170–71.

ference discussions were summarized, with policy recommendations, and were submitted as a draft report to the Standing Committee for its approval. If approved, the Secretariat transmitted the draft through the Party's regular policy ladder. Unlike its role in the GLF, the press took little part in this process; in fact, it reported very little about these drafts. And implementing policy by such stipulated rules and procedures tended to be routine rather than mobilizational.

Policy-making and implementation were closely related in this process. Indeed, policy was also made in the course of its implementation. Once a draft was transmitted, the feasibility of the center's intent became subject to judgment by local cadres. Thus its implementation was constrained by local conditions. This process fell into two categories. First, the localities in general (the "plane") more or less evenly implemented the draft (*p'ao-mien*); second, the Party center selected some special "spots" and allowed those places to carry out calculated experimentation under central or provincial direction or by squatting some work teams there (*tun-tien*). With respect to the Draft Sixty Articles on Agriculture, Anhwei and Honan experimented with variants of *san-tzu i-pao*. The combined efforts at the plane and the spots provided the center with more accurate information. On the basis of a calculation of risks and costs made available by the new information, the center amended the agricultural "Draft" into the "Revised Draft" (*hsiu-cheng ch'ao-an*) in September, 1962. Unlike the GLF, where the policy-maker (Mao) relied on an erratic policy process and on mobilization, in the adjustment period the policy-makers resumed a regularized process.

Local variations in implementation and diverging perspectives among the leadership invariably caused policy debates at the highest level. For example, when many localities lobbied for *san-tzu i-pao* and some central leaders supported them, Mao decided that the situation was getting out of hand. Since these kinds of policy difference could only be resolved at the highest level, the Party convened another central work conference for this purpose. It was at this level that ideology became one of the most important constraining influences on policy, even though the final outcome was predicated upon the relative power of those involved. At the Pei-tai-ho Conference of August, 1962, Mao vetoed the quest for *san-tzu i-pao* by interpreting it as a matter of class struggle. The Tenth Plenum then ratified the "Revised Draft" of the Sixty Articles.

A variant of this policy process occurred in the more specialized areas. Since these areas concerned some special localities or functional organizations, policy here was shaped through interaction between the Party-state authorities and the relevant constituencies. The Secretariat or the concerned central departments usually initiated proposals and organized task forces to investigate the policy options through such devices as "on-spot squattings" at factories, schools, and so on. In preparing "draft" regulations, the Party department convened more specialized central work conferences, attended by the relevant Party and state functionaries and representative practitioners, such as managers, educators, and writers. After having implemented the draft for a certain period, the department then solicited more suggestions from functional organizations such as schools or professional organizations such as the Chinese Writers' Association, and incorporated them into a revised draft. In this manner, the Pei-tai-ho Conference of August, 1961, produced the Seventy Articles on Industry and the Sixty Articles on Universities.

The total effect of these developments was to interpose intricate policy-making and implementing institutions between those at the pinnacle of power and the masses. It became impossible to obtain the kind of direct mass participation that Mao had urged in the GLF. The masses could only participate tangentially, more on some issues and less on others, or indirectly through a hierarchy of specialized organizations. In case these institutions failed to perform as expected, the architects of the recovery would seek a remedy through organizational reforms rather than through ideological rectification, and they would coopt diverse elements into such organizational structures rather than seek to train political activists.

Insofar as Mao's influence in the policy-making arena was concerned, starting from about the close of the GLF, he exerted primarily a veto power on existing policy through his power to challenge it ideologically. Even the new policies Mao supported had to go through the Party's regular institutional framework in order to be implemented. This did not constitute either an anti-Maoist conspiracy or a usurpation of the Party leadership by Liu Shao-ch'i. As Liu confessed in 1966, his responsibility for the work of the center lay in the fact that he let others propose policy innovations at the central conferences that he presided over while Mao was absent from Peking. Mao himself acknowledged his own responsibility for having voluntarily proposed the division of the Politburo and hence he was not being entirely candid in blaming Liu Shao-ch'i and Teng Hsiao-p'ing in

1966 for what took place. He was aware, perhaps correctly, that since the division of responsibility the central leadership had been "scattered" and that the leaders at the first line, particularly Teng Hsiao-p'ing, no longer consulted him on vital issues and had set up an "independent kingdom." [139]

Of the two trends that emerged in 1960–62—the ideological revitalization movement promoted by Lin Piao within the PLA, and the policy adjustments by Liu Shao-ch'i in the Party—Mao gave his support to the former. Mao did not, however, change either the existing policy practices or the current cast of the Party's top leadership. And the fact remains that while Mao's GLF turned out to be a colossal failure, the adjustments carried out under Liu's leadership proved successful in weathering the crisis created by the GLF.

The developments discussed in this paper led to a widening gulf between Maoist ideology and Party practice in policy implementation. And this gulf was the most significant legacy of the GLF for the subsequent political development leading to the Cultural Revolution.

[139] For Liu's responsibility, see "Self-Criticism," p. 361; for Mao's, see "Speech at a Work Conference of the Central Committee," October 25, 1966, *CB,* No. 891 (1969), p. 75.

RENSSELAER W. LEE III

The Politics of Technology in Communist China*

Political participation in Western democracies is essentially electoral participation, designed to exert popular pressure upon political decision-making. Political participation in Communist China serves the function of developing and maintaining commitment to officially sanctioned goals. The Chinese style of participation is on the whole concerned with implementing rather than with defining social policy. While asserting the sanctity of basic social norms and objectives, however, it includes within the realm of "politics" matters which in Western countries would be exclusively the prerogative of bureaucratic or professional elites. To a degree unparalleled elsewhere, it opens the performance of administrative and technical functions to popular scrutiny, suggestion, and innovation, even while denying to the populace the right to choose among alternative definitions of the national interest or to question the legitimacy of Mao's leadership.

Political participation in Communist China is closely linked to the practice of economic and technological change. Possibly the most important expression of the Chinese participatory style is in the technical sphere. At various times since the establishment of the Chinese People's Republic, the Communist leadership has attempted to institute a system of what might be called "technical democracy." Technical democracy seeks to promote the mass application of creative intelligence to improving the nation's productive capacity. It opposes

* I would like to thank the following persons for their guidance and support at various stages in the preparation of this manuscript: Robert North, John Lewis, Lyman Van Slyke, and Shao Wing-chan of Stanford University, and Ivo Duchacek of The City College of New York.

the concentration of technical control in the hands of a few authorities or "experts" and diffuses to broad segments of the population the right to participate in technical design and innovation. An important Communist rationale for the institution of technical democracy is that the inclusion of creative components in otherwise routine manual work can provide China's masses with a sense of being masters rather than appendages of their technological environment. Another is that effective innovation requires the integration of theoretical or "book" knowledge with the accumulated wisdom and insight that derives from productive practice.

The impact of mass participation in the technological sphere has been to level status distinctions within economic enterprises. Technical democracy demands the repudiation of traditional organizational hierarchies and the periodic merging of functions of those whose formal roles would otherwise confine them exclusively to "mental" or "manual" categories of work. The elimination of the so-called antithesis between mental and manual labor, a Marxist utopian aim, becomes in Communist China an ideological formula for opening the doors of technology to popular initiative and participation. The popularization of technology has tended to shift the locus of technical innovation from the technical department or laboratory to the production level. At this level, workers and technical personnel cooperate in designing new equipment, technological processes, and products. Communist propaganda has often focused on the worker as the initiator of suggestions for technical improvement or new designs, and has depicted the function of technological theory as one of summarizing and processing ideas that originate mainly from lower levels.

Technical democracy means, according to one article, that "everyone in the plant vies to be a path-breaker in technical innovations." [1] An integral part of Maoist development strategy, it means that arguments for mass innovation in China are couched in pragmatic as well as political terms, that they demonstrate commitments to modernization and industrialization as well as to social equality and mass mobilization. The Maoist rationale for linking technology with politics is a complex one. It derives partly from the proposition—now familiar

[1] "The Working Class Is the Master of Technical Revolution," *China Reconstructs,* XVIII, No. 4 (April, 1969), 29. Two Western sources which I found particularly valuable for this study are Barry Richman, *Industrial Society in Communist China* (New York: Random House, 1969) (especially Chap. iv); and Leo Orleans, "Research and Development in Communist China: Mood, Management, and Measurement," in Joint Economic Committee, Congress of the United States, *An Economic Profile of Mainland China,* II (Washington, D.C.: U.S. Government Printing Office, 1967), 549–78.

enough to all students of China—that the context of theoretical knowledge determines its validity or usefulness as an instrument for manipulating the environment; in simpler terms, theory must be integrated with and must serve the practice of production. Behind this rather obvious argument, however, lies an extremely important strategic consideration: the Chinese Communists are determined that China should follow a uniquely national road of industrial and technological development and that such a "Chinese" road is likely to evolve from a broad rather than a narrow distribution of change-producing opportunities within the society. On the enterprise level, the Communists see the separation of professional elites from "politics"—that is, their monopoly of technical power—as promoting the excessive or "slavish" imitation of foreign style and methods in technology. They feel, moreover, that the cumulative effects of such imitation will be to reinforce China's position of technological inferiority vis-à-vis the industrially advanced countries.

The relationship between technical democracy in China and the long-run economic objectives of the Communist leadership is the subject of this article. I intend to discuss this relationship on two levels, that of ideology and that of function, in order both to clarify Maoist conceptions of social change and to highlight some of the problems and alternatives facing latecomers to development in the modern world. Before embarking on an analysis of Maoism, however, I would like briefly to describe the evolution of Communist technological policies in China from the early 1950's to the present.

THE RIGHT TO INNOVATE

Chinese Communist conceptions of innovation have since 1958 stemmed largely from two propositions: first, that participation in labor is a legitimate source of ideas for technological change; and second, that the development of technology in China should depart as far as possible from foreign industrial models. Maoist ideology tends to view the relation of labor to the means of production as having broad implications for the nation's overall pattern of technological growth. The ideology closely links concepts of national and class alienation making national dependency upon foreign technical stereotypes the counterpart of workers' subservience to the tools and implements of manufacture. The most obvious though not the only factor in this ideological equation has been the so-called bourgeois expert, a model villain of Chinese economic life who not only disregards the creative potential of the working classes but also invokes foreign technical concepts as "doctrines" in order to deny them a share of technical power. Chinese Communist spokesmen since the Great Leap Forward have remarked on the obsequiousness of China's technical intelligentsia, its tendency to worship foreign books and theories, and to despise "the things created by China's working people in the course of practice" even where these might be better than their equivalents abroad.[2] Assuming the partial truth of this observation, to shift the balance of technical power downward within economic units could serve not only to encourage mass innovation but also to give a native bent to China's technological development.

Technological nativism has in recent years been a strong ally of technical democracy in China. It is noteworthy, however, that the concept of labor as a source of technical creativity made its appearance very early in Communist China. Party policy in the initial phase of Communist rule in China assigned to the working class a significant share of responsibility for the technical modernization of industry. According to Party dogma, the establishment of Communist power in 1949 had created an entirely new set of "production relations" within which work was no longer alienated labor and whereby workers were "the masters and not the slaves of their machines."[3] The Party's redefinition of workers as masters of their technical environment provided the ideological basis for a concept of labor that stressed creativity and problem-solving as well as ordinary manual work. During the early 1950's the Chinese Communists went to some lengths to promote the image of the worker-innovator, the technical virtuoso who could solve practical problems, make continuous improvements in the tools as techniques of production, and even invent some new items of equipment.[4] The technical exploits of individual workers such as Chao Kuo-yu, Chang Ming-shan, and Wang Chung-lun provided models for various innovations campaigns initiated in this period, including the New Production Record Movement (beginning in Manchuria in September, 1949), the Anshan Workers Inventions and In-

2 "Develop Science and Technology by Following Our Own Road," *JMJP*, January 24, 1966, translated in *SCMP*, No. 3632 (1966), p. 18.

3 Li Li-san, "Develop Emulation Campaigns—Celebrate the 30th Anniversary of the Party," *JMJP*, July 1, 1951, in *CB*, No. 112 (1951).

4 See "For National Industrialization, Unfold the Technical Renovation Movement," *JMJP*, April 16, 1954 (editorial). Also, Lai Jo-yu, "Labor Emulation Has Reached a New Stage—That of Technical Innovation," *JMJP*, May 27, 1954, p. 1.

novations Campaign of 1952–53, and the nationwide Technical Innovation Campaign of 1954.[5]

Communist technical policy shifted in the mid-1950's from sponsorship of "invention and creation" to an emphasis on raising technical levels, particularly through "learning and grasping advanced Soviet experience."[6] Statements anticipating the shift describe the 1954 innovations campaign as a deviation which "scattered the energies of the worker" and lowered productivity in some enterprises; moreover, they indicated that creative participation in technical matters was compromising the effectiveness of the new Soviet machinery and equipment being used to build or reconstruct the "core" enterprises of the five-year plan.[7] Recent Chinese accounts of the period 1955–57 attribute the decline of the worker-innovator image almost entirely to the increasing hegemony of Soviet technical and managerial doctrines over Chinese industrial life. In the early part of the decade, the argument runs, workers had considerable influence over technology and "produced outstanding results by native methods in the sphere of technical innovation and technical revolution." As time went on, however, the worker became subject to a "mass of foreign rules and regulations," and technical decision-making became the prerogative of "authorities" whose adoration of foreign experts was matched by their contempt for ideas and suggestions coming from below.[8]

The Great Leap Forward of 1958–60 marked the initiation of innovations campaigns aimed at "cutting a broad swath through the backwardness of Chinese industry"[9] and also at reducing China's dependence upon Soviet industrial models. The technological policies

[5] On the New Production Record Movement, see Lu ta tsung-kung hui (Lu-shun-Talien Trade Union Committee), *Ho-li hua chien-yi* (Rationalization Proposals) (n.p.: Hsin chung-kuo ching-chi chien-she yin-shua [New China Economic Construction Company Press], 1950), pp. 31–34. On the Anshan Movement, see "The Achievements of the Mechanization and Automation Movement at Anshan Are Very Great," *JMJP*, August 26, 1953, p. 1. For a good article on the 1954 campaign, see "For National Industrialization, Unfold the Technical Innovation Movement."

[6] Lai Jo-yu, "Report to the Sixth Meeting of the Eighth Session of the ACFTU Executive Committee," *KJJP*, March 11, 1955, p. 1.

[7] "Correctly Unfold the Technical Innovation Movement," *JMJP*, September 18, 1954, p. 1 (editorial).

[8] "Advance in the Direction of Independence, Self-Determination, and Regeneration through Self-Reliance," *JMJP*, May 20, 1969, translated in *SCMP*, No. 4433 (1969), p. 7.

[9] Soong Ch'ing-ling, "A New Revolution Pushes Back the Skies," *China Reconstructs*, IX, No. 6 (June, 1960), 4.

that emerged during the Leap comprised a kind of campaign against foreign standards—a campaign that took both direct and indirect forms. The former centered on modern, large enterprises using advanced equipment and complex production sequences. Here, employees were mobilized to overthrow "idols, conventions, and taboos" associated with foreign technique (notably, the belief that high-level technology was somehow unchangeable or untouchable) and to carry out thorough reforms of equipment, product designs, and technical regulations.[10] The "indirect" campaign, by contrast, relied on a broad industrial front to generate new ideas and experiences that could serve as "pioneers for the modern, large enterprises." [11] Central to this campaign was the assumption that "walking on two legs" (simultaneous use of foreign and indigenous production methods) involved the use of indigenous techniques as a long-term strategic policy, not as a temporary expedient where foreign facilities and equipment were lacking.[12] Such techniques, developed largely in medium- to small-scale enterprises with relatively few capital commitments and simple production technologies, were claimed to have "a great and promising future" and to be, in many cases, more advanced and scientific than foreign ones.[13]

The technical innovations campaign in the Great Leap brought technology to the masses both by broadly dispersing change-producing opportunities within Chinese society and by redistributing them at the level of the enterprise. On this level, Maoist policies present an apparent contrast to Western styles of change-management, which confine

[10] For a description of the campaign against "technological superstition" in the modern sector, see Chen Hsiu-cheng, "All Together for 150,000 Cars a Year," *China Reconstructs* VIII, No. 2 (February, 1958), 6–8. "Modernity," the author wrote, "has its drawbacks" because of the psychological barriers that it creates. The reference is to the Soviet-built Changchun Motor Car Works.

[11] See, for example, "Mass of Small Modern Enterprises Advances from Victory to Victory," *JMJP*, February 8, 1960, translated in *SCMP*, No. 2196 (1960), p. 4.

[12] "To Develop 'Small, Native' Enterprises on a Massive Scale with Revolutionary Spirit," *Chung-kuo ch'ing-nien pao* (Chinese Youth News), July 1, 1960, in URS, XXI, No. 10 (1960), 140.

[13] *Ibid.* Mao Tse-tung and Liu Shao-ch'i may have interpreted the "walking on two legs" formula differently, Liu stressing a dichotomy of foreign and native, and Mao the assimilation of the former by the latter. Liu's report to the Eighth Party Congress (second session) in March, 1958, indicated that technical revolution in China should consist of two complementary but basically distinct parts: first, the mechanization and semimechanization of backward enterprises; second, the "introduction of the world's latest techniques as far as possible." See Liu Shao-ch'i, "Report on the Work of the Central Committee of the Communist Party of China to the Second Session of the International Congress," May 5, 1958, *Second Session of the Eighth National Congress of the Communist Party of China* (Peking: Foreign Languages Press, 1958), pp. 16–66.

the innovation process mainly to specialized institutions well removed from the production level. In fact, the mass movement in Chinese industry during the Great Leap Forward resulted in the partial breakdown of professional boundaries separating technical personnel and workers. Technicians engaged in manual labor at production posts; workers participated in the designing of new tools, products, and processes. Technological change became an object of factory-wide participation, and expertise was downgraded, being often identified with "conservatism" or with "superstitious worship of foreigners, foreign books, and foreign methods." [14] Not only Chinese but also Soviet experts working in the newly built enterprises suffered a loss of prestige and status. Chinese antiforeignism, expressed in technical terms, may have rendered their advisory position untenable and undoubtedly hastened the break in technical relations between the two countries, which occurred in July-August, 1960.[15]

The mass innovations campaigns subsided in the early 1960's in favor of a new emphasis on adjustment, consolidation, and elevation of technical standards. Some curbs on innovation were doubtless necessary at the time: many of the masses' "creations" of the Leap showed little familiarity with machines or technical processes, as well as a complete disregard for scientific procedure, and were useless, if not harmful, to the development of production. Moreover, new rules and operating procedures had to be devised to implement in productive practice those items of innovation that showed some promise. The need to restore balance in the economy, to raise the quality of products, and to continue the operation and expansion of the modern sector in the absence of Soviet advisers had the effect of shifting the locus of technical power upward within the enterprise.[16] Communist publications now called upon enterprises to "fully develop the posi-

[14] Ho Chih-ping, "Help the Native to Digest the Foreign: Let Them Fly High Together," *JMJP*, August 28, 1958, p. 7. Note the stereotypes of "native expert" (*t'u chuan-chia*) and "foreign expert" (*yang chuan-chia*) in this article.

[15] For a recent account of the Soviet advisory role in China during the Great Leap, see O. Borisov and B. Koloskov, *Sovietsko-kitaiskie otnosheniya* (Moscow: Izdatel'stvo "Mysl'," 1971), pp. 154–70. See also Teng T'o's apparent reference to China's rejection of Soviet aid: "If a man with a swelled head thinks he can learn a subject easily and then kicks out his teacher, he will never learn anything." Quoted in Merle Goldman, "Party Policies toward the Intellectuals," in John W. Lewis (ed.), *Party Leadership and Revolutionary Power in China* (Cambridge: Cambridge University Press, 1970), p. 300.

[16] Partly because of the withdrawal of Soviet technicians and blueprints, China began in this period to show a new interest in acquiring technology from Western countries. See Cheng Chu-yüan, *Scientific and Engineering Manpower in Communist China, 1949–1963* (Washington, D.C.: National Science Foundation, 1965).

tive functions of technical personnel," and to practice democratic centralism (*min-chu chi-chung chih*) in the formulation and execution of technical policy.[17] According to this formula, projects under consideration would be open to "democratic discussion," but actual decisions would be made by the technical or administrative agency involved. Workers were admonished that differences of opinion on technical matters "could not be made into an excuse for disobedience." [18] Though worker-innovation continued to some extent in the post-Leap years, it was subject to strict bureaucratic controls, and the "nonintellectual expert" as a Chinese folk hero faded from public prominence.

The rehabilitation of experts and of professionalism in this period was further reflected in statements defending the "relative independence of theory in development" and the ability of theory to predict or to guide social practice. Such statements argued both that scientific theories with no tangible connection to production were not necessarily unreal or meaningless and that where the connection existed, it showed that technical inventions—for example, in the industrial revolution in the West—were often applications of pre-existing scientific laws.[19] These laws, moreover, were formulated through a process of deduction, and to demand, as the Maoists did, "the demonstration of every link of the deductive process with practical and material things" was entirely unreasonable.[20] (Benjamin Schwartz makes a similar case against Maoism in his contribution to this volume.) Probably because these arguments point to the reality of change-producing activity in modern industrial societies, Western observers tend to regard the aftermath of the Great Leap Forward as a stage of relative rationality in Party economic policy, in contrast to the irrationality of Maoist policies in the Great Leap Forward and the Cultural Revolution.[21]

[17] Kuang K'ai and Huang Ho, "Fully Develop the Positive Functions of Technical Personnel," *KJJP*, September 15, 1961, p. 4.

[18] "The Scientific Study and Discussion of the Policy of Actively Pursuing Technology," *Hung-ch'i* (Red Flag), June 1, 1962, p. 4.

[19] This argument probably applies best to the industrial revolution in its later stages. As one writer notes: "One looks in vain for actual applications of theoretical science as opposed to products of mechanical ingenuity before the middle of the 19th Century. By the last quarter of the century such applications were so obvious that it was no longer necessary to make a point of them." George H. Daniels, *Science in American Society* (New York: Knopf, 1971), p. 271.

[20] Fung Ting, "Concerning Redness and Vocational Proficiency," *KMJP*, June 12–14, 1962, translated in *SCMP*, No. 2776 (1962), pp. 12–13.

[21] Most Western writing on China still views Maoist policies as economically irrational, though perhaps "rational" from the standpoint of egalitarian objectives. My own view is

The relative separation of technology from politics that had occurred as a result of the problems and failings of the Great Leap Forward did not last long. Beginning in 1964, the regime launched another movement for technological innovation, centering on the revolutionization of designing work in industry.[22] The principal task of this designing revolution, according to one account, was to "use the thought of Mao Tse-tung to overcome subjectivism, dogmatism, and bourgeois individualism in designing ideology and designing methods."[23] Avowed targets of the new campaign were designers who were "isolated from the masses and reality," who regarded designing as the prerogative of specialists, and who considered that the masses were "laymen" who should "produce according to design and have no voice in designing itself."[24] Underlying these accusations of professionalism, however, was a renewed effort to emancipate China's technical development from the psychological residue of foreign industrial models. The "designing revolution" was largely an attempt to establish for China a separate technological identity, one based on the proposition that practical knowledge—that is, production practice—ultimately governs the development of scientific principles and that foreign "theory" is hence not immutable in the face of native ingenuity and experience.

In the opinion of some people, only things written in foreign books are scientific while things created by China's working people in the course of practice and, moreover, proved to be rational are not. New machines of foreign countries—despite the fact that they have obvious defects which are proved through their use and some of their parts are irrational—are all said to be scientific and cannot be changed, while innovations made by the Chinese people are arbitrarily described as unscientific, even though they have already proved rational in the course of practice.[25]

The renewed attempt to break away from foreign stereotypes and conventions and to establish a unique road of development for China

---

that egalitarianism and industrialization are not necessarily incompatible goals, at least at China's present stage of development.

[22] "Struggle for Revolutionizing Designing Work," *JMJP*, April 10, 1965, translated in *SCMP*, No. 3498 (1965), p. 7. For an extensive collection of Chinese articles on the designing revolution of 1964–65, see *Cheng-ch'ueh she-chi tsung na-li lai* (Peking: Jenmin jih-pao ch'u-pan-she, 1965).

[23] Fa Ting, "Revolutionize the Designing Work and Develop New Techniques," *Ching-chi yen-chiu* (Economic Research), No. 11 (November 20, 1965), translated in *SCMM*, No. 510 (1965), p. 24.

[24] "Correct Designing Comes from Practice," *JMJP*, April 22, 1965, translated in *SCMP*, No. 3459 (1965).

[25] "Develop Science and Technology by Following Our Own Road," p. 18.

required a new concept of technical designing, one which could "develop fully the tremendous role played by the broad masses of workers in science and technology." [26] Technical personnel were told to leave their offices, participate in productive labor at work sites, and integrate theory with practice by "earnestly summing up the inventions and creations of the masses in their designs." [27] The designing process itself became a cooperative enterprise, occurring largely "on the spot" at the production level and comprising the joint efforts of workers, technicians, and leadership cadres. Such three-way combinations "with workers as the mainstay" have, in recent years, allegedly created advanced equipment and technical processes which equal or even surpass world technological standards.

The link between mass initiative in the technical realm and China's emancipation from foreign technological models has been a consistent theme of innovation campaigns stemming from the Great Proletarian Cultural Revolution. The rhetoric of these campaigns invariably blames the limitations on workers' technical creativity in the pre-Leap and post-Leap periods on "foreign rules and systems," and "mechanical application of foreign experience," and on agents of revisionism within the Chinese Communist Party.[28] Such accounts, of course, never describe the decline of "politics" in the technical realm as the result of any inherent deficiencies of worker innovations themselves; nevertheless, they do point to the crucial role of nationalism in promoting the ascendancy of politics over technical administration by experts. The link between politics—defined in this context as a broadly based decision-making process involving producers as well as technical and managerial elites—and nationalism is provided in China by an ideology which closely identifies the oppression of classes in Chinese society with the oppression of the nation as a whole. Such an equation is, of course, not a new one in Chinese Communist ideology; its application to the technical sphere, however, is novel, as are the national stereotypes that result from this application. Replacing the "comprador" of old is the bourgeois expert who perceives modernization in imitative terms and so seeks (albeit perhaps unconsciously)

---

[26] "The Road for Fostering Scientists and Technicians in China," *JMJP*, January 20, 1966, translated in *SCMP*, No. 3632 (1966), p. 15.

[27] Fa Ting, "Revolutionize the Designing Work," p. 12.

[28] "Electro-plating Workers of Loyang Tractor Engine Factory Raise High the Great Banner of Mao Tse-tung's Thought, Defeat Bourgeois Technical Authorities, and Blaze a China-Type New Trail for Technology," *Hung wei-pao* (Red Guard Newspaper), September 14, 1966, translated in *SCMP*, No. 3793 (1966), p. 22.

to perpetuate China's position of inferiority vis-à-vis the rest of the world. And replacing economic exploitation is a new and more insidious variety—the deprivation of the natural right of workers to make creative contributions to building China's industrial future.

THE IDEOLOGY OF INNOVATION

Maoism as an ideology of development is largely a response to two forms of social stratification: that existing between China and the economically advanced nations and that separating technical and managerial elites from "the masses." In the first case, Maoism seeks to rationalize the disparity between Chinese and foreign levels of technological development by arguing that backwardness is, in fact, a source of strength: it represents a historical opportunity to remake old technologies and to fashion new ones that will catch up to and surpass world levels in the not-too-distant future. In the second case, Maoism tries to place modernization within an egalitarian framework by emphasizing that the masses are intelligent participants in the building of a new China, not passive objects of manipulation from above. These two themes—that backwardness is somehow a virtue and that the masses are "the creators of history"—converge in the Maoist theory of innovation, a theory which is ideological in its implications for patterns of stratification within and between nations but which may also offer some practical guidelines for technological change in underdeveloped countries.

Mao's theory of innovation may be analyzed in terms of these relationships in "contradictions" which have governed the cycles of revolutionary activity in China since the Great Leap Forward. First of these is the epistemological relationship between theoretical or book knowledge and direct practical experience; second is the relationship between "experts" and the masses, or between theory and practice expressed in class terms; third is the relationship between foreign industrial models and indigenous styles of technological development. Mao's visions of Chinese society have been fueled to a large extent by China's position of technological inferiority vis-à-vis capitalist or other socialist countries; hence, the third contradiction tends at times to determine the content of the first and second. In other words, by "theory" the Chinese Communists often mean doctrines derived from foreign sources; by "experts" they often mean technocrats who perceive modernization in terms of wholesale imitation of foreign methods. My intention is to show how creation of a "national" technology has served as a unifying theme of Maoist ideology in recent years, how it has determined the parameters of class conflict within Chinese enterprises, and also how it has developed from the special circumstances of industrial weakness and cultural borrowing in twentieth-century China.

THE ROOTS OF IDEOLOGY

Modern ideologies, one might argue, acquire strength by identifying the social distance between "elites" and "masses" with the effects of technological or cultural borrowing.[29] Chinese elites in the twentieth century have, in varying degrees, viewed modernization in terms of replacing the "backward" indigenous culture by the "modern" foreign one, and have, moreover, tended to define their social status in terms of the superior exposure to the latter. As Ting Wen-chiang, a member of China's early Westernized intelligentsia, remarked in 1923: "Only eighty thousand Chinese are college students who know a little about science and have read a few foreign books. If we are not the tiny elite, who is? If we do not have a sense of responsibility, who will?"[30]

The foreign self-definition of many of the educated served as a frequent target for leftist or Communist ridicule and, as far as the Communist movement itself was concerned, for criticism and re-education.[31] Mao Tse-tung, for example, noted in 1941 the tendency of some Party members and sympathizers to be "not ashamed but proud" that they knew nothing about Chinese history. Moreover, he said, "they return from Europe, America, or Japan, and all they know how to do is to recite a stock of undigested foreign phrases. They function as phonographs but forget their own responsibility to create something new."[32] The nativist emphasis of this and other statements, however, did not prevent the Communists in later years from establishing the invidious distinction between "foreign" and "indigenous" in a new and aggravated form. The triumph of the Communist movement in 1949 saw the initiation of the "lean to one side" policy, the internal conse-

[29] See the discussion in Robert Tucker, *The Marxian Revolutionary Idea* (New York: W. W. Norton, 1969), pp. 110–30.

[30] Charlotte Furth, *Ting Wen-chiang: Science and China's New Culture* (Cambridge, Mass.: Harvard University Press, 1970), p. 163.

[31] For some caricatures of China's foreignized intelligentsia of the 1930's, see Mao Tun, *Midnight* (Peking: Foreign Languages Press, 1957), p. 157; and Ts'ao Yu, *Sunrise* (Peking: Foreign Languages Press, 1960), pp. 63–64.

[32] Mao Tse-tung, "The Reconstruction of Our Studies," in Boyd Compton (ed. and trans.), *Mao's China: Party Reform Documents, 1942–44* (Seattle and London: University of Washington Press, 1966), pp. 62–63.

quence of which was to impose on Chinese the requirement of imitating "Soviet advanced experience" in virtually every professional sphere. The regime's conscious dependence upon the USSR as a prototype of China's industrial future required the resocialization of the bourgeois intellectuals—not in order that they might "create something new" but in order that they might change their pro-Western orientation for a pro-Soviet one. Sometimes, it seems, old loyalties died hard: ". . . at the bottom of their hearts some designing personnel are still infatuated with the technology of capitalist countries, considering the British and American technical standards and designing norms to be unbreakable and their experience to be irrefutable, and maintain a skeptical and even resisting attitude towards the advanced designing experience and technique of the Soviet Union." [33]

The Great Leap Forward marked the beginning of attempts by the Communist regime to incorporate distinctively native elements into the creation of an industrial society in China. The shift in emphasis from heavy dependence upon the USSR to assertions of native capabilities in technology and other fields could hardly fail to lower the status of professionals in Chinese society. Communist rhetoric now criticized the intellectuals not for having the wrong foreign orientation, but for having a foreign orientation at all. Their "feelings of self-abasement before foreigners," their "racial inferiority complex," their contempt for China's national heritage and for "the inventions and creations of their own people" contrasted sharply, according to the stereotypes invoked in the Great Leap, with the pioneering qualities of the Chinese masses.[34] The ideology of the Leap closely linked the ideas of native and mass, and virtually redefined Chinese "culture" as equivalent to work experiences created in the course of indigenous production. Innovations resulting from these experiences were viewed as the fountainhead of a distinctively native technology—which as a "culture-concept" had the apparent advantage of being able to satisfy the dual claims of nationalism and industrialization. The notion of a native technology, moreover, acquired during this period a certain historical legitimacy. "The forefathers of the Chinese working people were known for their creativeness," said a 1958 *Kung-jen jih-pao* (Workers' Daily) editorial. "Inasmuch as they could invent gun-

---

[33] "For Establishing Correct Concepts of Designing," *JMJP*, October 14, 1953, translated in *SCMP*, No. 669 (1953), p. 14.

[34] Nieh Jung-chen, "The New Climate in the Technological Revolution in the Factories," *Hung-ch'i*, No. 8 (April 16, 1960), translated in *JPRS*, No. 3591 (1960), p. 4.

powder, the compass, etc., can there be any doubt that the liberated working people of China today, led by the Communist Party, enjoying the advantage of the socialist system and becoming masters of the country will certainly invent new technology unknown to the world?" [35] Mass creativity and innovation, in other words, were defined as a part of China's cultural heritage, and one which promised to retain validity as China progressed toward industrialization and modernization.

MAOIST EPISTEMOLOGY AND THE PARAMETERS OF POLITICAL STRUGGLE IN ENTERPRISES

The conceptual basis of China's working class culture, and its continuing role during modernization, stems from an essentially Marxian principle, given particular emphasis by Mao, that all genuine theories stem from direct experience, particularly experience in the "struggle for production." The notion that production practice is the fountainhead of theoretical knowledge provides a convenient rationale for policies that make theory-building in the realm of science and technology a prerogative of those engaged in productive labor. Maoist doctrine defines the problem of class largely in terms of the exclusiveness of ideas. "Technology," according to a statement written during the Great Leap, "does not fall from the skies," but is the summation of labor in action. Hence, the argument runs, technology is nothing mysterious and can be easily grasped by the masses of people.[36] As the property of the masses, theories develop primarily on the basis of innovations and creations made in response to practical problems of production. To argue that theory is primarily deductive and develops according to autonomous inner laws is, the Communists argue, to defend the class nature of ideas, to deny the creative intelligence of the laborer, and to confine his role to the mere working out in practice of designs formulated by specialists.

The proposition that the masses' "rich experiences and creations in production practice are always the source" of science and technology makes little sense except as an ideological statement about class.[37] Communist dogma asserts that under the system of class exploitation, the opposition between classes, expressed in the division between men-

---

[35] "The Clarion of the Technological Revolution," *KJJP*, May 29, 1958, translated in *SCMP*, No. 1788 (1958), p. 8.

[36] "Carry Out the Technological Revolution," *JMJP*, June 3, 1958, translated in *SCMP*, No. 1788 (1958), p. 3.

[37] "On Scientific Experiment," *Hung-ch'i*, No. 1 (January, 1965), translated in *JPRS*, No. 28,667 (February 8, 1965), p. 37.

tal and manual labor, "separates the experts of science and technology who specialize in scientific experiments from the broad laboring masses." [38] Class exploitation greatly restricts the role played by the masses in innovation or experimentation, which are forms of mental activity denied to them by the social division of labor. Liberation from class exploitation, on the other hand, means that the masses' "inexhaustible wisdom and strength for creating new things" can come to the fore. In China, the Communists claim, Party policies of integrating mental and manual labor have enabled the masses of workers to engage in creative labor and make important contributions in revising outdated theories and in enriching the body of scientific and technological knowledge as a whole.[39]

The politics of technology in Communist China has greatly benefited from the nativist strain in Maoism, which has tended to characterize the relation between theory and practice as a cleavage between foreign dogmatism and the insight and experience of the Chinese working masses. The latter, according to recent stereotypes, "are the most intelligent, have the best practical experience, and have never nursed the fetish of foreign dogmas." [40] Technocratic elites, on the other hand, tend to "bury their heads in piles of foreign books" and to regard foreign technological theories and equipment as "inviolable." [41] It follows from this argument that the distribution of technical power to the masses (the subordination of technology to "politics") is likely to promote reforms in foreign technology, and to break new ground in the nation's industrial development. Such reforms typically follow, in Communist polemics, a confrontation between workers and experts over technical problems which according to foreign doctrines are insoluble or which the expert ignores as beyond the parameters of "science." Various accounts from the Cultural Revolution describe these confrontations as follows. Plant X imports a foreign machine. Workers operate the machine and on the basis of their practical experience discover defects and faults in it; they therefore insist on renovating the machine. The technical "authority" in charge, however, opposes the proposals on grounds that they "have no scientific basis,"

38 *Ibid.*, p. 38.

39 Chu Chi-lin, "The Technical Revolution Rolls On," *Peking Review*, February 9, 1960, p. 18.

40 "Doctrine of Trailing Behind at a Snail's Pace Is the Reactionary Philosophy of Slavish Comparadores," *Peking Review*, December 5, 1969, p. 26.

41 Pan Yu-ming, "I Will Integrate with Workers All My Life," *Hung-ch'i*, No. 1 (January 1, 1969), translated in *SCMM*, No. 642 (1969), p. 18; see also "Correctly Unfold the Technical Innovation Movement," p. 7.

"do not exist in foreign countries," "cannot be found in books," and
also on grounds that workers are "rough persons with no capacity
to change foreign equipment." The workers, on the other hand, argue
that "foreign equipment is a paper tiger"—imposing in its outward
appearance but possessing many inherent defects—and unable to
fulfill the urgent needs of the state.[42] In one case, notable as an illus-
tration of the dependency orientation of China's technocrats, workers
came up with ideas for reforming some imported machinery and the
"authorities" reportedly told them: "This is a foreign machine. Every
part of it is based on a scientific theory. You should not interfere with
it." The workers, however, went ahead and renovated the equipment
anyway, with good results.[43]

The peculiar juxtaposition, in Maoist ideology, between control over
technology, class relationships, and China's technological self-assertion
vis-à-vis foreign countries derives from the ambiguity of the technician's role within enterprises and within the nation's scheme of
modernization as a whole. The function and powers of the technical
professional are based on his supposed command of theoretical or
"book" knowledge. This knowledge, however, represents for the
most part a body of doctrine alien to China rather than a summation
of native experience in production. As a result, nativist emphases in
technological development have had the effect of forcing technical
personnel to "adopt the revolutionary style of penetrating practice
and aligning with the masses."[44] The creative powers of the masses,
the argument goes, are inexhaustible and are a rich source for the development of new technology. Separation from the masses and from
labor causes technicians to "entertain a superstitious belief in foreign
books on which they rely and from which they seek design blueprints."[45] As a result, they fail "to solve the problem of where new
technology comes from":

> Some designing personnel consider that if it is not foreign . . . it cannot be
> considered new technology, thus looking down on the renovations and innovations
> of the masses. . . . They have failed to solve the problem of where the new

[42] See, for example, "Anshan Seamless Steel Tubing Plant Increases Production through
Reform and Improvement of Foreign Equipment," *KMJP*, August 27, 1966, p. 3.

[43] "Technological Revolution Underway in Peking Printing Plant," NCNA (Peking),
November 20, 1968, in *SCMP*, No. 4306 (1968), p. 18.

[44] Fa Ting, "Revolutionize the Designing Work and Develop New Techniques," p. 23.

[45] "First Break the Cult of Foreign Technology and Eliminate Inferiority Complex:
Establish the Proletarian World Outlook and the Lofty Goal of Surpassing the Advanced," *JMJP*, November 13, 1965, translated in *SCMP*, No. 3588 (1965), p. 8.

technology comes from and the dependence of new technology on production practice.

. . . It is only when the designing personnel penetrate practice and earnestly sum up the renovations and innovations of the masses that it will be possible to contribute to the development of new technology.[46]

The postulated dependence of new technology upon the creations of the masses in China has led in practice to the institutionalized participation of workers in technical designing of new equipment, processes, and products. This aspect of Chinese Communist managerial doctrine is unheard of in most countries, where the separation between mental and manual labor in industry is epitomized in the distinction between laboratory and production line, between the drawing up of blueprints and their mechanical implementation in productive practice. The institutional form for mass participation in designing work in China is the so-called three-in-one combination of workers, technical personnel, and cadres. The focal point or center of gravity of the triple combination determines the degree to which workers exercise technical power within the enterprise. According to one article, written just prior to the Cultural Revolution, there are two possible "fronts" for the practice of triple integration: one is the office, the other is the actual production site. To make the office the front is a method "comparatively divorced from realities" and antithetical to the promotion of "technical democracy." To make the production site the front, however, allows for the "penetrating and thorough investigation of the situation" and allows the absorption of the "views of the broad masses of workers." [47]

A more recent article, written in early 1970, described the merging of designing with production in one factory in part as follows:

1. Sending some of the designing personnel to the workshops to study, labor, do designing, and carry out trial manufacture together with the workers so as to change the past situation of concentration of intellectual elements in the offices and their grave detachment from reality, from the masses, and from manual labor.
2. Merging some of the technological offices with the workshops they serve so that technological personnel could design or conduct research in the workshops and by the sides of machines and honestly learn from the workers.[48]

[46] Fa Ting, "Revolutionize the Designing Work and Develop New Techniques," p. 25.
[47] Chiao Jung-chang, "Industrial Technical Innovation and Technological Revolution in China," *Ching-chi yen-chiu,* No. 10 (October, 1965), pp. 49–50.
[48] "Educate Engineering and Technical Personnel with Mao Tse-tung's Thought," *JMJP,* January 10, 1970, p. 2.

The relocation of designers to workshops marks the end of a chapter in managerial relations in Communist China. According to Chinese claims in the aftermath of the Cultural Revolution, a new revolutionary technical intelligentsia has emerged to take the place of the bourgeois experts—a proletarian elite which has shed its intellectual airs and its faith in foreign doctrines after receiving "education and assistance" from the workers.[49] There is evidence, however, that the mass campaigns of recent years have carried the integration of mental and manual labor to a point unacceptable even to the Maoist regime. The stereotype of the revolutionary technician is clouded by recent Communist complaints that a number of scientific and technical personnel in the Cultural Revolution simply abdicated their intellectual functions entirely, having acquired (not surprisingly) in the ideological climate of the period "the idea that labor is safe and technical work is dangerous." [50] An effort is underway to divest theory of its bourgeois and revisionist connotations, and to assign to intellectuals a more creative role in technical innovation and change. Communist writers still perceive theory and research as serving a largely explanatory function (such as concentrating the experiences of the masses, providing scientific explanations for their innovations); moreover, the creation of new technology is still regarded as a cooperative enterprise of technicians, cadres, and workers. Nevertheless, the Communists seem anxious to define for theoretical work an image which, while proletarian in content, makes some concessions to the rules and procedures of science.[51] In so doing, they may be laying the basis for new hierarchies of technical management within Chinese industrial enterprises.

FUNCTIONAL ASPECTS OF TECHNICAL DEMOCRACY

Technical rationality is an important theme in the Communists' attempt to integrate theory and practice in Chinese enterprises. Communist sources in both the Great Leap and the Cultural Revolution have constantly emphasized that class hierarchies of ideas in which native or mass opinions were deemed inferior to "expert" or foreign

---

[49] *Ibid.*

[50] "Intensify Re-education of Intellectuals and Let Technical Personnel Play Their Parts to the Full," *KMJP,* September 7, 1971, translated in *SCMP,* No. 4978 (1971), p. 3.

[51] For a recent statement defending the legitimacy of scientific-technical work, see Ko Yen, "Strive to Make a Success of Scientific Research for the Revolution," *Hung-ch'i,* No. 11 (October 1, 1971), translated in *SCMM,* No. 715–16 (November, 1971), pp. 81–88.

ones often run counter to the requirements of China's industrial development. Reliance on the masses, on the other hand, leads to "greater, faster, better, and more economical results" in the development of technology. Note, for example, the following passage:

> The comrade workers of the electro-plating team of the Loyang Tractor Engine Factory carried out a complete and thorough revolution against imported Soviet doctrine—and created an automatic system for the productive process of electroplating. What were considered by technical "authorities" as old, big, and difficult problems have all been solved by us uneducated workers. We demolished the principle of smaller, slower poorer and less economical results of the "imported authorities" and blazed a new trail to greater, faster, better, and more economical results.[52]

The impact of workers' innovations upon the nature and direction of China's technical modernization may be summarized under two headings: first, the reform of foreign equipment and the development of an independent designing capability; and second, the use of medium- and small-scale industry to provide a broad "front" for experimentation and the generation of technical novelty.[53]

ASSIMILATION AND NATIVIZATION

Technical democracy in China is supposed, first of all, to promote the transformation of foreign technological inputs into something that is distinctively Chinese. The process of assimilating foreign technology and imparting to it "native" characteristics often involves a process of rationalization and simplification. There seems to be a law of decreasing complexity characterizing the progress of foreign blueprints or prototypes from the country in question to the hands of the Chinese working class. The "law of decreasing complexity" seems to be based on the proposition that such phenomena as "formalism," unnecessary complexity, and waste of raw materials in designing "are rather universal in foreign countries" and represent "dregs" which should be eliminated.[54] On the theory that the unity of theory

[52] "Electro-plating Workers of Loyang Tractor Engine Factory Raise High the Great Banner of Mao Tse-tung's Thought," p. 22.

[53] On the importance of an independent designing capability and China's problems in developing one, see G. Uchida, "Technology in China," *Scientific American,* CCXV, No. 5 (November, 1966), 37–40. For an excellent account of China's technological policy, see E. E. Wheelwright and Bruce MacFarlane, *The Chinese Road to Socialism* (New York: Monthly Review Press, 1970), pp. 162–79.

[54] "Break the Cult of Foreign Technology: Develop Creativeness," *JMJP,* November 13, 1965, translated in *SCMP,* No. 3588 (1965), p. 6.

and practice can accomplish "greater, faster, better, and more economical results," workers often play an important part in rationalizing imported machinery and in simplifying designs drawn from foreign
sources. An article written in 1958, for example, noted that at the
Shenyang Tool Plant workers, along with technical personnel and
administrative staff, were invited to modify the design of three
Soviet-type lathes and that their joint efforts resulted in the elimination of twelve hundred redundant parts (a procedure reportedly described by the workers as "cutting out the appendix"). As a result of
the success of this operation, said the article, "more and more machine-
tool plants are catching on to this idea and establishing native-style
designing institutes right inside the workshops." [55] Another article, also
describing the machine-building industry, noted that the effect of mass
innovation had been to break down many superstitious beliefs connected with designing, such as "the more materials we use in building, the stronger the machine will become," and "equipment of the
higher levels cannot be simplified." The same article noted that the
participation of workers of the machine-building industry in the renovation of machines "clumsy in build or complex in structure and low
in efficiency" was an example of the "thorough implementation of the
Party's policy for simultaneous attention to native and foreign methods
and walking on two legs." [56]

Communist writing since the so-called designing revolution of 1964–
65 has continued to emphasize the need for designers to overcome
their spiritual enslavement to foreign technique and to rely upon the
masses and on practical experience for creating rational, Chinese-
type designs.[57] Articles appearing during the Cultural Revolution have
been replete with instances in which three-way combinations or even
workers themselves created new machines that are simpler in structure and more efficient than imported machines of the same type [58] A
recent article has described "an important aspect of mass technical
innovation in China" as making "bold changes in the design of
products" and creating "new Chinese-type products characterized by

[55] Chu Chi-lin, "Machine-building Industry Races Ahead," *Peking Review,* December 9, 1958.
[56] "Workers of Machine-building Industry Revolutionize Old Products," *KJJP,* September 23, 1960, translated in *JPRS,* No. 7135 (November 30, 1960), pp. 2–3, 6–7.
[57] See "Break the Cult of Foreign Technology."
[58] For example, "Revolutionary Mass Repudiation Spurs Technical Innovations Campaign in Peking," NCNA (Peking), May 2, 1968, in *SCMP,* No. 4177 (1968), p. 20;
"Shanghai Technicians Refute Soviet Revisionist Slander," NCNA (Peking), October 9,
1968, in *SCMP,* No. 42,979 (1968).

their small size, lightness, high efficiency, and simple structure." [59] Another article described the process of rationalizing foreign patterns and stereotypes in technology:

Ordinary lathes of the C620-1 model, which represented the bulk of the output of the works, were products of a foreign pattern. To get rid of this label of a foreign pattern as quickly as possible, the revolutionary committee of the plant [the Shenyang No. 1 Lathe Works] closely relied on the masses to innovate the product and the design on a big scale. They boldly roused the masses to think about the matter and to suggest methods. They drew designs and conducted trial manufacturing simultaneously. They took less than half a year's time to cover the course from designing to trial production. After this innovation the number of parts of this new product decreased by 27% and its weight was reduced by 15%. [60]

Another important function of technical democracy in China, aside from improving and reducing the complexity of product designs, has been to shorten the production cycle, or the time elapsed from the initial conception of a required product to the product's actual manufacture. Lengthening of the production cycle results, according to Maoist industrial doctrine, "from the old convention of designing behind closed doors" and from overreliance on foreign books and technical data. Contraction of the production cycle results, on the other hand, from reliance on the masses and from adopting the method of simultaneously drawing designs and conducting trial manufacture. [61] Integration of technical designing with production is, in effect, a political formula for maximizing the speed of technical modernization in industry—one which demonstrates quite clearly the Communists' intention to combine economic and political forms of development in building a modern industrial state.

NATIVE AND MASS: THE CONCEPT OF EVOLUTIONARY POTENTIAL

The Great Leap and later the Cultural Revolution saw the appearance of numerous technological "miracles," created in the solving of practical problems of production, that confounded foreign scientific "laws" and practices. [62] Many of these miracles of technique resulted

59 Chi Wei, "China's Industry Is Forging Ahead," *Peking Review*, January 1, 1971.

60 "How an Old, Big, Foreign Enterprise Makes Still Greater Contributions to the State," *JMJP*, September 4, 1970, translated in *SCMP*, No. 4740 (1970), p. 94.

61 For example, see "New Situation of All-round Forward Leap on Industrial and Communications Fronts in Five Central-South China Provinces," *Hung wei-pao* (Canton), September 30, 1966, translated in *SCMP*, No. 3801 (1966), p. 14; "Advances Are Made through Struggle," *China Reconstructs*, XIX, No. 1 (January, 1970), 15–17.

62 Ho Chih-ping, "Help the Native to Digest the Foreign," p. 7.

according to Communist press accounts, from the use of native methods—"simple but by no means backward" [63]—and occurred within medium- or small-scale enterprises that were relatively lacking in specialized equipment, foreign technical data, and "technical forces." Some of these factories, Communist sources indicate, comprised only a few ramshackle bamboo huts, some old, broken-down tools and equipment, and a number of workers.[64] In the course of transforming these "poor and blank" enterprises, however, workers were reportedly able to create some new production techniques and even some advanced-type products which served as examples for enterprises employing the latest machinery and equipment from abroad.[65]

One may divide technical innovations campaigns roughly into two categories. The first involves foreign equipment and designs based on foreign books or prototypes and takes the form of a class struggle against "imported doctrines" and their technician-custodians. The second involves the creation of new techniques in enterprises which possess relatively simple equipment and are not bound to a given type of product or production procedure. Such "grass-roots" innovation reflects an extremely important tenet of Maoist doctrine, namely, that apparent backwardness can be a developmental asset and that an underdeveloped country such as China has certain evolutionary potentials that advanced nations lack. This argument for evolutionary potential appears most obviously in Mao's metaphorical comparison of China to a blank sheet of paper which lends itself admirably to receive the "newest and most beautiful words" and "the newest and most beautiful pictures." [66] What is important to note is that the responsibility for changing China's blank state lies, according to Maoist doctrine, largely with China's masses, using native methods to create inventions and innovations outside the framework of China's "foreign" industrial sector.

The native-mass concept continues to be a major theme of technical innovations campaigns in China. The Maoist view of blankness

[63] "Ko Ching-shih Analyzes Technical Revolution in Shanghai," NCNA (Shanghai), March 28, 1960, in *SCMP*, No. 2229 (1960), p. 27.

[64] Hsu Tze-hua, "Back-Street Rolling Mill," *China Reconstructs*, VIII, No. 8 (August, 1959), 12–13; Po I-po, "New Situation in the Technical Revolution," *Peking Review*, May 31, 1960, p. 20; Chang Wang, "A New Picture of Leap Forward in Economic Construction at Changhang," NCNA (Canton), September 29, 1966, in URS, XLV (1966), 294.

[65] See, for example, "Mass of Small Modern Enterprises Advances from Victory to Victory," *JMJP*, February 8, 1960, translated in *SCMP*, No. 2196 (1960), p. 4.

[66] Mao Tse-tung, *The Political Thought of Mao Tse-tung*, ed. and trans. Stuart R. Schram (New York: Praeger, 1963), p. 253.

as a virtue may be summarized in technological terms as follows: the less the capital outlay within a given enterprise, the greater the scope for technical innovation. "Medium- and small-scale enterprises," according to a recent *Jen-min jih-pao* editorial, "being a blank sheet of paper, are not laden with any burden nor restricted by rules and regulations. They can boldly create and carry out innovations and serve as pacesetters in the search for new techniques of all kinds." Those who "pursue large size and things foreign" do not understand that "continuous innovations in industrial technique can only come from production practice. The longer the production front is extended and the richer production practice becomes, the faster will be technological development." Also, said the article, a lengthened production front "will give the millions of masses a vast scope for working out technical innovations and give full play to the wisdom and ingenuity of our working people, so as to promote continuous development of technology and scale the peak of world science and technology." [67]

Continuous expansion of the industrial front means, in Maoist doctrine, that "the road of progress becomes broader and broader" for the Chinese. Promotion of "native-mass" industrialization seems to rest on the assumption that reliance on imported technique and large-scale "foreign" industries will force China into a sort of evolutionary cul-de-sac. The native-mass concept dictates that the smaller the factory, the less committed it is to a given production procedure, the greater the scope for experimentation and innovation. To rely on the masses and on native methods, according to this argument, will permit China shortly to reach and surpass world technological levels, if only because "native methods are clever methods" and can produce more results with the expenditure of fewer resources. [68]

CONCLUDING COMMENTS

The function of "politics" in Communist China is largely to redistribute opportunities of generating technological and cultural change. This redistribution occurs at the expense of professional elites and results in a close integration of change-producing actions with participation in labor. The integration of innovation and production, of technology and labor, presents an obvious contrast to the development process in modern industrial societies. Since the late nine-

---

[67] "Simultaneous Development of Large-size, Medium- and Small-size Enterprises," *JMJP*, August 24, 1970, translated in *SCMP*, No. 4731 (1970), pp. 73–75.

[68] *Ibid.*, p. 74.

teenth century, in fact, applications of theoretical science, as opposed to products of mechanical ingenuity, have increasingly governed the course of technical and industrial advance in the West.[69] Modern technological activity is, by all indications, thoroughly professional, based upon formal scientific training, highly specialized, and carried on in specific institutions (such as the industrial research laboratory) devoted exclusively to technological innovation.[70] Technological modernity means, or seems to, that scientific-technological theory is more likely to guide the development of productive practice than vice-versa (a point which Benjamin Schwartz makes eminently clear in his paper).

The Chinese Communists have partly repudiated these structural features of modernity in their approach to modernization. Their efforts to proletarianize the sources of innovation and change owe a debt to Marxism—certainly to Marx's views on labor and alienation —and, moreover, are not entirely unique within the Communist movement. In the Soviet Union, for example, writers point to technical creativity among workers as part of the gradual unification of mental and manual labor in the period of Communist construction.[71] Maoist ideology, however, has viewed problems of alienation not only in terms of the relation between mental and manual labor (workers' enslavement to machines, management of technology by experts) but also in

[69] See Daniels, *Science in American Society,* p. 271.

[70] See the discussion in Peter Drucker, *Technology, Management and Society* (New York: Harper & Row, 1970), pp. 56–62.

[71] See, for example, M. T. Yuvchuk, "The Social Significance of the Rise of the Worker's Level of Culture and Skill," *Soviet Sociology,* VI, No. 1–2 (Summer–Fall, 1967), 19–20.

Western managerial doctrines, though often addressed to the problem of alienation in industry, tend to define it mainly in terms of the subdivision of tasks. A typical, and not entirely successful, American solution to the problem is a practice called "job enlargement"—the redesigning of jobs to include a larger number of components of a given productive system. Job enlargement may give workers more responsibility and perhaps a greater sense of purpose in their work, but does not in itself prescribe worker participation in designing the equipment and processes that make up the productive system. This remains the prerogative of technical management. On this subject, see Louis Davis, "Toward a Theory of Job Design," *Journal of Industrial Engineering,* VIII, No. 5 (September–October, 1957), 305–7.

The Yugoslav experiment in workers' self-management does not seem to involve workers' participation in technical matters. "Workers councils" elect a management board which deals with such matters as pricing, production, and financial planning, statutes of the enterprise, allocation of net income, and budgeting. Normal operation of the factory is governed by a hierarchy similar to that in Soviet or Western enterprises. See Gerry Hunnius, "The Yugoslav System of Decentralization and Self-Management," in C. George Benello and Dimitri Roussopoulos (eds.), *The Case for Participatory Democracy: Some Prospects for the Radical Society* (New York: Grossman, 1971), pp. 151–61.

terms of China's technological relations with other countries. The addition of a foreign dimension to alienation has significantly increased the scope and intensity of innovations campaigns in China, and has subordinated technology to politics to a degree unprecedented elsewhere.

The Chinese Communists view mass participation in innovation as a method of incorporating distinctively native elements into the creation of a modern industrial state. Similarly, they equate "expert" monopolies over the sources of innovation and change in China with uncritical imitation of foreigners and with the failure to develop independent capabilities in the development of technology. The issue of whether or not to rely primarily on foreign technological models and on "experts" or on native initiative and "the masses" has been a major factor governing the cyclical changes in Communist economic policy over the years. But China has come a great distance since the years of "learning and grasping Soviet advanced experience," and it seems likely that the remaining technological symbols of China's dependency upon the outside world will be assimilated through innovation and ultimately replaced by "advanced Chinese-type designs." For this reason the equations of "foreign and expert" and "native and mass" faces an uncertain future in China. Distinctively native technical reference works and machine or product designs, reflecting the "rich experiences" of the masses in production, may become the source of new hierarchies in Chinese economic life. Maoist epithets such as "book worship," "fetishism of technology," "expert line," and "separation from the masses and reality" all retain connotations of foreignization; hence, one may wonder what will happen to Mao's egalitarian ethos as China attains higher levels of modernization and technological self-confidence. The worker-innovator figure is, in a sense, the fruit of more than a century of various eclectic formulas designed to adapt China to the challenge presented by modern industrialism. His tribulations as the appendage of foreign machinery, and his triumphs as the inventor of new Chinese techniques, symbolize to some extent the transition from alienation to independence which has characterized the learning process for China as a developing nation. His technical power may fade, however, where the problem of alienation ceases to reflect China's relations with foreign countries, but becomes a function of class hierarchies and factory technology alone.

❀❀❀❀❀❀❀❀❀❀❀❀❀❀❀❀❀❀❀❀❀❀❀❀❀

PHILIP L. BRIDGHAM

The International Impact
of Maoist Ideology

> Actually the situation within the socialist camp is quite simple.
> The sole question is one of class struggle—a question of struggle be-
> tween the proletariat and the bourgeoisie, a question of struggle between
> Marxism-Leninism and anti-Marxism-Leninism, a question of struggle
> between Marxism-Leninism and revisionism. . . . The question of class
> struggle [in China] is [also] a question of struggle between Marxism
> and revisionism. . . . It seems that it is better to rename Right oppor-
> tunism as revisionism in China.
>
> MAO TSE-TUNG, Speech at Central Committee Plenum,
> September 24, 1962

If Maoist ideology is defined loosely as a body of ideas derived from
Marxist-Leninist doctrines and shaped by half a century's experience
of the Chinese Communist revolution, this paper is then primarily
concerned with the international impact of the more extreme version of
Maoism which began to emerge in the fall of 1962 and eventually
culminated in the Cultural Revolution. In common with other ideologies, this more extreme variant of Maoism consisted of (1) a theory of
the nature of society (which explained human conduct as largely determined by "class nature"); (2) a program of social and political
change (featuring, as suggested by the quotations cited above, "class
struggle"); and (3) a call to action (a call addressed, in addition to the
domestic audience, to a foreign audience composed variously of governments, Communist parties, revolutionary groups, and other "revolutionary leftists" presumed receptive to this more militant version of
Maoism).[1] Although the international impact of this appeal to continue

[1] For a discussion of the components of ideology, see Maurice Cranston, "Ideologies,
Past and Present," *Survey*, No. 70/71 (Winter/Spring, 1969/70), pp. 3–11.

the revolution both at home and abroad provides the central theme, this paper will also discuss the reciprocal impact of developments abroad upon Maoist ideology.

It is a thesis of this paper that the more extreme version of Maoism that began to appear in the fall of 1962 was intended primarily to justify and legitimate Mao's rule in the face of domestic opposition within China. But while the claims that this leftist variant of Mao's ideology was the acme of Marxism-Leninism in the present era may have enhanced the authority of Mao within China, the increasingly overt and extravagant nature of these claims only served to affront foreign Communist parties intent upon following their own "national roads" to socialism. While the accompanying ideological and organizational challenge to the Soviet Union for leadership over the international Communist movement may have aroused a patriotic response and thus strengthened Mao's political position at home, the extreme lengths to which Mao was prepared to carry this challenge had the negative effect abroad of alienating friends and neutrals until China stood virtually alone among her former Communist allies.

Moreover, this challenge was accompanied by a widely publicized view that a revolutionary upsurge featuring armed struggle and employing Maoist strategy was imminent in the underdeveloped world of Asia, Africa, and Latin America. Again, while this view might have elevated Mao's prestige in China, the net effect externally of this more militant revolutionary posture was to alarm the national bourgeois governments in these areas—especially in Africa—and to dissipate the assets and good will built up laboriously over a decade by means of economic assistance, trade, and conventional diplomacy. Finally, although the utopianism and violence of the Cultural Revolution could be justified as essential to overthrow Mao's opposition entrenched within the Party bureaucracy at home, the overall effect abroad of this spectacle of licensed anarchism was to reduce China's international prestige to its lowest point in two decades, with only the student radicals of the "New Left" responding favorably.

If Mao's obsession with "class struggle" in the fall of 1962 [2] reflected also a genuine concern for continuing the revolution both at home and abroad, the opposition engendered by this simplistic and dis-

---

[2] Note, for example, Mao's statement at the Tenth Plenum: "From now on, we must discuss classes and class struggle every year, every month, every day." In "Speech Delivered by Mao Tse-tung at the Tenth Plenum of the Eighth Chinese Communist Party (CCP) Central Committee," *Talks and Writings of Chairman Mao* (*JPRS*, No. 52029 [December 21, 1970]), p. 29.

torted view of the nature of human society drove him further and further to the left in search of allies. By drawing ever more rigid and restrictive lines of demarcation based upon a metaphysical concept of class nature, Mao and his supporters found themselves increasingly isolated within the international community, the international Communist movement, and within China itself. To correct this "ultra-leftist" deviation, it was finally deemed necessary to point out (at another Central Committee plenum held eight years later in September, 1970) that, in addition to its "class nature," an equally important characteristic of Mao's thought was its "practicality." [3]

Underlining the close relationship between ideology and politics in contemporary China, the discussion which follows concludes that Maoist ideology has changed throughout the 1960's (moving first to the left, then even further left during the Cultural Revolution, and finally back to the right) largely in response to the requirements of political struggle. If the turn to the left which began in 1962 was basically a response to domestic political opposition, the turn to the right in recent years appears to have been stimulated not only by domestic but also by foreign political pressures, especially the growing military threat to China posed by the Soviet Union. Having veered sharply to the left during the Cultural Revolution in an attempt to revolutionize Chinese society and, in time, the world, Maoist ideology has been forced once again (as it did a decade earlier) to swing back sharply to the right in adjusting to political reality in China and the outside world.

THE TURN TO THE LEFT: PRELUDE TO THE CULTURAL REVOLUTION

In proclaiming his own "general line" for the Communists of the world in the summer of 1963, Mao Tse-tung issued an across-the-board indictment of Soviet "revisionism" as manifested in both foreign policy (peaceful coexistence) and domestic policy (the elimination of class struggle as a basic motivating force in socialist society):

It is wrong to make peaceful coexistence the general line of the foreign policy of the socialist countries. In our view, the general line [must also include] proletarian internationalism . . . and support and assistance to the revolutionary struggles of all the oppressed peoples and nations. . . . To deny the existence of class struggle in the period of the dictatorship of the proletariat and the necessity of

---

[3] "Conscientiously Study Chairman Mao's Philosophical Works," *JMJP*, October 30, 1970 (editorial), in *Peking Review*, XIII, No. 45 (November 6, 1970), 4.

thoroughly completing the socialist revolution on the economic, political, and ideological fronts is wrong, does not correspond to objective reality and violates Marxism-Leninism.[4]

In place of the false "revisionist" line of Khrushchev, Peking offered an "authentic Marxist-Leninist" general line for the international Communist movement embodying what has been called Mao's "optimum global vision"[5]—a world Communist movement reconstituted under Chinese leadership and dedicated to promoting revolution based on China's "revolutionary model" in the underdeveloped and oppressed areas of Asia, Africa, and Latin America. Implicit in this polemical attack was Mao's prescription of the proper way to build socialism after the seizure of power, a prescription featuring class struggle, heroic poverty, and collective enthusiasm and also based in large part on China's own revolutionary experience in Yenan. This attempt to recast Marxism-Leninism in the image of Mao's own experience in both revolution and construction would, by provoking further opposition at home and abroad, lead in time to the violence, extremism, and pariahlike isolation of China during the Cultural Revolution.

The strategy employed in the first stage of this swing to the left during 1963–64 was, in retrospect, relatively flexible and pragmatic. In its ideological and organizational challenge to the Soviet Union for leadership over the international Communist movement, Peking throughout this period championed the national independence of Communist parties; in place of Soviet domination, it offered a more benign organizational model for the movement in which China's leading role would be recognized voluntarily by the other parties.[6] The same, at least nominally, reliance on persuasion characterized the Chinese approach to "the great debate in Marxism-Leninism" with the Soviets throughout this period, viewed by Peking as an international rectification campaign designed to convince "the leadership of the Communist Party of the Soviet Union to correct its errors and return to the path of Marxism-Leninism. . . ."[7]

Mao's revolutionary doctrines appealed, moreover, to the leadership

---

[1] "A Proposal concerning the General Line of the International Communist Movement," *JMJP*, June 17, 1963, in *Peking Review*, VI, No. 25 (June 21, 1963), 15–16.

[5] Benjamin I. Schwartz, *Communism and China: Ideology in Flux* (Cambridge, Mass.: Harvard University Press, 1968), p. 186.

[6] Richard Lowenthal, *World Communism: The Disintegration of a Secular Faith* (New York: Oxford University Press, 1965), p. 260.

[7] "The Origin and Development of the Differences between the Leadership of the C.P.S.U. and Ourselves," article by the editorial departments of *JMJP* and *Hung-ch'i* (Red Flag), in *Peking Review*, VI, No. 37 (September 13, 1963), 20.

of a number of Communist parties who, viewing the Soviet emphasis on "peaceful coexistence" as harmful to their own revolutionary interests, were attracted by the anticolonial, anti-imperialist, and anti-American core of Maoist strategy. This was particularly true in Asia where by the end of 1964 the great majority of Communist parties (including the important parties in Indonesia, North Vietnam, North Korea, and Japan) had opted for Peking's more aggressive revolutionary strategy, in which United States "imperialism" was the main enemy and in which elimination of American power and influence from Asia was the common goal.[8] Despite a number of problems—logistical (distance), organizational (the pro-Soviet complexion of existing parties), and ideological (the competing revolutionary doctrines of "Castroism")—some progress in setting up pro-Chinese Communist parties was also achieved in Latin America during this early period.[9]

In Africa, however, even in this early period, Peking's attempt to project its influence abroad by advocating revolution based on the Chinese model received its first setback. As the second most important area of Chinese foreign policy, the newly independent nations of Africa had, up to this time, been cultivated by a broad-gauged program combining political blandishment, economic and technical assistance, and cultural diplomacy. But Peking's ideological pronouncement in late 1963 that "socialist countries were duty bound" to serve as "base areas" in support of "armed struggle" in "the extremely favorable revolutionary situation [which] now exists in Asia, Africa and Latin America," followed shortly by Premier Chou En-lai's observation (on completing a tour of ten African countries) that "revolutionary prospects are excellent throughout the African continent," could only be regarded with suspicion by Africa's new leaders.[10] As leaders of national bourgeois governments, it was a natural reaction to question whether they themselves were the object of the "armed struggle" emphasized in China's revolutionary model, the more so since that model called for "proletarian" leadership of the revolution at some point. In addition to this perceived threat of subversion, the new leaders of Africa were increasingly suspicious of Peking's efforts at this time to form a Chinese-led international "united front" directed at both the United States (imperialism) and the Soviet Union (revisionism) when

8 Donald S. Zagoria, "Asia," *Survey,* No. 54 (January, 1965), p. 102.

9 Ernst Halperin, "Latin America," *ibid.,* pp. 160 ff.

10 "Apologists of Neo-colonialism," article by the editorial departments of *JMJP* and *Hung-ch'i,* in *Peking Review,* VI, No. 43 (October 25, 1963), 10; "Premier Chou En-lai Speaks at Mogadishu Mass Rally," *SCMP,* No. 3156 (February 7, 1964), p. 24.

their own national interests dictated nonalignment and the acceptance of economic aid from both.[11]

Paralleling this undertaking to promote revolution abroad was the relatively moderate first stage of the Socialist Education Movement within China, a campaign designed to persuade the Chinese Communist Party and the Chinese people once again (after three years of privation and ignominious retreat from the original goals of the Great Leap Forward and commune programs) of the validity of Mao's approach to building socialism. As revealed in Mao's speech at the Tenth Plenum in September, 1962, it was agreed that for a time economic reconstruction would take priority over political and ideological reform. Mao stated, "We must not allow the class struggle to interfere with our work." [12] In this interim period extending through 1964, the Socialist Education Movement was focused on the countryside in a joint effort to reinstill a "revolutionary spirit" of self-sacrifice in the Chinese people and to re-establish control over agriculture as a prerequisite for new economic development.

Two developments in the winter of 1964–65 foreshadowed a further shift to the left in both domestic and foreign policy. As Lin Piao would subsequently point out in his political report to the Ninth Party Congress, the first of these occurred "at the end of 1964 [when] Chairman Mao convened a working conference of the Central Committee [at which] he denounced Liu Shao-ch'i's bourgeois reactionary line [and] clearly showed the orientation for the approaching great proletarian cultural revolution." [13] Convinced that the Socialist Education Movement had failed, Mao then began to plan a cultural revolution in pursuit of the same goals, but under new management (Lin Piao and others) and employing new methods (coercion and violence).

The second development was the confrontation in Peking between Chairman Mao and Premier Alexei Kosygin on February 11, 1965, during which Mao asserted that if necessary China would continue the struggle against the Soviet Union "for 10,000 years." [14] Perhaps based on the assumption that his previous ideological assault had, as a subsequent Chinese editorial put it, "hastened the bankruptcy of Khru-

---

[11] For a good discussion of Chinese policy in Africa during this period, see Robert A. Scalapino, "Africa and Peking's United Front," *Current Scene,* III, No. 26 (September 1, 1965), 1–10.

[12] "Speech Delivered by Mao Tse-tung at the Tenth Plenum," p. 31.

[13] "Lin Piao's Political Report to the Ninth CCP Congress," NCNA, April 27, 1969.

[14] See the account of this historic meeting by Premier Chou En-lai in the *Washington Evening Star,* May 21, 1971.

shchev's revisionism and [driven] its founder into the grave," Mao's decision at this time to intensify the struggle against Khrushchev's successors would have profound consequences.[15] It dictated the adamant refusal, announced the following month, to join the Soviet Union in any form of "united action" in aid of North Vietnam, a refusal justified by the unconvincing and paradoxical argument that in order to oppose successfully "United States imperialism" it was first necessary to oppose "modern revisionism." [16]

What is more, since in Chinese eyes Mao was now the fountainhead of authentic Marxism-Leninism, it was incumbent upon "all Marxist-Leninist parties," as emphasized in a subsequent major editorial of November 11, 1965, to accept this position and "to draw a clear line of demarcation both politically and organizationally between themselves and the revisionists, who are serving United States imperialism, and to liquidate Khrushchev revisionism in order to welcome the high tide of revolutionary struggle against United States imperialism and its lackeys." [17] Reflecting an unrealistic and distorted view of the outside world, this policy advocated simultaneous opposition, with equally acute antagonism, to both the United States and the Soviet Union. It was so extreme that within a matter of months China's only ally in what Peking described as "the broadest possible united front" was Albania.[18]

If this constituted a clear-cut example of "left deviationism" in "united front" theory, the intensified effort at this time to promote revolution abroad patterned after the Chinese revolutionary model constituted a form of "left adventurism"—namely, as defined by the Chinese themselves, an attempt to encourage "launching of a revolution before the objective conditions are ripe." The assertion in Lin Piao's famous treatise on people's war published on September 3, 1965, that "today the conditions are more favorable than ever before for the wag-

[15] "Refutation of the New Leaders of the C.P.S.U. on 'United Action,'" article by the editorial departments of *JMJP* and *Hung-ch'i*, in *Peking Review*, VIII, No. 46 (November 12, 1965), 11.

[16] "A Comment on the March Moscow Meeting," article by the editorial departments of *JMJP* and *Hung-ch'i*, in *Peking Review*, VIII, No. 13 (March 26, 1965), 13.

[17] "Refutation of the New Leaders," p. 21.

[18] Although most of the charges made against Liu Shao-ch'i for implementing a "revisionist" line in foreign policy prior to the Cultural Revolution are believed to be false, Liu is on record as denying, at least as late as November, 1963, the main premise upon which this extreme Maoist policy toward the Soviet Union was based. In an important speech at that time, Liu asserted that "the Soviet Union is still the chief enemy of, and the chief opponent to, the United States." See "Selected Edition on Liu Shao-ch'i's Counter-Revolutionary Revisionist Crimes," in *SCMM*, No. 653 (May 5, 1969), p. 14.

ing of people's wars by the revolutionary peoples of Asia, Africa and Latin America" was followed within a month by the disastrous coup attempt by the Indonesian Communists (in which Peking apparently was not directly involved), resulting in the virtual liquidation of the largest nonbloc Communist party in the world.[19] It was just at this time, moreover, that the Chinese Communists began to insist that their revolutionary model be followed not only in underdeveloped areas, but also in such advanced industrial nations as Japan. As the secretary-general of the Japanese Communist Party has recently charged, the Chinese Communist Party was guilty of "ultra-Left opportunism" when it attempted in 1965-66 to impose a strategy of "armed struggle" on the Japanese Communist movement.[20]

The final instance of a turn to the left in foreign policy in 1965 was the Chinese resort to arm-twisting and threats against Asian and African heads of state in its efforts first to hold a second Bandung Conference from which the Soviet Union would be excluded, and then to cancel this conference when it was discovered that the Soviet Union could not be excluded.[21] In this attempt to coerce foreign governments in the summer and fall of 1965, there was a hint of the violence and extremism of Red Guard diplomacy that were soon to appear as the hallmark of the Cultural Revolution in China's foreign relations.

The Left in Command: The Cultural Revolution

If the primary purpose of the Cultural Revolution was to restore Mao's political and ideological authority within China, an important means to this end was a concerted effort to demonstrate that Mao's thought, as the highest form of contemporary Marxism-Leninism, was held in high esteem throughout the rest of the world. As Lin Piao stated in May, 1966: "Chairman Mao has . . . developed Marxism-Leninism to a brand new stage. . . . Chairman Mao commands the highest prestige in the nation and the whole world. . . . If we don't see this, we won't know that we should elect such a great genius of the proletarian class as our leader." [22] This undertaking to transform

---

[19] Lin Piao, "Long Live the Victory of People's War," in *Peking Review*, VIII, No. 36 (September 3, 1965), 26.

[20] Quoted in Paul F. Langer, "The New Posture of the Communist Party of Japan," *Problems of Communism*, XX, No. 1-2 (January–April, 1971), 20.

[21] For an account of this episode, see Richard Lowenthal, "Communist China's Foreign Policy," in Tang Tsou (ed.), *China in Crisis*, Vol. II: *China's Policies in Asia and America's Alternatives* (Chicago: University of Chicago Press, 1968), 13.

[22] "Lin Piao's Address at the Enlarged Meeting of the CCP Central Politburo," *Issues and Studies* (Taipei), VI, No. 5 (February, 1970), 89–90.

the Cultural Revolution (a distinctively Chinese phenomenon reflecting a domestic power and policy conflict) into "a revolution of an international order" would embroil China in controversy with nearly every important government in the world.[23] Within two years' time, the extremism, violence, and utopianism of the Cultural Revolution would leave China almost completely isolated, dependent for visible signs of support from the outside world on Albania, an ill-assorted group of "Marxist-Leninist" splinter parties, and student revolutionaries of the "New Left."

With the unveiling of the Cultural Revolution at an expanded Politburo session in May, 1966, it was revealed that the main source of Mao's "revisionist" opposition within China was located at the highest level of Party leadership. Addressing a number of these top leaders in July, Mao disclosed that revolutionary students and teachers (the precursors of the Red Guards) were going "to impose revolution on you people because you did not carry out the revolution yourselves."[24] In this sense, then, the Cultural Revolution can be understood as Mao's last desperate attempt to seize by force what he could not gain through persuasion from his Party and society at large.

In carrying out this new type of forcibly imposed rectification campaign, the principal criterion differentiating "genuine" from "sham revolutionaries" and "Marxist-Leninists from revisionists" was "one's attitude towards Mao's thought."[25] As spelled out by Lin Piao in his keynote speech at a Central Committee plenum in August, 1966, the Cultural Revolution was conceived as "a general examination, a general alignment, and a general reorganization of the ranks of party cadres" directed at (1) "those who oppose the thought of Mao Tse-tung"; (2) "those who upset political-ideological work"; and (3) "those who have no revolutionary zeal." In addition to these (the rightists) who were "to be dismissed from their posts," there were those in an "intermediate state" (the center) who had made mistakes but who, "provided they accept education and resolutely repent," would be retained in their posts. The third category (the leftists), those who eagerly studied Mao, attached great importance to political-

[23] "Advance along the Road Opened Up by the October Socialist Revolution," joint *JMJP, Hung-ch'i,* and *Chieh-fang-chün pao* (Liberation Army Daily) editorial, NCNA, November 5, 1967.

[24] "Address to Regional Secretaries and Members of the Cultural Revolution Group under the Central Committee," in *Long Live Mao Tse-tung Thought (CB,* No. 891 [October 8, 1969]), p. 60.

[25] "Long Live Mao Tse-tung's Thought," *JMJP,* July 1, 1966 (editorial), in *Peking Review,* IX, No. 27 (July 1, 1966), 8.

ideological work, and were filled with revolutionary zeal, were to be "promoted." [26] As also indicated by Lin Piao, this undertaking to "revolutionize" the Party apparatus by promoting leftist cadres loyal to Mao to positions of leadership would be supervised by a newly formed Cultural Revolution Group composed of such top-level leftist Party leaders as Ch'en Po-ta, K'ang Sheng, and last but not least, Mao's wife, Chiang Ch'ing.

With this background in mind, it is easier to understand the momentous consequences which Mao's decisions to "revolutionize" the foreign affairs apparatus would have for China's foreign relations during the Cultural Revolution. The decision to revolutionize the foreign affairs apparatus within China would lead to the establishment of a "revolutionary rebel liaison station" within the Foreign Ministry assigned the dual function of investigating the loyalty (that is, their "attitude towards Mao's thought") and supervising the work performance of veteran cadres and diplomats, including nearly all of China's ambassadors recalled at the end of 1966 to take part in the Cultural Revolution. Foreign Minister Ch'en I became the principal spokesman for the career diplomats, voicing opinions such as this complaint in February, 1967: "Look what has happened to the ministry; there is no order, no organization, and foreign affairs secrets have been taken away." But because of these statements Ch'en would be subjected to a year-long campaign of Red Guard denunciation and attack for his courageous but unavailing effort to limit the authority of the "revolutionary left" within the Ministry of Foreign Affairs.[27]

Of far greater import for China's foreign relations during the Cultural Revolution, however, was Mao's second decision to "revolutionize" the foreign affairs apparatus abroad: "Let us have a revolutionization . . . of foreign affairs offices abroad; otherwise, it would be dangerous." [28] The effect of this decision, at least during the more extreme phases of the Cultural Revolution, was, in somewhat simplified terms, to convert China's embassies into centers for carrying the Cultural Revolution abroad. This concept of "revolutionary diplomacy," in itself a contradiction in terms, is so extraordinary that it deserves further discussion.

[26] For a discussion of this important speech, see Philip L. Bridgham, "Mao's 'Cultural Revolution': Origin and Development," *CQ*, No. 29 (January March, 1967), pp. 25 26.

[27] For a good account of the Red Guard attack on Ch'en I, see Melvin Gurtov, *The Foreign Ministry and Foreign Affairs in China's "Cultural Revolution"* (Santa Monica, Calif.: The Rand Corporation, 1969), RM-5934-PR, pp. 1–83.

[28] Mao, comment on a Red Guard letter, September 9, 1966, in *JPRS*, No. 42,359 (August 28, 1967), p. 15.

To the extent that there is a reasoned, coherent explanation for this practice of revolutionary (or Red Guard) diplomacy, it appears to be integrally related to the rationale underlying the Cultural Revolution within China. This rationale, as suggested earlier, was to explain opposition to Mao's thought and policies within China in terms of its "revisionist"/"capitalist" class nature, opposition which was therefore both illegitimate and, in the nature of things, bound to fail. By analogy and extension, the opposition to Mao's revolutionary goals and ideological pretensions outside China (which by the fall of 1966 included practically every major government in the world) was explained in terms of its class nature as "capitalist," "revisionist," or "reactionary" and as therefore also illegitimate and bound to fail. Both contributing to and resulting from China's position as an outcast in the international community, Mao's view of the world more as an arena of international class struggle than as a community of nation-states would dominate China's foreign relations during the Cultural Revolution.

The new militancy of China's foreign policy stance was revealed in the August 12, 1966, communiqué adopted by the Central Committee plenum which formally initiated the Cultural Revolution. In contrast with the more pragmatic and flexible formula advanced by Peking in June, 1963, as the "general line for the foreign policy" of all socialist countries (a formula which in featuring "peaceful coexistence" as one of three "interrelated and indivisible" principles represented an adjustment to the realities of the nation-state system), this communiqué emphasized that "China's foreign policy" would be "guided" thereafter by the one "supreme principle" of "proletarian internationalism" (defined as "support for the revolutionary struggles of the people of all countries").[29] That the new leadership selected at this Central Committee plenum favored a more active policy of promoting revolution abroad was also suggested by one of the charges brought subsequently against Liu Shao-ch'i—that prior to the Cultural Revolution he had advocated the "pacifist line" in foreign policy of "extinguishing the national liberation movement."[30]

The major premise underlying China's foreign policy during the Cultural Revolution—that it would be possible by means of the extensive dissemination of Mao's thought to stimulate and promote revolution abroad—reflected a basic idealistic tendency in Maoism to over-

[29] *Peking Review,* IX, No. 34 (August 19, 1966), 7.
[30] For a good discussion of the charges brought against Liu Shao-ch'i in the field of foreign policy, see Peter Van Ness, *Revolution and Chinese Foreign Policy* (Berkeley and Los Angeles: University of California Press, 1970), pp. 239–44.

emphasize the role of consciousness and the subjective factor in the unfolding of history. This emphasis on "the active role of the ideological factor in the progress of history" was hailed by Chinese propagandists during the Cultural Revolution as one of Mao's great contributions to the development of Marxist-Leninist theory.[31] Lin Piao, in his paean of praise to Mao Tse-tung's thought ("Marxism-Leninism at its highest in the present era") on the occasion of the fiftieth anniversary of the October Revolution, proclaimed that Mao's thought, "once grasped," would lead to "liberation" of "oppressed nations and peoples" in Asia, Africa, and Latin America, to delivery of the peoples living in socialist countries from their "revisionist" rulers, and, in fact, to revolution in all countries.[32] In this revolutionary manifesto, Lin did not discuss, however, the practical problem of how to persuade the peoples of these countries to "grasp" Mao's thought.

The issue of the exportability of Mao's thought lay at the very heart of the struggle between the "revolutionary left" and the professional diplomats within the Foreign Ministry throughout the initial stages of the Cultural Revolution. The record indicates, moreover, that the outcome of this struggle was a clear victory for the left. Addressing Red Guards in September, 1966, Ch'en I warned of the adverse consequences of this practice: "The thought of Mao Tse-tung is an out-and-out Chinese product. If we take it to foreign countries and people there say 'This is not our product and we don't want it,' what should we do then?" [33] Six months later, on March 10, 1967, after several public self-criticisms in the face of escalating Red Guard charges (including the charge that he "did not regard Mao's thought as an important force for carrying out world revolution and for aiding the people's revolutionary struggle abroad"), Ch'en recanted and, citing Mao's September 9, 1966, directive on revolutionizing China's embassies, ordered senior diplomats on their return abroad "to cooperate with the youth and propagate Mao's thought with every possible means, legitimate and secret," no matter what the local authorities might do.[34] Several days later, addressing a mass meeting of all embassy personnel who had returned to China for indoctrination, the foreign minister again criticized the ambassadors and leading Party officials for their failure to

---

[31] *Peking Review*, X, No. 42 (October 13, 1967), 11–12.

[32] NCNA, November 6, 1967.

[33] *SCMM*, No. 635 (December 2, 1968), p. 14.

[34] "Ch'en I's Speech [to] Persons in Authority Returning from Various Embassies Abroad," *Collection of Ch'en I's Speeches* (*SCMM*, No. 637 [December 16, 1968]), pp. 1–2.

"understand" Mao's September ninth directive, commending the example of some "intermediate level cadres" who, having understood the directive, "wanted to make a success of the work of our embassies and consulates, enlarge the influence of the Chairman's thought and China in the international arena, and give impetus to the world revolution." [35]

With the left firmly in command in the Foreign Ministry, China's foreign relations in the spring and summer of 1967 were characterized by a series of developments repeated with little variation in a number of countries: the transformation of the embassy and New China News Agency into centers for the propagation of Mao's thought and for the distribution of badges an.' other symbols of Mao's personality cult; an ensuing clash when local government authorities moved to curtail or prohibit these practices; various forms of retaliation by Peking ranging from sponsorship of Communist armed revolt (as in Burma) to, more commonly, Red Guard harassment of, and physical attacks against, the embassies and diplomats of the offending governments; and, in some cases, suspension of diplomatic relations.[36] Reflecting the leftist view that national sovereignty must give way to Maoism, *Jen-min jih-pao* (People's Daily) on July 10, 1967, asserted: "To propagate Mao Tse-tung's thought is the sacred and inviolable right of Chinese personnel working abroad." [37]

Reflecting the claim of universal validity for Mao's thought, this missionary effort encompassed hostile, neutral, and friendly countries alike, the latter exemplified by North Korea and North Vietnam, both of which protested in party publications against this attempt to impose Maoist ideology on their own national movements.[38] Expressing the same inner logic of the Red Guard movement within China, Peking's resort to Red Guard diplomacy appeared in essence to be an attempt to secure by intimidation what could not be gained through persuasion— namely, acknowledgment by the international Communist movement and the revolutionary peoples of the world of "Comrade Mao Tse-tung" as "the greatest teacher and most outstanding leader of the proletariat in the present era" and of Mao Tse-tung's thought as "Marxism-Leninism at its highest in the present era." [39]

[35] "Vice Premier Ch'en I's Talk to Comrades from Embassies Abroad," *ibid.*, pp. 15–17.
[36] Gurtov, "The Foreign Ministry," pp. 44 ff.
[37] *Peking Review*, X, No. 29 (July 14, 1967), p. 31.
[38] For the reaction in North Korea, see Joseph C. Kun, "North Korea: Between Moscow and Peking," *CQ*, No. 31 (July–September, 1967), pp. 48–58. The North Vietnamese response is discussed in Roger Salloch, "International Communism: A Survey," *Survey*, No. 70/71 (Winter/Spring, 1969/70), pp. 36–37.
[39] "Advance along the Road."

The unfolding of Mao's Cultural Revolution had brought China by the summer of 1967 to the brink of anarchy. A sharp turn even further to the left in foreign policy (blamed subsequently on an "ultraleftist" seizure of power in the Foreign Ministry) culminated in the ransacking and burning of the British Chancery and the manhandling of the British chargé on August 22. In domestic policy, the damaging effects of the new militancy of the revolutionary left were equally if not more serious, threatening the unity and stability of the People's Liberation Army. There was no choice in late August but to apply the brakes, pull back, assess the damage, and initiate a trend toward moderation in the Cultural Revolution.[40]

One of the many ironies of the Cultural Revolution is that the effort to propagate Mao's thought and thus promote revolution abroad should have its greatest impact not in the countries of the Third World (developing the national liberation movement) nor in the countries of the socialist camp (strengthening the "Marxist-Leninist" forces), as was predicted,[41] but rather in the advanced industrialized countries of the world where the Chinese Communists had seen little or no chance for revolutionary uprisings.

Still another irony is that the period of greatest influence of Maoist ideology on the student revolutionaries in Western Europe and Japan should come at a time (the spring and summer of 1968) when most of the radical elements in this ideology which particularly appealed to the forces of the New Left in the West had already been repudiated as "ultraleftist" and cast aside in China.[42] Attracted by the elements of utopianism (the attacks on functional specialization, inequality, and the pursuit of self-interest), anarchism (symbolized by the slogan "to rebel is justified"), and student elitism (the vanguard role assigned to youthful Red Guards) in Mao's Cultural Revolution, the rebellious students of the New Left in France and Japan who rose up to seize control over their university campuses as a first step toward "revolutionizing" society were protesting what they considered to be serious defects in the organization and functioning of their advanced industrial societies. To the leaders of the New Left, the fact that Mao's radical

---

[40] For a survey of developments in this period, see Philip Bridgham, "Mao's Cultural Revolution in 1967: The Struggle to Seize Power," *CQ*, No. 34 (April–June, 1968), pp. 24–27.

[41] See "Excellent Situation: East Wind Prevails over the West Wind," *JMJP* "Commentator" article, in *Peking Review*, X, No. 43 (October 20, 1967), 27–28.

[42] For a good analysis of this phenomenon, see Klaus Mehnert, *Peking and the New Left: At Home and Abroad* (Berkeley: Center for Chinese Studies, University of California, 1969), pp. 1–72.

prescriptions were addressed not to the solution of these problems but rather toward solving a constellation of political, economic, and social problems (in particular, the problem of restoring his own political and ideological authority) within China, was a matter of little consequence.[43]

Further illustrating the fortuitous nature of the influence of Maoism on the New Left, the anarchistic element in the Cultural Revolution which the revolutionary students found so appealing as an inspiration and justification for their own rebellion was directed not against bureaucratism and established authority as such, but against a specific example of bureaucratism, namely, the unresponsiveness of the Chinese Communist "Party machine" to Mao's revolutionary policies and programs. Also, the vanguard role which Mao assigned to the Red Guards in the Cultural Revolution was both temporary and controlled, an example of directed "revolution from above" rather than of spontaneous "'revolution from below." Once they had performed their assigned function of exposing, criticizing, and intimidating Mao's opponents within the Party (and gotten clearly out of hand), Mao then ordered the Red Guards to be packed off unceremoniously to the countryside.[44]

Indeed, one must be careful not to exaggerate the influence of Maoist ideology on the student revolutionaries of the New Left. In a searching examination of the intellectual roots of the New Left in the West, Richard Lowenthal and other knowledgeable observers have traced the principal characteristics of this new type of revolutionary movement (a faith in utopia and a cult of violent action) as much to the writings of Che Guevara and Regis Debray (the theorists of "Castroism") and of Herbert Marcuse (the American ideological critic) as to those of Mao Tse-tung.[45] Analysis of the radical student movement in Japan, which resembles in many ways that of the New Left in the West, reveals, moreover, that its ideology has been influenced by Trotsky as much as or more than by Mao.[46]

The most exaggerated estimates of the influence of Maoism on the

[43] For a thoughtful discussion of the influence of Maoist ideology on the New Left, see Stuart R. Schram, "What Makes Mao a Maoist," *The New York Times Magazine*, March 8, 1970, pp. 80–82.

[44] *Ibid.*

[45] See in particular the essay by Richard Lowenthal entitled, "Unreason and Revolution," in Irving Howe (ed.), *Beyond the New Left* (New York: McCall, 1970), pp. 55–84.

[46] Ichiro Sunada, "The Thought and Behavior of Zengakuren: Trends in the Japanese Student Movement," *Asian Survey*, IX, No. 6 (June, 1969), 457–74.

New Left have been made by the Chinese themselves, who were eager to claim credit for the student rebellions in France (and elsewhere) as both confirming Mao's prediction that "a great new era of world revolution" was at hand and validating their undertaking during the Cultural Revolution to "spur the development . . . of the contemporary world revolution [through] the extensive dissemination of Mao Tsetung's thought. . . ."[47] But these claims, accompanied by a series of mass demonstrations in which twenty million Chinese participated,[48] reflected the continuing effort by the revolutionary left to use foreign events and the reaction of peoples abroad to help legitimate and support Mao's (and their own) claim to power within China. It was at this low point in the international prestige of China and of Maoist ideology (its influence confined to Albania, a congery of "Marxist-Leninist" splinter parties, and a portion of the New Left) that, as subsequently revealed, the Chinese leadership first gave serious thought to remedying what had become an intolerable position of isolation and weakness for China in a hostile world.

The Turn to the Right:
Postscript to the Cultural Revolution

"[They say] I am also one who 'would not change direction until he comes to the end of his wrong course' and 'once he turns, he turns 180 degrees.' "[49] Mao gave substance to these words when in 1967 the direction of the Cultural Revolution was rotated from left to right. If the turn to the left in Maoist ideology which began in 1962 was basically a response to domestic political pressures, the turn to the right which began hesitantly in the fall of 1967 and has proceeded through several fairly well-defined stages up to the present appears to have been stimulated to a significant extent by external pressures, most specifically the growing military threat to China posed by the Soviet Union. Although mounting pressure to solve a host of domestic political, economic, and social problems no doubt played a more important part, the realization that, as a result of the provocative and self-defeating foreign policy of the Cultural Revolution, China stood isolated in the

[47] "A Great Storm," *JMJP*, May 27, 1968 (editorial), in *Peking Review*, XI, No. 22 (May 31, 1968), 10.

[48] *Ibid.*

[49] "Comment on the Article, 'How Should the Revolutionary Mass Movement Be Correctly Handled by Marxists,' " *Mao chu-hsi tui P'eng, Huang, Chang, Chou fan-tang chi-t'uan ti p'i-pan* (Chairman Mao's Criticism of the P'eng-Huang-Chang-Chou Anti-Party Clique) (n.p., n.d.).

face of a major threat to its national security has had, it is thought, a particularly sobering effect on the Chinese leadership. As a result, Peking's propagandists in their interminable discourses on doctrine no longer emphasize the revolutionary, class-struggle aspect of Maoist ideology but rather its "practicality." "Chairman Mao teaches us: 'The Marxist philosophy of dialectical materialism has two outstanding characteristics. One is its class nature. . . . The other is its practicality.' " [50]

The first stage in this painful and protracted process of retreating from left to right extended from the fall of 1967 through the summer of 1968 and was marked by the return of Premier Chou En-lai to a dominant role in foreign affairs. Speaking to workers in this field in December, 1967, Chou reminded his listeners that, like it or not, Peking had no choice but to deal with other countries primarily as sovereign states and governments: "In international relations, there are certain norms which we must respect. A majority of the countries we deal with are imperialist, revisionist or reactionary, not leftist." And he admitted that, since "ultraleftists" in the Foreign Ministry had ignored these norms, China during the preceding summer had in its foreign relations been guilty of "great-power chauvinism." [51]

The Chinese leadership also revealed a new awareness of the nationalist sensibilities of Communist parties and revolutionary groups throughout the world in a Central Committee directive issued in May, 1968. According to this secret Party directive (as reported subsequently by the Russians), Chinese propaganda directed at foreign audiences would no longer stress "the dominant role of China in the international workers movement" and statements about Mao Tse-tung being "the leader" of the international Communist movement and "the leader of the peoples of all countries" were to be avoided.[52] In accordance with this effort to make Chinese propaganda abroad more palatable, *Peking Review* discontinued publication at this time of its weekly column entitled, "Mao Tse-tung's Thought Lights the Whole World." Still another sign of Peking's growing sensitivity to foreign opinion was its shift not long thereafter from insisting on the universal validity of China's revolutionary model to an admission that it was necessary to

[50] "Conscientiously Study Chairman Mao's Philosophical Works," p. 4.

[51] For a good account of China's foreign relations when the "ultraleftists" were in command, see Gurtov, "The Foreign Ministry," pp. 33–61.

[52] See the editorial article, "The Mao Tse-tung Group's Policy in the International Arena," *Kommunist*, No. 5 (March 26, 1969), pp. 104–16.

"learn from the experience of revolutionary struggles of the peoples of all countries." [53]

The second stage in the trend toward moderation in Maoist ideology lasted from the Soviet invasion of Czechoslovakia in August, 1968, to the first Sino-Soviet border clash in March, 1969. Peking's initial response to the Soviet occupation of Czechoslovakia was, in fact, in the extreme ideological and confrontationist tradition of the Cultural Revolution: it consisted of an intensified attack on the Soviet leadership (now excoriated as "social-imperialist and social-fascist") and a solemn declaration (subsequently identified as Maoist) of the arrival of "a new historical stage of opposition to United States imperialism and Soviet revisionism." [54] At the same time, betraying apprehension that this Soviet military action in the name of safeguarding the interests of the "socialist commonwealth" set a precedent which might later be used against China, Premier Chou En-lai asserted (in a speech on September 2, 1968) that "the socialist camp" no longer existed and that it was therefore no longer possible to "talk about the defence of 'socialist gains' and the 'socialist community.' " [55] Peking's expression of willingness not long after this (in a November 26 Foreign Ministry statement)[56] to resume talks with the United States at Warsaw, though tentative and later withdrawn, also revealed concern about the possibility of a military confrontation with the Soviet Union and the desirability of adopting a more flexible foreign policy stance at a time of national danger.

The third stage, extending from the spring of 1969 to the spring of 1970, encompassed a series of border clashes with the Soviet Union which appeared to confirm Peking's worst fears that a general military showdown with its powerful "revisionist" neighbor was at hand. The progression of events begun more than a decade earlier when Communist China had sought to persuade Moscow as leader of the socialist bloc to adopt a more militant policy against the United States (the main enemy), followed by the increasingly left extremist line of the Cultural Revolution which had elevated the Soviet Union to a position rivaling the United States as China's principal enemy, had now turned

---

[53] "Advance Courageously along the Road to Victory," *JMJP, Hung-ch'i,* and *Chieh-fang-chün pao* joint editorial, October 1, 1968, in *Peking Review,* XI, No. 40 (October 4, 1968), 20.

[54] *Peking Review,* XI, No. 39 (September 27, 1968), 10.

[55] *Ibid.,* XI, No. 36 (September 6, 1968), 7.

[56] NCNA, November 26, 1968.

almost full circle: the Soviet Union had replaced the United States as China's number one enemy, with up to a million men arrayed menacingly (as the Chinese would publicly protest)[57] along the Sino-Soviet border.

Reacting to this military threat posed by a vastly superior technologically modern army, Lin Piao revealed at the Ninth Party Congress in April, 1969, Peking's intention to return to the more flexible, multifaceted "general line" which had characterized China's foreign policy before the Cultural Revolution. Lin pointed out that Peking, instead of relying solely on "proletarian internationalism" (the "supreme principle" which had guided China's foreign policy during the Cultural Revolution) was now returning to the more broadly based foreign policy formula of the June, 1963, "general line" comprised of three "interrelated and indivisible" principles. In addition to "proletarian internationalism" and support for the revolutionary struggles of oppressed peoples and nations, the third principle (the one of most immediate importance) was that of "peaceful coexistence" with countries having different social systems.[58] The utility, not to mention flexibility, of this concept of peaceful coexistence (based on mutual respect for territorial integrity and sovereignty) at a time of national weakness was soon demonstrated when in October, 1969, the scope of its application was extended to apply generally to all countries and in particular to the Soviet Union.[59]

Thus developments in 1969 support the judgment made a decade ago that a major consideration prompting the Chinese Communist leadership to shift from a "revolutionary model" (featuring revolutionary armed struggle based on the Chinese model against bourgeois nationalist governments) to a "nationalist model" (featuring an international "united front" with bourgeois nationalist governments against a presumed common enemy) of foreign policy was a perceived sense of national weakness.[60] This shift would be completed in the fourth and final stage of what might be called post-Cultural Revolution foreign policy, a stage beginning in May, 1970, and extending down to the present time in which the features of China's new "nationalist model" of foreign policy-making would be fully revealed.

[57] See the Chou En-lai interview in the *Washington Evening Star*, May 21, 1971.

[58] "Lin Piao's Political Report."

[59] "Statement of the Government of the People's Republic of China," October 7, 1969, in *Peking Review*, XII, No. 41 (October 10, 1969), 3.

[60] For an enlightening discussion of the "revolutionary" and "nationalist" models of Chinese foreign policy-making, see A. M. Halpern, "The Foreign Policy Uses of the Chinese Revolutionary Model," *CQ*, No. 7 (July-September, 1961), pp. 1–16.

The emergence of the nationalist model approach to foreign policy in the past three years constitutes in important respects a "turn of 180 degrees" from the revolutionary model which had dominated China's foreign relations during the Cultural Revolution. Instead of a policy proclaiming the need to promote revolution abroad in imitation of the Chinese model of armed struggle, Peking now poses as the champion of national sovereignty, claiming that it has always in its relations with other nations "faithfully abided by" Mao's injunction (delivered fourteen years ago) to "practice the well-known Five Principles of mutual respect for sovereignty and territorial integrity, non-aggression, non-interference in each others' internal affairs, equality and mutual benefit, and peaceful coexistence." [61] Instead of following a policy directed at a largely fictitious constituency of "revolutionary leftists" throughout the world committed to the Maoist goal of violent revolution, Peking has now reverted to the pre-Cultural Revolution Maoist concept of developing a broad international united front composed of governments and peoples (including, as evidenced by the recent venture in "ping-pong diplomacy," even the people of the United States) against what it likes to call the "big-nation hegemony" of the United States and the Soviet Union.[62] To promote China's revolutionary objectives abroad, Peking now relies heavily on such material incentives as economic aid and trade rather than trying to export primarily ideology, or Mao's thought.[63] Finally, instead of a policy based on such broad ideological considerations as promoting revolution abroad, Peking's policy is now defined more narrowly and pragmatically in terms of its own national interest.

Despite the many parallels, it should be noted that China's present course in foreign policy has turned even further to the right than in the years immediately preceding the Cultural Revolution. It appears, for example, that Peking has profited from some of the mistakes it made in the Third World, especially in Africa, during this earlier period, and is now concentrating more on diplomacy and state relations and less on insurgency and pro-Peking revolutionary groups in these areas.

There are indications, moreover, that Peking in its rapprochement with North Korea, North Vietnam, and Romania (not to mention the

---

[61] "Down with the Doctrine of Big-Nation Hegemony," *JMJP*, January 23, 1971 (editorial), in *Peking Review*, XIV, No. 5 (January 29, 1971), 7.

[62] *Ibid.*

[63] See, for example, the three recent trade and aid agreements signed with Romania in NCNA, March 22, 1971.

recent revival of diplomatic and economic relations with that arch-revisionist nation, Yugoslavia) is adjusting to the reality of national communism and is no longer exerting a major effort, as it did in the mid-1960's, to organize a new International composed of Communist parties subordinated to the ideological authority of a single center in Peking. Illustrating this new appreciation of the realities of the international Communist movement, Peking no longer characterizes the Cultural Revolution as "a revolution of an international order" but as one largely confined in its application to China.[64] What is more, authoritative ideological treatises on the status of the world Communist movement now stress that for a revolution to be successful every "proletarian party" must "make concrete analysis of the present conditions and the history of its own country, *and solve the theoretical and practical problems of the revolution independently."* [65]

Although further to the right than in the immediate pre-Cultural Revolution period, Communist China's current foreign policy strategy still differs in important respects from the nationalist model in what might be called its classic form during the period when the "Bandung spirit" was at its height (1955–56). Whereas the original Bandung strategy called for a "united front from above" at the national level (with local Communist parties instructed to seek a common front with the ruling national bourgeoisie) and thus implied the possibility of a "peaceful transition" to socialism,[66] Peking continues to insist today (as it has since the spring of 1964) that "violent revolution is a universal principle of proletarian revolution." [67] And despite the professed intention to conduct relations with all nations on the basis of "the Five Principles of peaceful coexistence" (which exemplified the Bandung spirit), China still asserts that its foreign policy is also based upon the contradictory principle of "proletarian internationalism"— that is, "supporting . . . the revolutionary struggles of the people of other countries." [68]

The shift to the right in domestic and foreign policy had become so pronounced by the fall of 1970 that it was necessary to explain to

[64] "Long Live the Victory of the Dictatorship of the Proletariat," *JMJP, Hung-ch'i,* and *Chieh-fang-chün pao* joint editorial, March 17, 1971, in *Peking Review,* XIV, No. 12 (March 19, 1971), 12.

[65] *Ibid.,* p. 9 (emphasis added).

[66] See John J. Taylor, "The Maoist Revolutionary Model in Asia," *Current Scene,* IX, No. 3 (March 7, 1971), 8–9.

[67] "Long Live the Victory of the Dictatorship of the Proletariat," p. 5.

[68] *Ibid.,* p. 12.

both domestic and foreign audiences why this shift had taken place. In time-honored fashion, it was decided, apparently at the Second Plenum of the new Central Committee held in late August and early September, to explain the excesses and violence and attendant policy failures of the Cultural Revolution as the work of an "ultraleftist group" headed, apparently, by the leading Chinese Communist ideologue and long-time confidant of Mao, Ch'en Po-ta.[69] Resembling the political indoctrination campaign undertaken in the early 1960's to extricate Mao Tse-tung from responsibility for the Great Leap Forward debacle, a new campaign was initiated at the Second Plenum for the whole Party "to study Chairman Mao's philosophical works" during which it was pointed out that "senior cadres" had been guilty of "idealistic and metaphysical" errors in their understanding of Mao's works and as a result had promoted an "ultraleftist" line during the Cultural Revolution.[70] This error of "left opportunism," according to an earlier definition by Chairman Mao, results generally from failure "to start from real life, to link oneself closely with the masses, to constantly sum up the experience of mass struggle and to examine one's work in the light of practical experience."[71] More succinctly and specifically, as indicated in an authoritative commentary on the "study Mao" campaign in late fall of 1970, this error of "left opportunism" during the Cultural Revolution had resulted from the failure to realize that "the Marxist philosophy of dialectical materialism" (or, rather, Maoism) is characterized not only by its "class nature" but, of equal importance, by its "practicality."[72]

While the domestic audience could only piece together what had happened by a close reading of murky ideological tracts, foreign audiences were treated to a much more revealing, if tendentious, account of recent Chinese Communist history in a series of interviews granted Edgar Snow by Chairman Mao Tse-tung and Premier Chou En-lai in the fall and winter of 1970. In a fascinating discussion of his "cult of personality," Mao described it as functional in origin, created "in order to stimulate the masses to dismantle the anti-Mao party bureaucracy" and thus enable him to regain "effective control"

[69] For one account of the fate of Ch'en Po-ta, who disappeared a year ago, see the article by Henry S. Bradsher in the *Washington Evening Star*, January 14, 1971.

[70] For a suggestive discussion of this campaign, see the *JMJP, Hung-ch'i*, and *Chieh-fang-chün pao* joint editorial, "Continue the Revolution, Advance from Victory to Victory," in *Peking Review*, XIII, No. 41 (October 9, 1970), 18–19.

[71] *Peking Review*, VI, No. 10–11 (March 15, 1963), 52.

[72] "Conscientiously Study Chairman Mao's Philosophical Works," p. 4.

(which he had lost by 1964) over the Party and state administrative apparatus.[73] The cult had "of course . . . been overdone"; the extravagant claims made for Mao had been "a nuisance"; and he had countenanced some of the more extreme manifestations of the cult (the slogans, pictures, and plaster statues), it was implied, only because the Red Guards had "insisted." [74]

In addition to disavowing the excesses of the personality cult, Mao also emphasized that he had "highly disapproved" of the violence, the factional armed struggle, and the resulting "great chaos" during the Cultural Revolution, much of it caused by the deceit and "lying" of those around him. Another thing which had made the Chairman "most unhappy" was "the maltreatment" of Party cadres by Red Guards and others during the Cultural Revolution, a practice which among other things "had slowed the rebuilding and transformation of the party." [75] Since Ch'en Po-ta, as head of the Cultural Revolution Group, had been entrusted with the task of purging and rebuilding the Party, the implication was clear that he, not Mao, had been responsible for much of the violence and extremism of the Cultural Revolution. This implication was strengthened by the disclosure in another Snow article that "the task of reconstructing the dismantled state and Party administrative apparatus" had now been entrusted to ("fell heavily on") Chou En-lai.[76]

Although it is dangerous to attempt to assign individual leaders to fixed positions in the Chinese political spectrum, it was symbolic that Ch'en Po-ta (the ideologue exemplifying the forces of the "revolutionary left") should now have been replaced by Chou En-lai (regarded as the foremost exponent of pragmatism and moderation within the top Chinese leadership). It was also indicative of the extent to which Maoist ideology, having veered sharply to the left during the Cultural Revolution in an attempt to revolutionize Chinese society and, in time, the world, has once again (as it was a decade ago) been forced to swing back sharply to the right in adjusting to reality.

CONCLUSIONS

As has frequently been pointed out, there is a basic contradiction between the scientific-analytic element and the revolutionary-activist

---

[73] Edgar Snow, "A Conversation with Mao Tse-tung," *Life*, April 30, 1971, p. 46; Snow, "Aftermath of the Cultural Revolution," *The New Republic*, April 10, 1971, p. 19.
[74] Snow, "A Conversation with Mao Tse-tung," pp. 46–47.
[75] *Ibid.*, p. 48.
[76] Edgar Snow, "The Army and the Party," *The New Republic*, May 22, 1971, p. 12.

element in Marxist thought. "Lenin often said that Marxism combines the greatest scientific strictness with the revolutionary spirit." [77] Even Mao has commented: "I am not more intelligent than others, but I understand dialectics and its use in analyzing problems. If the dialectical method is used to analyze an unclear problem, the problem soon becomes clear." [78] In addition to these two contradictory functions, there is a third and even more important function of Marxism-Leninism once it becomes the official doctrine of a Communist party in power—the function of legitimizing the regime and its authority in the eyes not only of the Communist rulers themselves but of the party and people as well. Ideology in this sense, then, becomes a self-justifying dogma, with doctrine manipulated to fit practical needs.[79]

If one places those parties in power which stress the scientific-analytic component of Marxism-Leninism on the right side of the Communist political spectrum, then the increasingly revolutionary and activist version of this doctrine which culminated in China's Cultural Revolution constituted a sharp swing to the left. The revival and intensification to unprecedented heights of a "cult of personality" which accompanied this shift to the left exemplified, according to Chairman Mao himself, the third function of Marxist-Leninist ideology, that of legitimizing and authorizing Mao Tse-tung's political rule in China.

It would be a mistake, however, to think that Mao in the Cultural Revolution was only manipulating doctrine in order to outmaneuver and discredit his "revisionist" opposition. There were also genuine policy differences between Mao and his opponents, differences which resulted in turn from divergent views of the nature of man and human society. At issue was a fundamentally different assessment of the extent to which the human factor (man properly motivated) rather than the material factor (objective conditions) should be relied upon in making revolution and building socialism. Since it is commonly recognized that there is a basic idealistic tendency in Maoism, it is fair to conclude that, even though he has shown tactical realism in the face of necessity, Mao in this sense has always been a leftist.

In domestic policy, the dispute centered on the crucial question of whether it was possible to apply the same "mass line" approach

[77] "More on the Differences between Comrade Togliatti and Us," *Hung-ch'i*, March 4, 1963 (editorial), in *Peking Review*, VI, No. 10–11 (March 15, 1963), 53.

[78] Mao Tse-tung, "A Talk with Comrade Mao Yuan-hsin," February, 1966, in *JPRS*, No. 49,826 (February 12, 1970), p. 30.

[79] For a good discussion of this third function of ideology, see Robert V. Daniels, "Doctrine and Foreign Policy," *Survey*, No. 57 (October, 1965), pp. 3–13.

which had proved so successful in the political and military struggles of the revolution to the more complicated task of attempting to modernize the backward economy and traditional society of China. When his "revisionist" opponents within China criticized this approach in the early 1960's as "anachronistic," [80] Mao responded by reasserting the necessity of "adhering to the mass line, [of] boldly arousing the masses and unfolding mass movements on a large scale . . . in both socialist revolution and socialist construction." [81] When carried to an extreme, this leftist "mass line" became the "ultraleftist" line—characterized by violence, armed struggle, and near anarchy—of the Cultural Revolution at its height.

In foreign policy, the dispute centered on the feasibility of attempting to promote revolution abroad by, among other means, exporting Mao's thought. The abortive attempt to revive China's "revolutionary model" as a major instrument of foreign policy suggests that this Maoist model, in its failure to account for the basic factor of nationalism in the contemporary world, is also anachronistic.

Although a secondary issue, there also appears to have been a difference of opinion concerning the proper tactics for conducting the Sino-Soviet dispute, with Mao insisting on more extreme measures (for example, a complete rupture of relations and the establishment of a new Peking International) than his domestic "revisionist" opponents. The failure of this attempt to re-establish a centralized international Communist organization, the result of not recognizing the reality and strength of national communism, suggests that this Maoist model for organizing the world Communist movement is also outmoded.

The basic cause for the failure of the leftist ideological offensive which Mao initiated nearly a decade ago was the complexity and intractability of the real world. Although all the returns are not yet in, the end result of Mao's attempt to revolutionize his own society by intimidation and coercion appears to be, as one observer has put it, a "utopia . . . run by the army." [82] Although again all the returns are not yet in, the end result of the concurrent attempt during the Cultural Revolution to revolutionize the world appears to be that the outside

---

[80] Mao Tse-tung, "A Talk with Foreign Visitors," August 31, 1967, in *SCMP,* No. 4200, p. 2.

[81] Quoted in "On Khrushchev's Phoney Communism and Its Historical Lessons for the World," *JMJP-Hung-ch'i* joint editorial, in NCNA, July 13, 1964.

[82] Schram, "What Makes Mao a Maoist," p. 82.

world, by exerting a moderating influence on that ideology, has triumphed over Maoism.

But what are the future prospects in the continuing interplay between the international impact of Maoist ideology and the reciprocal impact of developments abroad upon the substance and political coloration of that ideology? In the short term, there are still opportunities for rather easy Chinese diplomatic gains if Peking should persist in the present course in foreign policy, characterized by the pragmatism and maneuverability that have been so apparent since mid-1970. In time, however, it should become evident that these diplomatic victories will not significantly enhance China's capacity to project its influence abroad in the manner of a major power. In view of the limitations (such as economic underdevelopment and domestic political problems) that will continue to restrict China's influence in the international community, there may be yet another turn to the left (especially if Mao continues to dominate the government and people of China) in an attempt to surmount these limitations and advance once again toward Mao's revolutionary goals.

BENJAMIN I. SCHWARTZ

A Personal View of Some Thoughts
of Mao Tse-tung

During the turbulent years that have just passed, many of those involved in the study of contemporary China have been challenged to reveal whether they are for or against the "Chinese Revolution" and have been summoned to abandon forthwith the sham posture of "objectivity." The challenge is, of course, a reflection of the more general attack on the notion of objectivity and/or neutrality in the fields of human and social studies.

It seems to me that certain "social scientific" conceptions of objectivity are indeed vulnerable to this attack. There are still those on the academic scene who continue to believe that they approach experience with an assumptionless *tabula rasa*. When they employ "hypothetical models," they would have us believe that their choice of model has nothing to do with previously held tacit assumptions or general perspectives. Yet such models are never chosen at random out of the infinite realm of possibility: they are chosen because they seem "promising," and they generally seem promising because they conform to previously held views of how the world hangs together. No adult human being of any degree of intelligence approaches a vast area of human experience such as contemporary China with the Lockean blank sheet. He brings to his work his accumulated perspectives, both conscious and unconscious; and these perspectives certainly do not all derive directly and strictly from conclusions based on precise "empirical evidence," but from a variety of sources and a total life experience. This is hardly the place to plunge into the bottomless pit of genetic sociological or psychological theories of life-views, and it will suffice simply to note that all of us without exception have such assumptions, perspectives, and orientations. Indeed, they must exist if thought is to take place.

I would nevertheless maintain that none of this precludes the legitimacy of an aspiration to a certain definition of objectivity or to *Verstehen* in the Weberian sense. There are certain canons governing the validity of empirical evidence that can be accepted as norms by persons of the most varied assumptions and perspectives. One must thus accept the principles that assumptions *may* be undermined or seriously modified by empirical evidence and that empirical evidence contrary to one's assumptions must be accounted for. One may still aspire to consider all the empirical data that may be relevant to one's subject and to achieve an accurate understanding of contrary views concerning the same subject. One may also aspire to achieve an understanding of the orientations and life-views that are quite different from one's own.

Thus the type of interpretative writing that refrains from constant explicit reference to one's own premises and "value judgments" remains perfectly justified. The perceptive reader may discern the dialectic interplay between the author's perspectives and values and his treatment of the particular subject matter at hand. The fact that such assumptions have been discerned by no means invalidates the analysis. The reader must, in the end, judge whether the assumptions of the author have led to or inhibited fruitful understanding. In general, a straightforward analysis is much more worthwhile than a constant hammering on one's own value judgments concerning the experience at hand. And yet there may be occasions when the direct confrontation of one's own judgments concerning the matter at hand may be an exercise in intellectual self-clarification.

I do not propose in this brief article to pass any blanket judgment on that vast unfinished human experience called the "Chinese Revolution," since I remain utterly unconvinced that it is the kind of unitary entity which can be simply affirmed or negated. What we are dealing with in effect are some twenty-odd years of the history of Mainland China. During this period the People's Republic has undergone many shifts and turns, experienced many crises and many upheavals in leadership. At times the leadership has itself harshly condemned previous lines of policy which have received the blanket endorsement of those abroad who believe that the "revolution" must invariably receive total approval at any given point of time. It is thus quite possible to acknowledge the massive and undeniable accomplishments of the People's Republic in many areas without making any total commitment to an entity called the "Chinese Revolution" and particularly without accepting all of Mao Tse-tung's claims as a political and moral philosopher.

What I propose to deal with is not the Chinese Revolution but certain themes in the "Thought of Mao Tse-tung," particularly in their cultural revolutionary development. While these themes derive out of the matrix of his previous ideas, in their cultural revolutionary version they assume a particularly polarized form.

I shall not concern myself with the question of whether Mao is an "original" moral and political philosopher. It is probably quite true that if he had not achieved power, few of us would be interested in his metaphysical or moral-political philosophy. Yet the fact that those with political power are able, to a degree, to attempt to implement their ideas will always lend a peculiar interest to whatever ideas they may have. What is more, the ideas themselves concern fundamental issues—in my own view, issues fundamental not only to China in the last quarter of the twentieth century, but perhaps fundamental to all of us. In challenging the dogma that differences of culture and differences of "stages of development" preclude any sort of mutual relevance of thought, any kind of involvement in a common world of issues, Western admirers of Mao, whatever their limitations, have performed a distinct service.

Incidentally, the question of whether Mao's cultural revolutionary vision is relevant only to China's present condition (or, more broadly speaking, to "underdeveloped societies") or raises questions of more universal relevance is one that divides the defenders of the cultural revolutionary vision as well as the skeptics. Among them one can distinguish what might be called the "tough-minded" and the true disciples. The true disciples believe that all of Mao's words are to be taken at face value; the "tough-minded" believe in an exoteric and esoteric Maoist doctrine. In the latter's view, Mao, like all sensible leaders, is interested mainly in "modernization" as this term is understood in the West. He is fundamentally a theorist of economic development. He realizes that in a woefully capital-poor country such as China one must lean heavily on labor intensivity and hence he appeals to selflessness, austerity, and infinite self-sacrifice—to "moral incentives" in general—as the only way to mobilize the masses for development. As a consummate social engineer Mao knows quite well that this morality of sacrifice and collectivity is an interim, instrumental morality, that modernization will in the end lead to a society in which the dominant goals of life will be consumer pleasures and the pursuit of status; but he thinks of all these matters as a hard-headed strategist of development. He is, as it were, self-consciously creating his own version of a "Protestant ethic."   — debatable

Yet it is precisely this parallel to the notion of the Protestant ethic that leads one to ask questions about this whole approach. Neither Calvin nor his successors were strategists of development. They sincerely believed that their ethic was tied to man's eternal salvation and they were entirely unconcerned with the achievement of wealth as a "spin-off" effect. Nothing could have been further from their vision than an interest in "economic development." Indeed, if they had believed in the supremacy of the goals of economic development, they would have speedily abandoned their ethic of salvation. In his own exposition of this doctrine, Max Weber argued that the economic effects of the Protestant ethic were an unintended consequence. One can hardly claim that it had anything to do with conscious intentions.

To be sure, Mao's cultural revolutionary vision is explicitly committed to economic development and national power and even to the view that the Maoist ethic will spur on such development. This, however, by no means proves that Mao does not profoundly believe in his own image of the cultural revolutionary ethic as an ultimate end in itself. In certain varieties of Western liberalism, it has been argued simultaneously that individualism is good because it spurs economic enterprise and that individualism is good as an end in itself. The same may be equally true of Maoist collectivism. Thus in treating two themes of Mao's thought I shall accept the interpretation of the true disciples, who believe that Mao desires "modernization" but only the kind of modernization that can be achieved within the context of his vision of the good society. Finally, in dealing with these themes I shall not be concerned with the motives of Mao's behavior in the Cultural Revolution nor with the question of what relationship his doctrines bear to the actualities of Chinese politics in 1972. In fact, a good case can be made that at the moment we are witnessing in China a somewhat muffled retreat from any of the doctrines here described.

THE MAOIST CONCEPTION OF SCIENCE

What I here call the Maoist conception of science is an element of the cultural revolutionary syndrome that goes back at least as far as

Yenan and perhaps has its roots in Mao's earliest contacts with the concept of science in the writings of Yen Fu, Liang Ch'i-ch'ao, and popular tracts of the early twentieth century. At first approach, this concept of science seems to be based on an inductive-pragmatic view which has been common in the Anglo-American world. It is essentially a Baconian concept which emphasizes the centrality of induction from the observation of concrete facts, as well as "learning by doing." This view of science is related by Mao to the simple epistemology which we find in "On Practice." Concepts are immediately derived from percepts in the course of man's social practice and then immediately applied in practice. Mao, of course, shares with other Marxist-Leninists the conviction that the word "science" is just as applicable to the "truths of Marxism-Leninism" as to the truths of natural science. Thus, the epistemology of science described in "On Practice" is apparently equally applicable to the social history of man and to the natural sciences, although we shall soon find that there are in actuality considerable differences in the modalities of application in those two spheres. It seems apparent that this conception of science harmonizes most nicely with many other themes of both the Yenan and cultural revolutionary syndromes. Above all, it seems to involve an element of populism. If science is basically a matter of learning from immediate practical experiences, it should be a kind of common sense immediately accessible to all. Here one can find similarities between Mao's linkage of science to populism and John Dewey's linkage of his experimental-pragmatic view of science to democracy.

On its negative side, this view of science becomes a weapon for attacking those intellectuals who believe in the possibility of separating conceptual reasoning from immediate reference to the perceptual. They believe in the possibility of arriving at truth through sustained abstract ratiocination divorced from immediate practical experience. They are also excessively addicted to the mediated experience of book learning rather than to learning from immediate practical experience. Both the belief in the dynamic fruitfulness of abstract thought separated from immediate reference to concrete practice and the heavy reliance on past experience mediated through books involve the possibility that an intellectual cloistered in his study and divorced from political activity may independently arrive at truth.

Two questions face us at this point. To what extent is this view of science consistently maintained and to what extent is it valid? We will find that the first question is particularly relevant to Mao's view of the "science" of social history and to the supposedly populist implications of this view.

It might be illuminating at this point to compare Mao with Dewey. As we know, in spite of Mao's insistence on deriving truth from concrete situations, as in the case of Lenin and Stalin, "empiricism" is a bad word in his lexicon. Empiricism involves the failure to place newly experienced concrete situations within the pre-established framework of the "universal truths of Marxism-Leninism." (By now, we can perhaps add the "universal truths of the thought of Mao Tse-tung.") John Dewey also occasionally attacked the word "empiricism." What he meant by it was what he regarded as the "abstract" empiricism of Locke and Hume,[1] which attempted to reduce experience to universal elements, namely, sensations. To Dewey experience is made up of complex unique concrete situations. He objects to a "logic of general notions under which specific situations are to be brought" and is not prepared to admit the existence of any pre-established universal truth which may not be upset or modified by any new situation. All people, once equipped by education with scientific intelligence, will be able to solve the problems in their own situation in terms of those situations. They need not assume in advance that any a priori universal truth necessarily applies to their situation. The conclusions concerning the relations of general notions to specific situations will be drawn by those involved in the situations.

In Marxism-Leninism (including Mao's version of Marxism-Leninism), pre-established universal truths about the world as a whole certainly do exist. In Mao's thought there are some truths that are not only universal but even eternal, such as the famous "laws of contradiction." Other truths concerning the "laws of history" are not eternal but in principle universal during their period of application. To be sure, Mao informs us that Marx himself arrived at his "universal truths" from "detailed investigations and studies in the course of practical struggle."[2] Leaving aside the fact that most of the investigations and studies involved in *Das Kapital* took place in the dusty bookish archives of the British Museum at a time when Marx was most minimally involved in "practical struggles" (other than his personal struggles to support his family), there remains the old philosophic problem of how universal, necessary truth can be derived

[1] *Reconstruction in Philosophy* (New York: Mentor Books, 1949), pp. 84–85.

[2] "Rectify the Party's Style of Work," *Selected Works of Mao Tse-tung* (Peking: Foreign Languages Press, 1960), p. 40.

inductively from what must always be partial and contingent empirical data. In fact, some of the large universal categories of Marxism-Leninism derive from Hegel, who firmly believed that his major categories were based on a general contemplation of the total nature of the universe and not merely based on atomic empirical observations or "learning by doing."

Quite apart from the question of whether all the universal truths of Marxism-Leninism have been derived inductively, there is also the thorny question of who is authorized to relate pre-established universal truths to the specificities of new particular situations. The Leninist answer is that only the Party has this authority, while Mao informs us that "our comrades who are engaged in practical work must realize that their knowledge is mostly perceptual and partial and that they lack rational and comprehensive knowledge." [3] It is thus quite obvious that those who gather perceptual knowledge are not necessarily the same persons as those who derive the new rational and comprehensive concepts from this knowledge. It must be borne in mind that in the cases of Lenin, Stalin, and Mao the "application" of universal truth to concrete new situations generally involves the modification and constriction of previously held universal truths and hence a denial of their universality. Lenin and Stalin (however different they may have been from each other), no less than Mao, constantly spoke of "applying and extending" pre-established theory to new, unanticipated experience. In this sense they are all three "empiricists" and "pragmatists." Like Mao, both Lenin and Stalin "applied" the truths recorded in the canonical books to "life." Thus the Party, or the current leadership of the Party, or the Leader come to have the exclusive authority to interpret universal truths and to forge the linkage between the universal truth and the new lessons derived from new perceptual experience. What is involved is nothing less than the awesome authority to negate pre-existing universal propositions.

Thus at the heart of the Yenan *cheng-feng* (rectification) debates between Mao and those to whom he referred as "dogmatists" among the Communist intellectuals and cadres was not simply the question of whether truth is to be derived from pre-established truth and books or from direct, perceptual, "practical" experience. To the extent that Mao spoke of the universal truths of Marxism-Leninism he was referring to truths recorded in books. In essence he was placing the authority of the church to interpret the sacred scriptures above the

[3] *Ibid.*, p. 41.

scriptures themselves. He was by no means asserting that every man in the village has the right to interpret the scriptures in the light of his own "partial" reading of perceptual experience. It is probably true that Mao's reading of Chinese political and social realities in the Yenan period was generally more accurate than that of many of those whom he attacked, but embedded in his remolding speeches was the claim that the task of "synthesizing the experience of the masses into better articulated principles and methods" was the exclusive prerogative of the "correct" political leadership—"correct" not only because it could base its inductions on a broad view of the experiential landscape from the mountaintop but because it knew *how* to relate pre-established universal truths to new experience.

It may be maintained that Mao's inductive-pragmatic view of science is far less ambiguous and problematic when applied to the natural sciences themselves.[4] Here one might say that the populist implications are unambiguously clear. The man in the village or factory is unable to relate his own immediate "partial" experience to the total sociopolitical world and to the course of social history, but he is, after all, in immediate contact with physical nature. A worker or group of workers in contact with a machine may indeed be able to discover ways of improving it, and new inventions have been made by artisans down through the ages through "empiric" methods. To the extent that one identifies the history of science with the history of technological progress before the scientific revolution (and even to some extent after the scientific revolution), Mao's conception of "science" remains cogent. Indeed, as Joseph Needham has obsessively insisted, China may well have been in the vanguard for centuries in this old type of technological advance.

A more fundamental question than any we have yet considered is whether the Maoist conception is valid when applied to the science that has emerged from the scientific revolution. A layman's reading of many contemporary historians and philosophers of science such as Alexandre Koyré, Karl Popper, Stephen Toulmin, and Thomas Kuhn would suggest that the cutting edge of the scientific revolution in the "hard sciences" was not first and foremost the inductive method, accurate and exhaustive observation, or even experimentation as such,

---

[4] If one considers the whole sweep of the history of the People's Republic, one finds much less commitment than in earlier Soviet history to the application of Marxist-Leninist universal truth to nature (in the manner of Engels), although one occasionally finds references in cultural revolutionary literature to the application of "On Contradictions" to particle physics.

but the construction of fruitful deductive hypotheses of a logico-mathematical nature. Observation, experiment, and "practice" are crucial to the process of verification but not, we are told, to the process of discovery.

All this means that it may be precisely the ability of the human mind to abstract itself from immediate reference to concrete experience; its ability to conceptualize and to engage in sustained reflection and ratiocination is a crucial element not only in science but in intellectual endeavor in general. Indeed, to the extent that Mao Tse-tung is inclined to treat literature as a kind of applied science of social engineering, one must add that it is also true of the creative imagination. Mathematics, having played an enormous role in the scientific revolution, furnishes us with the paradigm case. To be sure, the scientific discoverer must in his reflection constantly refer to a vast accumulation of acquired human experience, but much of this experience may well be mediated through memory and books. The plain fact is that an Einstein could accomplish most of what he did apart from immediate "practical" experience.

One can still make an argument for many of Mao's maxims concerning intellectuals—scientific and others—on social ethical grounds, and such arguments have been made in many times and places. Intellection may lose its connections with "life" and become a self-contained scholasticism; people in the academy may lose the capacity to see the relationship between the printed word in books and the realities which they mediate. On the other hand, people involved in "social practice" may flatter themselves in the illusion that their "social practice" constantly reconfirms their general maxims when in fact it does nothing of the sort. Intellectuals may be enormously arrogant and may use the social advantage derived from their claims to knowledge to achieve special privilege. Whether they are more inclined to these infirmities of the flesh than "practical" revolutionary politicians whose social advantage derives from their positions in the political vanguard is, of course, questionable. Something may also be said for the view that in China in particular, with its long tradition of divorce of the literati from physical labor, some direct contact with physical labor may have some sort of wholesome effect; but whether it has all the intellectual and even moral effects attributed to it may well be questioned. It can also be argued that what a poor China requires in the first instance in science is not so much theoretical discoveries as their practical applications. Finally, the notion that in a vast and poverty-stricken country one should train large numbers of paraprofessional types of medical and technical personnel without insisting on a full mastery of the theoretical foundations of a given scientific discipline is a notion with considerable merit, even if it does not vindicate Mao's ideas concerning the foundations of modern science.

The main point at issue here is whether truths concerning society and the cosmos can be discovered by people in libraries, laboratories, and studies—people who do not occupy a position within or close to the present constellation of leadership. Viewing the whole matter from a somewhat negative perspective, the notion that truth can be discovered in this way challenges the leadership's monopoly of the privilege of "synthesizing the experiences of the masses into better articulated principles and methods." The present Maoist philosophy of education is designed to make education as strictly applied and practical as possible. While this again may be defended on the grounds of practical necessity, it also presumably reflects Mao's Baconian-pragmatic view of science. As for the synthetic universal principles required by the masses, they will, of course, be derived from the thought of Mao Tse-tung or whoever happens to be in a ruling position. The masses may thus be shielded against the corrupting effects of wrong "syntheses" derived from illegitimate sources.

On Bureaucracy and Domination

There is no element of Mao's cultural revolutionary vision that has had more appeal among many in the West than his attack on bureaucracy and on organizations in general. While the capitalist societies of the West have been a primary target, some of the most subversive implications of his doctrine apply not only to the Soviet Union as an ongoing society but also to pre-existent Marxist-Leninist doctrine in general. What Mao has done in essence is return to a position long shared by liberals and anarchists—namely, that the kind of social power and privilege which derives from the occupation of positions within a political institution or bureaucracy can be as primary and as autonomous a source of oppression, domination, and exploitation as the social power and privilege deriving from the possession of private property. We are now told that the bureaucrat who sits in his office shuffling papers (as the intellectual sits in his study perusing books) may be as far removed from the interests of the masses as the Western owner of property. The current Chinese doctrine concerning the capture of the Soviet state by the "bourgeoisie" is the confirmation of this doctrine. It obviously does not rest on the assumption that there exists in the Soviet Union a large class of people whose power rests on the private ownership of the means of production. As in so much of Mao's use of Marxist vocabulary, words are emptied of their concrete socioeconomic meaning and given largely moral references. The potent word "bourgeois" now simply means exploitative, oppressive, selfish, and so forth. The new "bourgeoisie" of the Soviet Union has been able to achieve its position precisely through the control of the organizational levers provided by party and state.

If we look back to all the writings of Marx himself, the issue is never simple. There is a theory claiming to derive from Marx that stresses the primacy and autonomy of political power—namely, the theory of Asian society. According to this theory, political organization—at least in Asia—was itself a primary class-forming agency of society. The question of what implications, if any, Marx drew from his theory of Asian society for the analysis of political power in the West remains a moot point. It seems to me that Marx simply did not think through the possible implications. It certainly did not prevent the predominance of a "vulgar Marxism" in which political power was treated as strictly "superstructural" and in which governments were treated as the "executive committees" of the ruling class. Again, the Marxist social democratic parties of the late nineteenth century, including the Mensheviks, insisted that their parties be organized along the lines of democratic constitutionalism. They by no means disdained the "machinery" of political democracy within their parties (in spite of the centralized, highly bureaucratic nature of the German Social Democratic Party). No pre-established harmony was assumed between vanguard and rear such as would render superfluous the machinery of constitutional controls of leadership. It was, on the contrary, sincerely believed that because the party represented the harmonious general will of the industrial proletariat, it would be precisely within the social democratic party that political democracy would find its true realization. It was such Mensheviks as the early Trotsky and Martov who immediately suspected a tendency in Lenin to create a new bureaucratic elite, and it was probably precisely their Russian environment that made it difficult for them to deprecate the social reality of bureaucratic power.

By the same token, it was precisely the Leninist strain within the Marxist movement that was most inclined to minimize the separate reality of political power and to emphasize its entirely "superstruc tural" nature, thereby invoking the vulgar Marxist notion that the state ruling power is merely the executive committee of the ruling classes. From this Stalin was later able to conclude that in any society, without the private ownership of the means of production, the existing state power—whatever its organization—necessarily represents the proletariat. To be sure, before his death Lenin had some dark premonitions concerning the resurgence of bureaucratic power, but he allowed himself to be comforted by the thought that the proletariat occupied the heights of power and that the Party continued to be the "virtual representative" organ of the proletariat.

Even under Stalin we find routine critiques of bureaucratism. But the attacks were directed mainly against the inertia and incompetence of party bureaucrats rather than their caste privileges and power to oppress; on the whole, the benign and "superstructural" nature of the new elite structure was stressed. Even the hounded Trotsky remained sufficiently imprisoned within his own post-October Leninism to refuse to admit the emergence of a "new class" in the Soviet Union.

With the Mao Tse-tung of the Cultural Revolution, as with Milovan Djilas (*ceteris paribus*), what we have is essentially the acceptance of the notion of the possibility of a new class. The kind of access to power and privilege that divides the occupants of party and government from the "masses" is by no means less real than the kind of access to power and privilege created by "relations of property." One may indeed use that most powerful epithet, "bourgeois," to describe both.

In the case of Djilas, this notion leads directly to a rehabilitation of all the tenets of constitutional democracy. If political power is a primary and formidable source of oppression and exploitation, the machinery created by liberal democracy with the aim of checking political power and making it accountable resumes its full validity. If the machinery is defective and fallible, it should simply be improved and made more effective.

In the case of Mao, it need hardly be pointed out that constitutional democracy plays hardly any role in his mental universe—and probably less during the Cultural Revolution than ever before. The machinery of constitutional democracy is, after all, machinery, and the spirit of the cultural revolutionary vision is skeptical of institutional machinery of all types. In the discussions of party-building that have taken place in the last few years and in the documents of the Ninth

Party Congress, we actually find a weakening of the kind of electoral machinery that has survived as a kind of ghost of constitutionalism within the structure of the Soviet-type Communist party. This has even led to Soviet attacks on Maoist leadership for undermining the "norms of intra-Party democracy" within the Leninist constitution of the Party.

Anarchism is the other major modern response to the perception that political power and organization are themselves a social basis of class domination. Nineteenth-century anarchism, when it did not simply call for an apocalyptic annihilation of all authority, tended to advocate the destruction of the nation-state and the creation of a network of small communitarian societies in which direct democracy would prevail to the extent that political organization was required at all. One of the influences behind this variety of anarchism was the doctrine of Montesquieu and Rousseau that democracy in any true sense of the term was only possible in something on the scale of a city-state.

The Paris Commune, which has played a distinct role in the writings of Marx and Lenin and which was invoked in China during both the Great Leap Forward and the Cultural Revolution, was in many ways an embodiment of certain nineteenth-century anarchist ideas. The accidental fact that its government was confined to Paris was precisely what made its anarcho-communitarian character possible, although Proudhonians and other varieties of anarchists also played a role in it. The acid test of whether it would have remained anarchist would have been faced if the Paris Communal government had extended its sway over France as a whole—a test it would probably not have met. In summarizing Marx's complex attitude to the commune, one might say that his passing enthusiasm for it was largely based on what he regarded as its revelation that a revolution in Europe was still possible as well as on the presence in it of prefigurations of his own vaguely articulated ultimate utopia, which would be anarchist in some sense.[5] To Lenin, the Paris Commune had a narrow polemical meaning: it proved that there could be no peaceable transition from capitalism to socialism and that the "old state machine must be smashed." The question of whether there was anything in the commune that prefigured a centralized, bureaucratic organization like the Communist Party is one he simply fails to consider.

[5] See particularly Avineri Shlomo, *The Social and Political Thought of Karl Marx* (Cambridge: Cambridge University Press, 1970), pp. 239-49.

In the case of the Maoist invocation of the Paris Commune, particularly at the time of the Great Leap Forward, one can perhaps discern a tendency to call upon some of its more anarchist implications. The communes of 1958 were depicted as being ideally autonomous cells of society which would carry on agricultural, industrial, cultural, and even military activities in a self-sufficient, highly autonomous way, thus greatly reducing the tasks of the central state organs. Their existence would lead to an enormous reduction in the size of the state bureaucratic apparatus, particularly in the agrarian sector. It must not be forgotten, however, that the centrifugal tendencies inherent in the image of the commune were to be quite effectively counterbalanced by the centripetal and unifying tendencies of the Party organization; even in 1958 the Party was ideally portrayed as being made up not of bureaucrats but of dedicated cadres. The unity of the Party, unlike the unity of the state, was not to be simply a function of its bureaucratic organization but of the selfless discipline of its individual cadre members who would be effective local leaders while maintaining their unquestioning loyalty to the authority of the center. Nothing could have been further from Mao's mind than the disintegration of China as a unified national society. Indeed, the tasks of the Party as an integrating nervous system would become heavier than ever.[6]

The Cultural Revolution goes much further. Here we have an attack not only on the state bureaucracy and organization but on the machinery of the Party itself. In spite of all the remolding of the previous years, the Party had, in Mao's eyes, proven itself susceptible to the same bureaucratic diseases as the state apparatus. Thus, the invocation of the Paris Commune under such circumstances would seem to have much more radically anarchist implications than during the Great Leap Forward. Indeed, some of the younger and more precipitous cultural revolutionaries leaped to the conclusion in 1967 that Mao was in effect calling for the abolition of the whole national apparatus of state and Party and for the implementation of the anarcho-communitarian Paris Commune ideal. In fact, there is no reason to believe that Mao had ever accepted this conclusion or ever wavered in his belief that within the national society there should be a central, supreme authority—a "center"—with overwhelming decision-making power. One might say

[6] Franz Schurmann has pointed out that the Great Leap Forward was actually preceded by a rectification movement directed against regionalist tendencies within the Party. *Ideology and Organization in Communist China* (Berkeley and Los Angeles: University of California Press, 1966), pp. 215–16.

that in early 1967 he had, in his own person, become the living embodiment of this central authority, although even then he relied on his cultural revolutionary group, the Red Guards, with the People's Revolutionary Army already lurking in the background. When the Red Guards proved susceptible to "anarchist" tendencies and the vicious "theory of many centers," he came to lean very heavily on that other crucial pillar of support of central authority, the People's Liberation Army.

Mao is, in fact, no anarchist. He has consistently followed his belief in vanguard leadership and political authority, both central and local. Since he obviously believes in the continued existence of China as a cohesive national society, he has never wavered in his conviction that the vanguard leadership must have a center of ultimate authority, just as in the Sino-Soviet polemics he has always claimed that a Communist bloc ought to have a spiritual center. In all the discussions of the dissolution of the division of labor in human society, in all the aspirations for the development of a man who will be simultaneously peasant, worker, soldier, and intellectual, Mao has not questioned the need for the ongoing division of labor between leaders and led.[7] The attack on bureaucratic machinery and highly articulate hierarchic organization does not necessarily imply the rejection of a ruling elite. One may simply dream of a ruling elite whose authority is rooted in the moral and intellectual quality of its members rather than in their organizational positions and functions.

Mao Tse-tung, like others in the Chinese Communist leadership, has concerned himself more than Communist leaders elsewhere with the problem of the territorial distribution of power within the state, with those problems of central versus local government that constitute a staple concern of Western "bourgeois" political theory. Mao obviously dreams of a local leadership that will be creative, take initiatives, exercise independent judgment, and be close to the masses, even while maintaining a profound loyalty to the policies of the center. This concern with local grass-roots government may reflect many of the particularities of Chinese Communist history. It does not imply any anarchist proclivities. The rather unexpected praise that the Chairman recently expressed in his interview with Edgar Snow for American techniques

---

[7] Mao has occasionally invoked the Marxist notion of the dissolution of the state, but his notion of the permanent revolution with its ongoing struggles and contradictions would suggest that the need for a social vanguard will continue into the distant future.

of local government—however seriously meant—would indicate how far he is from a rejection of the nation-state structure.

If one recognizes the sinister potentialities of political power as such and yet rejects the liberal democratic and anarchist ways of dealing with these potentialities, how then does one cope with the corruptions of power? The answer provided by Mao is a very ancient one and one with a long Chinese past: one moralizes the holders of power. The very language used to describe the virtues one wishes to attain in the power-holder is itself very ancient. One wants leaders who will be servants rather than masters, who will sacrifice themselves for the collectivity, live austerely, be humble, constantly scrutinize their own behavior, and be open to criticism. Yet, if the answer is ancient, it is nevertheless true that some of the methods suggested to achieve these ends are indeed new and bear consideration.

Both Western liberals and anarchists would be inclined to reject out of hand the notion that the problem is one of moralizing the holders of power. The whole rhetoric of moral improvement is alien to their discourse. Indeed, as Djilas has shown, liberals would be more inclined to feel that the rediscovery of the autonomous malignancy of political power vindicates the long effort to create effective constitutional machinery designed to check political power and render it accountable. And yet, as we are well aware, Western liberalism has its own problems. Not only do there remain vast concentrations of private power which are hardly subject to effective accountability, but the needs of the nation-state have created vast and distant bureaucratic machinery and executive power which are accountable in only the most indirect and long-term way. While many who call themselves liberals have been quite impervious to the belief in moral elites, they have not been equally impervious to the belief in technocratic elites—that is, the belief that many of the problems of modern society must be handled by "scientific" experts. There is an easy acceptance of the notion that such experts are wholly dedicated to the imperatives of their science, as well as an easy acceptance of their competence as scientists. Since they are in some sense ultimately accountable, the question of their corruption and abuse of power does not arise. Relatively speaking, liberal democracy has probably been more successful in the area of civil liberties than in creating an iron-clad machinery for assuring the accountability of power. The devices of corruption and abuse of power have proven more ingenious than the machinery designed to control them. Thus the machinery of political democracy has by no means rendered irrelevant the ancient and tragic question of the corruptions of power and domination. Conversely, one might add that a recognition of the reality of the fateful problem of political power may also vindicate the ongoing efforts to control power by constitutional machinery.

We are by now fairly familiar with the Maoist methods of moralization. The holders of power must not be separated from the masses. They must be in constant *gemeinschaftlich* contact with them. Higher cadres must constantly be "sent down" from their offices to learn from the masses. There must be a constant and unremitting inculcation of the Maoist ethic of self-sacrifice, self-abnegation, and so forth, and words must be closely tied to practice and immediate application. Administration must be simplified as far as possible. The local cadre must be subject to constant scrutiny by others who are constantly judging his performance. "Participation in labor" is felt to have especially powerful moralizing effects. Finally, the masses, who will have been thoroughly imbued with a Maoist ethic, will themselves exercise a moral control over their leaders. Furthermore, the aim is not only moralization but also effectiveness, and here we see how the Maoist concept of science neatly meshes with his methods of moralization. The cadre, by being in constant touch with the immediate local practice, learns from actual experience how to apply the general line to local affairs.

One of the first questions that arises here is, how simple can administration be in a regime that aspires to become a "rich and powerful" nation-state? Has Mao disproven Weber on bureaucracy? To what extent can any state that aspires to exercise authority over vast territories eliminate the tendency to bureaucratic differentiation and the chain of command? This is by no means a new problem of "modernization." It is a problem inherent in the effort to exercise authority over long distances, and the tendency toward division of labor in government rises out of the same imperatives as the division of labor in general. Given the goal of extensive control over vast territories, the time and energy of men can be most effectively used by specializing their activities rather than by leaving them diffuse. This specialization also inevitably involves hierarchy and chain of command. Ever since bureaucratic government has existed, men have bewailed its pathologies —the Parkinson effect, the inertia, red tape, the Kafka-like distance of the administrator from the administered, and the more common abuses and corruptions of power. In China there is a vast heritage of literature on all these topics. Indeed, among many Confucian thinkers there was a recurring call for "simplification of administration," although not, of course, for "sending down" officials to the village. In the vast sector of Chinese society that remains agrarian, the local cadres may indeed continue to be closer to the ideal of "all-around men." It would, however, be quite misleading to confuse the question of bureaucratic specialization with the question of hierarchy and domination. So long as the ambition exists to maintain vast territorial control from the center, so long as the modern ambition to extend the "wealth and power" of the nation is added to the traditional aims of the maintenance of peace and order, it will not prove possible to do without large-scale organization or to ignore the fact that it is more effective to employ the bulk of some individuals' energies and time in offices rather than "in the field."

If we can believe Mao Tse-tung's recent remarks to Edgar Snow, it is clear that he did not support either the extreme radicalization of foreign policy or the attack on the apparatus of the foreign policy-making machinery in 1967. The fact is that those leftist cultural revolutionaries who did opt for a radicalization of foreign policy had every reason to think that they were drawing the necessary consequences of Mao's cultural revolutionary doctrine. For one thing, the whole existing international world system itself embodied all those vices of bureaucratism that Mao had attacked. The diplomatic corps and even the foreign policy specialists in Peking were that part of the bureaucracy most clearly out of touch with the masses and perhaps the most vulnerable to "bourgeois" degeneration. If, as is now clear, Mao himself believes that it is to the strategic advantage of the People's Republic of China to maintain a dynamic and outgoing posture within the present framework of world politics, he must clearly will that China's foreign policy specialists, diplomats, and trade officials spend a maximum amount of their time and energies in exercising their taxing skills. He clearly seems to accept the whole elaborate protocol of the present system of international dealing, with its pomp, ceremonial airport receptions, limousine caravans, cocktail parties, and banquets. There may still be some practice of *hsia-fang* in the foreign policy organs of government; but one can hardly believe that it is allowed to occupy too much time, nor is there any evidence that the trend within these organs is toward the simplification of administration.

One suspects that if this is true of foreign policy organs, it is probably also true for most of the top-level power-holders in other bureaucratic sectors at the center. At this point, an anarchist might point to the contradictions involved in an effort to enforce the Maoist formulas for the moralization of power among the lower-echelon cadres while neglecting such techniques on the highest level. Thus one might ask whether a more unstructured power operating in close proximity to the masses is necessarily more benign than the power of distant bureaucrats. There is here a tendency to confuse domination with bureaucratic organization. The leader of an unstructured gang may surely be as dominant as a bureaucrat in an office. The fact is that, in the broad sweep of human history, men have suffered as much—if not more—from the oppression and brutality of immediate overseers, foremen, and corvée heads as from the distant bureaucrats. On the other hand, it has often been pointed out that in China and elsewhere despots have been hostile to bureaucracy because of the constraints it places on the exercise of arbitrary power from above. Certainly, if the authority of the local power-holder is entirely dependent on the local community as envisaged in communitarian anarchism, he will be entirely beholden to the local community.

Yet, as we have seen, the central Maoist cultural revolutionary doctrine never abandoned the notion of the subordination of local power-holders to higher instances of authority and to decisions made from above. Indeed, the sins of "tailism" still exist. When Mao speaks of the infallible wisdom of the masses, he is referring to the masses as a kind of abstract totality and not as empirical groups and individuals making up a whole. In spite of all the rhetoric about learning from the masses, there is always the proviso that one must not learn bad and incorrect things from the masses in the flesh. The wisdom of the masses finds its ultimate distillation and synthesis in the mind of Mao, but the masses in their plurality are quite capable of wandering from the true path. Their basic apprehension of experience remains one-sided and perceptual. Thus, even the cultural revolutionary cadre must not become an instrument of their errors and backwardness. When there is a tension between the errors of the masses and the general line, the good cadre must do everything possible to bring them to the truth, and therefore the dangers of commandism are always present. One may be driven to commandism in order to avoid the pitfalls of tailism and departmentalism.[8] Thus, the local cadre's interaction with the masses continually takes place in a context where basic policy and fundamental decisions are made at the center and higher levels of authority

[8] Departmentalism is a tendency to identify with particular vested interests whether these be geographic (village, province) or functional (the bureau or department).

—whether structured or unstructured—continue to exist. Whether the cadre's relationship with the masses is bureaucratic or *gemeinschaftlich* seems to have little effect on this basic fact.

Again, while it is no doubt a sound idea in China as elsewhere for "higher cadres" to "go down" to see how policies work in practice as well as on paper and to "learn from the masses," even the most self-less servant of the public must be concerned not only with his own direct conclusions from "perceptual" observation but also with the relationship of these conclusions to the whole drift of the general line which has been "synthesized" above him. If his reading the "little red book" has not overcome his selfish tendencies, the "going down" may turn into an entirely routine affair.

As for "participation in labor," it may indeed do something to over-come the traditional mandarin disdain for physical labor; but whether it has all the redemptive qualities attributed to it remains questionable. In the United States, where the disdain for physical labor is not really part of the cultural tradition, many have gone through the experience in their youth without its visibly affecting their adult behavior in po-sitions of authority, except as an occasion for boasts about the hard-ships of their own youth. There still remains the essential difference between those who possess the power to command and those who do not; there still remains the fact that the physical labor of cadres is intermittent. No doubt, the experience creates in some cadres a sense of solidarity with the masses (a sense of solidarity which may not always lead to enthusiasm for the current general line). To many others it may be an unpleasant ritual to be completed as soon as pos-sible in the happy realization that it is not one's life vocation.

None of this means that in the vast ranks of China's cadres there are not those who fervently and sincerely attempt to realize the tenets of the cultural revolutionary faith. There may also be larger numbers who belong to what Shao Ch'üan-lin called the "middling" type— those who attempt to realize the ideal but fail not only because of their inner weakness but because of sheer inability to cope with all the complexities mentioned above.[9] Unfortunately, it is still not clear whether the game can best be played by the sincere disciple or the

[9] The argument about the "middling" type relates to a conflict about literary policy in the early 1960's. Shao Ch'üan-lin, a literary bureaucrat, pressed the view that litera-ture should deal with men as they are—"middling," complex mixtures of good and evil. See Merle Goldman, "Party Policies toward the Intellectuals," in John W. Lewis (ed.), *Party Leadership and Revolutionary Power in China* (Cambridge: Cambridge University Press, 1970).

agile opportunist. While some of these techniques have their merits, it is still doubtful whether Mao's methods will in the end be more successful than others in moralizing the average power-holder (leaving aside the question of whether the Maoist ethic is itself an adequate life ethic).

The fact that the Chairman himself has doubts is indicated by his remarkable doctrine of the permanent revolution. The struggle between bourgeois and proletarian tendencies will continue on into the indefinite future. The unrelieved mutual scrutiny of groups, the supervision of the masses, the "struggle-criticism-transformation" sessions about which we know so little are all designed to maintain an unremitting revival atmosphere. The devil can be exorcized only by maintaining the battle at fever pitch. Whether men in general—including Chinese men—are willing to conceive of life in terms of permanent unremitting struggle is, it seems, a highly moot point. In any event, one can raise questions about the methods of struggle themselves. The "masses" are exhorted to supervise the cadres but only from a correct point of view, and the correct point of view continues to be determined at the center. To the extent that the center is Mao, to the degree that one believes that Mao infallibly synthesizes the wisdom of the masses, one may rest assured that all is well. But what if the center ceases to be occupied by Mao or any genuine adherent of the "Cultural Revolution Ethic"? Similarly, the technique of struggle-criticism-transformation with its malleable Maoist language can be used by all sorts of people for all sorts of purposes. The left deviationists of 1967 who had reason to regard themselves as the purest disciples of the Cultural Revolution were as vulnerable to the treatment as the capitalist-roaders themselves.

We have here considered two themes of cultural revolutionary Maoism. There are many other themes that might be considered, such as the question of self-interest and selflessness, the nature of mass participation, and the relationship of the masses to high culture and cultural revolutionary views on education. To the extent that Mao Tse-tung presents himself to the world as a social philosopher and philosopher of science, his doctrines can hardly remain immune to questioning. While he himself would no doubt strongly resist any effort to divide the philosopher from the king, we are free to do so and in doing so we are not rendering any sweeping judgment on that momentous slice of history known as the "Chinese Revolution."

Index

Academia Sinica, 180
Action: discussed with knowledge, 10-11
Aesthetics: debates on, 229-32
Africa, 327, 329, 330, 333, 337, 345
Age of Great Harmony, 14
Agitation: as function of ideology, 48, 50, 64-67
Agricultural crisis: the Chinese Communist Party's response to, 263-65
Agriculture, 86, 140, 202-3, 221, 244, 258, 263, 264, 265, 270, 281, 283, 290, 292-97 *passim,* 331, 365. *See also* Land
Ah Q, 79
Ahn, Byung-joon, viii, ix
Ai Ssu-ch'i, 242
Aisin-gioro, 62
Albania, 332, 334, 341
Alienation: Marxist theory of, 234
All-China Federation of Literary and Art Circles, 226, 253
Alliance Society. *See* T'ung Meng Hui
"Amateur ideal," 20. *See also* Levenson, Joseph
American Council of Learned Societies, ix
American Indian tribes, 103
An-p'ing, 275
An Tzu-wen, 297
Analysis: as second stage of ideological development, 124, 129, 132, 135-36, 138, 157
Anarchism, 24, 61, 70, 125, 217, 327, 339, 340, 361, 364, 365, 366, 367, 369
Anglo-American government and views, 185-86, 356. *See also* West
Anhwei, 120, 273, 290, 298

Anshan Steel Company, 263, 283
Anshan Workers Inventions and Innovations Campaign (1952–53), 304-5
Antibureaucratism, 14-18, 22, 28
Anti-Hunger, Anti-Civil War Movement, 172n
Anti-Japanese united front, 87, 88, 89, 90, 95, 97, 201n. *See also* Japan; United front; Yenan period
Antirightist Campaign, 231, 249, 262, 263, 281, 289, 294
Anyang Special District, 273
Army, 74, 93, 109, 177, 178, 179 and n, 196, 240, 267, 268, 269, 350; in Manchuria, 197, 198, 199. *See also* Military; People's Liberation Army; Soldiers
Art, 26-27n, 159, 230, 235, 277, 284; forms, and investigation meetings, 277
Asia, 327, 329, 330, 333, 337, 362
Assassinations, 173-74
Association for the Education of Workers, 133
Australian aborigines, 103
Authority: recentralization of, after the Great Leap Forward, 296
Autumn Harvest Uprising, 103, 157
Awakening Society (Tientsin), 61

Bacon, Francis, 356, 361
Bandung strategy and conference, 333, 346
Barnett, A. Doak, ix
Bedeski, Robert, ix
Behavior: as related to ideology, v
Belden, Jack, 215

373

CONTRIBUTORS

CHALMERS JOHNSON. Professor of political science and chairman, 1967–72, of the Center for Chinese Studies at the University of California, Berkeley. Member of the Joint Committee on Contemporary China since 1968. Author of *Peasant Nationalism and Communist Power: The Emergence of Revolutionary China, 1937–1945* (1962), *An Instance of Treason: Ozaki Hotsumi and the Sorge Spy Ring* (1964), *Revolutionary Change* (1966), and *Conspiracy at Matsukawa* (1972); editor of *Change in Communist Systems* (1970).

BYUNG-JOON AHN. Assistant professor of political science at Western Illinois University. Field research in Hong Kong in 1969–70. Junior fellow at the Research Institute on Communist Affairs, Columbia University, 1971–72. Author of *Ideology, Policy and Power in Chinese Politics and the Evolution of the Cultural Revolution, 1959–1965* (1972) and of an article in *Asian Survey*.

PHILIP L. BRIDGHAM. Research analyst at the Central Intelligence Agency. Has taught political science at the University of Hawaii, the Massachusetts Institute of Technology, and Dickinson College. His recent publications have focused on the origin and development of the Cultural Revolution.

JEROME CH'EN. Professor of history at York University, Ontario. Author of *Yuan Shih-k'ai, 1859–1916* (1961) and *Mao and the Chinese Revolution* (1965); editor of *Mao* (1969) and *Mao Papers: Anthology and Bibliography* (1970).

MERLE GOLDMAN. Professor of Chinese and Japanese history at Boston University and research associate at Harvard East Asia Research Center. Author of *Literary Dissent in Communist China* (1967).

JOHN ISRAEL. Associate professor of history at the University of Virginia. Author of *Student Nationalism in China, 1927–1937* (1966).

RENSSELAER W. LEE III. Instructor in political science, City College of the City University of New York. Doctoral work at Stanford University, with dissertation entitled "Technology and Political Development in China." Author of articles in *The China Quarterly* and *Asian Survey*.

SUZANNE PEPPER. Received Ph.D. in political science from the University of California, Berkeley, in 1972. Dissertation entitled "The Politics of Civil War: China, 1945–49." Author of articles in *The China Quarterly* and *Studies in Comparative Communism*. Field study in Hong Kong in 1969; currently in Hong Kong working on a study of education administration in contemporary China.

BENJAMIN I. SCHWARTZ. Professor of history and government at Harvard University. Author of *Chinese Communism and the Rise of Mao* (1951), *In Search of Wealth and*

Power: Yen Fu and the West (1964), and *Communism and China: Ideology in Flux* (1968).

RICHARD H. SOLOMON. Associate professor of political science at the University of Michigan and a research associate of the university's Center for Chinese Studies. Author of *Mao's Revolution and the Chinese Political Culture* (1971) and of articles in *The China Quarterly*.

LAWRENCE R. SULLIVAN. Instructor in Chinese politics at the University of Michigan, 1971–72. Currently engaged in field research in Taiwan and Hong Kong under a Foreign Area Fellowship Grant on his dissertation entitled, "Ideology and Political Communication in the Formative Stages of the Chinese Communist Movement."